MARGINAL NATIVES AT WORK

ANTHROPOLOGISTS IN THE FIELD

Morris Freilich

EDITOR

Schenkman Publishing Company

Halsted Press Division
JOHN WILEY & SONS
New York—London—Sydney—Toronto

Copyright © 1977

SCHENKMAN PUBLISHING COMPANY, INC.
3 Mt. Auburn Place
Cambridge, Massachusetts 02138

*Distributed solely by Halsted Press, a Division of
John Wiley & Sons, Inc., New York, New York.*

Library of Congress Cataloging in Publication Data

Main entry under title:
Marginal natives at work.

Earlier version (c. 1970) published under title:
Marginal natives.

Includes bibliographical references.
1. Ethnology — Field work — Addresses, essays,
lectures.   I. Freilich, Morris, 1928-   II. Freilich,
Morris, 1928-   Marginal natives.   III. Title.

GN346.M37 1977   572'.07'2   77-10539

ISBN 0-470-99306-5
ISBN 0-470-99307-3 pbk.

Printed in the United States of America.

CONTENTS

PREFACE

Fieldwork, in the mid '70s, is still "The Hallmark of Anthropology."[1] It is still the rite-of-passage which transforms an anthropological student into a real *marginal native*, into an anthropological researcher. It is still the method *par excellence* for getting to understand CULTURE (the general concept) by self immersion in *a culture*, a way of life. It is still the exciting, required but rewarding experience in which an anthropologist discovers whether he or she wants to dedicate a professional existence to probing the meanings of the word

---

1. See, "Fieldwork: The Hallmark of Anthropology" In *The Human Adventure: An Introduction to Anthropology* by Gretel H. Pelto and Pertti J. Pelto (pp. 13-31). 1976 New York: Macmillan.

"human." In fieldwork, we still discover the nature of the other person while uncovering hidden depths in ourselves. Yet fieldwork has changed, and for the better.

The mystique of fieldwork—the aura of magic, mystery and glamor which anthropologists once attached to life in the field—has gone. In its place we have an ever growing literature of what problems, pains and pleasures face the researcher in a foreign culture.[2] In less than a decade many of the problems caused by the "mystique" have been solved. And we are slowly gaining the benefits of sharing research experiences, benefits which I outlined in 1970, in the section "Whither Field-Work Culture?" (pp. 31-37 in the first edition of this book.) Anthropology is "Revolutionizing Field Work."[3] Once a revolution picks up steam it is difficult to know where it will take us. I like to believe that the first edition of this text which appeared under the slightly different title (*Marginal Natives: Anthropologists at Work*) helped to move the revolution in the right direction. I hope also that this book will continue to assist anthropologists in planning and doing fieldwork.

2. Among the texts which "tell it like it is" in the field, see:
   Berreman, Gerald D.
   1972 *Hindus of the Himalayas*. Berkeley: University of California Press.
   Gold, Peggy (Editor)
   1970 *Women in the Field*. Chicago: Aldine.
   Middleton, J.
   1970 *The Study of the Lugbara: Expectation and Paradox in Anthropological Research*. New York: Holt, Rinehart and Winston.
   Spindler, George D. (Editor)
   1970 *Being an Anthropologist: Fieldwork in Eleven Cultures*. New York: Holt, Rinehart and Winston.
   Wax, R. H.
   1971 *Doing Fieldwork*. Chicago: University of Chicago Press.
3. "Revolutionizing Fieldwork" is John Friedl's way of describing the great changes that have happened to anthropology in the recent past. See, his *Cultural Anthropology*. New York: Harper's College Press; and especially chapter 4 (Aims and Methods in Cultural Anthropology), 1976; pp 118-144.

PREFACE TO 1970 EDITION

The Marginal Man
is "one whom fate
has condemned to live
in two societies
and in two,
not merely different,
but antagonistic cultures."

Stonequist (1937)

The anthropologist has been a marginal man for most of anthropology's history. Regardless of time, place, or people present, he almost invariably "came on" as marginal to society. To members of his family he was "the strange one" who was more interested in primitive rituals (like how to make rain by dancing) than modern rituals (like how to make money by singing). To the neighbors his entrance into the community was a traumatic experience. He arrived with digging sticks, broken bits of pottery, masks, apelike heads of prehistoric men, and naked figurines. Once in, he held strange parties at which he offered his guests unsightly morsels, queer liquids that burned the stomach, and weird noises called "primitive music." At the university he was the professor who taught those wild courses on "Sex and

Magic Everywhere," and who attracted a following of disheveled students. Or were they really students? One could never be sure; perhaps they were informants brought back from some primitive tribe.

To social scientists who had a general idea of the nature of anthropology, the anthropologist was an object of ambivalent feelings. On the one hand, he had lots of interesting data always good for comic relief during a serious lecture; on the other hand, this cross-cultural researcher was intellectually perverse. He ceaselessly spoke of "what the data indicate" in ways unflattering to his audience. Social scientists were informed that their generalizations, looked at from a cross-cultural perspective, accounted for but 1 percent of the variance, although their theories did help to explain *some* of the behavior of freshmen students in nonsectarian liberal-arts colleges located in the urban centers of North America.

As the anthropologist found his way around to different departments, he informed geographers that geographic determinism was not a viable theoretical framework, no matter what Huntington had said, notified historians that history "existed" before writing, and suggested to psychiatrists that they take less seriously the Oedipus story and its Freudian interpretations. To their chagrin these latter gentlemen learned that all five-year-old boys do not hate their fathers; that indeed some "normal" kids, in the Trobriand Islands and elsewhere, loved their fathers and for some enigmatic reason hated their Mother's brothers. Economists were saddened to hear that "economic man," already considered quite sick by some, had, in actuality, "died."

Today, the anthropologist is still a marginal man, particularly in the field. At home, he is (almost) a solid citizen. The research method he fathered—participant observation—has been emulated far and wide, even by such rivals as sociologists. And his writings are being read by young and old, intellectuals and dilettantes. Anthropology has come of age; anthropologists have arrived. It is now possible to answer the old question of some students with a positive, "Yes! One can be an anthropologist and eat regularly!"

Anthropologists have been discovered by the students. The English literature-oriented co-ed is now reading *Patterns of Culture* and loving it. The brilliant senior once ready to set the world on fire via a doctorate in physics is thinking of a good graduate program with research opportunities in Africa, or perhaps Southeast Asia, or Latin America. Even the average student finds it necessary to take an anthropology course or two, for how else will he learn "in" terms like *potlatch* and *fête* and put-downs like, "Having met you, I better understand the mentality of Australopithecus." Some students are currently developing such a passion for this discipline that they have demanded extra ethnography courses.

The remarkable growth of cultural anthropology, particularly in the last decade, is due to many factors, including (1) the fact that, due to the revolutionary changes in transportation and communication technology, the lives of peoples all over the world have become more familiar, meaningful, and important to us; (2) the growing importance of such related disciplines as sociology, psychology, economics, and political science, and the realization by many that effective work in these sciences is greatly helped by some knowledge of cultural anthropology; and (3) the growing realization that the natural sciences cannot solve the major problems of the modern world: wars, racial and ethnic conflicts, crime, poverty, and overpopulation.

As more and more students become involved in collecting cross-cultural ethnographic data, and as such information progressively becomes more important both as a basis for scientific generalizations and as a guide for social planning and political action, it becomes the duty of professional anthropologists to see that data collection follows rigorous, scientifically sound procedures. Unfortunately, sound research methods have not been adequately developed in anthropology. The novice, off to live among "primitive" peoples for the first time, has often been dispatched with minimal training and a "sink-or-swim" philosophy.

In order to develop a rational and comprehensive program in anthropological research, it is necessary to discover how such research has been done in the past by anthropologists working in every part of the world. The contributors to this book are anthropologists truly interested in field research. Their interest goes far beyond the mechanics of research: they wish to share their experiences so that life-in-the-field will lose some of its mystery and apprehension. Each informant is a well-trained and experienced field worker. Each has successfully passed through the two *rites-de-passage* required of the professional anthropological researcher: *academic competence*, measured by graduate degrees, and *research competence*, measured by his survival and his return with valuable data. To achieve success in both these areas requires a unique mixture of talents: an ability for introvertive, ivory-tower scholarship, and an ability for extrovertive field work.

Contributors were sent an outline suggesting that each chapter be presented in three parts: Project 1, Project 2, and Comparisons. It was also suggested that the description of each project be structurally similar, with sections discussing (1)

Problem, Theory, Research Design, (2) Passive or Adaptational Research, (3) Active Research, and (4) Summary and Evaluation.

Each contributor was thus asked to think of field research as work involving two distinguishable stages: (1) adapting to a novel environment, and (2) solving a research problem. Each stage was described as having a major goal and a number of related problems. The problems of one stage did not disappear in the next stage; rather they assumed different meanings. For example, a major problem of the passive-research stage is "getting and maintaining rapport." Clearly, this problem exists throughout the research period, but in the active-research stage, maintaining and developing rapport becomes of greater importance than "getting" rapport.

Within the limits of this general structure, the contributors freely wrote what they did, thought, felt, and believed. Within the limits of accurate first-level interpretation, I have summarized some of the information presented by contributors and have gone on to derive generalizations, models, research strategies, and orientations for which the contributors are not responsible.

The essays that follow indicate the stylistic differences in anthropological research. Such differences are due in part to differences in the anthropologists' age and personality, the research sites worked in, and the problems around which data collection was oriented. However, additional and important differences stem from the paucity of theory directly relevant to anthropological research. These essays thus show the creative and bold attempts of individual anthropologists, working with a minimum of guidelines, to solve research problems.

A preface is a ritual and traditional one that ends with grateful acknowledgments. This book, while not traditional in many respects, does toe the line on ritual when gratitude is involved. I thank the contributors for their readiness to enter this "public confessional" and thereby help disperse the myths of life-in-the-field. It takes special people with a very special type of courage to allow an unknown public to look in on intimate and personal matters pertaining to life with the natives.

A host of colleagues and students are thanked for their comments, criticisms, and suggestions, all of which have improved this book.

M.F.

Boston

FIELD WORK:
AN INTRODUCTION[1]

Morris Freilich

When an anthropologist speaks of "going into the field to do field work," the field refers to the place where the group he plans to study resides, and field work includes living as well as working in this place. The culture being researched is assumed to go through all of its major temporal variations in one year, so the anthropologist generally remains in the field for at least that long. Although anthropologists use a number of methods to collect data, the basic method associated with field work is *participant observation*. This means observing the behavior of a group while participating in its community life.

---

[1] The writer is much indebted to Rose Coser, Pertti Pelto, Norman Whitten, Munro Edmonson, and Robert Maxwell for critical and constructive comments on an earlier version of this essay.

The field anthropologist attempts to become part of the culture he is studying. Depending on his personality, the peculiarities of the group being studied, and contingent factors operating at the time of the study—wars, revolutions, prosperity, famine—the anthropologist acts in one of a variety of possible stylistic modes. At one extreme, he may "go native," in which case his speech, dress, eating and sleeping habits, interactions, social relations, and personal identification all begin to approximate community norms. Or, at the other end of this role-playing continuum, he may become a "privileged stranger," a stranger with rights to live for an extensive period in the community, to question community members extensively, and to record what he observes and hears. More often, the anthropologist's role is somewhere in between "native" and "privileged stranger."

Irrespective of what role he assumes, the anthropologist remains a *marginal man* in the community, an outsider. No matter how skilled he is in the native tongue, how nimble in handling strange social relationships, how artistic in performing social and religious rituals, and how attached he is to local beliefs, goals, and values, the anthropologist rarely deludes himself into thinking that many community members really regard him as one of them. This is true even when he gets "adopted," as I was by the Mohawk steel workers. It was true for me even when Trinidadian peasants asked the clearly rhetorical question, "Mr. Morris, you one of us, yes?"[2]

The role of marginal native is not an easy one to play, for the real natives are often suspicious of the anthropologist. Although his credentials appear legitimate, his goals honorable, and his behavior friendly, his work is of a kind that few, if any, have ever heard of before. At best he is a collector of *loshon hora* (literally, evil talk or gossip), as one of my informants put it. At worst he must be lying, for the question remains: Who could be paying him to collect information on land holdings, economic behavior, kinship relations, sex and mating practices, religion and magic?

The real natives quickly develop their own explanations for the sudden entrance of a stranger into their community life. Mohawk steel workers, for example, thought I was some kind of scholarly tramp looking for a home, since I was constantly sitting

---

[2] Most people in Anamat, Trinidad, called me "Mr. Morris." I interpreted the "Morris" as a sign of friendship, and the "Mr." as indicating some respect for my position of high status in the community. The concept of "high-status friend" (Freilich, 1964) appears to describe well both the position I attained in the community and its functional meaning.

in "their" bar, without displaying any interest in finding a job. Trinidadian peasants thought I was an income-tax spy, a reasonable deduction, since I set up residence in a government-owned building (a dilapidated former schoolhouse) shortly after the passage of an income-tax bill.

The belief that the anthropologist is some kind of spy—that he is not what he pretends to be and that he is gathering information for some purpose harmful to the community—is quite common. Many Nova Scotian Negroes thought the Whittens were spies; two Samoan women spread rumors of Robert Maxwell's "spying" activities; some of the Toro of Uganda thought that Melvin Perlman was a government tax spy; Mandaya cultivators were concerned that the data Aram Yengoyan was collecting would be used to increase their taxes. Some Oshogbo initially viewed William Schwab as a potential tax collector, or as a harbinger of the white man's imponderable laws; and the Slave and Cree Indians thought that John Honigmann was spying on a U.S. military air base. The anthropologist must counter these and other false beliefs of the natives with information that truthfully describes his work, yet "makes sense" to the highly pragmatic natives. With the help of a few special informants, the marginal native gets to know some of the stories that are being circulated about him and discovers what description of cultural anthropology and of a cultural anthropologist will be convincing to them. Out of this knowledge he is able to construct a "story" that the natives find believable. For example, I described my interest in modern Mohawks as part of a fascination for Iroquois history and for the way of life of the descendants of the great warriors of old. In Trinidad, I defined myself as a student of tropical agriculture and related cultural practices.

An educational role—student, teacher, professor, scholar, writer—is one that an anthropologist frequently finds useful in order to describe himself and his activities. The teacher role was so used by Nancie Gonzáles among the Cakchiquel Indians, by Robert Maxwell among the Samoans, and by Norman Whitten in Nova Scotia. In Tripoli, John Gulick presented himself as a "professor-scholar-writer," a role similar to that used by Melvin Perlman among the Toro. These and other role descriptions that anthropologists use do not immediately convince all the natives that the anthropologist can be trusted with personal information. At times the anthropologist has little control over his role assignment. For example, among the Oshogbo, William Schwab was assigned a quasi-political role, and in Gwelo he could not escape the Africans' image of every white man as an "inimical authority." However, presenting one's self and one's project in ways meaningful and flattering to the people being studied, and in a friendly and humble manner, will generally provide the anthropologist with a number of informants who will be willing to work with him. As Pertti Pelto points out, many of these initial collaborators are, like the anthropologist himself, marginal members of the system being researched.

Despite the many problems of the role of marginal native, this role permits an intensive involvement with community members and maximum opportunities for participant observation. Participant observation is a method to which anthropologists are intellectually and emotionally attached: they believe in its efficacy, they like to use it, and they enjoy discussing it with colleagues and students. Strangely enough, they are often loath to write about it in a personal way. That is, they only rarely publish accounts of their own experiences as participant observers. The method of participant observation is anthropology's special contribution to the study of man. The dearth of published descriptions of field experiences and methods used by anthropologists in various parts of the globe is, therefore, quite an enigma. My interest in this puzzle is not solely a matter of intellectual curiosity. Solving this enigma will, I maintain, produce a deeper understanding of the nature of field work and will thus lead to superior field research.

My explanation for this enigma is complex. It includes several interrelated, casual "variables," referred to respectively as (1) field-work culture, (2) problems of field research, (3) common self-evaluations of anthropological researchers, and (4) unwillingness to present a "true" self to an "unknown" public. Each of these variables will be briefly discussed below.

FIELD WORK CULTURE

Anthropological field work in its modern form—carried out by a social or cultural anthropologist, who lives with the natives, speaks their language, and, to a certain extent, practices their culture—is a relatively new phenomenon.[3] Its roots, however,

---

[3] British and U.S. anthropologists who study on-going social systems do much the same thing, but use different terminology to describe it. The British say they engage in *social anthropology*, an activity that focuses on the social relations of primitive and complex societies. The Americans think of themselves as students of culture, focusing on the goals, values, beliefs, symbols, and rituals of primitive and complex societies. They thus define

lie deep in history in the first-hand reports of historians, explorers, travelers, fur traders, missionaries, and others whose interests or vocations have led them to reside among peoples with "strange customs." The data provided by these amateur ethnographers are not uniformly valid: some writings are moralistic or fanciful accounts of "life among the savages"; others are factual descriptions of native life. Irrespective of their validity, many of these reports are rambling and poorly organized. The writers, possessing neither specialized theoretical terms nor systematic theory, were guided by popular opinion coupled with personal interest.[4]

The nineteenth-century scholars who were interested in "primitive" societies used these data to develop universalistic generalizations concerning man's history and the nature of primitive culture.[5] The fact that such data were used extensively and often uncritically by scholars is itself a phenomenon that requires much explanation. Suffice it to say that these men were children of the Enlightenment. Behind them stood the remarkable achievements of Kepler (1571–1630), Galileo (1564–1642), and Newton (1642–1727), scholars who formulated principles of great generality and predictive power and freed their intellectual offspring from the dogmas of the Middle Ages. Behind them too stood the British empiricists John Locke (1632–1704), George Berkeley (1685–1753), and David Hartley (1705–1757), the Scottish moral philosophers David Hume (1711–1776), Adam

---

their field as *cultural anthropology*. Since it is impossible to study social relations without studying culture at the same time and vice versa, the distinction between social and cultural anthropology is purely academic. For a different view see E. E. Evans-Pritchard, *Social Anthropology and Other Essays*, New York, Free Press, 1964.

[4] Evans-Pritchard has pointed out that no one sees reality without some kind of "theoretical frame." "The student [of anthropology] makes his observations to answer questions arising out of the generalizations of specialized opinion, and the layman makes his to answer questions arising out of the generalizations of popular opinion. Both have theories, the one systematic and the other popular." (1964:65)

[5] The word *primitive* as used in such contexts as "primitive society," "primitive culture," and "primitive man" is a rather unfortunate term that is now deeply embedded in anthropological terminology. It does not mean inferior, of lower quality, or anything else that suggests a position subordinate to "civilized" or "advanced" society, culture, and man. Nor does the word *primitive* group social systems and individuals into a homogeneous class of phenomena. In its modern usage the term *primitive society* refers to social systems that are generally small in scale (with regard to size of territory inhabited, number of members, and range of social contacts) and lack a written history, a complex technology, and a highly specialized economy. Further, in primitive societies, familial ties and kinship relations are generally the focus of much social action. Anthropologists often place quotation marks around the term to indicate its specialized meaning; they also use as synonyms the terms *tribal, nonliterate,* and *preliterate,* none of which really describe these systems very adequately.

Smith (1723–1790), Thomas Reid (1710–1796), and Dugald Stewart (1753–1828), and, in France, Montesquieu, the Encyclopaedists, the Physiocrats, and Saint-Simon (1760–1825). These philosophers rejected Cartesian notions of innate ideas and focused on sense experience. They believed in the possibility of a science of society (called "sociology" by Saint-Simon's famous disciple, Auguste Comte) and in societies as natural systems with functionally interdependent parts. These systems, they believed, must be studied empirically and inductively. In these men strong beliefs in the "environmental determinism" of social life, in progress and the ultimate perfectability of man, were aligned with a strong interest in formulating general principles about man and society.

The intellectual climate seemed to be right for the creation of a science of man. Unfortunately, most of the nineteenth-century scholars who were interested in such an endeavor set out to create, instead, a history of mankind. Furthermore, perhaps because they were eager to emulate the achievements of the physical scientists, the fathers of anthropology were in a great hurry to generalize. Given the sparsity of data on primitive man, the poor quality of much of these data, the frequent labeling of almost all non-Western cultures as "savage" or "primitive," the generally accepted (although dubious) proposition that living primitives represent prior cultural stages of all mankind, and the scholars' inexperience in handling anthropological data, it is understandable that most anthropological generalizations of the nineteenth century can hardly be described as "science." They are more accurately "creative speculations."[6]

These speculations on the origins and history of man were often presented scientifically. Data were analyzed within a theoretical framework—evolutionary change and progress—and logical reasoning was used to buttress the conclusion reached. Using scientific models, Gustav Klemm (1802–1867), J. J. Bachofen (1815–1887), Lewis Henry Morgan (1818–1881), Theodor Waitz

---

[6] The lack of sophistication in handling ethnographic materials continued in the early twentieth century and is well exemplified in the writings of Edward Westermarck. In R. H. Lowie's words, "The profusion of Westermarck's documents has blinded some critics to his amazingly uncritical use of them. Not only are there inconsistencies . . . but bad, good, and indifferent sources are cited indiscriminately. . . . In short, Westermarck neither appraises his evidence discriminatingly nor becomes absorbed in his cultural phenomena." (1937:98–99) Marvin Harris describes other scholars of this same period in equally unflattering terms. Comparing these men with Franz Boas, he writes, "[T]here was nothing illusory about the shoddy standards of his contemporaries . . . [many of whom] were temperamentally unsuited to scientific discipline. It was an age in which the license to generalize on the basis of fragmentary evidence was claimed by second- and third-rate people." (1968:253–254)

(1821–1864), Adolf Bastian (1826–1905), and John McLennan (1827–1881), among others, fitted the available data into a variety of conjectural histories. Working with great energy, enthusiasm, and imagination, these scholars and some of their contemporaries developed what I have called the "rubber-data" stage of anthropology, a period when the information available was both "stretchable" and "stretched."[7]

To judge the scholars of the rubber-data stage too harshly would be to ignore their important contributions. As they struggled to make sense of the available information on primitive societies, they developed some categories and concepts that are now basic to anthropological thinking. In their arguments concerning the nature of "savage" life and in their passionate defense of a particular scheme of evolution, they gave meaning to barren data. The intellectual excitement they generated captivated many brilliant minds for service in the development of a discipline yet in its infancy. Finally, the scholars of the rubber-data stage created the conditions necessary for the development of a science of man. That is, they brought to the study of primitive societies an interest that underlies all scientific endeavor: *an interest in making generalizations whose claims to "correctness" are linked to empirical data.* Very clearly, these scholars laid the foundations for modern anthropology.

Factors conducive to the development of a more scientific discipline were present even during the rubber-data stage. First, many of the scholars of this period themselves took a critical view of the type of data that was being used for generalizations. As early as 1859 Herbert Spencer delineated the type of data that is necessary in order to understand "how a nation has grown and organized itself."

---

[7] The aptness of this label is attested to by the following statements of Lowie and Evans-Pritchard: "Able travelers mingled fancy with observation, indulged in the superficial psychologizing that duped Klemm and otherwise twisted the facts from initial bias." (Lowie, 1937:70) The missionaries and administrators, although frequently "men of greater culture than the gentlemen of fortune of earlier times" (Evans-Pritchard, 1964:67) were themselves often far from objective in describing primitive society and culture. Their data was therefore also to some extent a "twisting of the facts."

By the time the synthesizers had added their own interpretations and had completed their attempts to fit the data into preconceived theories of evolution and progress, descriptions of primitive society were far removed from the reality being depicted. Thus, Sir John Lubbock, an eminent prehistorian, could conclude from his readings that the Andaman Islanders have no sense of shame and have many habits that resemble "those of the beasts," that the Greenlanders, Iroquois, and Fuegians have no religion, and that almost invariably "savages are cruel." (1872:430–570) And Lowie could write of Morgan's *Ancient Society*, "the total picture of ancient society that resulted was curiously distorted." (1937:57)

. . . an account of its government; with as little as may be of gossip about the men who officered it, and as much as possible about the structure, principles, methods, prejudices, corruptions, etc., which it exhibited. . . . Let us of course also have a parallel description of the ecclesiastic government . . . of the control exercised by class over class, as displayed in social observances—in titles, salutations, and forms of address. Let us know, too, what were all the other customs which regulated the popular life out-of-doors, including those concerning the relations of parents to children . . . [and of the] superstitions . . . the division of labor . . . the connection between employers and employed; what were the agencies for distributing commodities; what were the means of communication; what was the circulating medium. Accompanying all of which should be given an account of the industrial arts technically considered . . . the intellectual condition of the nation . . . the degree of aesthetic culture . . . a sketch of the daily lives of the people—their food, their homes and their amusements. And lastly, to connect the whole, should be exhibited the morals, theoretical and practical, of all classes as indicated in their laws habits, proverbs deeds. (1876: iv–vi)[8]

In line with this, Lewis Morgan and James Frazer tried to obtain superior data by using a "mailed questionnaire" technique: they asked missionaries, traders, and consular agents who were living among primitive peoples to describe the cultural practices of their hosts. In addition Morgan did his own field work for some of his writings, thus exemplifying the potential benefits of this activity for anthropology.

Second, the functional thinking that pervaded evolutionary treatises (Freilich, 1967) set up its own demands for data collection. In the words of E. E. Evans-Pritchard,

But once it was accepted that a custom is more or less meaningless when taken out of its social context it became apparent both that comprehensive and detailed studies of primitive peoples in every aspect of their social life would have to be undertaken, and that they could only be undertaken by professional social anthropologists who were aware of the theoretical problems in the subject, had in mind the kind of information required for the solution of them, and were alone able to put themselves in the position where it could be acquired. (1964:55)

---

[8] With the aid of three assistants, Spencer began a work in 1870 that was to provide summaries of existing knowledge on a great variety of sociocultural systems. Under the title *Descriptive Sociology* the following volumes were published during the period 1873–1934: (I) *English;* (II) *Ancient Mexicans, Central Americans, Chibchans, Ancient Peruvians;* (III) *Types of Lowest Races, Negritto and Malayo-Polynesian Races;* (IV) *African Races;* (V) *Asiatic Races;* (VI) *North and South American Races;* (VII) *Hebrews and Phoenicians;* (VIII) *French;* (IX) *Chinese;* (X) *Hellenic Greeks;* (XI) *Ancient Egyptians;* (XII) *Hellenistic Greeks;* (XIII) *Mesopotamia;* (XIV) *African Races;* and (XV) *Ancient Romans.*

Third, the scholars of the rubber-data stage did not write solely on evolution. Some of their works were very much concerned with specific subareas in sociocultural life, and such writings did much to stimulate future research by anthropologists concerned with collecting specific data. For example, the works of Waitz and others on primitive mentality were later used as a base for systematic research by W. H. R. Rivers among the Torres Straits Islanders, Morgan's writings on kinship developed the field of comparative kinship studies and sent several generations of anthropologists into the field to collect kinship data, and Frazer's notions of primitive magic, science, and religion challenged many anthropologists to do in-depth studies on these and related phenomena.

Fourth, the writings of Charles Darwin (among others) demonstrated the value of careful empirical studies of phenomena in their natural environment. As Darwin's work was followed up by prehistorians whose careful and persistent research uncovered evidence of the Iron, Bronze, and Stone ages, considerable pressure was exerted on anthropologists to make analogous contributions through research with living aborigines. As R. H. Lowie notes (1937:22), "prehistory proved evolution by the rigorous technique of geological stratigraphy at a time when ethnographers were still groping for proper methods of investigating living aborigines. No wonder that ethnographers leaned heavily on the staff of archaeology."

Fifth, the times produced a number of great men, among the most influential of whom was Edward B. Tylor (1832–1917). With a strong sense of probability, Tylor spurned data that many of his contemporaries found acceptable, assembled a vast mass of authentic data, derived concepts therefrom, and defined terms critical to the new discipline: *culture, religion, local exogamy, teknonymy, cross-cousin marriage.* By emphasizing the importance of weighing the evidence, Tylor provided a model for future theorists and thus helped steer anthropology in the direction of science.

It is beyond the scope of this essay to discuss further the many scholars, events, and convergent trends whose work and influence led to the demise of the rubber-data stage of anthropology. Suffice it to say that by the time the nineteenth century had passed so had the rubber-data stage.[9] Twentieth-century an-

---

[9] According to Sol Tax, between 1860 and 1890 cultural anthropology had grown "from nothing to maturity" (1955:466). I would say, rather, that during the period 1860–1900 cultural anthropology grew from "infancy" to "childhood." By 1900 Boas' expeditions to Baffin Island and British Columbia and the British expeditions to Torres Straits had been completed. Such investigations took anthropology out of its "infancy," but hardly represented

thropologists have assumed the duties—with their concomitant pains and pleasures—of collecting ethnographic data and have given more and more thought to the validity of ethnographic descriptions and to the degree of fit between such information and the generalizations and theories that continue to develop.

To guide them in their field work, the anthropological researchers of the early 1900s could refer to various models. There was Morgan's field work among the Iroquois, which led to his book *League of the Ho-de-no-saunee, or Iroquois* (1851), and his expeditions through Kansas and Nebraska, to Hudson's Bay, to the Rocky Mountains, and up the Missouri as part of his study of comparative kinship structures. There were the works of such pioneer ethnographers as Henry Schoolcraft, one of the founders of the American Ethnological Society, W. H. Holmes, Otis T. Mason, Alice Fletcher, and James Mooney. There were the ethnographic descriptions of Henry Callaway, R. H. Codrington, H. A. Junod, B. Spencer, and F. J. Gillen, the work of Franz Boas in Baffin Land (1883–1884) and in British Columbia (started in 1886), and the British expeditions to the Torres Straits regions of the Pacific in 1898 and 1899 by A. C. Haddon, W. H. R. Rivers, and Seligman and associates. Anthropologists who had themselves done field work and who had a university base were able to impart to their students the importance of this activity and some of the basic problems associated with reaching its goals. These teachings fell on receptive ears and, often, on brilliant minds. As students became researchers and teachers and as their students in turn continued to file into the ranks of professional anthropology, a culture of field work slowly developed. Before presenting my description of this culture, let me, at the risk of sounding like a page out of the Old Testament, list some of the people who helped develop this tradition.

A. C. Haddon and W. H. R. Rivers trained A. R. Radcliffe-Brown, whose study *The Andaman Islanders* (1922) represents a landmark in ethnographic achievement. This was the first attempt by a social anthropologist to describe the social life of a primitive society in such a manner as to represent a test of current theory of primitive society. Seligman helped train Bronislaw Malinowski, the first anthropologist to conduct a long and intensive field study through the native language. Malinowski

---

the labors of a mature science. For further discussions on this and related topics, see Sol Tax, "From Lafitau to Radcliffe-Brown: A Short History of the Study of Social Organization," in *Social Anthropology of North American Tribes*, ed. F. Eggan, Chicago, University of Chicago Press, 1955, pp. 445–481, and Marvin Harris, *The Rise of Anthropological Theory*, New York, Crowell, 1968, particularly pp. 142–216.

trained Raymond Firth, Evans-Pritchard, Hortense Powdermaker, Isaac Schapera, and S. F. Nadel, among others, who in
turn have trained many well-respected and renowned anthropologists.

Franz Boas, and the anthropologists who studied with him,
set the tone for the development of cultural anthropology in
America. Included among those who took a degree with Boas at
Columbia are A. L. Kroeber, Albert B. Lewis, William Jones,
R. H. Lowie, A. A. Goldenweiser, Paul Radin, E. Sapir, F. C.
Cole, L. Spier, Ruth Benedict, M. J. Herskovits, Margaret Mead,
G. Herzog, Jules Henry, and M. F. Ashley-Montagu. Among
others who spent some time studying with Boas or doing research
under his guidance were R. B. Dixon, Clark Wissler, J. A. Mason,
J. R. Swanton, and Ralph Linton.[10]

The modern masters—Boas, Radcliffe-Brown, Malinowski—
taught much that was similar, but they differentially emphasized given aspects of field work. Boas taught that a field
study should include a "thoroughgoing description of all cultural
data . . . House types, basketry, social structure, beliefs, and
tales must all be registered faithfully and with the fullest detail
possible." (Lowie, 1937:131) Further, like Malinowski, on the
other side of the Atlantic, Boas insisted that a command of the
aboriginal language was a requisite for effective data collection.

From Radcliffe-Brown came the emphasis on studying social
relations and attempting to show their harmonious equilibrium:
their function for the system (i.e., structural-functionalism).
From Malinowski came the insistence that intensive involvements with the (real) natives in terms of their culture was a
necessity in field work. He stressed that such research would enable the investigator to demonstrate that man (even in "savage"
societies) was not a puppet on cultural strings, but a decision-
maker who at times opted to go against cultural rules and to
accept the sanctions such behavior called forth. He argued that
without an intensive involvement with the native it is not possible to understand local meanings, functions, and structures.

Through the sharing of a common publication language—
English—and through other communications between the modern
masters and their students, a common information pool developed

---

[10] Others include L. E. W. Benedict, T. Waterman, H. K. Haeberlin, M. W.
Beckwith, Manuel Gamio, Louis R. Sullivan, G. Reichard, I. G. Carter,
Erna Gunther, Erich F. Schmidt, Ruth Bunzel, T. M. Durlach, R. Sawtell,
Anita Brenner, H. A. Carey, R. F. Fortune, M. C. Jacobs, Frederica De
Laguna, E. Phelps, M. J. Andrade, B. W. Aginsky, E. G. Aginsky, Marcus
Goldstein, E. A. Kennard, C. A. Lewis, Ruth Underhill, and William
Whitman, III.

for British and American anthropologists concerning the nature and goals of field work. This information pool can be referred to as field-work culture.

Field-work culture—particularly in its early developmental stage—stressed goals rather than the means (methods) of attaining them. The reasons for this are as follows. First, statements concerning what needs to be done logically precede statements describing *how to do it,* but anthropologists had had too few field-work experiences to be able to formulate such a description. Second, the interests of many early anthropological field workers were focused on the collection of cultural data—beliefs, values, rituals—rather than data on social relations—roles, relationships, rights, and duties. Cultural data are of much greater variety than data on social relations, and it was thus assumed that getting such very "different" data from societies around the world required a host of different procedures, methods, and approaches. Not only were cultures considered to be very different from each other, but it was widely believed that, when all the "parts" of a particular culture were "put together," they became a unique system, each system requiring a unique methodological set for obtaining rapport and collecting data. Third, there was no general agreement that anthropology was a science (a few anthropologists still say it is not), and this lack of consensus was not conducive to an emphasis on methods. Men of such widely different backgrounds as Evans-Pritchard and Lowie argued for a "common-sense" approach to field work, an approach that lets the culture under investigation be the guide for both what to study and how to study it (Lowie, 1937; Evans-Pritchard, 1964).

Fourth, there was, particularly in America, the strong influence of Franz Boas, whose disciples had one major goal: to get data. As M. Smith, himself a student of Boas, put it: "Boas' emphasis on systematic fieldwork led to the collection of whatever data became available. . . . [There was here] a fascination in following the details of a subject just for its intrinsic interest." (1959:54) [11] Fifth, in the early years of field work, a curious relationship developed between the anthropologist and the tribes

---

[11] It might be said that Boas' teachings helped cultural anthropology change from a rubber-data stage into a holy-data stage. In the words of Marvin Harris (1968:257), "Unprecedented also was the precise quality of Boas' devotion to the collection of facts. There is a strong puritan element in his outlook. For him, science was very much a sacred enterprise. Those who rushed to conclusions without proper attention to facts were in effect desecrating a temple." This influence of Boas, while undeniable, is still somewhat strange, since in some of his own work he developed problems that were so sharply defined as to allow for solutions through ethnographic research. See Lowie's chapter on Boas in *The History of Ethnological Theory* (1937).

he studied that in some ways is analogous to the relationship between many psychotherapists and their patients. Anthropologists became "possessive" of their tribes, and the "my tribe" or "my people" approach to field work was a strong factor in holding back replications of given field studies. Since no anthropologist was supposed to study someone else's tribe (just as no psychotherapist is supposed to treat another's patient), and since it was believed that each tribe was unique and required unique approaches, what was the point of describing one's methodology and the various environmental facts that in part were responsible for it? Further, what one does with one's tribe (or one's patient) is a personal matter not "decently" discussed at length. A lack of regular discussions of these "private" matters functioned to keep methodology an underdeveloped phenomenon in field work.[12] Sixth, ethnographies existed that were written by laymen. Since some of these were and still are considered excellent, the professional anthropological field worker could argue, "Why should I worry about methods? I'm already 'ahead' of these laymen of good judgment and keen sensibilities, and unlike them, I know much ethnography and some theory."

Seventh, anthropologists were constantly adding to their field-work goals. Due either to the influences of books and articles or to the direct requests of colleagues, teachers, and high-status friends, anthropologists collected an ever-increasing variety of "data." They looked for and stored local plants, herbs, leaves, and roots; they took head measurements; they recorded dreams; they administered various psychological tests; and they observed and recorded the activities of young children (Powdermaker, 1967, particularly pp. 96–97). In thus carrying out the cross-cultural work of the botanist, physical anthropologist, and psychologist the goals of the field worker ever increased and took much time and energy away from methodological concerns.

Finally, the above factors and their consequences—a lack of emphasis on methodological procedures and a sparsity of guides for field work—forced the anthropologist to resort to his own

---

[12] The public nature of all aspects of a scientific project is considered basic to modern science. It is interesting that as both cultural anthropology and psychotherapy are becoming more scientific, these public "broadcasts" are becoming more common and more complete. In anthropology we now have such writings on field-work experiences as Gerald Berreman's *Behind Many Masks* (1962), Hortense Powdermaker's *Stranger and Friend* (1967), and Bronislaw Malinowski's diary materials (1967). In the literature of psychotherapy it is becoming more common for a therapist to describe precisely what, when, how, and why given techniques are used. Some clinicians even permit others to observe the actual process of therapy, either directly or through tape and/or films. See John G. Watkins, "Psychotherapeutic Methods," in *Handbook of Clinical Psychology*, ed. B. B. Wolman, New York, McGraw-Hill, 1965, pp. 1143–1167.

devices in solving field problems. In a process that is often seen in cultural systems and that helps to explain many cultural complexes, this behavior developed its own rationalizations. That is, *a necessity was transformed into a virtue.* The good professional came to be one who went into a "mysterious" situation (the field), gained rapport through a likeable personality and an imaginative mind, and collected valid data through hard work and creative thinking. The researcher was regarded as a creative problem solver, and the field as a place full of unpredictable situations. The result was that few anthropologists attempted to develop sophisticated field-work procedures, for within this framework such attempts appeared foolish. After all, how can one program the unpredictable?

Field-work culture—a system of implicit and explicit rules for field work—developed over time under the influence of a complex set of factors: the excitement and optimism of the Enlightenment, the work of amateur ethnographers, the creative hypotheses of "rubber-data" professionals, the work of sister-disciplines, the scarcity of professional ethnographers, the presence of a variety of types of great men, and the novel nature of field work itself. These and related variables developed field-work culture into a system that has much in common with other cultural systems. It includes methods for selecting new members and for achieving rank and status. Moral and ethical rules exist and function as both community solidifiers and guides for behavior. Science, magic, art, and economics are all to be found in this cultural system. And, though this characteristic is somewhat underplayed in the current neo-functionalist era of anthropology, field-work culture has as many inconsistencies and incongruities as any other ongoing and viable system. Let me illustrate this with a brief description of two complexes within field-work culture that taken together provide considerable inconsistencies. I will refer to these respectively as the "field-work mystique" and "field work as science."

When anthropologists get together and discuss field work, something happens to the immediate environment. The term *field work* is so packed with meanings, highly prized sentiments, and basic beliefs that its powers to influence anthropologists border on the magical. The term conjures up happy thoughts, pleasant memories, and exciting expectations. That the term should have these powers is not surprising, for it belongs to a category of terms describable as "environmental transformers." Among other environmental transformers are the terms *fête* and *puja.* At the mention of *fête* the faces of Trinidadian Negroes take on an ecstatic glow. *Fêtes* represent the good life, when one is living in a truly meaningful way. In Hindu Indian culture, the term *puja* designates good living. At a *puja*, or family prayer meeting, a man is surrounded by his family as he sits facing the *pundit*, whose prayers will assure the future well being of all who participate.

For the young graduate student preparing for his first field trip, field work represents mystery, opportunity, and excitement. Field work is also a trial through battle in a war for which the novice has little preparation. The student knows that this is a challenge he will have to face, a major *rite de passage* that will provide him with the opportunity to prove his ability, courage, and temperamental suitability for the profession. He knows that, in doing field work and in working with the ethnographic data he will collect, a number of transformations will occur. Basic anthropological concepts—culture, community, family, values— for which he previously demanded unique operational definitions will become "understood." By living in a strange cultural tradition he will somehow learn what culture "really means." By living among strangers whose good will is a requisite for survival, he will somehow learn to achieve enough rapport to collect personal information concerning sex, family, education, economy, polity, and religion. By attempting to change his "raw" field notes into artistic and anthropologically meaningful essays, he will somehow learn to analyze and draw generalizations from ethnographic materials. No specific techniques exist to help the young ethnographer transform a group of hostile natives into friendly informants; no specific and operationally useful rules exist for obtaining valid data; no program exists for translating raw data into information that is meaningful for anthropological analysis; and no specific techniques exist for drawing predictive generalizations from such information. Much like the *rites de passage* of many primitive societies, success in field work is more a function of personal ability than of previous training in specific techniques. Success in field work proclaims manhood and generates a major transformation: a student of culture becomes an anthropologist. Along with this new title come the rights of a real marginal native: to have one's "own" tribe and to be considered a specialist of an ethnographic area (i.e., the continent in which the tribe resides). The young anthropologist also becomes the owner of his own data bank, which can be used for teaching and for publications.

The mystique of field work—the magical properties of the term, the mysterious aspects of the work involved, the wonderful transformations that occur through living and working "in the field"—never disappears. Although field work develops more profound and subtle meanings after many field trips, its magic and mystery somehow remain. The field stands forever as a direct challenge to one's ability to be a real marginal native. Time and again I have heard experienced anthropologists—respected for their many successful field trips and publications—speak eagerly of plans for yet another field project. In their eagerness far more was involved than the added prestige they expected through the collection of new data and further publications. They were interested in reaffirming their right to be considered real, working anthropologists. Much like the knights of old who periodically had to legitimatize their status by yet another involvement in mortal combat, the anthropologist must periodically return to the "combat" of field work, so as to demonstrate that he is still an effective professional. The first field trip provides membership in the anthropological fraternity, but those who rest on the laurels of their *rite de passage* research become marginal members of this fellowship. To have status of a full participating member—a first-class anthropologist—one must think constantly of the next field trip, plan for it, and periodically carry out the plans. Field trips subsequent to the initial trip are thus *status-maintenance rites* and, I would claim, purification rites. An individual who decides to become an anthropologist enters into this profession with a variety of conscious and subconscious motives. Those motives that are more idealistic and more noble are reinforced through graduate training, and the anthropologist's personal involvement with them reaches a peak during his first field trip. After a period back in his own comfortable and materialistic world, the anthropologist may forget some of the important goals that drew him into this discipline. A return to the field thus functions as an intellectual, emotional, and spiritual "cleansing."

Each field trip is thus, in part, both a mystical experience and a sacred ritual. Somehow important data are collected, and somehow desirable transformations occur. The techniques for reaching desired goals have been set down by the modern masters (the "High Priests") and their disciples; they are thus susceptible to little critical evaluation. If traditional techniques are followed, the desired goals will be reached. If traditional techniques do not produce success, then it is the person, not the tradition, that is at fault. Success is assured for the ethnographer who is in a state of anthropological "grace"—with sincerity of purpose, emotional maturity, adaptability, sensitivity, friendliness, honesty, and a readiness to sustain much physical and psychological discomfort. Given the very general methodological guidelines that tradition provides we can better appreciate Lowie's ideas of a good ethnographer (1937:6) : "It is when a talent for observation accompanies both protracted residence and contact with professional ethnography that we obtain such superb results as mark the work of Snr. Nimuendaju."

The field-work mystique—field work as a "mystery" to be solved by doggedly following tradition and being of right character and personality—exists alongside a complex based on a very different set of principles. This complex, here designated "field work as science," includes a slowly expanding pool of information that instructs the field worker to do the following: (1) to gain knowledge of the language of "his tribe"; (2) to read up on all available ethnographic accounts of the area in which his research is planned; (3) to use the general methods of observation and participation, special informants, and informal and formal interviews; (4) to collect life histories and genealogies; (5) to check frequently on the reliability of both given bits of information and of information sources; (6) to develop controls for generalizations by designing studies such as "natural experiments" (Freilich, 1963); (7) to develop a host of related techniques for gathering, storing, retrieving, and analyzing data; (8) to develop programs for efficient use of time in the field; (9) to be concerned with reciprocities in field work (i.e., what informants can and do get in return for providing valid data); and (10) to use some of the research designs, techniques, and methods that have been developed by sister sciences such as sociology and psychology.

All anthropologists are commited to *some* aspects of the field-work-as-science complex, and most of them are also strongly attached to the field-work mystique. Somehow, these two somewhat contradictory complexes remain part of the field-work culture.

In summary, in this century field work developed a tradition or culture that guided (and continues to guide) both the training of anthropologists and the activities of field workers. Fieldwork culture, a system where goals rather than means are emphasized, includes mystical notions and "sacred" beliefs, as well as methodological and theoretical concerns related to "science." The underemphasis on science, the focus on goals, ritualism, and artistry have all functioned jointly to keep discussions on methodology to a minimum.

LIFE IN THE FIELD

Anthropologists have regularly left for field trips with only a scant knowledge of what awaits them and how best to achieve their research goals. Life in the field is rarely free of problems. Many of these problems are novel and difficult to handle, and the anthropologist often solves them in ways that are far from satisfactory. A second explanation for the dearth of published accounts of field experiences is, then, that such works would have to reveal the anthropologist's ineffectiveness or inefficiency in dealing with such problems. This explanation, which is supported by discussions with colleagues, friends, and students, general readings in anthropological literature, and my own field work with Mohawks, Trinidadians, schizophrenics, Hasidim, and rural Missourians, needs considerable explication.[13] Such an explication is attempted in the analysis that follows, which could be labeled the "natural history of a field project."

Traditional anthropological field work includes two distinguishable although overlapping stages. The first stage is primarily an adaptation period when the anthropologist must learn how to survive physically, psychologically, and morally in a strange setting. The second stage consists of the anthropologist's attempts to obtain the data pertinent to his research problem. The adaptation period involves activities that I will call *passive research,* and the second period involves activities that I will call *active research.*

Passive research is difficult for both the experienced researcher and the novice. The anthropologist generally arrives in the field with a broadly defined problem and a limited budget. Traditionally, the "field" is in some far-off place and involves groups about which little is known. When this is the case, the researcher is often wise to allow the field experience itself to guide him in formulating specific research problems. A strategy that is often used is to begin a project with a problem of wide generality. This strategy produces meaningful research problems and provides the anthropologist with a considerable work load. The researcher's limited budget means that he can rarely afford to pay for all the assistance he needs, so he must collect most data by himself. Working long hours, and often seven days a week, he is well aware of the size of his task and the brief time allotted for it, and thus he often begrudges the time he must spend in "passive" research.

The passive-research period is, however, the time when the anthropologist's efforts serve to solve basic field problems. It is

---

[13] The study in Missouri attempted to arrive at what I have called *mental-health culture.* In this study involving thirty-four rural communities, a mixture of anthropological and sociological methods were used. Ministers and medical doctors living in the communities were used as special informants on matters relating to local beliefs, values, and attitudes concerning mental health and mental illness. Similar data were collected in a much more "sociological" manner from representative household heads. For a summary of the initial findings of this research, see *Mental Health Culture in Rural Missouri,* St. Louis, The Social Science Institute, 1967.

during this period that he learns to restructure his views of social and cultural reality. To attain maximum rapport, he learns that he must accept the community's definitions of cultural reality. At the very least, he must learn to act *as if* the community's cultural world is a reasonable alternative to his own. During the passive-research period the anthropologist occupies the status of an insufficiently socialized child: he frequently acts inappropriately by community standards, and he receives negative sanctions for doing so. As he learns more and more about the culture of the community, two different and often incompatible sets of values govern many of his social interactions: those of his own culture—the *culture of orientation*—and those of his community's culture—the *native culture*. As the anthropologist attempts to develop a set of norms that integrates the culture of orientation with the native culture, he discovers that successful field work frequently requires *replacing* old cultural rules rather than integrating them with new ones, and this discovery often results in considerable internal conflicts.

The situation is exacerbated by the fact that the anthropologist is actually dealing with three, rather than two, cultures during this research stage: the culture of orientation, the native culture, and the field-work culture. While the latter should ideally provide many rules for learning the native culture, it actually lays down only a few and very general guides. Further, the difficulty of knowing how, when, and if to follow even these few guides in particular situations increases the problems of passive research. So the field anthropologist discovers rather quickly that he must work out his own research program and develop styles of work suitable both to the native culture and to his own personality. The novice, who is forced to rely heavily on his common sense, finds all too often that what is common sense in his culture of orientation is nonsense in the native culture. The more experienced field worker is in a superior position, for some of his problems are quite similar to those he faced in previous field sites. However, even anthropologists on their third and fourth field trips encounter novel problems requiring creative on-the-spot solutions.

The anthropologist deals with at least four types of problems while doing passive research: (1) physical survival, (2) psychological comfort, (3) everyday pragmatics, and (4) moral dilemmas.[14] The problems of physical survival are considerable in

---

[14] Like many other problems of passive research, these are present during the active-research stage also. However, by that time the anthropologist can deal with them more effectively due to his understanding of native culture.

most field-work situations; they are particularly difficult to handle in primitive societies. Finding a suitable dwelling, a steady and "interesting" supply of food, keeping either warm enough or cool enough for comfort and good health, and protecting oneself and one's possessions are problems not easily solved. Among the Mandaya in the Philippines, Aram Yengoyan was fortunate to have an abandoned dwelling "loaned" to him. His food, however, had to be transported by horseback and human carriers, and catsup became a necessity to mask the other food he had to eat. The problems of physical survival are aggravated when climatic conditions are difficult. John Honigmann, for example, had to allot a considerable portion of his field work time to collect and cut wood and to carefully nurse the stove in his cabin during his research among the Kaska Indians. Low temperatures and nearly constant winds caused the Honigmanns considerable problems in Baffin Island too. And although Professor Honigmann spent much time dressing for the cold, he suffered several mild cases of frostbite during his work with the Frobisher Bay Eskimos. In Ecuador, Norman Whitten developed a series of light fevers and intestinal problems and lost about twenty pounds. In Samoa, Robert Maxwell suffered from infected mosquito bites that left his body flecked with white spots and for two months he had an eye infection that kept his lids swollen and inflamed. Melvin Perlman and his wife contracted malaria while living among the Toro, and William Schwab, while working with the Oshogbo, also became quite ill with malaria.

The problems of physical survival, if unsolved, may lead to death and, if poorly solved, to physical sickness. The problems of psychological comfort, if unsolved, could lead to insanity and, if poorly solved, to periods of deep depression, anxiety, or related psychological states. The kinds of efforts needed to make a good psychological adaptation to field work are suggested in Napoleon Chagnon's description of the scene he encountered upon his arrival among the Yanomamö Indians in Venezuela.

> The excitement of meeting my first Indians was almost unbearable as I duck-waddled through the low passage into the village clearing. I looked up and gasped when I saw a dozen burley, naked, filthy, hideous men staring at us down the shafts of their drawn arrows! Immense wads of green tobacco were stuck between their lower teeth and lips making them look even more hideous, and strands of dark-green slime dripped from their noses. My next discovery was that there were a dozen or so vicious underfed dogs snapping at my legs. . . . Then the stench of decaying vegetation and filth struck me and I almost got sick. I was horrified.

This situation, described in Chagnon's *Yanomamö: The Fierce People* (1968), is an extreme one. The typical situation is much easier on the researcher's psyche, although it presents a considerable number of psychological problems. For example, Honigmann describes his short stay among the Slave and Cree Indians as a "dreadful seven weeks" that included "loneliness occasioned by separation from my family, claustrophobic fear of isolation brought on by the flooded rivers, and . . . interpreter and informant problems." Gulick, too, found the separation from his family a heavy burden, and Yengoyan speaks of the need he had to get away from the field to maintain his sanity. Maxwell speaks of a need to leave his village periodically to communicate with the Samoan élite, a need he could not meet, since, as he puts it, "The élite were so clean cut, and they placed so much stock in appearance that I found it embarrassing to present myself to them." In *Stranger and Friend,* Hortense Powdermaker writes of the times when she was "totally fed up with life and with native life" (1967:100), a psychological state I experienced during my research with Mohawk Indians and Trinidadian peasants.

Problems of "everyday pragmatics" include (1) *how to program one's time in the field:* when to get up, when to eat, when to sleep, when to relax, when to look for informants, when to allow informants to visit, and when to write up field notes; (2) *where to "hang out" during the quiet times of field work:* the docks, men's houses, gambling places, local rum shops, bars, other native spots; (3) *how quickly to accept and reciprocate friendly overtures from natives:* to get intimate quickly with community members who show obvious signs of desiring such a friendship, or to discover first how marginal these would-be friends are and what the other natives think of them; (4) *how to handle local commerce (if such exists):* where to purchase food, liquor, other consumable supplies, and hardware items, how to select a store for shopping, and how to allocate one's purchases among several stores; (5) *what exchange "currency" to use as payment for services rendered:* whether to pay informants, provide them with valued goods (cigarettes, liquor, food), offer them valued services (help in the fields, help with housebuilding, rides, the use of equipment, or use a combination of "payments"; (6) *how to deal with local "con men,"* i.e., people who want to "borrow" money or sell things the anthropologist doesn't need; and (7) *how to handle community schisms.* Almost invariably, the anthropologist will find himself in the midst of some kind of community conflict based on ethnicity, race, caste, or class. What kinds of roles can he play that will both enable him to maintain the respect of the natives and allow him to keep his own self-respect?

The following passage describing my field work in Trinidad highlights some of the problems of "everyday pragmatics":

Shortly after arriving in Anamat, Trinidad, I entered a general store in an area called "The Village." I introduced myself to the proprietor (Bram, an Indian in his fifties), who agreed to cash checks for me (a small one first, followed by larger amounts), to send orders up to my house, and to order special things for me from Port-of-Spain. For several weeks Bram was my sole Anamatian supplier, although I was aware that other stores like his existed in Anamat. I was happy with Bram's services and according to our cook—a daughter of a local peasant farmer, and an extremely bright woman—rightfully so. I was not being overcharged for anything, and I received services not generally afforded Anamatians. I never thought to ask her what in retrospect appears to be a most obvious question: What do the Anamatians think of Bram? Do they like him? Quite accidentally I discovered that I was losing rapport with both Indian and Negro informants because of my business relations with Bram, a man who was disliked by many of the community. My situation with the Indians was aggravated by the fact that another local and general store was owned and run by Maj, a man who belonged to the most prestigious Indian family in Anamat. For a variety of reasons I did not think it wise to immediately change my buying habits in a drastic fashion. Instead I slowly began to divide my purchases between the stores of Bram and Maj.

I had developed the habit of "hanging around" the post office when I had nothing else to do. Mr. Rapas, an Indian who had been introduced to me by the school teacher, was often to be found there. Rapas and I soon became quite friendly. We bought each other cold drinks while waiting for the postmaster to sort out the mail (the post office doubled as a "parlor," a general store, and a rum shop), and we exchanged house visits. I was later to discover that many of my initial problems with some members of the community stemmed from my habit of loafing at the post office (considered a lower-class hang out), and from my friendship with Rapas. Because of his constant fights with his brothers and his mother, Rapas was generally avoided by the prestigious Indians of Anamat. He was also disliked by most of the Negro peasants.

The moral dilemmas of field work arise when the anthropologist must decide whether to continue acting in the role of anthropologist—marginal native—or whether to temporarily assume the role of "real native"—an individual who can behave in ways he thinks "right," "just," and "human." The marginal native observes, listens, copies behavioral modes, feels, thinks, and records. The real native is often in a situation where his moral training or personal feelings incline him toward *active intervention*. Irrespective of the influences that lead the anthropologist to play the role of "real" native and irrespective of the effects on field work of playing this role, the practice raises several moral questions: Does the anthropologist have the right to interfere with the way of life of a community? Does his "contract" with the natives—in which he is alowed to live and work in the community in return for documenting their way of life, aiding in world peace, and so forth—allow or prohibit periodic attempts to intervene in the community life of the real natives? These are questions that plague both the novice and the experienced researcher. My own handling of one situation may throw additional light on the dimensions of this dilemma.

A Negro friend—who was also a good informant—came to my house one day, specifically to invite me to attend a "curing" session for his brother. The event was scheduled to begin around midnight, and was expected to continue until the early hours of the following morning. My friend's brother was described as a "wild man" who was always insulting people, who was not willing to work, and who repeatedly ran off into the woods and disappeared for days. My informant had been saving his money for nearly two years to pay for the services of an Obeah man (the charge was $300!). Through contacts (which he declined to discuss) he had found a "bush doctor, a great Obeah man," in Port-of-Spain, who had a fine reputation for treating people like his brother. The treatment, I was told, would include tying the patient to a tree, drenching him alternately with cold and hot water, beating him, and chanting secret "prayers." My dilemma—to stick to the role of anthropologist, show up with a camera and notebook and get a complete record of an interesting event, or to be a humanist, and try to save my friend from wasting his hard-earned savings and his brother from useless suffering—was "solved" by giving myself a short vacation. I invited my friend to have lunch with me and made my pitch. I argued eloquently against the value of using "doctors" who did not really understand what was actually mental illness and not a spell cast by another Obeah man. I offered to help him get psychiatric help for his brother in Port-of-Spain. As I kept talking and replenishing his glass with rum, his resistance to my arguments slowly faded. Finally, my friend was convinced. He promised to call the whole thing off. Satiated with food and somewhat high, he left to get a message off to the "doctor" about his change of plans. I sat a while gloating over the success of my strategy: alcohol mixed with reason.

The next day another informant told me of an interesting event that had taken place during the night. He was surprised that I had not been there so that I could learn "the way we do things for people who are crazy in the head." As the informant walked off I began to brood on the wisdom of "attacking" a curing-complex that in its own way (as a form of shock therapy) might be just as effective (or just as ineffective) as the psychiatric treatment I believed in. I remained in a depressed state for the rest of the day, alternatively worried about my interference, and upset by its failure.

Theoretically, optimal solutions exist for all passive-research problems, but the anthropologist is rarely lucky enough to hit on them. His major fear is that a particular solution will hinder his field work, will hurt his public image in the community, will force him to lose rapport with his informants, and will cut him off from given types of data. Such a fear is quite realistic.

As problems follow each other in rapid succession, and as some attempted solutions fail, the anthropologist develops strong doubts about his ability to conclude the project successfully. He is concerned about the passage of time and dissatisfied with his image in the community and with his relations with the real natives. The passive-research stage thus tends to be an emotionally painful time, marked with periods of anxiety and depression. Feelings experienced during psychotherapy are not significantly different from those the researcher develops while adapting to a native culture. Both the patient and the anthropologist have strong feelings of personal inadequacy, and both must look deeply into themselves and learn to change well-integrated behavior patterns, beliefs, values, and emotions. These highly personal experiences are not easily revealed to an impersonal public in cold print. If they are communicated at all, it is to long-time associates and friends "who understand." Even then, alcohol is often required to loosen the anthropologist's tongue on these sensitive topics.

It is important to emphasize that during the passive-research stage some information is gained relative to the project's end. As the anthropologist solves his adaptive problems—finding a site for his tent or finding a hut or house in which to live, stocking his new home with utensils, arranging for a regular food supply, acquiring efficiency in a "strange" language, hiring help, learning how to get around with ease (how to paddle a canoe, ski, handle a machete, or drive on the "wrong" side of the road), learning the route to central meeting places, and developing rapport—he is gathering much information about the native culture. However, at this stage, the information is often too novel and traveling toward him at too fast a rate and in too great a volume to be adequately decoded. Some of this information is received on a cerebral level, some gets picked up on a subconscious level, and some is completely missed. Thus, although the researcher has some general knowledge of the native culture at the conclusion of his passive research, he has little data of whose validity he is certain.

Once he has obtained shelter, developed a system for feeding himself, gained some rapport, learned to communicate, and learned the rituals for different types of encounters, the anthropologist systematically begins to collect the data for his research problem: he embarks on *active research*. The good personal feelings that were anticipated when passive research terminated actually occur, but only for short and infrequent periods. Active research rarely follows the ideal patterns described in textbooks on scientific method. The information the anthropologist obtained while doing passive research often indicates that some of his previously made plans either cannot be used or will not work. For example, a strict sampling may not be possible if local customs prohibit him from interviewing particular people or groups; if the subject matter central to the project's goals is too sensitive to be researched, due to the internal problems of the system being studied; or if important informants do not cooperate with the researcher because of his nationality, race, sex, or religious affiliation. If these or other obstacles arise, the anthropologist often has to give up an artistic and scientifically sound research design—one in which much hard work has been invested—for a less sophisticated but more practical project. Such changes are rarely made easily or without considerable pain.

Often, part of the suffering that occurs at these times is due to the anthropologist's unawareness that his colleagues are facing the same kinds of problems. This ignorance leads him to believe that his difficulties are due to his personal inadequacies. Isolated from the physical and psychological benefits of his culture of orientation, and away from family, friends, and colleagues, he has frequently lacked the comforting knowledge that, in field work, we are all "in the same boat."

Traditional anthropological research had as its goal the complete description of a way of life. Unfortunately, little consensus exists among professional anthropologists as to what a "complete" description of a culture is. To operationalize the term adequately one needs a theory of culture presented in language that is meaningful to the field anthropologist, but such a theory of culture currently does not exist. Working without one, the field worker who is engaged in a traditional study has few guides for deciding what data are relevant, marginal, or irrelevant for a given subject. Without a formal model, which would set the boundaries for data collection, the typical field study has no logical end.[15] A common cry of the anthropological field worker is:

---

[15] Margaret Mead has described this situation as follows: "The anthropological approach is to go into primitive societies without any too specific theories and ask instead open-ended exploratory questions. How do male

"I could have gone on and on, there was so much to be done." The logical question, but one rarely asked, is: "If I had as much time as I desired, how would I know when the study was completed?" Hence, when the time comes for the anthropologist to leave the field, he has a strong sense of "unfinished business."

In sum, the many problems faced in the field, the poor solutions used to solve some of them, the dissatisfactions with an uncompleted task, and a lack of knowledge of the similar plight of other field workers often lead the anthropologist to leave the field with an unduly harsh evaluation of his own performance. He blames himself for the generality of his research problem—forgetting the sparse data he had with which to develop a more complex design. He is upset by the length of time it took to achieve enough rapport to begin active research—forgetting the many novel rapport problems he had to face. He chastises himself for having spent some time away from his field site—forgetting the physical and emotional states that prompted his flight, and the recuperative value of such holidays. Often reasoning in terms of Protestant-ethic values, he wrongly believes that with harder work and less time "wasted" for "fun," he could have accomplished a much more successful project.[16]

Upon his return from the field, the anthropologist busies himself analyzing and writing up his field notes. When he is finally ready to publish his work, he generally presents the central focus of the study as a thesis, a monograph, or a book, and writes up the other data for scholarly journals. At this time one might assume that his data on field experiences and methods would be brought together and handled in a manner analogous to other data collected during field work, but generally this does *not* occur. Although field-work culture stresses the importance of sharing ethnographic data with the anthropological community as soon as it can be analyzed and written up, it has traditionally provided only minimal encouragement to publish on

---

babies and female babies learn their social roles in different societies? What types of behavior have some societies classified as male, what as female? What behaviors have they failed to treat as sex-typed? How like have some societies felt males and females to be—and how unlike? . . . how different peoples expect infants to behave, how they use the difference in sex to define difference in role, and how they succeed in evoking the expected responses." *Male and Female: A Study of the Sexes in a Changing World*, New York, William Morrow, 1949 Ch. 2.
[16] This point is well illustrated by Malinowski's diary materials. For example, Malinowski was upset that he did not work hard enough, and that women excited him: "I turn in too late, I get up at irregular hours. Too little time is devoted to observation, contact with the natives, too much to barren collecting of information. I rest too frequently. . . . I must never let myself become aware of the fact that other women have bodies, that they copulate." (1947:247–249)

methods and field experiences. Lacking such encouragement and often unaware that the "goofs" of other anthropologists are as many and as serious as his own, the researcher delays writing up these painful experiences. These delays are often life-long and most understandable.[17] One resists publishing material that appears to document one's inadequacies in the field, particularly since competence in field work is considered the mark of a real professional.

An institution that probably contributes to the lengthening of these delays is the "bull session" on field work that often takes place at anthropological conferences. After a day of listening to and presenting scholarly papers, anthropologists generally get together at little parties where the talk frequently turns to field work. In an atmosphere made cheerful by alcohol, and often in the presence of envious graduate students yet without field experiences, these discussions of life in the field almost invariably omit certain kinds of information. Much time is spent presenting bits of data that throw new light on a given theoretical problem or that make a traditionally accepted ethnographic description either doubtful or in need of some revision, and considerable time is spent recalling the "joys" of field work. Happy solutions to field-work problems, prestigious meetings with high-status officials—chiefs, tribal leaders, and the government élite—and wonderful parties with exotic food and entertainment are discussed at length, but it is rare indeed to hear a speaker describe the emotional pains of field work, especially those of the early "culture shock" period. Rarely mentioned are anthropologist's anxious attempts to act appropriately when he knew little of the native culture, the emotional pressures to act in terms of the culture of orientation, when reason and training dictated that he act in terms of the native culture, the depressing times when the project seemed destined to fail, the loneliness when communication with the natives was at a low point, and the craving for familiar sights, sounds, and faces.

What happens to these memories of pain, anxiety, and sorrow? Anthropologists, either consciously or unconsciously, attempt to forget the more stressful and unhappy times of field work. Such attempts are facilitated by and indeed casually related to a number of phenomena. First, anthropologists are dedi-

---

[17] Professor Powdermaker writes that when many of her contemporaries heard about her book *Stranger and Friend* they claimed that they too had often thought of doing such work (i.e., one describing in an intimate fashion the experiences of field work). Since Professor Powdermaker's contemporaries began their research careers in the exciting days when the masters were teaching anthropology, these scholars have already delayed quite a while.

cated to field work; they consider it both a mission and a privileged duty. It is understandable, therefore, that the memories that surround field work should be selectively weighted toward the pleasant. Second, the meaning, sentiments, and feelings conjured up by the term *field work* are such that unpleasantness is not easily linked to it. As highly selective recollections are shared with colleagues, friends, and students, positive and pleasant meanings are reinforced, and the magical qualities of the term are strengthened. Third, by maintaining and developing the fiction of the pure joys of field work, the anthropologist can conveniently repress some of the misinterpretations he has made of his own field-work performances. That is, since he often believes that many of his field problems are signs of personal incompetence, since he has much other evidence of his competence as a field worker, and since he would rather believe the positive "data," a useful bit of self-deception is to forget the bad times. By such mental manipulation a number of elements of field-work culture can remain in equilibrium: (1) in the field the anthropologist can continue to attribute many of his problems and errors to personal inadequacies; (2) after leaving the field he can continue to forget field problems, aided both by the tradition of not writing up field experiences and by discussions centering on the "joys" of field work; and (3) by maintaining an image of himself as a good field worker and of the field as an exciting and pleasant place, he can continue to plan future field trips with self-confidence and happy anticipations.

The forgetting process is probably far more complex than this, and it probably is closely related to the personality of the anthropologist and the degree to which he is able to practice self-deception. However, I submit that such forgetting occurs with considerable regularity and contributes greatly to the dearth of writings on field experiences. To summarize, the following "variables" jointly function to inhibit the writing up of field experiences and methods: field-work culture, problems encountered in the field, the habit of defining many field problems as a function of personal inadequacies, and the repressing of painful times and events in the field.

But why, you may ask, is there also a shortage of published accounts describing the happy events of field work? Why are descriptions of the latter by and large limited to bull-session discussions? Precisely what do anthropologists find enjoyable about field work, and why are these pleasures rarely shared with the scientific community?

It is difficult to present a list of experiences related to field work that *all* anthropologists will describe as joyful and pleasant. Obviously, many such phenomena are matters of personal taste and are related to the different personalities and backgrounds of field workers. However, some phenomena exist that most anthropologists would probably describe as pleasurable and personally rewarding. Among these I would isolate (1) the professional and personal "stock taking" that accompanies the planning stage of a new project; (2) the excitement of field preparations and early field-work experiences; (3) the intellectual challenge of field work; and (4) the opportunity it offers to escape from normal routines, i.e., to change one's life-style.

Life in the field shows strong discontinuities with life in one's culture of orientation. New field projects thus become "time markers" in the life of the anthropologist: they close one period and herald the start of another, and they present the anthropologist with an opportunity to review his basic ideas, beliefs, values, and goals, a mental exercise that is personally very satisfying. This review is also useful for field work, for it helps the anthropologist to develop a project that *really* interests him by incorporating theories and methods that he has come to believe in. Further, it brings to a more conscious level the self-doubts and fears that accompany new challenges, allowing them to be handled more rationally and thus more effectively.

Preparations for field work invariably generate considerable excitement. A combination of real and unreal anticipations, hurried attempts to complete travel arrangements, "goodbye" parties, and attempts to contact scholars familiar with the culture to which one is bound all put the researcher into a state of euphoria.

The intellectual challenge of cross-cultural research is also a source of considerable personal and professional satisfaction. In finding solutions to the many problems that field work provides, the anthropologist's analytical and creative powers are often taxed. The joys experienced in solving vexing field problems are later relived when the data are being analyzed. The data analysis and synthesis necessitate a rethinking of current anthropological theory. Often this leads one to develop new categories and theoretical modifications that better explain the findings of the study. In brief, the challenges found at every stage of a field project, and the solutions developed around them, provide the anthropologist with considerable satisfactions. The latter increase as the researcher publishes and otherwise communicates his findings and as he receives valuable feedback from his peers and students.

Finally, field work provides a kind of "escape" from normal routines. In attempting to carve out some kind of consistent set of behavior linking together the culture of orientation, the field-work culture, and the native culture, the anthropologist develops new roles and new routines that provide him with an opportunity to be himself or, better, his selves. A discussion of the pleasures of field work of necessity becomes a discussion of the type of person who seeks and enjoys such pleasures. The anthropologist is often a person with idealistic beliefs about man's ability to improve his way of life, with romantic notions concerning the good human relations and noble goals of primitive societies, and with strong humanistic feelings for people of all races and cultures. He also has a strong belief in the mission of anthropology: to collect data from fast-disappearing primitive societies, to get laymen to understand the relativity of culture, so that prejudice is given no basis in fact, and to communicate ideas about the basic dignity of man.

Many anthropologists traditionally have shown a disdain for the comforts of modern Western societies and a disregard for the findings of modern medical research, at least as they apply to many health problems in the field, yet these same anthropologists are deeply interested in the problems of the modern world. Convinced that cultural anthropology has much to offer in easing race relations, ethnic conflicts, and world tensions, some anthropologists have recently attempted to maximize their contributions by following ever more strictly the dictates of the scientific method.

This portrait of the anthropologist as an idealist, romantic, humanist, scientist, adventurer, and man with a mission is not easily presented to an impersonal public. Indeed, it is not easily acceptable to the anthropologist himself! These various traits rarely "sit well" in one body. If he thinks of himself primarily as a scientist, the anthropologist may well be unhappy with the "impurity" of his motives for doing anthropology. That is, he may not realize that an individual must have a rather complex set of motives to leave the comforts of understood environments for the world of native cultures. The more he thinks about the experiences of field work—both the pleasant and the painful ones—the more he is forced to look into himself in order to understand his reactions to the various field situations he encounters. This kind of self-analysis is not easy, and if accomplished, the findings are not easily communicated via the cold and impersonal media of the printed page. The anthropologist who plays "center stage" in a "strange" society for a year or more is reluctant to present his real self (or selves) to members of his culture of orientation.[18]

---

[18] It is interesting to compare my portrait of a typical field worker with Evans-Pritchard's description of the qualities that make for a perfect field worker (1964:82): "To succeed [in field work] a man must be able

WHITHER FIELD-WORK CULTURE?

The consequences of anthropologists' reluctance to publish their field experiences and their widespread disinterest in developing a systematic methodology for field work are quite serious for a discipline generally classified as a science. It has meant that for many anthropologists, and for most anthropological graduate students, field work is still a venture into a mysterious world: rules for survival, for work, and for play are both sparse and very general.[19] If field experiences were shared, many common errors could be avoided, and many successful strategies, methods, and ways of coping emulated.

The anthropologist experienced in field work has much valuable information to share. With every field trip he learns to work more effectively and more efficiently. He learns how to obtain rapport faster, how to avoid with less embarrassment and difficulty excessive involvement with marginal members of the community, how to better utilize his personality for the project's ends, how to better understand his own particular tendencies to misinterpret some kinds of phenomena, and, by paying more careful and studied attention at these times, how to achieve greater objectivity in his research. He learns to develop more and better field tests to validate given conclusions, and to discover quicker ways of finding situations where data flow freely and better means of avoiding situations that produce little information relative to the time and energy invested. His reactions to an informant's communication signals and symbols are more often correct. He is better able to decode signs of boredom, fatigue, resistance, hostility, and cooperation. He learns to avoid

---

to abandon himself without reserve, and he must also have intuitive powers . . . ability, special training, and love of a careful scholarship . . . the imaginative insight of the artist which is required in interpretation of what is observed, and the literary skill necessary to translate a foreign culture into the language of one's own. . . . he must have in addition to a wide knowledge of anthropology, a feeling for form and pattern, and a touch of genius."

[19] Learning a native culture is still, for many anthropologists, a procedure not unlike seducing a woman. Success is made more probable if one knows the language, if he is passionately attached to his goal, if he has the charm and style to gain good rapport, if effective use is made of special informants, and if the project is vigorously pursued with a high investment of time and energy. Questions concerning very specific techniques, operationally described, are rather indecent.

hasty interpretations. He learns how to broadcast his project in ways that the natives find more understandable and acceptable. He learns to estimate more accurately when to arrive at functions and when to leave, when he is being used as the group's goat, and when his work is being taken seriously. He is able to predict with greater accuracy how he is likely to react to given field situations: what kinds of field experiences he will find enjoyable and what kinds of situations will make him anxious or depressed. These kinds of understandings are vital for effective field work; put to use regularly they also make for more efficient field work.

The average graduate student leaving on his first field assignment knows little about these matters. The prospect of the mysterious "field" makes him quite apprehensive, and he is anxious to pick up any bit of information he can get to make his assignment more predictable. Gerald Berreman makes this point very clearly (1962:3):

> Not so many years ago, when a group of us were preparing to leave the relative security of the teaching assistant's room for the entirely mysterious world of the "field," we went to one of our teachers and asked him to tell us what it was like. We also expressed some doubts about our capacity to carry on "field work" in spite of the steady diet of ethnographies which for months had been ours. . . . the council fell rather short of our expectations, not because we had wanted solemn warnings about unlikely diseases or sanitation problems, but because we had wanted to know "what it is like" rather than "how to do it."

In anthropological field work a close relation exists between the questions "what is it like?" and "how do you do it?" What it is like includes feelings of frustration, fears, hopes, isolation, exciting "on-stage" performances, euphoric heights, and deep depressions, and these feelings must be understood both for the anthropologist's psychological comfort and for effective research. Learning to understand them is a basic part of "how to do it," for in anthropological research the field worker is not just a dogged follower of an artistic research design; he is not a puppet programmed to follow automatically a plan of research operations; he is not just the bearer of research tools; he is not just a "reader" of questions found on questionnaires; and he is not just a dispenser of printed schedules. He is the *project:* his actions will make the field trip either a success or a failure. What he does in the field will tend either to attract or to repel information. He is the information absorber, the information analyzer, the information synthesizer, and the information interpreter.

The flow of information toward the field worker—its frequency, amount, and validity—depends to a large extent on his image in the community. Are his "on-stage" performances consistent? Are they honest? Are his beliefs in racial and cultural democracy sincere? Is private information safe with him? Is it rewarding to treat him as a friend? These and similar questions are silently, but regularly, put to the anthropologist by his informants. The answers informants receive come in large part from the anthropologist's actions while in the community. His public image becomes either that of an individual who should be avoided, one with whom only brief discussions are wise, or one with whom it is rewarding to converse at great length. The information the anthropologist receives can be totally false, slightly misrepresented, the very bare facts, or facts and interpretations presented as completely and as honestly as possible. The nature of the information he receives depends largely on his public image. A favorable public image requires some "impression management"—a process much facilitated if the anthropologist is emotionally calm and if he has an understanding of his mental states. Such self-knowledge also helps to develop the kind of rapport necessary for receiving complete and honest data. As information of various kinds flows toward the anthropologist, it is his internal states that by and large determine how it is received. That is, such data are caught, fumbled, dropped, or completely missed, largely depending on the state of the marginal native's psyche. If the anthropologist is constantly plagued by fears, anxieties, and desires to please everyone at all times, much information will either pass him by or will be completely misunderstood.

As the raw data are analyzed, synthesized, and interpreted, errors made during data collection can be highly magnified, partly because anthropology currently lacks well-developed, formalized methods for decoding field-work information. The analysis and synthesis of the data are very much at the mercy of the individual researcher, and the anthropologist with psychological problems and little insight concerning them produces analyses that are quite suspect. His final presentation of findings merits investigation: Were the natives really that paranoid? Or is the paranoia more in the researcher than in the cultural world he is depicting? Were the natives really that angry, anxious, hostile, and megalomanic? Or were these traits more a part of the basic personality of the researcher than of the culture he studied?

The point is, the critical tool in anthropological research is the researcher himself. This is why it is so important that he be ready to meet the many challenges of his work. To prepare well-fashioned field workers a pool of information and training programs are needed that will permit the following kinds of questions to be answered: (1) What is it like in the field? (2) How is field work done by experienced anthropologists? (3) How *should* field work be done? (4) How am I, the novice preparing for a first field trip, likely to perform in the field?

A discussion of how field work should be done and how to gather the kind of information that will permit a novice to make good predictions about his future performances in the field is delayed for the final chapter of this book. Here I am concerned with how to make field work a more public experience. It seems clear that field work will become more public only if individual anthropologists are ready to make it so. The gaining of much more data on *what it's like* and *how it's done* requires answers to a very basic question: Why should the field worker present his real selves—his problems, mistakes, and satisfactions—to an impersonal public? My answer is, because he will find it "pays" to do so. I believe it is demonstrable that the net benefits from such writings (the positive feedback *minus* any negative sanctions) are greater than the net benefits from following present field-work culture.

What predictable reciprocities are there to tempt a field worker to relive his field experiences for thousands of readers? What kind of "compensations" can marginal natives hope to receive for the time-consuming and difficult introspective work necessary to transform field notes on methods and experiences into meaningful essays on life in the field? Two kinds of "payments" will be forthcoming from such efforts. First, writings that demand deep introspective thought will help the anthropologist to achieve a superior knowledge of himself, a deeper and more objective self-awareness. As he relives fearful, stressful, and tension-creating field experiences, he will get deeper insights into his fears and anxieties. Second, not only will this superior understanding of himself better enable him to handle similar field situations in the future, but verbalizing painful times of the past actually reduces the fears that may have generated them in the first place.[20] Writing on field experiences thus represents a kind of self-analysis: an analysis of internal mental states focused around experiences in the field. By getting to understand his field-work fears and anxieties, the anthropologist may be able to handle situations previously considered difficult. In brief, at the very least, such writings will permit the researcher to relive fearful times "on paper" and make his future

---

[20] Systematic desensitization as a therapeutic method is well described by Joseph Wolpe in his paper "The Experimental Foundations of Some New Psychotherapeutic Methods," in *Experimental Foundations of Clinical Psychology*, ed. Arthur J. Bachrach, New York, Basic Books, 1962, especially pp. 564–566.

adaptations to analogous situations more effective. At best, such situations will no longer be conceived as fearful. In either case superior field adaptations will result.[21]

The benefits of this focused self-analysis are far greater than merely reducing the problems in the field. As previously indicated, the internal mental state of the anthropologist is a prime determinant of his presentation-of-self in his research community. His presentation-of-self leads to a public image that attracts or repels valid data. Indirectly, therefore, the anthropologist's internal mental state greatly affects the nature of the messages that are "sent" to him. Further, his internal mental state is an important determinant of what happens to the data that are sent: how much of it he "receives," what meanings he gives to it, and the closeness of fit between the "meanings" informants intend and the "meanings" the anthropologist decodes. In short, other things being equal, the greater the reality-orientation of the anthropologist, the more likely that his raw data and his interpretations are valid. Hence, anything that tends to increase the field worker's reality-orientation makes him a superior field worker.[22] Once field workers realize that writing about their life and work in the field increases their reality-orientation, they will write more on these phenomena.

The long-term benefit of such writings is the development of an ever-widening pool of information on field experiences and practices. This matter has already been discussed and needs but a brief review. Personal field-work errors will become under-

---

[21] Often a researcher with some insight can reinterpret a troublesome situation to his advantage. For example, after several very difficult weeks at the beginning of one of my field trips, I fell into a state of deep depression. A psychotherapist, after a few sessions, pinpointed my anxieties by asking me the following question: "Do you want to do a good project, or do you want all your informants to like and admire you?" It soon became clear that I wanted both "instant" popularity with the natives and the satisfaction of doing a good project. I somehow learned to accept my position in the community as that of a marginal native who in time could develop enough rapport with the real natives to complete the project successfully. I was helped to reinterpret a situation—the passive-research period—that I had successfully adapted to in several previous projects. I might well have been spared this depressing period had I previously written up my field experiences.

[22] This argument provides support for the belief held by many social scientists that some kind of psychotherapy is a valuable adjunct to other forms of field-work training. Margaret Mead has for a long time been a vigorous proponent of this position. It has also received published support by Hortense Powdermaker, Herbert Gans, and Morris and Charlotte Schwartz. The Schwartzes discuss the possible harmful influences of one's feelings toward the informants and their culture and conclude, "Only by increasing awareness of his own feelings and their effects will the researcher be able to counteract their destroying influence." See "Problems in Participant Observation," *American Journal of Sociology*, LX:4:343–353.

stood for what they usually are—the common experiences of researchers working in strange and minimally understood environments. Self-castigations for poor decision-making in the field and the concomitant effects of such self-blame—a lowering of self-confidence and the development of a cycle in which foolish mistakes keep increasing due to increasing concerns with one's performances—will by and large disappear. The mistakes will also decrease because the researcher will be constantly learning from the field experiences of others. The constantly increasing pool of information on field experiences and methods will enable anthropologists to develop a sophisticated set of methods, strategies, and theories for use in field research. Field work culture can, in this manner, evolve from a system that includes magic and mysticism to one firmly rooted in science and its methodology.

In summary, the sparsity of writings on anthropological field methods and field experiences is explained by, first, a field-work culture that underemphasizes methodology and supports private rather than public communications of field experiences, and, second, the "rewards" field workers receive for keeping their errors and their personalities hidden and for maintaining a romantic attachment to the field-work mystique. It is suggested that anthropologists will receive valuable personal and professional rewards by writing on their field-work methods and experiences. I would add that irrespective of the benefits that individual anthropologists will get from such writing, they have a duty to their discipline to make field experiences public information, for it is only through a regular sharing of field methods and experience that anthropology can develop a truly scientific methodology. As Joseph McGrath reminds us (1964:534):

> Differences in research methodology *do* make a difference in the yield of research . . . . When we choose one methodology over others . . . , we are thereby affecting the kinds and amount of information which we can obtain from results of that study . . . . It follows that we should choose the methodology that we will use in a given case on the basis of the kinds of information we are seeking (i.e., the nature of the problem we are studying), and we should choose so as to maximize the amount of information which we will gain about that problem . . . . When we choose our methodology for reasons of personal preference, familiarity, or operational expediency, we are changing the nature of the problem about which we will gain information, as well as altering the amount of information which we can gain from our study.

Differences in research methodology do make a difference in the research yield. To take a hard line, the meaning of data is intrinsically connected to the manner in which they are collected. It is clearly of critical importance that anthropologists state fully, frankly, and unapologetically what they do, and when, how, and why they do it. The gains from such expositions will be high: the data from anthropological research will be more understandable, the methods available for anthropological research will be better and more widely understood, and individual anthropologists will more objectively do their work, due to a superior reality-orientation. Taken together, this will mean that anthropological field work will be able to evolve from an art only slightly touched by science into a science that permits its practitioners ample opportunities for artistic expression.

COMPARATIVE FIELD TECHNIQUES IN URBAN RESEARCH IN AFRICA

William B. Schwab

Social anthropology is not an experimental science. We cannot tear apart our raw data, build it up, or modify it in any way. Nor can we conduct rigidly controlled scientific experiments that lend themselves to duplication or verification. Far less than in any physical science are we able to approximate an isolated neutral system of relationships and determine its functions. Yet social anthropology strives for a theoretical understanding of human behavior. It sets out to isolate and expose the regularities manifested in social behavior and to present a rational description of these relationships. Thus, it shares a general orientation with those sciences that endeavor to discover and analyze the regularities in nature.

It also shares with the natural sciences many of the same

problems of demonstrating the validity of theory, methods, and reality. One can argue that if there is a trinity in anthropology, it is the relationship of method and theory to the reality of the collected data. The anthropologist must determine whether the data he has collected reflect real behavior in the society he is studying. If the raw data are questionable and if serious doubts develop with regard to their reality, he must re-evaluate his theory and/or his method. Until recently, many anthropologists carried out their research in small-scale communities in which the populations rarely exceeded 2,000 inhabitants. Because the universe under study was small, the anthropologist was often able to establish social relationships with the total population that provided him with a means of checking on his raw data. Many anthropologists tended to ignore theoretical considerations and let the data "speak for itself" in leading the way to theoretical formulations. Some collected data widely, hoping that if sufficient data were collected, the pieces would fall into their respective places, and the raw data would reflect the true real behavior in the society.

Recently anthropologists have begun to make use of more precise methodology and to pay more attention to theoretical implications than they did previously. This has been particularly true with regard to urban or large-scale studies where the communities under investigation have exceeded 5,000 inhabitants. In communities this large, reality is difficult to ascertain, and the universe may not be reflected in the raw data unless precise tools are used. The anthropologist is unable to meet and know all the inhabitants, and individual and institutional behavior is much too vast and complicated for one observer to record. Nevertheless, more precise tools and greater attention to theory can turn a difficult and complex urban field study into a relatively manageable field-research project.

This chapter will compare the methodology employed in two large-scale urban field studies that I carried out in Africa in the 1950s. I have indicated the flaws, difficulties encountered, and the achievements accomplished in both studies. I have made some attempt to assess the implications of the methodology and theory employed in both studies. The first field venture was an analysis of the Yoruba city of Oshogbo in the western provinces of Nigeria. The second project was a study of Gwelo, a Rhodesian city in the high ridge country between Bulawayo and Salisbury. Oshogbo is a mud city of approximately 150,000 inhabitants, and Gwelo is a European-dominated urban center of 32,000 people.

My interest in Africa was stimulated and developed by the professors with whom I studied. After World War II, I was for-

tunate to work under Dr. Hans Wieschhoff, one of the few out-
standing Africanists in America at that time. Dr. Wieschhoff
conveyed to me, and to others, his intense interest in Africa and
his concern with the lack of behavioral research in Africa. To
him, Africa was a scientific enigma that most social scientists,
particularly American anthropologists, had ignored. He saw
Africa as a land of mystery that had to be scientifically investigated before its people could be properly understood. Africa, to
Wieschhoff, was a vast anthropological laboratory from which
could be abstracted basic laws and generalities concerning human
behavior.

For many years, I had been concerned with the problems of
urbanism in America. As my interests in Africa developed, my
concern with urbanism shifted to Africa. In 1949 Africa was
the least urbanized continent, and few analyses had been made
of its urban centers. The British Social Science Research Council was interested in an analysis of a traditional African city,
and, when my interests coincided with theirs, our only problem
was what city or people to study. At the time, it was apparent to
me and other anthropologists that the Yoruba were the most
urbanized people in Africa. When I left America for England,
I had agreed to conduct an urban study of a Yoruba city in Nigeria. The exact city was to be decided in England in consultation with the British Social Science Research Council, the Nigerian Government, and British anthropologists.

My second field project was partially determined by my first
study. I was interested in comparing Oshogbo with other African
urban centers, and I sought a city that had been affected by similar factors of change. I was searching also for an African city
that had a structural composition different from Oshogbo's and
a city that reflected a geographical background and cultural development different from that found in West Africa. For these
reasons, I rejected most of the traditional urban centers of East
and West Africa. Southern Africa, with its Rhodesian and South
African cities, seems to embody the elements of change and
structure that I was seeking, but population size, racial conflicts,
economic complexities, political tensions, and marked ethnic
diversity and heterogeneity forced me to discard this area, too.
By elimination, I was left with the Rhodesias from which to
select a city for the second project. I felt that my final decision
could best be made in London in consultation with British anthropologists, the Rhodes-Livingstone Institute, and officials of
the Rhodesian Government.

A number of personal details affected both studies. In the
Oshogbo project, I had no children, and my wife participated
fully, collecting much of the data pertaining to women. When I

undertook the Gwelo project, we had one child, and so my wife was not able to participate as much as she did in Oshogbo. However, the addition of my son did not present any other problems. His activities were carefully supervised by a nursemaid, and he was able to make friends with the children in the neighboring European households. The operation of our household during both projects was taken care of by the servants I employed. The well-being and operational efficiency of most Europeans in the tropics is usually dependent on the competence of their servants, and I was fortunate in being able to employ extremely skillful and loyal Africans whose efficiency made my own life and activities much easier.

Housekeeping details are essential to the successful operation of any anthropological field study, and probably the most important is to locate a place to live. To find permanent living quarters in Oshogbo was difficult, as there were no vacant houses, spare accommodations, or facilities that we could rent. The African population lived in massive mud compounds and were not receptive to European outsiders residing with them and invading their privacy. In small village studies, the community often builds the anthropologist a house, but this is rare in larger, more complex, and more impersonal communities. In Oshogbo, the indigenous leaders were not inclined to either build or loan me a house, since they considered me to be the responsibility of the colonial power, which politically dominated the community. The European population was made up of ten resident colonial and commercial officials, who resided in a small quarter outside the town limits. Even if I had wanted to live in the European section, I would not have been able to, for there were no houses available in the area. The only other accommodation in the town was a "rest house" or small dried-mud catering hotel that had been built by the Colonial Administration within the town to house transient officials. When my wife and I arrived in Oshogbo, we were temporarily assigned quarters in this rest house. Obviously, we had to find some neutral quarters that would not irritate the Africans, would satisfy the Colonial Administration, and would still allow us to observe and participate in the life of the community. After considerable search and consultation, the only possible solution appeared to be the rest house, and the Colonial Administration, at the suggestion of the local District Officer, permanently assigned to us a section of the rest house consisting of three small mud rooms. The quarters were adequate and clean and allowed us to participate, to a limited degree, in town life. Our greatest difficulty was the lack of privacy, as we were constantly under the scrutiny and surveillance of the Africans who lived in the vicinity. Although the quarters were cramped, and at times quite hot, we eventually made them comparatively comfortable and looked upon them as home.

In Gwelo our housing problem was not so complicated. In London we inquired through the Colonial Office and the Rhodesian representative about a house in Gwelo. Since by Rhodesian law we could live only in the European quarter, our problem was much easier to solve than it had been in Oshogbo. After a short wait, the Rhodesian representative in London informed us that a modern European house would be available to us when we arrived in Gwelo five months later. Unlike our quarters in Oshogbo, it was spacious, cool, and pleasant and contained modern water and sanitation facilities.

Most field workers in a tropical climate fall prey to various illnesses. In Oshogbo, I was quite sick with malaria and dysentery, to which our rather primitive quarters and food contributed to some degree. In Gwelo, I was not seriously ill, for our better living conditions helped us remain healthy and possibly more efficient. As important as good living conditions can be, few studies fail because of the lack of them. It is only when ill health and extremely bad living quarters coincide that the field venture is seriously hurt and severe damage is done.

Finally, there is an excitement and sense of adventure and purpose that accompanies the anthropologist's first field venture that is usually missing in later studies. It is his "first love," and although he may be more efficient in later studies and accomplish much more, his first love is rarely ever replaced.

PART I: OSHOGBO, AN URBAN
COMMUNITY IN NIGERIA[1]

Problem, Theory, and Research Design

In 1949, I left America for England and Africa, on a British Social Science Research Council grant, to carry out a field study of a Yoruba urban community in Nigeria. The Yoruba people, who have occupied the western section of Nigeria for many centuries, are probably the most urban of all African peoples. They live mainly in large, densely populated, mud cities, which in re-

---

[1] Sections of this chapter were previously published in *Human Organization*, 13:2, and 24:4. The papers were entitled "An Experiment in Methodology in a West African Urban Community," and "Looking Backward: An Apraisal of Two Field Trips."

cent times have ranged from 10,000 inhabitants to well over 150,000. At the time of the study, late 1949 to early 1951, little was known about the Yoruba, as no systematic analytical research had been conducted among them. There existed no pertinent analysis or description of the indigenous social, economic, or political structure of the Yoruba people or their towns. We knew that changes induced by foreign influences since the advent of the British in 1900 had proceeded far and rapidly, but the direction and scope of these changes had not been investigated. My problem was clear: to make an intensive anthropological survey of the social, political, and economic organization of a Yoruba city. What city to study and what methods to employ had still to be determined.

Before going to Nigeria, I spent most of 1949 in London learning Yoruba, perusing the literature and the Colonial Office files for information about the Yoruba, absorbing British anthropological knowledge, and determining the Yoruba city to be studied and the methodological procedures to be pursued in the field. The methodology that finally emerged was to a large extent a result of the many discussions I had with British Africanists in London. It was quite clear from the very start of the research that such traditional anthropological methods as participant observation, interviewing selected informants, collecting case histories and genealogies, and observing group and individual activities, would not be adequate.

The methodological problem was further complicated by factors inherent in Yoruba urban communities. The population size of Yoruba towns, the great variation in behavior and norms, the extensive social differentiation, and the marked heterogeneity indicated the necessity of using some kind of measurement techniques. These critical social conditions suggested that the selection of reliable and representative informants would be crucial to the success of the project and difficult to obtain. It was not only a question of whether an individual or group was typical or atypical and this is difficult in any study, but also the need for selecting informants who would represent the marked diverse social components of a Yoruba community. These four factors, (1) the inherent complexity and size of Yoruba towns, (2) the enormous variation in behavior, (3) the diverse social components, and (4) the need for a sophisticated measurement technique, that necessitated the use of sociological survey methods and sampling techniques. Questionnaires, field guides, random sampling, and other sociological devices had to be employed. We would also need field assistants to help collect the raw data, as one scientific observer would be unable to observe or record the diverse patterns of behavior. It was apparent also that a random-sample census would be necessary to establish a reliable scientific base for the study that could be used as the basis for future research as well.

But there was another factor that had to be considered. Since British contact in 1900, numerous external forces had exerted profound influence on the internal structure of Yoruba communities. For over forty years, European trading concerns, governmental agencies, and missionaries had been active in Yorubaland. New occupations had developed, and the scope of economic mobility, both horizontal and vertical, had widened considerably. As inadequate as our London sources were, they indicated that we would find a marked variation in wealth—an economic continuum in which the polar ends were the rich and poor. Further, both Christianity and Mohammedanism had become intertwined with the indigenous religions to form a new religious base. We could assume also that new political concepts had been introduced and that those previously ineligible for political office had begun to achieve political power.

As a consequence of this increased multiplicity of social patterns and the introduction of new social forces, we expected to find a complexity and diversification not known before. Consequently, we felt the need for some precise scientific methods with which to collect the raw data and to analyze these complex and rapidly changing social relations and institutions. It was my hope that, through sampling and other quantifying devices, we could isolate the various dependent and interdependent social forces that enter into a rapidly changing network of social relationships.

Our emphasis on quantifying devices was not an attempt to reduce social relations to mere statistics, but rather a recognition of the fact that statistics and other quantifying mechanisms when used properly can be excellent scientific tools. Statistical data in itself does not usually provide the theory or conceptual framework, but it can add the substantive flesh to the theoretical skeleton. By this I mean that statistical data when properly collected and analyzed will reinforce or substantiate the researcher's hypothesis or theory. The difficulty that develops is that statistical data can often be analyzed and interpreted in different ways. Thus, it is possible for a scientist to develop support for different theories with the same statistical data, depending on how he manipulates, interprets, or analyzes the data. Nevertheless, there is little doubt that methods that utilize statistical and other mathematical tools tend to yield results that are more invariant with respect to individual observers. They may reveal also complex linkages between variables that otherwise might remain obscure. In addition, statistics may widen the range of our perception and reduce to practicability problems that otherwise could not easily be handled.

At the same time, I wanted information and insights that are not ordinarily amenable to survey and statistical methods. I hoped that by combining survey and statistical methods with traditional anthropological field techniques we would be able to collect data representative of the entire community and at the same time able to provide cultural insights, details, and nuances. The two methods are not incompatible; in principle each should support the other. Our aim was to develop hypotheses through the information obtained from individuals, and to test these hypotheses in the sample survey. In turn, the survey data was to lead us to formulate new questions and make additional interpretations that could be investigated in depth. Thus it was hoped that the pitfalls and the inadequacies of both methods would be avoided.

The problem of selecting a Yoruba city to study was less complex than that of selecting the methodological procedures to be employed in the field. Although reliable Yoruba data were limited in London, we located some material that indicated general population size, social heterogeneity, and tribal subdivisions of Yoruba cities. After much searching and consideration, we selected Oshogbo, which our data indicated would range in population from 75,000 to possibly 125,000 inhabitants. This population range appeared to be typical of the major Yoruba towns and could be studied by a team of ten field assistants. Oshogbo was 200 miles inland, in the center of Yoruba country, and was inhabited by either Oyo or Ilesha peoples, both major tribal subdivisions of the Yoruba. It was a rail and road center, and we assumed it would have the elements of change that we were seeking. Colonial office files indicated that the town was ruled by an educated king who was not hostile to Europeans. Oshogbo appeared to be a typical Yoruba city. When the Nigerian Government, whom we had consulted, suggested Oshogbo as their first choice also, we were ready to begin our study.

In September, 1949, we arrived in Lagos, the capital of Nigeria, after a pleasant voyage down the west coast of Africa. We spent eleven days in Lagos, where we were briefed by colonial officials and interviewed by the governor. We acquired a pickup truck and gathered together the supplies and gear we would need for at least a three-month stay in Oshogbo. During our stay in Lagos, the Nigerian Government agreed to make line maps of Oshogbo from aerial photographs. Our future area sampling was to be based on these maps, which were to be ready in a month's time. Early on the twelfth day we left Lagos for Oshogbo. As we left Lagos, the capital and port city of Nigeria, we were symbolically and realistically cutting our links with the outside world. Once we were in the interior, communications would be difficult, and until stable relationships were established, we would be isolated from the indigenous population.

The anthropologist under the best of circumstances never becomes a fully accepted member of the culture he is studying, nor does he want to become a member. Usually the people look upon him as being outside the indigenous culture and do not expect him to follow their cultural norms, which both protects him and allows him greater freedom of action. However, this situation has its drawbacks for the anthropologist, because he is often emotionally isolated and almost totally dependent on his own internal resources. Most often he is alone in the field; only rarely is he fortunate enough to have a trusted assistant or informant with whom he can discuss his crucial decisions. The anthropologist must scrutinize his own behavior carefully, for incorrect actions and decisions may mar his standing in the community or weaken a favorable image that he has established. The anthropologist always makes mistakes, but the more emotionally secure he is, the less isolated he is, and the more people he can trust, the less is the probability that he will make serious and irrevocable mistakes.

We arrived in Oshogbo two days before the Great Beirum festival, the major holy day of the Moslim religion, and were greeted by the Assistant District Officer, the colonial administrator for the area. He had booked us into the rest house for three days. The information about our study of Oshogbo had not reached him, and he was rather shocked to learn that we would be with him in Oshogbo for the next two years.

Passive or Adaptational Research

There necessarily must be an initial period of orientation and contact in any field trip (Vidich, 1955). This serves many purposes for the anthropologist and for the people he is studying. It enables the researcher to begin to communicate.[2] It permits him to adjust his language and symbolic systems, so that the meanings he assigns to events and questions or answers can approximate those commonly assigned by his respondents. At the same time it enables the people to assign an identity to him. He is fitted into a role that has some meaning within the culture and that provides a basis for reaction. Typically both the image of

---

[2] We are assuming here that the researcher can speak the language of the people or that he is able to communicate through interpreters, administrators, or a common language.

the field worker and his understanding of the symbols and language of the people are continuously redefined during the course of the field work.

In Oshogbo, during the initial period, which lasted for several months, I had four specific goals. The first was to obtain a broad skeletal outline of the underlying principles of the Oshogbo social system. Very little was then known about the Yoruba. At this stage, I was not interested in obtaining detailed or even necessarily precise information. What I sought was a very general understanding of the forms of relationships and patterns of behavior so that I could begin to isolate sets of relationships and attitudes and thus start to ask meaningful questions.

My second goal was a practical one. Social anthropologists require an adequate framework of demographic data, but none was available for Oshogbo. I began, therefore, to make plans for a sample census with the object of obtaining information on age, sex, ethnic composition, kinship and family composition, occupation and income, education, religious affiliation, and other relevant data. Before any statistically reliable census could be undertaken, the area had to be mapped, and so I was fortunate in having been able to persuade the Nigerian Government to take aerial photographs of Oshogbo from which line maps were made. These maps incorporated every building in the community, and the boundaries of every compound and separate building were marked on them.

My third objective was to hire field assistants and gradually introduce them into the community. Initially, we employed ten assistants. The Africans selected had to meet certain minimum requirements. They had to be the equivalent of our high-school graduates, and they had to be bilingual in English and Yoruba. They could not be natives of Oshogbo but had to be Yorubas from neighboring towns. Initially, they were to indicate the boundaries of all the compounds in Oshogbo on the town map and begin to work on the sample census.

The fourth and possibly the most critical goal was to encourage the Oshogbo people to form a favorable image of me as a field worker and to obtain their permission for the studies. I had come to Oshogbo with the active support of the colonial administration, but I assured them that I was not part of the government and not a missionary or a trader, nor did I have any other role with which they were familiar. Despite my self-definition as a research worker only, which of course was entirely alien to them, I believe my initial image was ill-defined and vague, but nevertheless closely associated with government. I believe the people looked on me as a strange and deviant colonial administrator. This image changed during my stay in Oshogbo. Gradually, over time, I became more and more identified as a friend, and eventually I was assigned a quasi-political role and was known as Oyinbo Atoaja (the Oba's white man).[3] Having found a place for me within their own social system, the people could reorient their behavior. With the change in their attitude the quality of data we collected also changed, for the better.

The main problem, however, was to secure the consent of the community for the study and to begin to establish effective rapport with the people. With the support of the Ataoja, the king of Oshogbo, and the Assistant District Officer, the colonial administrator in the area, I was able to hold a number of open meetings attended by the chiefs, educated members of the community, and other influential people. At these meetings I presented the purposes of the study, defined my role as an investigator, and gave the townspeople an opportunity to question me extensively. At each meeting, I was cross-examined extensively. The chiefs and literate members of the community desired to know what material benefits, if any, would accrue to the community as a result of the study. Although I was unable to promise them any positive material results, I was able to point out the intangible benefits of the study: greater community prestige and possible future governmental developments. Once I had convinced the chiefs and other influential members of the community that the study would bring no harm to the community and might be beneficial, their approval was secured. These meetings culminated in a reception in my honor where the chiefs and other influential people publicly promised their support and cooperation in the study.

During this early period, I did not attempt to begin investigations in the town proper until I had the consent of the ruling hierarchy. The approval of the chiefs and the other literate and influential members of the community did not ensure the approval and cooperation of the people, but it was a necessary prerequisite to gaining the confidence of the community at large. Other methods and activities had to be employed to win the support of the people.

With the sanction of the chiefs, I began to move about the town, meeting and talking with as many individuals as possible until I was no longer a stranger to the community. The people were quite willing to talk to me and responded in a friendly

---

[3] "Oba" is a common Yoruba term applied to any paramount chief among the Yoruba. By assigning to me the term of "Oba's white man" the Yoruba were indicating the close and honored relationship that had developed between the king and myself.

manner as long as I refrained from asking personal questions. The educated people and chiefs, who had had extensive contact with governmental and European trading agencies, accepted me as a scientific investigator, but the uneducated viewed any European investigator as a potential tax collector, or as a harbinger of an imponderable law of the "white man," and thus regarded him with distrust and suspicion. These reactions were not entirely baseless, since previous experiences with most Europeans had led to either increased taxes or unwanted laws; the concept of a scientific investigator was alien to them. By assiduously avoiding the role of an investigator at first, and by attempting to establish warm interpersonal relationships with as many diverse individuals as possible, I found I was able to implant a notion of my purpose in the community and to abate their anxieties concerning increased taxes or other evils. Moreover, the approval of the chiefs and literate people, who used their considerable influence and authority on my behalf, helped to mitigate the peoples' fear and apprehensions. Their efforts, together with my own attempts to explain and publicize the study, succeeded in minimizing anxiety to the point where I felt initial work could be attempted. My task was also made easier as I had the active support of the colonial administration and the hospitality and friendliness of the Yoruba people.

When it seemed apparent to me that I was no longer causing suspicion, I began to question and interview the people. Although their fears and distrust of me were diminished at this time, it was not until many months later that their feelings were fully dissipated.

I spent the next several weeks defining my role and purposes and making preliminary studies of the political and historical background of Oshogbo. Historical and political data are usually not difficult to obtain, and the people of Oshogbo were proud of and willing to speak freely about their history and political hierarchy and about family life and economic organization. The main purpose of my inquiries was not to acquire details or even very precise information, but to obtain the general knowledge necessary to initiate a census. Since no reliable records were available, I had to take a sample census to secure basic demographic and other social data. The objectives of the sample census were not to enumerate heads, but rather to obtain information on the characteristics of the community, and to collect reliable and representative data concerning family organization, occupational structure and the religious, educational, and age composition of the community. It was my intention to select from the census a subsample of families on the basis of the economic differentiation of the male heads of household and to subject these families to intensive investigation for the remainder of the study.

The town was divided into four areas, each of which had markedly different social characteristics. The largest section in both population and area was the old city, inhabited mainly by the indigenous Oshogbo Yoruba people, who live in the traditional Yoruba mud compounds. Physically, a compound is a collection of buildings, usually adjacent, with defined and recognized boundries in which a lineage or several lineages live. The average population size of a compound was 150 inhabitants, but some exceeded 500 individuals. We estimated that between 70,000 and 90,000 people lived in the old city, which took in over three-quarters of the town, including 580 compounds, and extended for approximately two miles around the central market. The smallest area was the Hausa quarter, with 42 compounds, located on the northern limits of the city and inhabited only by Hausa traders and cattle dealers. The third area was the commercial district. Lining either side of the main thoroughfare of the town (Station Road) were approximately 250 small trading stores owned or rented by men and women who had left their native towns to settle in Oshogbo. Most of the inhabitants of this area had become permanent settlers in Oshogbo and were making conscious and positive efforts to be incorporated into the social, political, and religious life of the community. Finally, there was the section classified as the Foreign Quarter. It was the home of temporary immigrants: government clerks, employees of European-owned concerns, teachers, and transient laborers. It was the sophisticated quarter of the town where night clubs, dancing, and intellectuality existed. The typical Yoruba compound structure was absent in this quarter, where most houses were "European" mud or stone dwellings. There were 87 dwellings and buildings in this quarter.

In as orderly a geographic fashion as possible, each compound, store, or separate building was assigned a number on the town map, and a list was then compiled of the names and numbers of each. From this list every tenth name was selected in each of the four differentiated areas. The entire population in the various buildings and compounds selected in the sample was to be enumerated. A total of 94 compounds, stores, and buildings were included in the census.

At the start of the survey, I had hoped that it would be possible to employ educated inhabitants of Oshogbo as my field assistants, but it soon became apparent that the townspeople were too involved in local pressures and commitments. Moreover, the prestige that accrued to the field assistants as members of the survey was of considerable significance. Had the assistants been inhabitants of Oshogbo, this prestige could have created significant complications within the internal political structure. Although the assistants I finally obtained were more Westernized in manner and thought than the local townspeople, they were cautioned to adhere constantly to all local customs and traditions.

In order to facilitate the practical operation of the census, as well as for physical expediency, we divided the town arbitrarily into eight geographical zones. At least one field assistant was assigned to each zone. Four weeks before the census began, the field assistants started to contact the residents of the 94 compounds and other buildings that were to be enumerated. We then estimated the population and the religious, occupational, and educational composition of each compound or store, in order to provide some basis for a check on the reliability of the census. The chiefs and other influential people supported the census publicly and the official messengers and bellringers publicized it among the townspeople.

During this four-week contact period, there was little manifestation of the distrust and suspicion that had been evident immediately after my arrival. Initially, all the compounds granted us permission to conduct the census and indicated their willingness to cooperate with us. However, as soon as the practical operation of the census began, opposition to it developed, some of which had not been apparent previously. Much of the opposition can be attributed to factors rooted in the culture of the people, but some was to the methodology we employed. Our sampling techniques, for example, were incomprehensible to the people. The residents of the compounds selected were unable to understand why they had been chosen in preference to neighboring compounds. As a result, they refused at first to cooperate. Moreover, the residents of a compound are a corporate group, and as such they required what is, in effect, the unanimous approval of the group; at times the dissent of only one man was sufficient to block the census. In addition, the men refused to enumerate their wives and children in the compounds. At this point, it became quite apparent that their previously expressed fears of increased taxation and conscription of women and children into labor gangs and armies had not been fully dissipated. There was also a deep-rooted belief that counting one's children would bring them harm. At times, children up to the age of five were frequently omitted from the census as the people did not consider them to be permanent members of the family, since there was such a high mortality rate among young children. We found also that the literate townspeople who had volunteered originally to assist in the census refused to participate, since they were unable to withstand the pressure from some segments of the community who were opposed to the census. In those few cases where the literate townspeople or school children cooperated and provided us with information, they were publicily chastised and accused of being informers by members of their compound.

Many of these difficulties were overcome by repeated visits to the compounds and by enlisting further aid from the chiefs and other influential members of the community. By concentrating our efforts on the influential compounds in the census, we were able to convince them to cooperate and that the census was harmless. They, in turn, often were able to sway the more obstinate and recalcitrant compounds.

There were also two other significant factors that, I think, contributed to the ultimate success of the census. In the first place, I had no official attachment to the Colonial government, and thus the people knew I was not in a position to impose taxes or unwanted laws. Second, the people of Oshogbo knew that I was not a transient and thus could be held accountable for my actions. At the end of ten days of concentrated effort, only two compounds remained recalcitrant, and they were replaced by alternates. Eventually, 6,241 individuals were enumerated in the census.

Active Research

Once social and demographic data were obtained, more intensive work could begin. A subsample of families was selected on the basis of the occupation of the male head. We studied these families intensively for over a year, taking genealogies and case histories of each family and making a detailed examination of its social and economic organization. Our object was to understand the networks of role relationships that linked the members of a family to one another and to the structures of the wider society.

Research was carried out in the main by field assistants directed by questionnaires and field guides. The questionnaires were employed primarily for the collection of quantifiable factual data and were designed to elicit information relating to specific issues. However, after some experience with the questionnaires, it became evident that they were unsatisfactory for any complex situation. In these circumstances, the field assistants used guides suggesting the lines the investigation should follow. The guides formed the basis for qualitative reports.

There were no formal interviewing procedures, and the form of questioning varied from one field assistant to another and often from one family to another. This approach has the possible disadvantage that the data collected may be uneven. On the other hand, it led to the establishment of excellent rapport and probably led eventually to more accurate and complete knowledge. Since all the assistants followed identical guides and questionnaires, it was possible to check on the reliability of the data of one against another. I should like to stress here that much of the success of this aspect of the study depended upon the intelligence, ingenuity, and loyalty of my field assistants, as well as on the continuing cooperation and good will of the people.

During the period that the field assistants worked with their selected families, I used traditional participant-observation methods throughout the community. I collected geographical and historical data, participated in political councils, and observed and took part in religious and other rituals. In my work the representativeness of an informant was not a primary consideration. On the contrary, I made an effort to seek out those who were best informed about a subject in which I was interested or those persons with whom I could develop closer relationships. With some individuals and families the relationships grew into intimate friendships; with others the links were not so close. To the extent permitted by each relationship, I tried to share in the ordinary day-to-day activities of the people and in the nodal events of their lives.

The use of a combination of survey and participant-observation methods in a single study poses three primary questions. How successfully can the methods be combined? In what areas is each most effective? How consistent are the results of different methods? There were areas of inquiry in the Oshogbo study for which one method or the other was obviously better suited. For example, demographic material in a community the size of Oshogbo could not be obtained except by some sort of survey. But most of the areas of inquiry could be approached by using either or both methods. As the study progressed, several facts began to emerge that helped to guide me in making optimum use of the combined methods. It shortly became evident that the formal underlying structural principles of the social system could not easily or economically be obtained through survey procedures. My conceptual models were largely derived from personal observation and inquiry. The data from the survey families served in several ways to correct and elaborate my conceptualizations. They made possible a closer examination of the empirical fit between the actuality of behavior and the formal rules of social life or between what people do and what they say or feel they ought to do. In even the most stable social system, there is an important gap between the formal rules of behavior and the interpretation and manipulation of these rules. In a social system that is undergoing profound changes in its legal and moral precepts and in its forms of behavior, as the Oshogbo system was, there was an even more urgent need to examine the difference between social theory and social reality. Certainly this was possible without using survey methods. But, because survey methods can reach so many people, they yield a greater insight into the range of the variations and changes that are occurring and hence a better understanding of social process.

But survey techniques, though their range is wide, can penetrate only to certain levels. Consider one aspect of the Oshogbo religious system as an example. We learned, through the survey, that 80 percent of the Oshogbo community called themselves Muslim, 13 percent were Christian, and the remainder adhered strictly to traditional religious beliefs and customs. It was also possible through the use of questionnaires or guides to arrive at some understanding of the motivation for the changes in religious affiliation and to assess some of the conflict between traditional and modern religious rules and beliefs. But the more complicated and frequently more obscured reasons for shifting religious affiliation, the uses to which these changes were put, and the ambiguities about religion were best brought into the open by long and informal personal discussions. Further, I doubt if there is any survey method that would show with such startling clarity at least one important aspect of current Yoruba religious belief—the acceptance of inconsistencies—as did the following event. One Friday afternoon I intended to visit the chief priest of a major native cult whose festival had been celebrated the previous day. I arrived at his house as he was leaving to worship in the central mosque. He was a devout Muslim, too!

Occasionally, there were significant incongruities between my conceptions and the data of the field assistants. These could often be reconciled easily, but at times they required additional interpretations, reformulations, or more information to resolve them. Not every inconsistency that arose was or even perhaps could be reconciled, but, with enough insight and information, the two methods led in every important area to basically compatible results.

Inconsistencies and contradictions in the data were also resolved in another way. Each field assistant was assigned twenty families for intensive study in the same geographic area and worked with these families for a period of a year. Thus, the assistant was able to establish contact not only with the compounds in which his designated family units were located, but with other compounds in the area, and was able to draw upon a large segment of the inhabitants of his area for additional information. In this way, the field assistants worked on two levels of investigation. On one level, their research was concerned with family units; on the other level, they were concerned with the dynamics of the wider community. Where contradictions or inconsistencies arose in the analysis of the data collected from the selected family, checks could easily be made in the wider society with different informants, and the reliability of the data could quickly be ascertained.

Interviews, either by myself or my field assistants, were conducted in Yoruba, the indigenous language, but answers to questionnaires and data collected for the reports were recorded by the field assistants in English. Eventually my own rapport and that of my field assistants became sufficiently well developed with the community that we were able frequently to record the answers to the questionnaires at the time of the interview. The consolidation of reports occurred, however, only after many interviews had been completed. The assistants usually visited each of their families at least once a day, collecting their data over a long period of time. Often these visits were of a purely social nature, designed to promote friendly relationships between the assistants and their informants. With these techniques, the field assistants were continually reviewing and checking their collected data.

For many of the problems investigated it was possible to limit the time slice utilized, but in other cases it was necessary to investigate the problem throughout a major portion of the survey. For example, agricultural data were collected on many different occasions, depending on the variations in the farming cycle. On the other hand, it was possible to collect data concerning marriage and divorce rates, diets and birth rates, within a limited period of time. It was necessary to review at least once many of the more fundamental categories—such as kinship, which was operative in many different aspects of the society— so that the additional material accumulated could be synthesized with the earlier date.

The ease with which data were collected varied considerably depending on the social circumstances. I had anticipated resistance from the women, but we soon found that most of them had little hesitation in discussing their lives and social activities. Serious resistance was encountered in the collection of data pertaining to income and expenditures, and in some instances the people were reluctant to discuss certain ritual procedures and illnesses. It was only after we had resided in Oshogbo for a long time that barriers to acquiring this information and other sensitive data were overcome.

In the early phases of the field study, I had hoped that the literate members of the community might supply significant clues to the analysis of the traditional social structure, but with rare exceptions the family studies, and the illiterate informants who had spent most of their lives in Oshogbo, provided more accurate data. In many instances these data contradicted the information gathered from the literate people. Because of the lack of higher educational facilities in Oshogbo and the demands of their professional or commercial activities, most of the literate people had spent many years away from Oshogbo and were not so familiar with the traditional ways of life. Nevertheless, although the literate people were poor informants about traditional Yoruba behavior patterns, they were able to provide valuable information and insights concerning the changing structuralization of the society and the new values and ethics that were developing. Moreover, they were invariably strong supporters of the survey and, at times, provided the necessary help to overcome difficult situations.

As I look back, it is clear to me now that my role in the Oshogbo study assumed almost a dual aspect. In the first instance I was director of the survey and, as such, conducted field work parallel to that of my staff. Second, it was my role to provide those data that could not be obtained by survey methods and without which the structural framework of the wider society could not be formulated. However, a social fact is often not significant in itself, acquiring full meaning only when it is understood in its historical perspective and in its functional and structural relationships to the society. Thus it was also my job to provide the theoretical skeleton and the structural framework upon which all the social facts collected by the team and myself had to hang. It should be realized also that the data collected by me and that of my staff could not be treated as isolated and unconnected entities. Neither sets of data could be considered as complete or separate. They were, in fact, complementary, with the divisions between them somewhat artificial. Each was a stimulus to the other, for it was the data collected by the field assistants that provided the substantiating facts for a continuing sequence of ethnographic hypotheses.

Bowing Out

After reviewing what we had done and checking and rechecking our facts, figures, and theories, we came to the conclusion that the Oshogbo survey had been completed. For over a year and a half we had been living with and observing the people of Oshogbo. Seasonal, ecological, structural, and cultural effects had been studied and noted, and their effect on the changing behavior patterns of the people recorded. Like most other anthropologists on their first field trip, we had exhausted our check lists and believed that we had scrutinized all forms of behavior so that future analysis could be reliably determined. We were aware of the perimeters of behavior and were confident that we could easily ascertain normal and abnormal behavior in the town. It was not until we had left the field that we became cognizant of a number of factors that we had overlooked. Fortunately, they were not crucial factors and were easily remedied.

It was difficult to leave Oshogbo and bring to an end some extremely meaningful relationships. I had learned not only to respect and admire the king, but had developed a warm camaraderie with him that one rarely achieves with another individual. I was his "Oyinbo" or "white man," and he was my "chief clerk." There is no question, at all, in my mind, that much of the success of the Oshogbo study was dependent on the excellent rapport that I had with him. There were others with whom relationships were almost as close: Old Ajayi, the returned soldier, the catholic schoolteacher, the town councilor, and the Ifa priest. Separating from my team of African field assistants was even more difficult, complicated, and beset with emotions. We had worked together as a team for well over a year and a half and had bulit a strong relationship, akin to a father-son relationship. It is interesting to note that all the young Nigerians who worked for me eventually achieved high university degrees, most obtaining Ph.D's. Before I left Oshogbo I had to see that each field assistant was placed in a job commensurate with his talents, education, and desires, for they were dependent on me for their future activities as I had been dependent on them in the Oshogbo study. It was hard to separate, but we celebrated our departure at a small feast in my three-room mud house where we toasted the study.

Our last day in Oshogbo sadly came. The Atoaja arrived at 5:00 A.M., we said goodbye, and with all my field assistants aboard my truck, we drove off to Lagos. A week later we boarded ship for England. The Oshogbo field venture was over.

Summary and Evaluation

The Oshogbo study was a successful field venture, from the point of view of our objectives. Our goal had been an intensive anthropological survey of a changing Yoruba city. We had examined the major social components that determined behavior in Oshogbo, and we could clearly indicate the traditional organization of the city. Briefly, the city could be viewed in terms of three fundamental principles: patrilineal descent, residential association, and political organization. The ultimate judicial and administrative authority was vested in the paramount chief, the Atoaja, who was regarded as the executive head, the supreme adjudicator, the legislator, the ritual leader, and the military commander in chief. Below the paramount chief were a series of hierarchical lines of chiefs, military, administrative, and ritual, to whom the king delegated responsibilities, duties, rights, and privileges. At the base of this essentially pyramidal political structure were the residential units—the compounds. To facilitate administration, the community was divided into somewhat amorphous and mutable clusters of compounds, each administered by a chief. Each compound contained large aggregates of domestic families, often bound by patrilineal ties, that acknowledged the authority and jurisdiction of their senior male. Residence was patrilocal and polygyny the desired marital state. The compound, with a membership varying from 15 to 500 persons, was in a sense the structural epitome of the political organization, and it was in the compound that the matrix of the jural and administrative organization was to be found.

In common with many West African peoples and, indeed, with many other societies outside of West Africa, kinship was the articulating principle of social organization and the primary determinant of behavior in every aspect of social life in Oshogbo. Descent was traced through the patrilineal line; kinsmen sharing common patrilineal ties formed corporate units or lineage groups.

The Yoruba lineage group was the largest group of living agnates to trace descent from a common male ancestor; marriage and sexual relations were forbidden between them. Their lineage was not an agglomerate of undifferentiated individuals, but a highly segmented structure.

Each lineage group, or a large segment of it, shared a common residence, although the limits of lineage and residence units were not necessarily coterminous. Frequently, two or more lineages lived in a single compound or members of a single lineage resided in two or more compounds. Although the lineage as such did not have explicit functions in the political organization, the highest political offices were vested in certain partilineages. The occupation of each male was determined by lineage affiliation, and male members of a lineage followed the same occupation. The vast majority of lineages were engaged in agricultural pursuits, and subsistence cultivation of the soil was the primary means of livelihood of the Oshogbo people, who lived in the town proper and farmed the peripheral lands. Often the farmers made a daily journey to and fro, although during crucial periods of the farming cycle they might remain in temporary shelters on the farms for a period of a fortnight or more. Other male occupations, such as blacksmithing, drumming, and carving, were regulated by the male members of traditionally designated lineages.

All able women in Oshogbo worked, and almost all were petty traders, but a woman's occupation was not, as was the male's, a function of lineage affiliation. The lineage exercised certain rights in real property and inheritance over its members, regulated marriages, and determined the native cult adherence. Patrilineal ancestor worship was a fundamental part of the religious system. The dead were buried beneath the mud floor of the room in which they had lived.

Thus, Oshogbo was a large community characterized by the close integration and interweaving of its social, economic, religious, and political aspects. Limited economic, differentiation and specialization existed and were intimately associated with the lineage structure. Apart from the usual differentiation of social roles, based on sex, age, and economic specialization, individuals were differentiated in accordance with political rank and power. Kin and residential groupings provided additional social differentials.

A number of factors contributed to the successful development of this study, the most important being the operation of the team. The field assistants collected large quantities of scientific data and functioned with a high *esprit de corps*. They were liked by the people and were able to establish an excellent rapport with large segments of the community. The cooperative spirit that pervaded the team permitted checking and comparing of collected data as part of normal procedure. We were also fortunate in the excellent relationships that I was able to develop with the king, who was my major informant, and other key individuals in the community. Without the information and advice that the king and the other key informants gave us, the study might have proceeded at a much slower pace, and our insights into the behavior of the people of Oshogbo might have been reduced. The excellent relationships that existed between the townspeople and myself and the team increased the quality of the data collected and allowed us to rapidly check the data and quickly ascertain reliability. These factors probably outweighed our difficulties and brought about the successful conclusion of the study.

But mistakes we did make, and the most serious was the census. We underestimated the opposition and resistance to the census and obviously missed many clues that would have reduced and possibly eliminated the census conflict. Closer attention to the census opposition, which we were cognizant of, and broader and deeper knowledge of the Yoruba culture might have alerted us earlier to the census difficulties and given us a greater opportunity to nullify the resistance among the people to the census. However, once the people recognized that we were their friends, would cause them no harm, the census conflict was resolved, and we were able to collect data with few difficulties. In the later analysis of Oshogbo, the census, demographic, and other statistical data proved to be extremely useful in understanding Oshogbo.

We also overestimated the reliability and usefulness of the educated people as informants. Many had spent years away from Oshogbo and could be classified as deviants to the traditional culture. We had expected them to give us much more critical aid than they were able to do, but, as I have already indicated, they were extremely useful in our general understanding of Yoruba culture and the town. Finally, it is now clear to us that we attempted too much. Our subject was too broad, our goal too difficult, and we became involved in too many activities. It is possible that we could have penetrated deeper if the scope of the problem had been reduced and our energies channeled into more specific problems.

PART II: GWELO, AN URBAN COMMUNITY IN RHODESIA

Problem, Theory, and Research Design

In 1955 I was awarded a Ford Foundation grant to carry out a study of an urban community in either Northern or Southern Rhodesia. The grant included a three-month stay in England to examine and locate comparative data, contact British anthropologists who had worked in similar areas, and to select the town to be studied. After considerable correspondence with the social scientists of the Rhodes-Livingstone Institute and lengthy discussions with British anthropologists, I decided to study a town in Southern Rhodesia. Few, if any, urban studies had been conducted in Southern Rhodesia, and the Rhodes-Livingstone Institute had carried out considerable urban research in Northern Rhodesia (Zambia), so it seemed logical for me to concentrate on a town in that area. My aim was twofold: to discover the underlying principles of organization and the form and content of the social relationships that make up the social systems of Central African towns, and to shed some light on the complex problems of adaptations, modifications, and changes in the social patterns that have occurred in Africa as a result of Westernization and urbanization. I also wished to select an urban community that was representative of the towns of Southern Rhodesia and generally reflected the over-all pattern of change that was developing in this part of Africa.

Using these objectives as my major criteria, I began to scrutinize the Colonial Office files and other London sources for reliable data on Rhodesian towns. It soon became clear that my choice was restricted to the seven major towns of Rhodesia; Salisbury, Bulawayo, Umtali, Gwelo, Gatooma, Que Que, and Fort Victoria. These towns had been established by Europeans, since cities, large or small, did not exist in the Rhodesias before the advent of European domination and colonization. All the towns were located in the high ridge country and had climates that were extremely agreeable to Europeans. Since we were seeking a comparatively small city with few complexities, Bulawayo and Salisbury were eliminated as too large and too complex. Fort Victoria was excluded as being atypical and Gatooma as lacking the major elements of change we were seeking. Que Que lacked economic diversification, and Umtali was geographically remote with ethnic and economic complexities that could cause difficulties. Gwelo, by elimination, seemed to be our choice, but Gwelo's vital statistics reinforced this decision. The town was not too large, having a population of approximately 25,000 Africans and 7,000 Europeans. It was the commercial and industrial hub for the surrounding farmlands, and Western economic, social, and political forms seemed to provide the basic social matrix. It appeared to be a city of flux and change with a highly migratory and unstable African population and a rapidly developing European core. Our data in London indicated that Gwelo was typical of the Central African towns and appeared to be an excellent choice. When the High Commissioner for the Rhodesias informed us that it was possible for him to rent and reserve a modern house for us in Gwelo, months before we arrived, the selection became final.

With our city chosen, we could turn to a consideration of the methods to be employed in the field. Our field methods were determined by our previous experiences in Oshogbo, our discussions in London, and the working conditions we expected to find in the city of Gwelo. The population of Gwelo was much smaller than Oshogbo, and the town was administered by Europeans, so it appeared that a team of six to eight field assistants would be more than enough to carry out an efficient field study. Although our data indicated that Gwelo would have a more transient African population and be tribally more heterogeneous than Oshogbo, we did not think that these factors would increase the complexity to such an extent that more than eight field assistants would be needed.

As in the Oshogbo study, we planned to employ statistics and questionnaires wherever possible, to use random-sample devices and a sample census, and to pilot-test all questionnaires. We also faced the probability of making our working sample larger than the normal 10 percent. We were quite sure that the high degree of transiency among the Africans would gradually reduce the number of informants we would be able to retain in the study. We assumed that the longer the study ran, the greater would be our loss of informants. This problem could be overcome by making the original sample larger and gradually adding randomly picked new informants as the older informants dropped out. However, after six months of field work, we assumed that a cut-off point would develop, and that it would no longer be feasible or practical to add more informants to the sample. We also intended to base the census and statistics on area sampling, since we knew that line maps of Gwelo and Southern Rhodesia were available.

But other social factors complicated our field methodology. We were quite aware that Central Africa, and particularly Southern Rhodesia, were plural societies characterized by their social conflicts mainly between Europeans and Africans. The Rhodesian towns were created by Europeans, and virtually all power was vested in them. Socially as well as economically, Africans were subject to rules and rigid constraints that had no applicability to the white segment of the population. These barriers could result not only in apathy and frustration, but could engender bitter resentment causing marked cleavages between black and white in all aspects of social life. Most of the African population, by Rhodesian law, lived in segregated areas or locations on the periphery of Gwelo in the periurban area. These locations were built and owned by the European municipality. When an African found a job, he was assigned living quarters in the location by the Office of Native Affairs. The rent that was assigned to each African was paid for him by the European concern that employed him. Loss of a job by an African usually caused his eviction from his quarters on the location. By Rhodesian law only Africans could live in the locations. The exception was the European supervisor who administered the location. Around Gwelo were four African locations and one Coloured location that housed the majority of Africans and Coloured people. Europeans were allowed to live in the municipal township and by law forbidden to live in the African locations. Our original objective was to study a plural society composed of both the African and European cultures. Under these circumstances we assumed that racial difficulties would develop with both the White and African populations. Gwelo was obviously a city of intense racial antagonism, as were all Rhodesian cities, and it did appear that good rapport with one racial group would antagonize the other racial group. While we were still in London, our limited data indicated that initially we would probably receive some cooperation from both major racial groups. We had no method by which we could determine how long this initial or superficial cooperation would last, nor could we determine whether the hostility of either group was sufficient to prevent the study from moving beyond its initial and superficial stages. These were intangibles that could only be answered in the field, and we had no alternative but to assume that we would be able to carry the study to completion and be unmolested by the government, racial groups, or any other unit during our stay in Gwelo.

But we were faced with other difficulties. We were unable to locate in London any maps, statistics, or data about any of the four locations. Thus the decision of which locations to study had to be put off until we arrived in Gwelo, and much of our early specific planning, which usually eases the initial contact period, had to be postponed. However, all general planning could be and was developed to a much greater extent than had been possible in the Oshogbo study. It was quite clear to us, however, that the intangibles in Gwelo could be major obstacles to any depth analysis in Gwelo. The racial antagonisms and conflicts indicated to us that our future in Gwelo was marked with uncertainties and social difficulties.

Passive or Adaptational Research

After a fruitful three months' stay in London, we sailed for South Africa and in early September, 1955, landed in Durban. From Durban we drove via Johannesburg and Bulawayo to Gwelo, where we found a modern European home awaiting us. According to Rhodesian law we could live only in the European areas. We could visit the African locations as much as we desired but not live there. The Director of Native Affairs issued us a pass that permitted us to go back and forth to the location undisturbed by the police or civil administrators.

The initial weeks in Gwelo presented a number of interesting problems. We had some advantages that we had not had in Oshogbo. Available to us were the results of studies of other towns in southern and central Africa that were not unlike Gwelo, and these provided us, in the early phases of the study, with critical insights, essential clues, and bases for comparisons.

We were also operating in a European-imposed economic and social framework with which we were familiar. The Europeans were not a mystery to us, and we could associate with them and gain knowledge of their values and behavior patterns. We were not culturally isolated or cut off from the outside world as we had been in Oshogbo, and as a result initially we had a better understanding of our field situation. These facts and experiences made our initial orientation in Gwelo somewhat easier.

But there were critical problems in Gwelo, too. There was an obvious absence of any traditional organization that tended to structure the social life of the Africans. There were many factors contributing to this. The most important included the ethnic heterogeneity of the African population, its transience and lack of commitment to town life, and the insurmountable barriers to economic and social achievement placed before the Africans by the Europeans. Our initial probing also indicated a paucity of formal associations. In addition, the administration of the location rested exclusively in European hands. In many Rhodesian towns there are African Advisory Boards, which, in principle, help administer the locations. In Gwelo the Board was defunct. Thus there were no formally constituted or acknowledged native authorities through whom the people could be reached and the purposes of the study publicized and explained.

We had already visited the four locations in the Gwelo area and had decided to concentrate on the two largest: Mambo-Monomotapa and Senka. The Mambo-Monomotapa location was built by the municipality and administered by it, but Senka had been constructed by the central government and was controlled by a supervisor appointed by the central government. Senka had a population of approximately 1,500 people and was nine miles from the center of Gwelo, while Mambo-Monomotapa had been built five miles from the city and had more than 9,500 inhabitants. The other two locations appeared to be atypical, one extremely small and too far away to be conveniently worked, and the other inhabited only by railway workers. It was quite obvious, even with the most superficial inquiries and investigations, that Senka and Mambo-Monomotapa were the key locations in the Gwelo area. Neither of these locations had any apparent African leadership or any structure of government.

Our difficulties in publicizing the study and explaining our purposes to the Gwelo community were resolved with the help of the African field assistants whom we hired in the first few weeks we were in Gwelo. Each field assistant had to speak and read English and be conversant with two of the major indigenous tongues, preferably either Shona or Ndebele and Bemba. The two major ethnic groups in Gwelo were the Shona and Ndebele peoples, and knowledge of Bemba would be helpful with immigrants from Northern Rhodesia, present-day Zambia. Since there were few secondary schools in Southern Rhodesia and few graduates of these schools, we were forced to accept men who had graduated from primary schools. This caused difficulties, in the later stages of the study, since with more education the field assistants would have been able to handle the more complex questionnaires more easily and more rapidly.

We were not greatly concerned with the ethnic identity of the field assistants, since tribalism in a culturally heterogeneous community is not usually very significant. When an African comes to an urban community in Central Africa, he must accept the concept of strangers, for he is usually forced to work, associate, and live with people of different tribal groups. Since the African populations of all Central African cities have been reared in their traditional rural villages and have migrated to the urban centers, there was no possibility of hiring field assistants who were Gwelo-born. We received three experienced field assistants, with qualifications similar to the three we hired, from the Rhodes-Livingstone Institute, with whom I had excellent working relationships.[4] Since strangers were accepted in Gwelo, we had no problems in introducing our field assistants into the locations.

Our procedure in publicizing the study was to visit the churches and schools on the locations with the team of African field assistants and explain the study and its purposes. The schoolchildren would usually carry the information about the study to their parents, relatives, and neighbors, and the church members would relate the information to their friends and associates. Notices and stories about the study were placed in the African and European newspapers. Finally we received permission from the municipal authorities to announce our plans about the study over the public-address system, which is an essential feature of most African locations. The information was announced over the public-address system in six different languages for a period of a week, three times daily, allowing us to contact all the different cultural groups in Gwelo. Thus we were able to achieve considerable publicity, and the African populations of both Mambo-Monomotapa and Senka locations quickly learned about the American, his study, and the team of African re-

---

[4] I was fortunate in establishing close working relationships with the Rhodes-Livingstone Institute in the early stages of the Gwelo study that resulted in my being able to borrow three of their field assistants for the duration of the study.

searchers that were working for him. However, because of the absence of any African leadership or any meaningful African social group that might give a stamp of approval to the work, apart from the churches, which were socially isolated from one another, we received no sense of acceptance or consent from any segment of the African community. On the other hand, there was no overt hostility to our proposed work from the Africans so we felt that far more concrete and intensive work could begin.

In the initial phase of the study, which lasted approximately three months, we were able to achieve a number of our objectives. We planned, as we had previously done in Oshogbo, to base our random-sample census on area sampling. In Gwelo, maps of the location were available that listed every structure and assigned to each building or residence a number. The major location, Mambo-Monomotapa, was divided into living quarters for married men accompanied by their wives and children, and residences for single men or men whose wives and children were not with them. The houses in Mambo, the area for married men, were all the same. Each house had four rooms: two bedrooms, a livingroom, kitchen, bath, and lavatory. Each house contained running water, electricity, and a wood stove. In Monomotapa, the main area for single men, the housing structures were quite different. Each structure contained between twenty and forty rooms with central bathing and lavatory facilities. Four men were usually assigned to one room regardless of ethnic origin, education, or work. It was quite possible for men speaking four different languages to share the same room and act toward each other as distinct strangers. Our procedure in Mambo was to include every tenth house in our sample and in Monomotapa to select 10 percent of the rooms in all the structures. All the individuals residing in the selected houses or rooms were included in the census. We divided Mambo-Monomotapa into six separate areas, and each assistant was assigned an area where he worked for the duration of the study. Each assistant was allotted forty rooms or houses to enumerate during the census. During this period of orientation, each field assistant visited his area daily and established relationships with the people to be enumerated and others living in the same area. The objective of each field assistant was to develop rapport with as many informants as possible in his area and thus have a check and comparison on the people included in the sample census. The sample census included 2,500 people.

The census in Gwelo was intended to collect data in depth, and in this sense each interview resembled a case history. We were interested in the entire development of each individual and recorded all data available from birth to the present. We made a complete record of each person's early childhood, education, occupations, marriages, divorces, wives, children, bride-price payments, movements to and from traditional birth place, membership in associations, religion, ethnic status, and kin and village relationships. We intended to collect as much data as we could in the initial interview, but before the census interview took place each field assistant had, at the most, been able to develop only a superficial relationship with his selected informants. Although no deep relationships were established, the census was surprisingly very successful. There was little discernable opposition to it, few recalcitrant informants, and no organized resistance. There were several reasons for this favorable response to the census in Gwelo. The life of an African in Gwelo was regulated and largely determined by a seemingly endless series of forms, questionnaires, and passes. He was accustomed to them and intimidated by them. He saw the census as just one more inevitable and incomprehensible form to which he must submit if he was to remain working in town. He also saw it as an act of a European against which he had no organizations or leaders who might act as a focus for resistance. Had there been, the census might easily have been prevented. In this particular situation, the formlessness of the internal political system in Gwelo was a strong factor in our favor.

Besides taking the census and interviewing informants in the random sample, we also wished to establish a panel group that would operate as a sounding board for us and allow us to test our ideas and hypotheses and review the questionnaires. Immediately upon our arrival in Gwelo, we began to compile a list of the important, respected, rich, successful, and educated Africans. In a short period of time, we had a list of twenty men whom the Africans classified as successful. These men, for the duration of the study, met in my house twice a week and openly discussed a variety of subjects. At the meetings, which usually lasted for three or four hours, we discussed racialism, African migrations, marriage laws, kin groups, ethnic hostilities, budgets, wages, and similar topics. My function was to get the group to start talking and then withdraw, entering again only if there was a lull in the conversation. Usually the conversation was quite heated as the Africans attempted to analyze and explain their behavior and cultural world. Since any subject was permitted, I was unable to record these conversations until after the meeting was over. These discussions could be viewed as revolutionary, antiwhite, and seditious, and even though the Africans trusted me they feared the repercussions if a record of the talks fell into the hands of the white authorities. We also had to be careful not to break any of the racial laws, or the meeting would have been forbidden by the municipal authorities.[5] Probably the most important aspect of the panel board was that it was a check on the data collected by the field assistants and vice versa. Every questionnaire that we used in the field was pretested through the panel, and this enabled us to avoid many mistakes. The panel thus acted as a testing ground for each major questionnaire. Moreover, since we were working on two levels, we were able to see and collect behavioral data that we might otherwise have missed.

It is clear to me now, although I did not realize it at the time, that participation in the panel group conveyed high prestige on its members. It appears that in a cultural atmosphere in which racial stratification is dominant, close association with a member of the dominant racial group may bring to the depressed group greater prestige and higher social status. This kind of social relationship also allows avenues of communication to develop that may result in greater emotional and material benefits for the depressed individuals. If a crisis or critical situation develops, the member of the dominant social group becomes a channel or source that may possibly help to alleviate or reduce the severity of a difficult situation. In Gwelo, this could mean protection from the police, the waiving of minor infractions or misdemeanors, such as improperly made-out passes or breaking the curfew, and the possibility of achieving a more rewarding job. In other words, I became a social mechanism by which the extreme racial laws and prohibitions in Rhodesia could be diffused or blunted. Another reason for the success of the panel group was that we liked each other. I found the Africans to be interesting, and they were curious about an American whose major activity seemed to be associating with Africans.

In Gwelo, as in Oshogbo, the identity assigned to me and the image the people formed of me were of central importance. I wished to develop in the early months of the study good rapport with all sections of the community, but in Gwelo this was difficult, since great hostility and enmity existed between the African and European populations. I immediately disclaimed any any association with the government, which had given its somewhat unenthusiastic acquiescence to the field work, and attempted to identify myself as a research worker and as an American. The success of these efforts was minimal, for the

---

[5] Laws prohibited Africans from drinking alcoholic beverages, being in the municipal township after 6 P.M., and wandering around the city without specific permission between the hours of 6 P.M. and 6 A.M.

Africans saw me—as they see every white man—as an inimical authority. Despite my continuous efforts to modify it, this initial image did not change basically. In retrospect it seems clear that, almost inevitably, this had to be so. In a society in which racial tensions and conflict is the predominant theme underlying all relationships between black and white, it is unrealistic to expect an African to react on any other basis. However, in the early phases of the study, it was our hope that in time the ascription could be changed.

We also had to contend with the European community. In our original plans, we intended to study a plural world, both the African and European cultures. Initially, our relationships with the Europeans were excellent. It was rather easy to make friends, and we quickly had access to documents and people. However, when I indicated to the town council that I intended systematically and scientifically to examine the behavior of the European community, as well as the African, difficulties developed. The Europeans regarded themselves as being the same as any other European or white community and could not understand why I should want to study them. In their view, it was quite proper to analyze the African but not the European world. They saw the study as a threat to their world and as a criticism of their behavior and policies. Despite much discussion and much pleading on my part, the town council refused to cooperate and indicated that the town would not officially sanction the study. They did agree to allow any European who so desired to participate in the study. Needless to say, without the "blessing" of the community most of the Europeans refused to cooperate. We were given access to documents, could delve into the history of the town, peruse maps and study the town layout, but we were refused permission to attend council meetings, examine the files of the department of native affairs, or systematically and randomly interview Europeans. Thus we were forced to alter our plans and to concentrate mainly on a study of the African locations.

Once we began to contact and interview the Africans, a disturbing situation began to develop. My field assistants reported that African policemen were interrogating our African informants after they had completed their interviews with them. The police were trying to discover what information the informants were conveying to us. It was quite obvious to us that if the police continued to interrogate our informants, the study would abruptly end. The Africans would begin to refuse to talk to us, and what little data we received would be unreliable. For the study to continue, the harassment by the police had to end. Since the Gwelo study had the approval of both the British Colonial

Office and the Rhodesian Central Government, it would have been quite awkward and embarrassing for the Gwelo authorities if we were forced to discontinue the study because of overt local hostility to the project. I mentioned this when I met with the head of Rhodesian intelligence in Gwelo to complain about the interrogation of our informants, and he agreed to countermand his original orders and end the harassment.

Nevertheless, the threat of harassment hung over us for the remainder of the study, and our relationships with the European community never became friendly. With the exception of a few close friends and some European informants who were friendly, most Europeans were civil, but basically uncooperative. The study was allowed to continue but without the cooperation or participation of the European population. The European community regarded us, throughout the duration of the study, as a threat to their way of life and they viewed us with hostility.

These initial encounters in Gwelo during the contact period point up two fundamental differences between the Gwelo and Oshogbo studies that greatly affected both field ventures. The first was the more random and unstructured system of social relationships that operated among Gwelo Africans as compared to the highly complex and organized system in Oshogbo. The second was the very minimal amount of racial antagonism in Oshogbo as compared to the deep cleavages and hostilities between blacks and whites that permeated all aspects of life in Gwelo.

Active Research

Our intensive study of Gwelo presented a number of interesting problems, many of which were quite different from those in Oshogbo. In Gwelo there was no institutional focus or principle of organization that provided a common framework for behavior apart from the remote and broad structuring provided by European industries, administration, and social behavior. Our task was to discover the types and channels of social interaction in this community characterized by ethnic heterogeneity, the absence of discrete groups, high mobility, incomplete families, a disproportionate sex ratio, and economic and social barriers of great magnitude.

We selected from the original census a subsample of heads of households based on occupational differentiation and tribal affiliation. The unit picked for intensive study was not necessarily a family, since much of the Gwelo population was composed of single men or men who had left all or part of their families in the reserves. In this part of the study we had two major aims. The first concerned migration, urban and job stability, the composition of urban families, and other relevant sociodemographic data. The circulation between town and reserve and among towns posed a number of problems. Why do people come to town? How long do they stay, and why do they leave? What are the attractions of town life that cause so many men to trek so far? How do factors such as age, education, occupation, and residence of family influence urban stability and commitment? In what explicit ways do the social and economic constraints hamper the development of a stable urban population? What are the pulls toward and pushes from town life that properly belong to the reserve?

The second part of the study dealt with the network of social relationships an African established in town. Because the range of kin present in Gwelo was almost inevitably incomplete and because many of the rights and obligations that give substance to traditional kin bonds were absent, each person had to discover and establish his own set of relevant kin bonds. What, then, were the kinship obligations in Gwelo, and to whom did they extend? To what new uses were kinship bonds put, and in what situations were they recognized?

Tribalism offered another category of interaction that could be drawn upon and put to new uses. All Africans in Gwelo were born and reared in traditional villages. They grew up with people whom they usually knew from birth, and were members of the same tribe. Social relationships were personal, and each individual established and maintained a web of personal ties that was based on traditional life and activities. Strangers and members of different tribes were rare visitors, and few behavior patterns existed to deal with them. The world of a villager was relatively simple and well structured. When a villager migrated to town, however, he had to live in a culturally heterogeneous world and associate with tribal groups that were different from his own. He had to accept strangers and learn how to associate with them without conflict. He had to move and live in a world for which his socialization process and previous experiences had not prepared him. It was this new way of life, how old patterns were changed and new ones accepted, the problems and difficulties that arose with the retention of old patterns, and the manner in which adjustments were made that concerned us.

We were also interested in neighborhood ties, the more formal associational relationships that provided alternative links between people, and the bonds of friendship and work that could rival the claims of kinship. Were new friendships mainly established from work and neighborhood, or were new relationships kept to a minimum by the bonds of kinship and village ties? The new political relationships between Europeans and Africans also interested us. In 1955 racial tensions and conflicts were increasing and were manifested in all aspects of Rhodesian life. It was essential to understand the new attitudes and values that produced these sharp tensions and conflicts and created a highly structured political world.

Finally, we were interested in examining the forms of institutional life that existed in the location. In the villages, the life of an individual was molded by traditional patterns of behavior, and an individual was anchored by many stable institutions. The world of the location was a world of change and a place where traditional institutions were being remodeled or new forms of behavior being created. For example, religion has been one of the cornerstones of traditional behavior in Africa. In the location, religion seems to dominate many aspects of life and, for most of the people, the Christian church appears to be the stable force around which much of their lives is built. It becomes a place of social interaction, where new ideas and concepts are developed, but where stability still exists. The church, for the African appears to be one of the major links between his traditional world and the new changing world of the location. Thus it was our hope that by studying these institutions and relationships we could discover the intersecting networks and new institutions that gave a measure of order and stability to the Gwelo African social system.

To a very large extent, we depended upon questionnaires and interviews by field assistants to provide information in Gwelo. Much of the material was easily adapted to this particular method, but I think we might have achieved more understanding in many areas had we been able to use a less structured interviewing technique, as we had in Oshogbo. Several factors made this virtually impossible. The use of field guides involves repetitive visits and very informal relationships and thus requires that one have informants who are positively involved in the study. This was not true in Gwelo. For the most part our informants were passive. They were willing to answer questions, provided that the interviews were not too lengthy or the questions did not probe sensitive areas. The expectation that in time our relationships might improve and our informants become more responsive was not realized. On the contrary, some informants became less docile and more reluctant to answer any question as the study continued. As the study progressed many came to realize that I had very little, if any, actual authority or power over their lives and that they were not compelled to cooperate with me. At the same time, we were unable to build up a great enough fund of good will upon which to draw. The tensions between black and white and even between black and black precluded, I think, the development of relationships that would permit the kind of intensive questioning that had taken place in Oshogbo. In addition, less structured field guides also required field workers who were better trained and more capable than those available for the Gwelo study. The resistance of our informants and the performance of my assistants necessitated that I continuously cross-check and test the data, and this made the use of structured interviews more convenient. We also faced one other problem in our interviews in Gwelo that did not exist in Oshogbo. This was a consequence of the residential unstability of the Gwelo population, which we had anticipated and had hoped to control. It was our intention to interview the sample households continuously for a nine-month period, replacing the drop-outs wherever possible. During this time a not insignificant number of our informants left Gwelo either to return to the reserves or go to another town, and we found that many of them could not be replaced, so that for a portion of our sample the data are incomplete.

The barriers and reluctance manifested in the interviewing phase of the Gwelo study were reflected in my own work. The initial reaction to me, by the Africans, was determined mainly by the single criterion of my white skin. This reaction was modified but not basically changed during my stay. I was able to form some relationships that were relatively free of the consciousness of color, but for the most I remained primarily in the role of a white man, a role that carried with it a considerable, though in my case ill-defined, threat. One important consequence of the almost uniform, although largely passive, antagonism toward whites was that all black-white relationships had to be maintained on a level that prevented the hostility from erupting into the open. This limited the type of question I could ask, as well as the quality of data I could obtain. There were many areas of Gwelo social life that were accessible to me, but there were others that remained closed for the duration of the study. The most notable example was our inability to either visit or study the beer hall. We were interested in the leisure activities and habits of the Africans after their work had been completed for the day. Most Africans, living on the location, relaxed in the beer halls where only native beer was sold. The beer hall was built and run by the municipality, and most Africans view it as a black retreat or sanctuary. Three times I attempted to visit the beer hall, and on each occasion I was forced to leave. My field assistants were permitted to use the beer hall, but they could not interview anyone there since the Africans clearly indicated that they would not talk while under the influence of alcohol. The hostility of the Africans was great enough to block any further attempts to study them in the beer hall.

Furthermore, even when I was permitted to observe social behavior, I usually felt that my presence not only constrained this behavior but altered it. However, I *was* able to form close relationships with the panel group, who met with me regularly. They were a verbal and cooperative group whose insights guided me in formulating hypotheses and questionnaires. Without the help and insights of this group, the study would have been much more difficult to carry out.

The conditions in Gwelo led to a field situation in which my own researches and those of my staff were more independent of one another than they had been in Oshogbo. In many areas we had to depend either on the questionnaires or on my interviews and observations. There was not the continuous feedback between the survey data and my own material that had existed in Oshogbo. Thus in many areas we were not able to obtain the multileveled understanding and additional insights that more integrated methods might have afforded. Nevertheless, the two methods were certainly supplementary and, given the particular circumstances in Gwelo, probably yielded more than either method could have alone.

Bowing Out

In planning the Gwelo study we had allotted a year for field work. Since we were attempting less and were more experienced than in Oshogbo, we had estimated that a year would be sufficient time to carry out the Gwelo study. As the later stages of the study developed, we began to check off completed items and to re-examine our data. After carefully reviewing our work, we came to the conclusion that we had collected more than sufficient material to satisfy the objectives of the study. We could articulate the Gwelo social system and understood the major tenets that controlled behavior on the location. To stay longer would require us to enlarge the scope of the study and redefine our goals. It became clear to us that the study was over; it was time to leave.

There was an even more practical reason for leaving. We had enough funds for one year in the field and to stay longer would have required securing additional funds.

It was not difficult to leave Gwelo. With few exceptions our relationships to both Africans and European were distant and formal, for we had been generally unable to develop close ties or establish intimate friendships. Both the Africans and Europeans viewed us with hostility and as a threat to their existence. We were not accepted or trusted, nor did we trust the Africans or the Europeans. The cultural atmosphere in Rhodesia, with its emphasis on racial conflict and prohibitions against Africans, was a constrained atmosphere in which we had to be very careful not to break any laws and to follow the correct behavior for Europeans. We were constantly being watched. It is not easy to live in a society in which behavior is so restricted and guarded, and we left Gwelo with a sigh of relief, as though a heavy weight had been removed from our chests. We were free once more and could behave without closely guarding our actions.

Most social situations are two-sided, and it was not easy to leave my field assistants, with whom I had established very satisfactory relationships. In these relationships the norms of Gwelo did not prevail, and a healthy bond existed between them and me. During the study, I saw them at least twice a day, and usually more often. When we left, new jobs had to be secured for them, and they had to be protected from any hostility that the study may have engendered against them. We were fortunate in being able to secure fairly safe jobs for three of the assistants, whose new employers had full knowledge of their work with me and felt that it added rather than detracted from their skills. The three field assistants who had been sent to me by the Rhodes-Livingstone Institute decided to return to Lusaka and continue their work with the Institute.

I also had excellent relationships with the members of the panel group. Before leaving Gwelo, my obligation to these men was to safeguard them from possible harassments by the white community in the future. To some extent they were protected by the positions they held, but the white community was fully aware that they met with me regularly. To what extent this was resented was difficult to ascertain, but any extensive relationships between white men and Africans were frowned upon. Again we were fortunate in being able to contact their superiors, who viewed the study and their relationships to me sympathetically.

In the final days of the study an interesting phenomena was brought to my attention by the panel group. At our last session some of the participants indicated to me that I had overlooked a number of individuals whom the African community felt had high status. It had never been our intention to invite *all* the Africans of high status but only a select few. A discussion group becomes unwieldy if it is too large, but some of the men whom we did not invite greatly resented having been overlooked. Apparently, membership in my panel group increased the status of an African, while those who were not included lost prestige in the eyes of the community. If we had acquired this information earlier in the study, we would have taken some action to correct our unintentional oversight.

Another difficult and embarrassing problem confronted us in the last days of the study. Because of the racial situation in Rhodesia and the hostility of the European population to the study, I had refused to grant any newspaper or radio interviews about it. I was concerned that the interviews would be used against the study or against the African people. Nevertheless, I had become quite friendly with a newspaper reporter who persistently pleaded for a story, and a week before we left Gwelo I granted his request. We gave him a carefully worded statement about our results and work, and he promised that it would be published without alterations. We felt that the publicity would be good for us, for our staff, and for future social studies in Rhodesia. We assumed the good faith of the newspaper. When the story was published two days later, it had been modified to support European racial policies in Rhodesia. The reporter apologized and explained that his editor had made the alterations over his objections. Even more embarrassing was the fact that the newspaper would not publish our denials and objections to the story. We had been naive in assuming that we could get a story published in the Rhodesian press that was favorable to the Africans and not to Europeans. Fortunately, the study was over and the harm was not too great. We were able to counteract some of the effect by publishing our original story in the African press.

Finally the end of the Gwelo study came. We had our last farewells in my Gwelo home, and the following day we boarded a train for Beira, a major East African port in Mozambique, and began the long trek home.

Summary and Evaluation

Although the Gwelo study was conducted in a cultural atmosphere marked by extreme racial hostilities and tensions, it was, in my judgment, relatively successful. It is true that we were not able to pursue our original goals, but the limited objectives that we finally achieved produced some rewarding results. We could clearly indicate the behavior of Africans on the location, and we had some knowledge of the problems confronting a plural community as a whole. Briefly, Gwelo was a European community of 7,000 Europeans and 25,000 Africans that had been founded in 1896. Like most of the other towns in Rhodesia, Gwelo was the commercial and industrial hub of the surrounding area. The African populations living on the location in Gwelo were tribally heterogeneous, with the great majority of Africans divided between the Shona (60.5 percent) and Ndebele (13.6 percent) tribes of Rhodesia. There were, however, also Africans from Portuguese East and West Africa, Zambia, South Africa, and Malawi.

The average Central African man is a highly transient and migratory individual. Typically, he leaves his traditional rural village to seek work in European-created industrial towns. Most often he comes alone, leaving his wife and children behind to tend his fields or cattle in his native village. After a considerable period of time in town, he returns to his traditional village, regardless of whether he has accomplished his objective or not. His goals were usually economic. The average African male sets out to seek capital to finance new equipment, to educate his children, and to buy seed, more cattle, or more land. Usually he returns to his village in debt, since living expenses on the locations absorb most of his wages. Eventually, after an undeterminate period in his village, he will return to the same town or even to a different one. This circulation between town and rural areas may continue for the greater part of his life.

There are two other major themes that pervade all aspects of social life in Gwelo. The first is the cleavage between black and white. Each color group forms a stratum in society clearly separated by customary and statutory laws. Virtually all power in the society is in the hands of the Europeans, who control the major mechanisms of coercion, whether they be political, social, religious, or economic. Europeans construct all laws, control the police and armed forces, dominate the expenditure of all funds, indicate who can be educated, and determine, with rare exceptions, what economic pursuits an individual can follow. The only recourse to European domination that the Africans have who reside in the urban location is to leave and return to their traditional villages. Thus, any African migrating to town must accept domination by the white man and be prepared to be coerced into specific areas of behavior.

The second pervasive characteristic of the African community in Gwelo is the discontinuities in the two social systems. With extremely rare exceptions, all Africans are born in their traditional villages and, although the most remote villages in Rhodesia have had some measure of contact with urban industrial patterns and European way of life, the average African male is still primarily a subsistence farmer conforming to traditional patterns of behavior. The essential elements in his social world are familial obligations and personal ties and contacts with his traditional village. When a traditional African man migrates to town, the patterns of urban life are imposed upon him. He must live and work in a world marked by a complex network of strange, unfamiliar, and conflicting relationships and roles. Most often the new network is disturbing and forces him to perform tasks and duties that may be repugnant to his traditional values. To a very large extent, his position in society and his economic and social relationships in the location are now determined by what he does as an individual and not by the traditional groups to which he belongs. His position in the productive system is the critical factor, not kinship, age, and sex, which are usually the major factors determining behavior in traditional structures. He begins to move in a world where relationships tend to be impersonal, amorphous, and transitory. New values and incentives begin to develop that are based on the urban world and have no relationship to the older traditional patterns. Often the new values threaten the old ways of life and are deeply incompatible with traditional social forms. The African stands alone, his old patterns of security are gone, and few counterparts to his traditional security system have developed in his urban world. Thus, when an African migrant comes to the urban world, he enters a social system marked by conflicts and tensions and lacking most traditional forms of security.

Another significant factor in the Gwelo social system is the marked discrimination in roles and occupations between Europeans and Africans. Occupational stereotypes have developed, and by custom and law certain specific categories have been marked off for each color group. Wage differentials are maintained, and professional and managerial roles are virtually barred to Africans. Education for Africans is very limited, but some Africans have received sufficient education to become clerks or schoolteachers with a very narrow range of responsibility and authority. Some commercial traders and skilled artisans have developed among the Africans, but they are allowed to operate only on the location and are not permitted to transact business in Gwelo proper. The vast majority of Africans inhabiting the Gwelo locations are unskilled, illiterate laborers or domestics performing menial, unrewarding tasks for which they receive wages barely sufficient to maintain them in town. Virtually all functionally significant roles are reserved for the white segment of the population.

Although Africans coming to town are forced to accept new patterns of behavior, some of the traditional differentiating characteristics, such as age, sex, kinship, and hereditary political rights, still persist in town, even though they have been greatly modified. Among these, kinship is probably the most important as it still provides some basis for relationships in the Gwelo location. People come to town because their kinsmen are there, and our data indicate that more than 50 percent of the men came to work in Gwelo because a kinsman was already there. A man has the right to seek food, aid, and shelter from his urban kin, and he is rarely refused. Most urban Africans will turn to their kin when such all-important events as death, sickness, marriage, births, loss of a job, and financial embarrassment occur. The importance of kinship is emphasized by the fact that a man in Gwelo almost invariably looks forward to returning to his kin and traditional village permanently. Thus an African in town has divided allegiances, for he must live in the urban world and still accept some of the traditional patterns of behavior that persist in town.

This, then, is Gwelo, a town of conflict and tension. It is a town in which the European dominates, and the African keeps shifting between the urban location and his traditional village. Finally, it is a world of shifting value systems in which the African is creating a new network of social relationships.

In retrospect the relative success of the Gwelo study can be attributed to three factors: the successful operation of the team, the panel group, and my own individual contacts. Although my field assistants had many deficiencies, they also had certain attributes that were an asset in Gwelo. Most important was the fact that we were able to weld them into a team with an *esprit de corps*. As the members of a team they supported each other and helped each other in their work. Although each field assistant worked independently and collected his data separately, they all compared notes and experiences and passed on their accumulated skills, knowledge, and contacts to each other. Sometimes, when the field situation was conducive to it, and the field assistants knew the same informants, they worked together. The assistants were also informants to me and to each other. At times, I discovered significant and key bits of information through the constant discussions and examinations of the data that the team performed as a whole. Each questionnaire was carefully reviewed by the team, and extraneous and faulty probes were eliminated. At our daily meetings a lively discussion took place in which faults were corrected, suggestions made, and new clues passed around. It was this cooperation and exchange of ideas and facts that overcame many of the team's deficiencies.

Nevertheless, the capabilities of the field assistants were limited by their education. They could handle only highly structured questionnaires and were constantly in need of direct supervision. Less structured questionnaires would have created too many difficulties to have been successfully employed by them. It took the field assistants many weeks to complete even the structured questionnaires. Obviously, more educated and talented field assistants would have allowed us to penetrate more deeply and collect more data about the population of Gwelo, but this was not possible at the time of the study. Today, it is conceivable that, in Gwelo, we could hire more educated field assistants and resolve many of these problems.

In many ways, the team of field assistants cannot be separated from the panel group. The panel met at my home, and under my direction they would discuss the problems we were experiencing in the field. They knew the values and problems of their people and often had invaluable suggestions and leads for they possessed insight and knowledge that were quite different from the field assistants' and that often opened up for us new areas of investigations. Although we never attained the flow and feedback of data that we had in Oshogbo, we were able to have considerable exchange of data between the team and the panel group, with me as the intermediary, as little actual contact existed between the field assistants and the panel members. One of the major difficulties in Gwelo was this lack of contact. If we had had more direct communication between the field assistants and the panel group, I think, in retrospect, that we would have achieved greater efficiency and possibly greater depth in the collection of data, even though the panel members perceived my field assistants as Africans with low status. However, I think in time healthy working relationships would have developed between the two groups.

My work was to direct the activities of the team, coordinate and manage the panel group, and collect data from informants. My rapport with the Africans was generally not nearly so good as that of my field assistants, but at times, in difficult situations or with people of high status, I was able to achieve sufficient rapport to collect reliable data. I also collected institutional data by visiting churches, schools, and governmental agencies, where I had less difficulty in establishing rapport. It was also my task to deal with all Europeans, and, fortunately, I was able to develop good rapport with a few Europeans who gave us considerable information on the history, government, demography, and social welfare of Gwelo. Although my activities, at times, were limited and although definite hostility existed toward me, I was still able to overcome many of these difficulties and create a relatively successful study. I have no doubts, however, that if we could have reduced the hostility of both the Europeans and the Africans toward us and created a better image in the society, we would have been able to penetrate deeper into the structure of the society and accumulate more significant data.

Probably the most difficult problem to contend with was the racial conflict between the white and black populations. It affected all aspects of the study and limited my own activities and those of my field assistants. It was quite obvious to us, after the first few months of the study, that neither the European or African populations trusted us. Both perceived us as a threat. It was beyond our powers to affect the racial situation in Rhodesia, nor were there other ways in which we could have reduced the hostility of the two groups toward us. It is interesting that we were able to collect large quantities of data, despite the hostilities.

Because of the transient nature of the African population, many of our informants left Gwelo during the study either to return to their villages or to move on to another town. Although we replaced many of these early drop-outs, we never did develop a satisfactory solution to this problem. Increasing the amount of time allotted to the field work might have alleviated the problem, but the African migratory patterns were an ongoing continuous process. Eventually with rare exception, all Gwelo Africans will leave the location and return to their traditional villages. Consequently, our data are not as complete as they could have been for approximately 15 percent of the sample. Unfortunately, I do not think there is a solution to this type of field problem.

There is one behavioral area where we could have achieved much more than we did, and that is in collecting data on African women. Most of our data on women were collected by men, as I had no female field assistants on my staff, nor were we able to hire any. Data on the personal and sexual behavior patterns of females were secured by my wife, for the women in Gwelo would not talk about their personal and sexual activities to men. An educated African female assistant would have been very helpful and could have collected much more data than we did.

Finally, it should be repeated that the Gwelo study was conducted in an atmosphere of violence, hatred, conflict, and tension. Under the circumstances, we did well, but many of the critical factors were beyond our control.

PART III: COMPARISON OF THE OSHOGBO AND GWELO STUDIES

In both Oshogbo and Gwelo the aim of our study was twofold: to discover the underlying principles of organization and the form and content of the social relationships that made up the social systems of these towns, and to shed some light on the complex problems of the adaptations, modifications, and changes in social patterns that are occurring throughout Africa today as a result of Westernization and urbanization.

Gwelo and Oshogbo share many common characteristics. Each has a high population density. Oshogbo has a population that exceeds 120,000 Africans. Gwelo, although considerably smaller, numbers about 25,000 Africans and 7,000 whites. The underlying factors causing change in both towns are intrinsically similar and have been grouped under the headings of colonial rule, industrialization, or commerce. Their social systems are characterized by increasing social differentiation and economic diversification and specialization. The introduction of Western institutions and values has given rise to new sets of interests and values that are often deeply incompatible with and threatening to traditional social forms. Thus both Oshogbo and Gwelo are characterized by the existence of contradictory sets of interests and relationships, by the exacerbation of traditional conflicts and the development of new ones, and by many ambiguous choices that may be interpreted and manipulated differently by individuals or groups.

There are also striking differences between Gwelo and Oshogbo. Gwelo, a commercial and industrial hub for the surrounding farmlands, typifies the towns that predominate in central and southern Africa. They were created solely by Europeans and have grown largely in response to the needs of a European market economy (see Schwab, 1961). Western economic, social, and political forms provide the basic social matrix in Gwelo. Oshogbo, on the other hand, was a large, dense, and permanent settlement before European contact. Many of the existing Yoruba towns, including Oshogbo, were probably founded in the eighteenth and nineteenth centuries. Today Oshogbo has an indigenous Yoruba population that is ethnically homogeneous and stable. Although there are some strangers who have migrated to Oshogbo, and others who have left Oshogbo to seek work or education in Ibadan and Lagos, migration plays virtually little or no part in the life of the community. In Gwelo, the African population is tribally heterogeneous, polyglot, migratory, and unstable although most are Shona and Ndebele. Typically, an African leaves his traditional village to seek work in town. After some time in Gwelo, he will return to his village. The circulation between town and rural village may continue for the greater part of a man's life. Unlike Oshogbo, there are only a very few Africans in Gwelo who are committed to town life and regard Gwelo as their home.

Oshogbo is mainly an agriculture community, but the economy in recent years has expanded, new occupations have developed, and there is a new emphasis on a market and impersonal monetary system. The Africans in the Gwelo location participate in a Western economic system mainly as unskilled laborers. When an African migrates to town, the patterns of town life are imposed on him, and he must live and work in a world characterized by unfamiliar and conflicting sets of roles and relationships. The transition from the rural economy to urban industrialism is abrupt, and the African is forced to reject traditional patterns and familial obligations. The African in Oshogbo has a kin-bound social system (see Schwab, 1955) based on segmentary lineages; the rules of kinship regulate and coordinate social behavior in almost all spheres of activity. The centralized administrative and jural authority is composed of a paramount chief (Oba) and a series of lesser administrative and ritual chiefs. Gwelo is controlled by a European minority in whom virtually all power is vested. Every aspect of life, social, economic, and political, is dominated by the cleavages and conflicts between Europeans and Africans. In Oshogbo, the effects of Western industrialized civilization have been less direct and more diluted than in Gwelo. There are no permanent settlers in Oshogbo, and no large-scale alienation of or sale of land to outsiders or Europeans has yet occurred. In Gwelo Europeans own at least 5 percent of the best lands, and fourth-generation Europeans are beginning to exert themselves. Finally, the people of Oshogbo live in a highly complex, organized, and structured system, whereas the Africans of Gwelo are unorganized and have a more random and unstructured system of social relationships.

I think that there is no doubt that the Oshogbo study was more successful than the Gwelo study. Although the methods employed in both studies were quite similar, the range of material covered was wider and we penetrated deeper into basic social processes in Oshogbo. The Oshogbo material is also more valid in the sense that it conforms more closely to social reality. There are many reasons for this. The field assistants in Oshogbo were better educated and more capable. They were able to act independently, handle complex problems, and manage the unexpected. They were capable of developing interviewing techniques and employing complex questionnaires and guides. Eventually they were able to function without direct supervision and gradually developed the ability to recognize what was important and to penetrate beyond the superficial facts and behavior. My field assistants in Gwelo were limited by their education and their command of written languages. Complex interviewing techniques or questionnaires could not be used by them, and they were unable to comprehend the social process to the same extent as my Oshogbo assistants. Also, my Oshogbo assistants were Yoruba and had been reared in the culture they were studying. They spoke the language fluently and understood the shadings and nuances of the culture. It was easy for them to establish rapport and develop relationships with their informants. These relationships deepened over time and resulted in a fuller understanding of behavior than would have been otherwise achieved. Because Gwelo is ethnically heterogeneous, polyglot, and basically European dominated, we could not fully duplicate this field condition there. Nevertheless, at times ethnic ties helped to increase rapport in Gwelo, since half of my team and half of the sample were Shona. But the cultural and racial atmosphere in Gwelo was such that ethnic ties were usually pushed into the background. In fact, the hostilities in Gwelo were great enough to reduce relationships and rapport over time. In many instances, the longer my field assistants continued their relationships with their informants, the less responsive the informants became.

There are other reasons too for the greater success of the Oshogbo study. I think the cooperation I received from the colonial administration in Oshogbo helped facilitate our work. After the initial difficulties of housing, the colonial administration was fully cooperative and put no stumbling blocks in my way. We had no difficulty in securing access to official information, and whenever possible the colonial files were open to our inspection and perusal. In Gwelo the situation was reversed, because the European administration was hostile to us, did not approve of the study, and put obstacles in our way as often as they could. Most of the Europeans were uncooperative, and access to government files and information was difficult. Considering the political and racial circumstances, it is doubtful that we could have improved our rapport with the European community.

Some of the differences in the results of the two studies can be traced to important dissimilarities in the two social systems. The stability and structure of Yoruba society provided an almost built-in analytical framework that made the field work easier. They had not been subject to the massive amounts of Westernization and industrialization that the people in Gwelo had, and the changes that were taking place in Oshogbo were within a social system that had basically remained intact. Gwelo, on the other hand, was characterized by instability, heterogeneity, and the absence of articulating principles of organization. Contrasts between traditional rural life and the industrial modes of town were sharp, and the people were forced into many unfamiliar roles and social situations. In other words, because a man brought many aspects of tribal behavior with him into town, he alternated between urban and tribal forms of behavior according to the social situation that involved him at any given moment. Thus the social system in Gwelo was marked by ambiguity and inconsistency and made for a more difficult field situation.

But most important were the hostility and defenses exhibited by the Gwelo Africans, who feared, hated, and distrusted all white men. The political, social, economic, and religious prohibitions that the Europeans forced on the Africans did not allow them to develop any image of the Europeans other than a hostile one. Under these circumstances, I do not know of any techniques that can clear away such deeply embedded antagonisms, especially when the populations are large. It is conceivable, where populations are small, that time and understanding could reduce the hostilities. By using African field assistants, creating an African panel group, and publicizing the study and the fact that I was an American, we initially assuaged some of their fears and hostilities toward us, but when we continued to question and probe, the basic hostile attitudes and values of the Africans began to re-emerge. In Oshogbo, our rapport deepened with time, and our relationships became friendlier as our stay increased. In Oshogbo, I was the Ataoja's "white man" and he was my "chief clerk." The hostility and fears of the Africans in Gwelo limited the operation of the study and reduced the amount and depth of the data that we could collect. However, it is interesting to note that when we could establish personal relationships, as I did with my field assistants and panel-group members, many of the hostilities and fears evaporated.

Much has been written about the effects on an anthropological study of the attitudes and values of the people among whom the study is undertaken. But what about the effect of the attitudes and values of the anthropologist on the success of the field work? We all admit that the objective anthropologist free from prejudice and preconception is a myth, so, because I suspect that my own reactions played an important if not easily discernible part in the two field studies, I must make some reference to them. I responded to the people in Gwelo very differently from the way I had responded to the Yoruba. A good portion of this difference in feeling can be attributed to the deep and disturbing racial tension in Gwelo. My conscious sympathies were with the Africans, for I was bitterly angry at the degradations and restrictions imposed upon them. At the same time, I was a white man and perforce treated as one by the Africans. This involved more than their restricting my questions and observations. It also involved a subtle personal antagonism, which in turn must have generated feelings of hostility and anger in me. Although I was largely unaware of such feelings while in the field, in retrospect I must question whether my ability to be objective and to gain insights was not in fact hampered by these tensions.

I reacted to other elements in the cultures as well. The Yoruba are a colorful, exuberant people with a great capacity for fun and enjoyment. Their relationships have many dimensions, and their culture has been enriched by its strong traditions, its rituals, and its songs and dances. Little of this ebullience and creativity is evident in Gwelo. Indeed, there were times when I came to think of the Gwelo African community as a kind of Black Necropolis. Some of the inertia and flatness that mark Gwelo is without doubt derived from the repressions of the whites and from the painful adjustments of the Africans to town life. But some of it is simply that the peoples of Gwelo do not have as rich, varied, and enjoyable a culture as the Yoruba. I have no doubt that in both field situations my own personal attitudes and reactions were unconsciously carried over into and affected the research. Thus it is difficult to dismiss them as negligible, even though now I have great difficulty in assessing them.

VILLAGE
AND CITY
FIELD WORK
IN LEBANON

John Gulick

Sometime during the period 1946–1951, when I was an anthropology student (undergraduate and graduate) at Harvard, a visiting anthropologist shocked some of us by declaring that he really hated some of the people among whom he had done field work. Our shocked reaction was the result of what we were being taught explicitly and also implicitly by innuendo: that all cultures are inherently equally lovable and that, if one does not come away from a field trip loving those whom one has studied, one has failed as a field worker and therefore as a true anthropologist.

Since our visitor was unquestionably a "genuine" and accomplished anthropologist, we decided (in those halcyon days of Freudian ethnography) that he must have many unresolved conflicts and problems that had somehow survived the subjective analytic experience of field work. "Be psychoanalyzed before you go," we were advised by another mentor, with little regard to feasibility. If you aren't, the implication seemed to be, you will certainly feel as if you ought to have been before you are through. Some of the recent pronouncements of Lévi-Strauss, and the adulation with which they have been received, suggest that this point of view—equating field work in part with an initiation ordeal and in part with mystical experiences—still has wide currency. The implications of this point of view are as deceptive as the old marriage-manual dogma that a couple who fail to achieve simultaneous orgasms are failures not only personally but also in their "true selves" as man and woman.

When the anthropologist is in the field, field work is his total life. He copes with it by using his whole body and personality in the same way that he copes with life when he is not in the field. This is the fundamental difference between anthropological field research and sociological survey research, which is not only not a total life situation but can even be (and frequently is) done entirely by someone else. Life in the field involves the same emotions as life at home: elation, boredom, embarrassment, contentment, anger, joy, anxiety, and so on. To these are added, however, the necessity of being continually on the alert (of *not* taking one's surroundings and relationships for granted), and the necessity of learning new routines and cues. These necessities are likely to force a heightened awareness of facets of one's personality of which one had not been aware before. This can be an emotionally devastating experience, but it is by no means inevitably so. The emotional and situational factors are so varied and complicated in their relationships that no safe predictions in the abstract can be made on this score.

Why has the performance of this important professional role of the anthropologist been caricatured in terms of either/or emotional extremes and veiled in mystical claptrap? Is it possible that many anthropologists are attracted to the field less out of love for other cultures than out of the feeling of being inadequate in their own? Could it be that many anthropologists are also ambivalent about various aspects of field work, regarding it chiefly as a means to the end of contributing to knowledge, rather than as an end in itself? Could it be that many successful episodes in the field come about through good luck as much as through sophisticated methodology, or that many unsuccessful episodes come about through bad judgment as much as through bad luck?

Indeed, it could be! And once these possibilities are accepted, it is more readily understood why so many anthropologists have been unwilling to be forthright about their field experiences.

Fear of violating the field-work mystique, and of being professionally downgraded because of this, has been a major cause of this lack of honesty, and so the mystique has become self-perpetuating.

This book is an attempt to improve the discipline of anthropology by breaking up this conspiracy of silence. This does not imply, however, that all reticence can go by the board. Field work, being a total life situation, involves some personal reactions that are generally considered to be private. Although much can be done to replace mystique with specific information, there are limits of privacy beyond which most anthropologists (and most people generally) will probably not allow others to intrude. In other words, although we can help each other by sharing our experiences far more than we have in the past, each of us must, ultimately, find his own way.

PART I: VILLAGE FIELD WORK

Problem, Theory, and Research Design

The Arabic-speaking culture of the Middle East had, by 1951, intrigued me to the point of my wishing to study it professionally. This came about through my experiences in the Middle East during World War II and the enthusiasm of one of the very few senior anthropologists, Carleton S. Coon, who was interested in the area's present-day culture. There was very little else upon which to build. What material existed consisted of some out-of-date ethnographies, mostly of nomadic groups whom I knew to be peripheral in fact, though not in reputation, to the mainstream of the culture. Although some socioeconomic monographs existed, many of them substantial but often slanted toward ulterior political aims, there were no intensive community studies of the sort that formed the very foundation of ethnography in other areas, and there were only a few theoretical or problem-oriented anthropological studies. The simple fact was that the contemporary Middle East had been ignored by modern anthropology.

Where and with what problems should I begin? The possible answers were as limitless as the lacunae in Middle Eastern ethnography. In 1949, however, I had written a B.A. honors thesis on the Maronites, a Christian Arab subculture surrounded by Muslims that had adapted itself to the mountainous environment of Lebanon, and this gave me a start (Gulick, 1949). In my thesis, I had had to piece together a composite picture of Maronite family life, kinship, and village structure, for there was no single study that encompassed all of these subjects— either for the Maronites, or for anyone else in the Middle East. The sources indicated in a general way that endogamous patrilineages located primarily in endogamous villages were the rule. The lineages were composed entirely, it seemed, of extended family households. Household, lineage, and village were all described as being cohesive in-groups, each opposed to "outsiders." How, I wondered, could patrilineage endogamy be reconciled with a rule forbidding *bilateral* first-cousin marriages? How, in reality, could household, lineage, and village be cohesive in-groups *simultaneously* for the same individual? How could *all* households consist of extended families at the same time? And how could a system of strong unilineal kin groups be functionally consistent with a system of kinship terms that G. P. Murdock had just christened "Sudanese"? (*Social Structure,* 1949.) I began to suspect that, aside from possible inaccuracies, the various sources expressed idealized norms more than they did generally observable realities. Obviously, only field work could provide answers to these questions.

On the matter of multiple in-groups, my reading of Evans-Pritchard's *The Nuer,* with its concept of balanced antagonisms and related matters, created in my mind an image of a complicated real world of mixed motives and situationally varied cues that was not even hinted at in the literature itself. Here was fascination and challenge combined. In 1951, I proposed to my dissertation committee that I do a village study in Lebanon focused upon these problems. Preferably, it would be a Maronite village, but the particular sect of the village was, as far as I could see, of secondary importance, for the same phenomena were apparently present in all villages, including Muslim ones (except with respect to some details about cousin marriage). The core of my method would be a thorough household survey, establishing the exact composition of each unit and the relationships among them both within the village and outside it.

The committee gave me its blessing, but otherwise I found myself to be on my own. The first reason for this was that the committee, though composed of experts on social structure and complex peasant cultures, did not include anyone with Middle Eastern experiences or interests. In fact, one member of it even exclaimed, "*Lebanon!* What do you want to go to *that* greasy place for?" Second, although four budding young anthropologists of my own age had just returned from field work in Lebanon, they were reticent about their experiences and obviously were not willing to give me entrée into the particular villages they had studied, although they were very generous with the names of other contacts. Third, pressed for funds and concerned (perhaps overly so) about how our three-year-old and one-year-old sons might fare, my wife and I decided that I should go to Lebanon alone. In retrospect, I wish that we had done otherwise. It would be idiotic to claim (as I have heard others claim under similar circumstances) that it would have been a great experience for the children, for they would hardly have remembered it, but the many pains of separation were a burden I could well have done without. Furthermore, I believe that it is very important for anyone, even under "ordinary" circumstances, to have access to at least one other person with whom he can constantly test out his reactions and try out his ideas. If it is important under ordinary circumstances, it is absolutely essential in the field. This other person can be another member of a formal research team, or a spouse, or both, or someone else, but it must be someone who can be completely trusted, emotionally and intellectually, for benevolent candor. (Ten years later, in 1961, when my wife, sons, and daughter went to Lebanon again for field work the validity of these points was amply borne out.)

Passive or Adaptational Research

My original plan was to spend a year in the field, September, 1951, to August, 1952, but red tape about visas and like matters delayed my arrival in Lebanon until the beginning of November. In Beirut, I immediately set out to find and buy a used car, which took some time, and to establish contacts at the American University, using references that had been given to me. From this base, my hope was to establish further contacts who would introduce me into a suitable village.

In regard to selecting a village, one of my acquaintances had said, before I left America, "Well, drive around everywhere you can get to, looking them over. When you find one you like the looks of—especially one with a great view—just move in!" Easier said than done, of course, but although it sounded appealing, it did not match my cautious temperament. Had I been part of a team, as the speaker had been, it might have been different, for a casual, unsponsored entrée into a Lebanese village could have distinct advantages over a formal, sponsored one. The "passive" stage of field work might take longer, but one could hardly start off on a better foot than by saying, "I would like to live in your village for a while because it is so beautiful!"

I quickly discovered that Beirut was full of Lebanese people who had village identities but who were living in the city because village life was, for them, boring and uncomfortable (especially in winter) and unremunerative. My desire to live in a village was thus in a direct countercurrent to the desires of many of my Lebanese acquaintances. To only some of them did the explanation that it was a requirement of my training have much reality. All readily agreed that the Arabs were very badly misunderstood in America. They were, for instance, all regarded as nomads with no fixed abodes, an old romantic notion that happened to fit in well with the aims of Zionist propaganda. Some of my acquaintances assented to the idea that, if more accurate information were made available, it might help to offset these misunderstandings, but what, they asked, is to be learned in villages? Seventy-five percent of the Arabs live in villages, I replied. Yes, they said, but village life does not matter; it is in the cities where our civilization is. Even in this "passive" phase of field work, some of the major conflicts in values and social cleavages in Lebanese culture were having their impact on my plans. I also discovered that none of my contacts at the American University had any suitable Maronite contacts, nor any contacts at the Université St. Joseph, also in Beirut, where there were many Maronites.

A reference to persons in the Catholic and Maronite hierarchy outside of Beirut took me to a village very high in the mountains. The priest received me very kindly, seemed to understand my objectives, and invited me to stay. However, he was not a native of the village and did not know all the families well, and the village, which was often snowbound in the winter, was to a considerable degree depopulated for that season (a common phenomenon). I decided, reluctantly, to keep on looking.

An employee of the American University to whom I had explained my mission some time before then told me that she had mentioned me to a young man from her own Orthodox Christian village who happened to be in town. She said that he was the son of the priest who was a native of the village and would know the kinds of things about families in which I was interested. If I would like to visit the village with him, I would be welcome.

Accordingly, that night we drove to the village, and I spent several days with the young man, his father, mother, and younger brother. A married sister lived in Beirut. The village, which is fully described elsewhere (Gulick, 1955:20–46), is located on the northern coast of Lebanon, about halfway between Beirut and Tripoli. The shoreline at that point consists of eroded layers and big, broken slabs of limestone. A paved highway and a railroad run north-south along the shore, but the land rises almost immediately from the sea in the form of ridges (running east-west) and intervening arroyos. No ground water is available, and the only source of water throughout the year is what is collected in cisterns during the winter rains. Much of the land consists of naked limestone outcrops, but earth has been conserved in some places by means of retaining walls that form terraces. Olives and figs are the main crops. The sparse natural vegetation consists mostly of low, thorny shrubs.

In 1951–1952, the village consisted of a small, subsidiary hamlet on the highway (which has subsequently grown considerably) and a cluster of about a hundred stone houses half a mile inland and up from the hamlet. The main house-cluster consisted of irregular rows of houses at various elevations along the southern slope of a ridge. The top of the house-cluster was on the crest of the ridge 750 feet above sea level, and the lower end of the house-cluster was at about 500 feet. These top and bottom points were about half a mile apart. I lived in the main-house-cluster, but the leader of the faction to which most of my informants were opposed lived in the hamlet on the highway.

The priest did indeed have genealogical information about the village's families, marriages, and occupations. As a priest, it was his business to know these things, but he knew them also by virtue of his being a native of the village. He would be glad to help me, he said, but what was I going to do with the information? I said that I was going to put it into a book whose purpose would be to give people in America a better idea of what life among the Arabs was really like. Whether or not he and the other villagers then believed that I would write such a book, I do not know. There was no reason they should have, except that they knew I was a scholar associated with an institution of high prestige in their culture. I knew that books and a person's associations with books were highly prestigious in these peoples' eyes, but as far as "role-playing" is concerned, it is important to note that it was indeed my intention to write such a book, that subsequently I *did* write it, and after less than four years a copy of it was in their hands. In the Lebanese culture, my role as a scholar was to some degree compatible with the native system of role values, although a social-science study of a village was not. The problem of the anthropologist whose role in the field is not at all conceivable to his informants, and who must therefore define himself in other terms, is obviously different from what mine was.

Because my informants to some extent understood my role, I had one immediate advantage: the period of "passive research" was very short, and I was soon (just after New Year's, 1952) at work with the priest and asking directly for the information I needed.

The priest's family did not have space for me in their two-room house, so I rented a room in a house that would be vacant until the middle of the summer. This was a strictly business arrangement, for I dealt with the owner's brother as agent and there was little haggling, as it was obvious that any sum of money at all would be sheer profit for the owner, who lived in Beirut during the winter.

I took my meals with the priest's family. Hospitality is a matter of great pride among the Arabs. Although there are definite limits to hospitality, more is expected and more is given than in America, especially with regard to food. I had been warned not to make the mistake of trying to pay for what was intended as hospitality, and I was also very conscious of trying to avoid the reputation of Americans as people who thought they could get anything they wanted just by paying for it. But were these meals hospitality or not? I was not sure, and my guess is that the priest's family was not sure either, for though the meals themselves betokened hospitality (for which the host would certainly not ask for payment), the protraction of the service was wholly unprecedented. In any event, neither party was able to suggest that this be made a regular business arrangement, and we entered into the relationship with only my verbal assurances that from time to time I would be pleased to show my gratitude for their generosity. Subsequently, at irregular intervals, I made gifts of money that I felt sure were more than adequate compensation for the food, and at the end I gave them a large polished veneer table that I had had made according to their specifications. Several years later, I learned that they had indeed felt anxious and tense about the whole arrangement and that they would have preferred regular, fixed payments, but apparently they felt unable to raise the issue. At the time, I felt the tension but could not identify its source. This was an instance, I believe, where both the foreigner and the natives were deluded by an ideal norm in the culture, namely that the "spiritual" rewards of hospitality take precedence over fair recompense for services rendered. In practice, the priority of values is the reverse whenever the direct choice must be made.

Active Research

Census and household survey. In establishing a working relationship with the priest, I entered into the active phase of the research. My aims were to obtain, first, a map of the village showing every house (occupied, unoccupied, and ruined—the last being a sign of an emigrated family), second, an exact census of every household, including the name, age, and sex of every occupant, their relationships to each other, any unrelated residents, whether or not spouses were natives of the village, nonresident members of the family and where they were living, occupations of all adults, degree of education of all children, and other details; and third, a genealogy of the families of the village.

The priest had such a genealogy. It was written on a large sheet of paper and was of a style that is standard in Arab culture —present and past, Muslim and Christian. It is a schematic tree and is literally called a tree *(shajarat)*. It shows only males, each represented as a circle (if there is room) with each one's progeny attached as if on stalks. It took some time to decipher the names and to make a version in English with the generations reconciled. I knew that the chart, lacking females, was worthless for any genetic study and that it might be inaccurate in other ways, but it enabled me to begin to piece together the relationships of the twenty-one named lineages in the village. The priest and I worked on this at the same time that we began to work on the census. An individual's lineage name is not ordinarily used in the village, because everyone knows everyone else, and repeatedly I had to remind the priest about it, except when he remembered my interest and supplied the name himself.

For purposes of the census I had prepared some mimeographed forms on legal-size paper. The priest and I usually worked in the evenings, and sometimes in the afternoons, in the reception area of his house. Other family members came and went, sometimes joined us, and, particularly in the evenings, various cronies and other relatives appeared. While we were working, I deliberately left these forms out in the open, so that anyone could see what I was asking and what the priest's answers were, and I let others interject comments or questions. Often these led to long digressions and diverted conversations.

What with the interruptions and variations in mood and my policy of not striving for completion too persistently, all this took a long time. Repeatedly I had to press the priest for specific information on certain individuals, but I did not want to be too persistent. Perseverance is reported not to be a usual characteristic of Arab personality, but through the months, the priest and I persevered together until all 580 residents of the village were recorded in several different ways. Throughout it all, an informal check (but admittedly not a systematic one) was provided by the fact that our discussions were public and that there were many comments and corrections from others.

Meanwhile, one of the villagers who was a trained surveyor was, in company with the mayor, making a cadastral survey of the village. The surveyor made a sketch map of the village—its paths, houses and other buildings—and with it in hand I tramped all over, taking photographs and checking on each structure. Early in this process of checking houses against households, some of the complexities of the ecological realities of the village became evident. In particular, I discovered that many of the households identified with certain houses were absent, in whole or in part, during the winter. This discovery led to a whole line of questioning in regard to occupations and residence elsewhere, to the reasons for and occasions of visits to the village, and to the whole matter of commuting to Beirut and Tripoli. I also discovered that "outsiders," people not on the priest's genealogy, were living in some of the vacated houses. These discoveries introduced many economic factors into the household survey and into the conversations that I recorded in my field notes.

The surveyor was reluctant to talk about land ownership. The mayor himself was also reticent on this subject, although he was vociferous about the necessity of improving the economy of the village itself. He also had a good deal to say about the nefarious influence of Communists, and he made more than one remark about black people. (He had spent several years as an immigrant in Vicksburg, Mississippi.) He said nothing about America's support of Israel, but he did speak disparagingly of the education "for no practical purpose" that seemed to him to be the policy of the American University of Beirut. In contrast, the priest and his friends, with no experience in America, continually badgered me on the matter of Israel and greatly lauded the intellectual importance of the American University. (On the Arab-Israeli question I had to try to defend my country and at the same time acknowledge what I personally felt to have been its excessive zeal in supporting Zionism at the expense of so many Arabs.)

Factions and the role of the ethnographer. I discovered that there were ideological differences of great significance in this village for which I was a sounding board. I do not think that I appreciated their full significance at the time, but I began to realize that the priest and the mayor were members of opposed factions, and that my involvement with one had already gone so far that I did not see how I could make up for it to the other.

This was not a factionalism of simple distinctions between lineages or places of residence, although these factors played some part in the situation, but rather an ideological factionalism. Ideological factionalism, supported by friendships and family ties, and felt to be mortally threatened, can result in a steadfastly defensive possessiveness. Since kinship ties and marriage relationships are properly the province of the priest, and since these were my major interests, too, then my major relationship should be with him. But the priest was also a member of a faction, and as another member of that faction once said to me, "You belong to *us*."

This status of being adopted into a faction was reflected in the names I was given. Some people called me Sayyid John ("Mr. John"), an expression of formal distance. Others called me either John or Hanna, its Arabic equivalent, an expression of familiar equality. But the name by which I was referred to and the one by which, I understand, I am still remembered, was Hanna Khoury. Khoury literally means priest, but it is also a common family name among Lebanese Christians, although it was not the family name of the priest in this village. Normally, in this culture, a person's second name is that of his or her father, or a suitable substitute, while the third name (rarely used) is that of the lineage. I had no lineage affiliation, and though the priest was obviously not my father, I was very clearly identified with him in a style that was compatible with the patterns of the culture.

Techniques. In addition to the census, I kept written field notes on conversations, observations, hunches, and subjective reactions. I found it impossible to separate the recording of "objective data" from the recording of my own reactions and day-by-day activities. One of my professors had advised keeping "field notes" and a "journal" for these dual purposes, but I was not able to separate the two. If one is recording the highlights of a conversation, how does one select those highlights and determine the mood and intent of the informant, especially if the conversation concerns attitudes and values? Is he serious or joking? Is he reiterating stereotypes or expressing a critical judgment? The context of the conversation, including the ethnographer's own state of mind at the time, may provide clues to answers, and these must be recorded along with direct quotations, if the notes are to have any value.

The use of tape recorders does not obviate these problems, except for those ethnographers (if such there be) who keep no records of their field work except tape recordings. As in ordinary life, invaluable information and insights often come to me through some unexpected encounter, and any ethnographer worth his salt must be prepared to cope with such events and write them up effectively. Although I do not deny the value of tape recordings under certain circumstances and for certain kinds of material, I do not believe that they can displace the "old-fashioned" field notes.

I always carried with me a small pocket notebook in which

I jotted down specific information, such as names, dates, and other numerical figures. I also wrote down the spellings of words and names in Arabic, always allowing my informants to see these spellings and therefore anything else that might be on the same page. It always amused them, I think, to see samples of my somewhat clumsy, schoolboyish Arabic characters, but it also pleased them, for one of their assumptions (generally well-founded) is that Americans don't know how to write Arabic.

For the main flow of a conversation, I relied on my memory. I never tried to copy down the other person's discourse, for I knew that to do so would have destroyed not only that particular conversation but very likely the whole relationship as well. I discovered that my own attention span was limited to about an hour and that in longer encounters much was lost as far as my notes were concerned. During the day I would try to retire to my room and record my impressions as soon as possible after a particular event. Often, however, I would have to wait until the evening to do this, and tired though I usually was at the end of the day, I found that it was essential to write the day's notes before going to sleep. If I failed to do this and postponed note writing till the next day, I found that the notes were useless, except insofar as they might contain simple factual information. The subtleties of cues and responses—some of which one can catch in notes if one writes them soon enough—became lost in sleep, and what I wrote the next day was essentially a second-hand account, an oversimplified version, in which the events and my reactions to them were truly blurred.

If one is to catch the immediate realities of life in field notes, one must write them as nearly as possible as one lives the events. They must be raw, fresh, undigested, yet organized enough to be coherent for future reading and analysis. It was and is impossible for me to record field events according to some preconceived system of coded headings for the purpose of facilitating analysis. There is time enough for coding and sorting later on. Impressions, hunches, and "hard" information all should go into the notes together as they come into one's consciousness. Epistemologically, they must not be confused with each other, however, and that is why notes must be recorded promptly.

Note-taking of this kind is difficult and time-consuming. It is also the very essence of real field work. In rereading notes that spanned a period of several months, I have repeatedly discovered discussions of events or ideas that I had completely forgotten, as well as other impressions of phenomena that I subsequently had learned to take for granted and was actually no longer seeing at all.

I wrote my notes on 5″ × 8″ sheets of paper, using a pen,

dating each sheet, and numbering all sheets consecutively. I kept the originals and mailed carbon copies to my adviser at Harvard for safekeeping and for his comments. The previous summer I had been employed by the Harvard "Rimrock" Project to read the field notes of one of the participants, assigning to each paragraph Human Relations Area File code numbers according to the contents. This analysis was intended to facilitate the crossfiling of the notes and the sharing of notes with others.[1] Subsequently, as adviser and critic myself, I have read the field notes of others and, on the basis of these experiences, I think that unless the adviser is also in the field, the usefulness of his comments is rather limited. However, he can comment helpfully on the precision of the recording. For instance, my adviser, in response to my writing that I thought an informant was joking when he said something, would point out that I should also have noted what evidence I had, if any, that the informant was joking.

On the basis of these experiences, I also question both the wisdom and propriety of sharing one's field notes with others, unless, perhaps, the others are simultaneously working in the same locale on coordinated research (although under these circumstances one would expect one's co-workers to be orally sharing their findings and problems). There may be those who record field notes with readers other than themselves in mind, and they may be good field notes, but I know that if I wrote field notes this way I would feel constrained in organization and restricted in expression, and no ethnographer should feel so constrained and restricted.

Extensions of the Field

During the preliminary period of my stay in Lebanon, I had agreed to give a course of lectures on anthropology at the American University of Beirut during the spring semester. I made

---

[1] In the late 1940s and early 1950s, the Harvard Department of Social Relations sponsored a coordinated cooperative research project (now called by the code name "Rimrock") on five different cultures in the Southwest (Mormon, Navaho, Spanish-speaking, Texan, and Zuni). Students and faculty members did field work at the same time, and in order to facilitate communication among them, their field notes were typed on ditto masters, and the contents of each page of notes was analyzed in terms of the inventory of culture content devised by the Human Relations Area Files at New Haven. Each item in the inventory has its own code number, and so each page of notes acquired from one to half a dozen numbers, depending upon how its contents were analyzed. A copy of each page of notes was then filed under every content category involved. A participant in the project would then be able to refer quickly to the numbered headings in the file to see what others besides himself had recorded on a large number of predefined subjects.

this commitment, because I wanted a genuine affiliation with the institution, not a token or merely courtesy one. I also had hoped that my interactions with the students would provide me with an additional dimension of significant contact with Lebanese culture.

When the time came, and as the spring progressed, I found that the teaching itself made greater demands on my energies than I had anticipated. Also, it often removed me from the village, and it undoubtedly slowed down my work there. However, it enabled me to share the commute with many of the villagers, for I often served as a taxi driver and a carrier of messages and packages. My original research design had not envisaged this urban extension of village life, but research in the village had revealed it, and my commitment at the University gave me some first-hand experience with it. In retrospect, I wish that I had concluded my work in the village earlier and turned my attention more fully and systematically to the villagers who were living in the city. The latter, however, were physically dispersed, and at the time, my primary responsibility seemed to be in the village itself.

My students did not become informants, as I had thought they might, but my contact with them was revealing in a number of significant ways. The tensions in their lives, especially those connected with intergenerational conflicts due to revolutionary cultural change, were obvious. Also obvious was the inadequacy, in helping them to identify the sources of their tensions, of their intellectual models and the formal curriculum imposed on them. Arabic intellectual exercises consist of memorizing normative systems of abstractions. The use among Lebanese students of sociology and anthropology textbooks written by and for Americans was, ironically, compatible with these traditional exercises, but not in the least suitable for elucidating local cultural problems. These texts provided normative abstractions to be memorized, but an inductive approach to actual behavioral patterns (or lack of them) was judged unworthy of systematic effort. The Arabs take the same approach to their own language. Only classical, literary Arabic is considered worthy of formal study, though much of it is archaic, whereas the colloquial dialects are academically beneath contempt. The students were not interested in the village materials I attempted to feed into the course; they thought that they knew all about village life, or they had rejected it, or both.

Part of these failures might be attributed to my inexperience and the fact that my field data were incomplete. However, in the intervening years I have discovered that others have had the same experiences, both in the Middle East and in other areas.

The reluctance or inability to distinguish normative patterns from behavioral practices and the great difficulty in generalizing about behavioral practices without parroting normative abstractions appear to be prevalent in many cultures. They constitute barriers to communication not only in field research but also in the transmission of interpretations and conclusions.

Bowing Out

I had originally told the villagers that I would stay only until sometime in the summer, so there was no difficulty in announcing and taking my leave when that time came. I had completed the household survey by the time that I was ready to go, and in that sense I had "finished" my work. Of course, by that time, I was very much aware of the many avenues of inquiry which, ideally, I should be following, or should have followed. Because of this awareness I felt a profound sense of unfinished business.

In saying my goodbyes in the village, I made a special effort to call on everyone with whom I had had contact, even though the contacts had not been frequent or recent. I made a particular point to call on the mayor. At the time, I felt that this was simply a common courtesy that was incumbent upon me, and I still think so. However, according to the oral report on professional ethics presented by Professor Ralph Beals at the Meetings of the American Anthropological Association in November, 1966, such courtesies are apparently not practiced commonly enough by the brethren. Perhaps if they were redefined as "field techniques" they might be taken more seriously.

Summary of Findings and Evaluation of Accomplishments

My publications based on this study provide descriptions of the material culture of the village, which was at that time without piped water or electricity yet was linked rather closely to urban centers through the educational and occupational aspirations of its people. Considerable attention is given in the publications to the decline of farming and the increase of wage labor and white-collar work as substitute means of subsistence, together with the associated commuting and urban-residence patterns.

A major conclusion is that, despite these important socioeconomic changes, loyalty to and identity with large kinship groups, sect, and village as a whole remain essentially intact. Although this conclusion is interpreted in terms of the abstractions of equilibrium theory, it is very similar to more recent findings by others in the same area, particularly in regard to the continuing importance of kinship groups, despite the decline of peasant-type agriculture. Large kinship groups continue to be important because they provide their members with help and security in times of radical change.

My original topic grew, because of the revelations of the household study, to include occupations and the whole urban dimension. I probably could have followed these matters even further than I did. I think also that the younger people became bored with my basic approach, and that I may have missed an opportunity in not trying to get them to talk more about their problems as they saw them, their fears, hopes, and aspirations (or lack of them).

My entrée to the village households was through the priest. If it had been through the mayor, who represented the opposing faction, I might have collected a different order of data on the culture of the village. Once embarked with one faction, however, I do not think that I could have been successful in establishing equivalent contacts with the other without jeopardizing my relationships with the first.

The prospect of my writing a book about them may have led the villagers to withhold certain information or to slant their communications in certain ways. The factional split, its causes, reinforcements, and results, were, I suspect, purposefully minimized on this account. I myself, in fact, contributed to this by never reacting to the personal remarks that were often made. In fact, I sometimes frustrated some people by refusing to state or support the either/or preferences for things and people that were often asserted. In the absence of a "natural" crisis, some cther anthropologist might have involved himself in the factional split, risking becoming a target in the hopes of becoming a catalytic agent of actions that might reveal more about the phenomenon. Such involvement might be regarded as sophisticated, gamesmanly field work. I would regard it as unethical, because I do not think that the field worker has the right to interfere in the affairs of the culture he is studying, especially when he himself will not have to live with and bear the consequences of his interference.

I may have defined my role and purposes as unnecessarily narrow and thereby made it difficult for myself to widen my inquiry. Be this as it may, the field work made it difficult for myself to widen my inquiry. Be this as it may, the field work yielded the type of information that I originally had planned to obtain in sufficient amount to permit an analysis along the lines originally projected, and it opened new vistas to me that subsequently led to further research in the area. More immediately, it led to the publication within three years of two papers and a monograph (Gulick, 1953, 1954, 1955).

PART II: CITY FIELD WORK

Problem, Theory, and Research Design

Nine years elapsed before I returned to Lebanon in 1961 for another year of field work, this time in the city. During the intervening period, my interest in Middle Eastern culture did not abate, but I digressed from it to some extent by undertaking the direction of a field-research project among the eastern Cherokee Indians (Gulick, 1960). Simultaneously, my interest in the urban dimensions of culture became more and more focused. I participated in a multidisciplinary study of the cities of the Piedmont Industrial Crescent of North Carolina and acquired some first-hand knowledge of, and experience with, sociological survey techniques (Gulick, 1962; Gulick, Bowerman, and Back, 1962). The popular tendency to equate urban life with impersonal and superficial relationships had a considerable philosophical and theoretical history that was being challenged in a number of quarters (including my own), although social scientists persisted in talking in terms of it. Did they not also *think* in terms of it, despite their disclaimers? The concept of nonpolarized but nevertheless distinctive rural and urban subcultures comprising a more inclusive national culture certainly seemed (and still does seem) worth exploration.

It occurred to me that the impersonal nature of survey research itself might imperceptibly reinforce the old, oversimplified assumptions about urban life in the minds of survey researchers, census-tract analysts, and so forth. As to urban research outside the industrial West, too much of what existed seemed to be a "replication" of methods developed for American cities, and the results were very disappointing.

When undertaking a sociological survey, there is a great temptation to obtain a large amount of data in quick interviews in the belief that there is security in large numbers. It is quite true that the larger the population under research, the larger and more diversified the study samples of it should be. But as an anthropologist, I feel that the advantages of large survey samples are sometimes negated by relying on purely verbal responses and by a lack of concern with the actual environment of the respondents. Ideally, a large, complex system such as the population of a city should be approached through both surveys and the intimate, intensive methods of anthropologists. Such a combination, however, usually calls for a team project. Not wishing to undertake team research in a Middle Eastern city without first having done urban research there myself, I decided to study a Middle Eastern city "anthropologically" and supplement "participant observation" with questionnaires, content analysis of the mass media, and whatever other strategies I could put into operation in the field.

I was already familiar with Lebanese culture, others had done anthropological studies there, and the country was open for social-science research. So I decided to study one of the Lebanese cities. The choice is a narrow one: Beirut or Tripoli. Beirut is entirely too large for one person to tackle meaningfully in a limited time, and besides, some survey studies had already been done there. Beirut is also so heterogenous that, fascinating though they would be, findings on it would very likely not be typical of the Middle East as a whole, and the Social Science Research Council, to which I had applied for financial support, was understandably loath to support research in an "atypical" city. So I chose Tripoli, the second largest city of Lebanon, a stronghold of Muslims, and in this respect, if no other, typical of the Middle East.

The inhabitants of the village that I had studied in 1951–1952 had commuted to both Tripoli and Beirut for work. I had been through Tripoli myself a few times, but had encountered very little published information on it. In fact, many people at first thought I meant the better-known Tripoli in Libya. Those who knew Tripoli in Lebanon described it as provincial and narrow-minded, the site of an oil terminal. Compared to Beirut, Tripoli was the equivalent of Peoria to Chicago, Springfield to Boston, and Fresno to San Francisco. These attitudes, as I eventually encountered them in Beirut, were hardly more tolerant or informed than they had been ten years earlier in regard to villages.

The existing city of Tripoli (not including earlier settlements on the same site) had been in continuous occupation for 770 years and had recently greatly increased in size. I assumed therefore that it probably had two large populations: one with few if any village ties, and another with strong village ties. My research proposal was to compare the two types of population to see what their significant differences and similarities might be. In particular, I proposed to seek comparative information on household structure, occupational patterns, neighborhood relationships, and participation in other types of groups. My plans were to live successively in several different parts of the city so as to check migrant and nonmigrant characteristics, if any, against different environmental factors.

Passive or Adaptational Research

A city the size of Tripoli (about 180,000 people) in a nation the size of Lebanon (about 1.6 million people) is not a separate entity that can be studied as if it were isolated from the rest of the culture.

Accordingly, as soon as I arrived with my family in Beirut in September, 1961, I began taking field notes on my observations, even though they were not on Tripoli itself. Of particular interest to me were the many changes that had occurred in the intervening years since I had last been in Lebanon, changes to which I eventually became accustomed and of which I would probably have ceased to be aware if I had not made note of them when they were new and striking to me. These changes included increased informality between men and women in public and a far greater number of Western-style commercial enterprises.

I established a home base for my family in Beirut, where the school facilities were suitable for the children, and, as before, made an arrangement with the American University of Beirut to give a seminar in exchange for all the privileges of visiting faculty, including the services of graduate-student assistants in the Sociology and Anthropology Department. I no longer had any illusions about using my students as informants, but I correctly foresaw many advantages in associating myself with the prestigious university.

I decided to play my role—that of a university professor—as straight as possible, even though this role would cut me off from the people of the "culture of poverty," whom Oscar Lewis has studied with such remarkable results. This role, however, would open doors to me that would otherwise be closed, particularly the doors of people who had general information about the city and influence in it. It would probably restrict my informants to "middle-class" people, but I could not be all things to all men in field work any more than I can in life away from the field situation.

I had two references in Tripoli. One, who proved to be very helpful, was a schoolteacher and a life-long friend of a Lebanese-Amercan sociologist whom I knew. The other was a close relative of a person with whom I had become acquainted in America during the previous year. The second reference turned out to be a member of the same small sectarian group as the first, and they were close acquaintances.

One day late in September, I hired a car, went to Tripoli, and sought out the teacher at his school, only to discover that he was still at his summer retreat in the mountains. There he received me very kindly, particularly in response to greetings from the sociologist in America, originally a fellow-villager known to have made a name for himself in the New World. It was helpful in explaining my own mission to be able to say that I was professionally interested in many of the same kinds of information as his sociologist friend was and that I had done a village study in Lebanon ten years previously. Reprints of the papers and a copy of the monograph I had published on the village were available to anyone who was interested in them. I explained my interest in learning more about the relationships between village migrants to the city (of which he was one) and city-dwellers who had no village ties, and I asked him to help me find households in various parts of the city in which I could room and board. He mentioned a couple of possibilities and suggested I look him up in Tripoli later in October when the summer was over.

Meanwhile, I intensified my search in Beirut for sources of information (both written and live) on Tripoli. What I did essentially was to make known among my friends in Beirut the type of information I was looking for, in the hope that eventually some fruitful suggestions would be made, and, indeed, some were. A brief visit to the city (during which the native driver lost his way in the bewildering maze of streets) had reinforced my need for a good, detailed map, but none seemed to be available. Then someone mentioned that a Palestinian city planner who had worked in Tripoli not long before and was now working in another Arab country might be able to help me. I wrote to him and had the good fortune to receive a reply that referred me to a new contact in Tripoli who did eventually provide me with a good map. There were two books on Beirut in print, one socioeconomic and the other urban geographic, but there was nothing of the kind on Tripoli, except for one or two sources that emphasized Tripoli's early architectural monuments. One potential source of information on Tripoli was the Tripolitan students at the American University, but I decided not to approach them until I had much more first-hand knowledge of the city. Because of the dearth of published material, this was not an easy task. No census had even been taken in Lebanon since 1932, and those figures were hopelessly out of date.

The living pattern I had decided upon—a few days in Tripoli alternating with a few days in Beirut—was ideally suited to the wide-net, follow-up-every-lead approach that became indispensable as time went on. For example, since Tripoli was a Muslim city, I wanted to find out if anything remained of the traditional institutional structure of urban Islam on which there was considerable, but extremely dated, literature. What I eventually learned in Tripoli itself led directly to questions on twentieth-century Islamic institutions, especially modern Islamic education, and these questions led me to contacts in Beirut rather than in Tripoli.

In the middle of October, I returned to Tripoli to find a family with whom to live. Two prospects had been found by my primary contact, both of them members of his own sectarian subculture (Christian and definitely a minority group in Tripoli). To each husband and wife I explained my purposes, just as I had to my contact. One of the couples finally decided that they could not accommodate me, because the wife would be out of town during the next few months caring for a married daughter and her first baby. The second couple agreed to provide me with room and board. They had in their apartment a spare bedroom occupied only occasionally by a daughter who was away at college. They were also experienced in this type of arrangement, for during World War II, in another part of Lebanon, they had accommodated British government personnel who were strengthening their command of the Arabic language by living in Lebanese homes.

I had learned a lesson from my previous experience in Lebanon: the room and board arrangement I was making was not a conventional pattern of Lebanese culture, and there was no point in pretending that it was. Accordingly, I suggested paying them a flat weekly fee, an amount that I was sure would more than cover any extra expenses that they might incur on my account. After some discussion, but no haggling, they accepted my suggestion. I also proposed that we initially plan on my staying for five weeks only, as I wished to live in different parts of the city successively. The short-term commitment in itself may well have facilitated the whole arrangement, though it was ostensibly a statement of research strategy.

Toward the end of the five weeks, neither they nor I had said anything about its being time for me to move. Indeed, I had been so busy becoming acquainted with the city, getting introductions to various people, and making initial contacts with them, that I had made no moving plans. My hosts were very helpful, and we were getting along well together. In fact, I did not want to move. Nevertheless, I broached the subject because of our agreement. My hosts said that if I wished to continue to stay on with them, I was most welcome. I felt that they were not being falsely hospitable, and so I accepted their invitation "for a while longer," asking them to assure me that they would tell me if things became unsatisfactory.

During late November and early December, I began to struggle with several questions regarding my course of action. I had good rapport with a number of the members of my hosts' sub-culture. Though they were generally "middle class," they included native Tripolitans and immigrants, elders and adolescents, and professional people who had many pivotal contacts with others in Tripoli. If I were to content myself with them as my base, however, I would be very unlikely to get any direct or intensive information on Muslim family and neighborhood life. Counter-balancing this serious limitation were two other major consider-ations.

First, my own self-generated pressure to live in several parts of the city became greatly lessened once I realized how compact Tripoli was (about 1.5 square miles) and how I was already directly immersing myself in the ambiances of its var-ious sections by walking all through all of them at all times of day. Would finding and getting settled with new hosts in an-other part of town be worth all the trouble? Not, I decided, unless the new hosts belonged to a different subculture, preferably Muslim.

Second, my hosts' subculture was a Christian minority group, many of whose behavioral practices in the domestic and private aspects of life could not automatically be generalized to apply to larger segments of the population. But I did not need to con-centrate my ethnographic work on these particular aspects of culture, nor had I ever intended to limit my study to them. There was much else to be studied: the basic ecology of the city, its growth patterns and commercial structure, the location of its subcultures, its immigrant enclaves, and governmental and sec-tarian institutions, activities, and interrelationships. In addition, there was the entire matter of Tripoli's place in the larger cul-ture. Unless some very much better opportunity arose, I began to think that I would do well to make the most of the base I had already established. As members of a minority, the members of my hosts' subculture had adapted themselves in various ways to Tripoli, and so they were consciously aware of many facets of its culture. Allowing for their sectarian biases, I found some of them to be very informative on many subjects.

Besides all this, I liked my hosts, I was comfortable in their home, and they were apparently comfortable with me. I was beginning to be able to test out hunches in a relaxed, informal manner with them, just as I was already doing, at greater re-move, with my Lebanese friends in Beirut.

As December progressed, I became torn between getting myself into a Muslim household in another part of town, and trying to manage the move without hurting the feelings of my hosts and cutting myself off from their group. I mentioned the possibility of living with a Muslim family to friends of my hosts who had Muslim friends, but I did not pursue the matter, because I sensed that my raising the subject was being taken as a sign of dissatisfaction with my hosts' hospitality (which was far from the truth), rather than as reflecting an impersonal "scientific" procedure. To approach some of the Muslims whom I had met might evoke the same reactions with added complications of intersectarian gossip and backbiting. Even if another suitable family could be found, the costs might cancel out any hoped-for gains.

I was still struggling with these issues at the beginning of January when Lebanese politics decided the matter for me. An attempted *coup d'état* on December 31, 1961, created a state of crisis that continued till the time we were to leave Lebonan for good. Roadblocks, searches, sudden arrests, mass detentions, and rumors of atrocities created an oppressive atmosphere throughout the country. I was obliged to stay in Beirut for the first three weeks of January, during which time I began a systematic survey and analysis of Lebanese magazines and newspapers, which I continued throughout the rest of the project.

When things had cooled down to routine crisis proportions, I returned to Tripoli and discovered that my hosts did not wish to dissociate themselves from me. Americans were not implicated in this particular crisis, but the wariness of the Lebanese among themselves had been greatly intensified, and I had no desire to risk stirring up any further tensions by trying to shift my base of informants from one sect to another. So it was that I remained with my original hosts until my departure in June.

Like any student of Lebanon, I had long been aware of the explicitly sectarian structure of its national social system, but mine had been a rather abstract awareness until I came face to face with it in everyday life. In my initial plans for research in Tripoli, my concentration on the rural-urban frame of references had led me to underestimate the possible effects of sectarian and social-class differences on the issues with which I was concerned. After a few months in Tripoli, I was very much more aware of it.

Active Research

In January, 1962, the "passive phase" of my field work ended with the procedural decision to stay with my hosts. The "active" phase of research, however, had long since begun. The two phases overlapped, and the resulting feedback caused a subtle but important shift in my perception of my field-work role and in my goals. My original plan envisaged intensive ethnographic work on and in two "populations" (native urbanite and migrant). Circumstances did not lead me to any such discrete aggregations, however, but rather to a corporate group whose membership comprised both native urbanites and migrants. With this group as a base, I embarked upon a broad sociocultural analytic inventory of the city. At the Symposium on Urbanization, Annual Meeting of the American Anthropological Association, November, 1966, Peter Gutkind distinguished between microcosmic and macrocosmic studies of cities, emphasizing the usefulness of both. My shift of orientation was, I suppose, from the microcosmic to the macrocosmic. In other words, I went from a concentration in depth on a small segment of the population (relegating the rest of the city to a mere backdrop) to a consideration of all discernible aspects of the city's culture. Since neither kind of study had been done before in Tripoli, either would contribute knowledge and greater understanding of the city.

My key informants were mostly members of the host group, although Muslim informants provided details on Muslim marriage and household composition, physicians and nurses with wide social-class experience related their impressions of different class patterns, business leaders briefed me on commercial conditions and organizations, and various government functionaries provided information on government operations and institutions, etc.

Without disclosing sources and as tactfully as possible, I tested the remarks of one informant against the reactions of others. For example, when one Muslim estimated that 2 percent of the Muslim marriages in Tripoli were polygynous, that the co-wives generally lived in separate establishments, and that the practice was becoming increasingly a lower-class one, I asked other informants to tell me about any specific cases of polygynous marriages with which they were acquainted. In this way I gradually built up a series of native generalizations on many subjects (some factual or purportedly quantitative, others normative or qualitative), backing them up where possible with data on specific cases. Some cases were consistent with the generalizations, others were inconsistent, and others ambiguous. When it was available and relevant, I added documentary evidence on Tripoli (scholarly, journalistic, and official) to this body of information, as well as similar evidence from elsewhere in Lebanon or from other Muslim Arab cities.

Instead of limiting myself to a household, genealogical survey, as I had in my earlier village study, I gathered information from as wide a variety of sources as possible. My organizational frames were (1) the city of Tripoli and any aspect of culture, as anthropologically defined, pertaining to it, and (2) the culture

of Lebanon and any generalizations about it that might apply to
Tripoli. For example, when a news item or a feature article on
Tripoli appeared in a Beirut paper or magazine, I would discuss
its contents with Tripolitans to get their reactions. With Tripolitan informants I discussed general articles on Lebanon on such
subjects as education, the status of women, or any other subject
of current interest to see to what extent they felt the articles
were applicable to the city. Conversely, I discussed feature articles in the local Tripoli press with Beirut informants to gain
perspective on Tripoli from their point of view. In other words,
I attempted to stimulate as much feedback among my various
sources and types of information as I could.

I kept field notes on my observations, discursive conversations, and formal interviews in the same way as I had in the
village study, except that I more frequently inserted excerpts
from and interpretations of published materials. Otherwise, my
discussion about note-taking in the village applies equally to
my work in Tripoli.

In addition, I built up files of newspaper and magazine
clippings and took notes on the numerous mimeographed reports,
unpublished theses, and other fugitive sources that came into
my hands. The Tripoli telephone directory became a source requiring much investigation after I discovered that from it could
be drawn samples indicative of the areal distributions of certain
occupations, the relationship of place of work to place of residence, and large, residential kinship clusters.

My informants eventually fell into two types. The regulars
were people to whom I could and did repeatedly return without
any further explanation of my purposes or presence. Of them,
my hosts were, of course, the most regular. Another regular
informant was a businessman on whom I dropped in when I saw
that he had no customers. A supplier to building contractors, he
did not have a steady stream of customers and therefore had
time to talk to me. Unlike my hosts, he was a native Tripolitan,
not a migrant. The other regulars, all busy people, had to be
contacted by telephone or other message when I wanted to see
them.

The other type of informant consisted of "specials," with
some of whom I had one-shot interviews arranged in advance
either for reasons of courtesy or to enable them to prepare certain types of information. Special informants included the
mayor, the manager of the city's Muslim endowed properties,
and the mufti (nominal head of the Muslims in the city). In
Beirut, two of my "specials" were the secretary of the grand
mufti of Lebanon and the head of the Muslim educational system
(a former Tripolitan). I was not always successful in obtaining

information from the special informants, but even when they were evasive the experience in itself was informative in one way or another.

Other special informants, with much persistence on my part over a long period of time, provided data on enrollment figures on the sectarian schools of Tripoli and on the government schools, institutions that were extremely important and intricately involved in the value system and culture-change problems of many people. In this task, whether I used the direct approach or enlisted intermediaries or both, all relationships were focused on a particular, special purpose.

Following the city planner's lead, I eventually got an excellent map of the city that showed all streets and built-up blocks as they had been just before the great spurt of growth that began in 1948. It seemed like miraculously good fortune, too, that superimposed on this map were the outlines of all the planned future streets. With a simplified version of the map that I prepared, I was able to make my own up-to-date map of the built-up parts of the city. It was not easy to acquire the map for it seemed to be regarded by the person I first approached as a classified document. It was only after repeated visits and many assurances that I would not divulge the locations of the as-yet-undeveloped new streets that he gave me a copy of it. Much later, when I was working out the conceptual relationships between the administrative districts and the informal quarters of the city, a higher official gave me an annotated copy of the same map without any "security" cautions whatever. Actually, the map was no more detailed than the street maps one can buy in almost any big-city book store in the United States or Europe, but in Lebanon not only was it not publicly available but it also seemed to be considered something secret. One of my regular informants told me that once, when he had tried to get or see a copy of it, he had been refused. I gathered that difficulties arising out of land speculation were one reason for the generally withholding attitude, but I suspect that there may have been a more deep-seated feeling that surveyed, scale maps, like all kinds of accurate knowledge, are more likely to be used as weapons than as the stuff of neutral enlightenment.

For this same kind of reason, the act of taking down peoples' words as they are spoken, the most elaborated form of which is the questionnaire, was suspect. Questionnaire studies had recently been done in Lebanon, some in an institutional setting, others on the hit-and-run principle in the field. The latter was, and is, repellent to me, and it might have been disastrous to my study in Tripoli, even if I had wanted to undertake it there. The very idea of a questionnaire, as well as the idea of my taking photographs during my wanderings in the city, was horrifying to my regular informants. Long experience with predatory governments has caused Middle Eastern people to resist strongly having their words written down and thus taken out of their control. Furthermore, they have not learned to play the question-and-answer game epitomized in the American questionnaire poll. Sophisticated Middle Easterners feel that the American predilection for taking photographs of them indicates insensitivity and condescension, and they believe that the photographs will be used to show them in an unfavorable light. Less sophisticated people, sometimes including policemen and the military, often seem to regard foreigners' photograph-taking as an act of aggression, and they may respond in kind, so besides disliking questionnaires and photograph-taking, my informants were also apprehensive that any trouble I might get into because of such activities might have repercussions on them.

I recognize the usefulness of questionnaires for some purposes, however, so I constructed one to be taken by the Tripolitan students at the American University of Beirut. My affiliation with the University greatly facilitated the identification and location of these students, of whom there were about sixty. Thirty-five of them (male and female, Christian and Muslim) answered my call. This was in May, after I had had full opportunity to consider what items would be most useful. The questionnaire included an application of two of Kevin Lynch's questions on socially significant visual perceptions of the city, and a long series of questions on village ties, location of relatives and friends, household composition, and social class.[2] Though the sample was small, it nevertheless yielded some very interesting information, much of which was meaningful in terms of other studies as well as to my own.

As a visiting professor at the American University of Beirut, I was affiliated with an institution of considerable interest to some of my informants. In Lebanese culture, a link with someone who has an institutional tie of this kind is automatically regarded as a potential source of special advantage. In a couple of instances, I was asked if it would be possible for me to help

---

[2] Kevin Lynch is a city planner at the Massachusetts Institute of Technology. He has done field rseearch among small samples of inhabitants of Boston, Jersey City, and Los Angeles, asking them what parts or aspects of their cities are important to them, having them draw sketch maps of their cities indicating significant features, and accompanying them on walks during which their verbal reactions to their surroundings were recorded. The results of this study can be found in Lynch's book, *The Image of the City* (1960). In the case of my Tripoli sample, I asked the question about significant parts of the city, and I asked them to draw a sketch map.

influence some decisions that would be beneficial to those making the requests. I knew that I was being put into the role of an intermediary, but I could hardly refuse to help people who were being helpful to me. At the same time, I understood the university system, and I knew that it would have been most inappropriate for me to try to exert any influence on it, even if I had had any, which I did not. What I did was to make some legitimate inquiries at the University, transmit the information to my friends in Tripoli, and volunteer some advice. This was not what was really wanted, but I had at least made a bona fide effort to help. I could have played the expected role and raised their expectations in hopes of a payoff of some sort, but I did not do so, nor would I do so another time if a similar situation ever arose.

As in the case of the village study, "bowing out" posed no particular problems, because I had prepared my informants for it from the beginning, and the concept of my being a temporary visitor with responsibilities elsewhere was entirely comprehensible to them.

An evaluation of the effectiveness of my field techniques must depend on a study of my Tripoli publications (Gulick, 1963a, 1963b, 1965a, 1965b, 1967), and it really should be left to others. I can, however, mention a few matters concerning the outcome of the study. My original research aim, to study two discrete populations in Tripoli (native urban and ex-rural), was not realized for reasons already explained. Instead, my findings on subcultural differences were cast more in terms of sect and social class. In some cases, the boundaries of sect or social class were isomorphic with native urban or ex-rural groups, but this was not true in most cases. The reality was more complex than I had originally envisaged.

As of 1967, my publications on Tripoli constituted the only comprehensive descriptive analysis of a present-day Arab city readily available in print. This analysis includes a thorough physical description of the city that is related to the history of its growth and changes through time. The impact of this manmade environment on some of its inhabitants is also dealt with. Subsistence patterns, in the form of businesses, both traditional and modern, are discussed, as are the governmental institutions of the city viewed locally and from the perspective of the national culture. Major attention is paid to kinship and neighborhood groups, sects and social class, with emphasis on the internal divisiveness manifested in these groups (but generally neglected in most publications on the Middle East, including my own earlier ones). A basic theme in the study is that, although Tripoli is "modernizing" in many respects, the lives of its people have not been impersonalized, and although Tripoli's modernization has not been heavily industrial, there are symptoms of "alienation" among its inhabitants.

COMPARISONS AND CONCLUSIONS

In both studies, my methods were similar in that I relied primarily on my own powers of observation and anthropological skills in eliciting and recording information and feelings from other people. The differences between my methods in the two studies resulted in part from the fact that in Tripoli I was more experienced, more self-confident, and better able to avoid conceptually painting myself into corners merely for the sake of orderly inquiry.

In Tripoli, I had an obviously much larger system to study, and my method of coping with it essentially consisted in making myself the center of a series of communication networks. Tripoli was small enough to be systematically comprehended, once I became familiar with it. Also, like the village, it was virgin territory for anthropological research (or any other kind of social-science research), and I believe the one-man research effort was methodologically justified on this account. To argue that *only* a team project and/or a massive survey is suitable for the study of a population the size of Tripoli's is not valid when nothing systematic is known about that city. Some of the information I laboriously gathered there is of the type that is routinely available, prepackaged as it were, in Western cities, where the random-sample survey has been so much used. Yet, if the time ever comes when both survey research and studies of the Oscar Lewis type are feasible in Middle Eastern cities, I think that the practitioners of these very different methods are likely to continue to talk past and around each other rather than to each other, unless they both can find a way to relate themselves to the same holistic conception of their subject. This conception, so far, seems to have been produced by individual minds. Perhaps computers will make these holistically-thinking minds obsolete, but before they can do so, far more information than is now available will have to be fed into them, at least as far as places like Tripoli are concerned.

It would seem logical to assume that the larger the subject of study, the longer should be the amount of time allowed for it. One could easily illustrate this logic by itemizing the array of specialized studies that, ideally, one "should'" do in Tripoli as opposed to what one "should" do in a village of 500 people. It does not necessarily follow, however, that knowledge and understanding of a culture increase in direct ratio to the amount of time one lives in it, and I became aware of this during my Tripoli study. As I have mentioned before, reviewing my earliest field notes revealed to me how, in only a few months, I had internalized, and become unconscious of, a number of items in the culture, despite the fact that my role was that of observer. I did not cease to be an observer, but I became a specialized one, and adaptation to my surroundings involved routinization, just as does enculturation in general. I was even more impressed with this phenomenon after my encounters with Americans who had lived in Lebanon for many years. As individuals, they did not predictably provide any more (or less) insight than did Lebanese individuals, for they too had been enculturated and, except for isolated incidents, had forgotten the process of enculturation.

A two-year field study *may* be twice as fruitful as a one-year one. It is not the mere time that makes it so, however, but rather the carrying out of successive phases of research that continually requires the anthropologist to reset his sights and take stock of his findings. To do this, regardless of how strong his empathy for his hosts may be, he must to some extent always remain consciously and subjectively what he is objectively: an alien in another culture.

CAKCHIQUELES AND CARIBS: THE SOCIAL CONTEXT OF FIELD WORK

Nancie L. Solien González

This chapter will compare and contrast four different field-work situations involving two distinct cultures and the variations that may occur due to the nature of the investigator's contact with the natives.[1]

I lived in Santa María, a Cakchiquel-speaking Indian village in Guatemala, for a period of two months in the summer of 1955, during which time I concentrated primarily on recent ac-

[1] The field work was supported in 1955 and 1956–1957 by the Henry L. and Grace Doherty Foundation and by travel assistance from the United Fruit Company. The later research, extending from 1961 to 1964, was carried out while I was employed as research anthropologist by the *Instituto de Nutricion de Centro América y Panama* (INCAP). Grateful acknowledgement is made to all.

culturation in the domestic domain—foods, weaving, gardening, and child-care. Seven years later I returned to the village to do research on a more or less "eight-to-five'" working-day schedule for two or three days a week for about eighteen months. In this later period I studied social structure in relation to beliefs and practices concerning health, nutrition, child-bearing, and child-rearing as part of a larger comparative study involving Guatemalan Indians, Ladinos,[2] and Caribs, both rural and urban.

The second culture is that of the Black Caribs residing in Livingston on the north coast of Guatemala. I spent thirteen months there in 1956–1957 doing a community study that concentrated on the relationships between family and household structure and the economic system. I returned twice to Livingston in 1963 to gather additional data for the comparative study mentioned above. At this time I also collaborated in a study of blood types among the Caribs.

PART I: THE CAKCHIQUELES

Problem, Theory, and Research Design

In the summer of 1955, having completed my master's degree in anthropology, I sought and received a grant from the Henry L. and Grace Doherty Charitable Foundation for two months' field work in Guatemala. I had no particular anthropological reason for choosing this country at this time. I wanted to improve my Spanish and I wished to find out whether I could adapt to the exigencies of field work and living in a foreign culture before I went on for a Ph.D. I had already invested in a B.S. and a year's graduate work in nutrition, only to find that I was temperamentally unfitted for the kind of work I had been trained to do— administrative dietetics. If I was to have another disillusionment, I wanted to have it before I went any further in anthropology. I contacted the directors of the Institute de Nutricion de Centro América y Panama (INCAP), and they encouraged me to come to Guatemala.

The Doherty Foundation granted me $500, which I supplemented by persuading the United Fruit Company to give me a free round trip on a passenger freighter sailing the New Or-

---

[2] *Ladinos* are persons of Latin, as opposed to Indian cultural background. Although they are predominantly mestizos racially, this is not their most important identifying feature.

leans–Puerto Barrios route. Upon my arrival in Guatemala I was received warmly by INCAP. Although we had no formal agreement, this organization helped me in making my arrangements. The personal assistance of Dr. Richard Adams, an anthropologist, and his wife Betty, a Guatemalan citizen, was also invaluable. They introduced me to people, helped me arrange inexpensive living quarters in the city, loaned me books and field equipment, gave me counsel and advice, and extended unlimited hospitality to me in their home. I chose the village of Santa Maria largely on the advice of Dr. Adams, who provided me with field notes of his own and of others who had worked in this village at various times previously. Since I had no particular problem to investigate, I was glad to take advantage of this advice, and ended by making a simple analysis of the kinds of changes that had occurred in the few years since INCAP had started its work there.

Environment of the Group Being Researched

Santa Maria is a community of Cakchiquel-speaking Indians in Guatemala's western highlands. It is situated 24 kilometers west of Guatemala City at 6,000 feet above sea level. Although well below the Tropic of Cancer, the temperature is moderated by the altitude. The rainy season lasts from May through October and, although Guatemalans like to say that theirs is the land of eternal spring, foreigners are often tempted to add, "a very early and wet spring." A light jacket was necessary in the evenings and early mornings, and on overcast days I usually wore a sweater all day. In July, when I was there, the actual temperature ranged between 60° and 75° F. during the day, dropping as low as 50° at night.

When I first began field work in Santa Maria in 1955, the population of the village was about 650. In 1962 when I returned, the population had grown through natural increase to 1,053. No new families had made the town their home, and the increase seems to have been due almost exclusively to the lowering of the mortality rate.

The houses of Santa Maria, built of adobe bricks or wattle-and-daub, are set about a central plaza in a grid-iron pattern. Most houses are screened from the street by high adobe walls that enclose the entire yard, within which there may be two or three structures sheltering members of an extended family. Each household is thus ensured of its privacy, and one does not casually intrude without advance warning.

The Indians, using digging sticks, machetes, and hoes, cultivate extensively the surrounding hillsides and valleys. They grow maize and beans for home consumption and vegetables and fruits for sale largely to the non-Indian population in nearby towns and cities. The village has no market of its own, but itinerant peddlers occasionally pass through selling dried shrimp, cheese, bananas, yarn, thread, woven cloth, and other items. When I was there two Ladino-owned *tiendas* (small general stores) sold a variety of candies, spices, staples such as salt, sugar, coffee, and bread, school supplies, and patent and herbal medicines. Two similar smaller stores with a much less varied and plentiful inventory were operated by Indian families. Another Indian operated a meat market, offering beef and occasionally pork about once a week. The supply depended upon the availability of animals. The owner usually purchased one animal at a time, slaughtered it himself, and simply closed up shop when the meat was gone, always the same day the animal was slaughtered.

There were no full-time specialists in the village, although a number of persons had a special skill or enterprise. An Indian from the nearby town of Santiago owned a corn-grinding machine in Santa Maria that was well patronized. One Ladino had a small tavern, patronized occasionally during the week, more so on Saturday evenings, and quite heavily on fiesta days. The customers, almost exclusively men, bought small bottles of local rum there, which they drank off the premises. Indian women also drank this rum on special occasions, but almost always at home.

A few Indian men supplemented their incomes by local carpentry and masonry jobs, and one man (two in 1962) was a curer, using traditional herbal and magical remedies, as well as modern patent medicines. Two midwives attended virtually all the births in the village, although some women sought the assistance of practical nurses who visited the town regularly. A few men occasionally worked outside the town, traveling to the coffee plantations during harvest season, or working on highway construction, but migratory wage labor was not an important source of income for the village as a whole.

Although the Indians kept chickens, ducks, and in a few cases pigs, these were thought of primarily as nest eggs for a rainy day rather than investments for capital gain. They sometimes had the latter function, but this tended to be incidental, and in some cases the keeping of domestic fowls and animals was a losing proposition. No special arts or crafts existed as income resources.

Although there was a Catholic church in Santa Maria, there was no resident priest, and the town's inhabitants maintained the church and its grounds, the saints' statues, and even conducted regular prayer meetings. Two small Protestant congregations also existed; by 1962 they claimed 12 percent of the total population.

A public school offering grades one through six plus preparatory first year of "Castellanización" (teaching of the Spanish language) was a unique feature in a village of Santa Maria's size. A small clinic, maintained by INCAP, offered simple medicines and routine first-aid procedure, its primary interest being health research. This clinic also was a departure from the services usually available in such villages, and Indians from the surrounding area often came into Santa Maria seeking medical assistance from the practical nurses stationed in the village five days a week.[3]

Entry Problems and Initial Copings

On my first visit to Santa Maria, I was accompanied by a professional nutritionist who had carried out dietary surveys there under the auspices of INCAP. Although a native Guatemalan, she was an urban middle-class Ladino with a kindly, but patronizing, attitude toward the Indians there.

Most Ladinos, or persons of Latin-American culture patterns, tend to regard the local Indians as a somewhat inferior species, an attitude that goes back to the Spanish conquest. The Indian is expected to defer to the Ladino in all matters. The more "enlightened" Ladino recognizes that the differences between him and the Indian are cultural, but his behavior toward the other is similar to that shown a child. The fullest description of the interrelationships between Ladinos and Indians is that by Melvin Tumin (1952), but see also Richard Adams (1957).

My guide took me almost immediately to the schoolhouse, where I was introduced to the Ladino teachers who welcomed me politely and enthusiastically. Arrangements were made for me to move into one of the schools' smaller rooms for my two-month stay. The school, in addition to the clinic, was the only structure in the village with running water and toilet facilities, both of which were thought essential for my comfort. Furthermore, there were no empty houses, and I had neither funds nor equipment to establish housekeeping, even had there been such available. The Indians' houses were crowded, and they were not accustomed to accepting boarders—especially foreign women. Although I might have made arrangements to live with a Ladino

---

[3] Since this is not intended to provide a complete description of the culture and history of the highland Indians of Guatemala, the reader is referred to the following works for general background: Tax, 1939; Tax, 1952; Reina, 1966; Wagley, 1949.

family, this alternative was not immediately available, so I accepted the offer made by the teachers and my nutritionist guide without much further consideration. Arrangements were made for me to eat with the family who owned the tavern, which also seemed satisfactory to me at the time. After a casual tour through the village, during which my companion exchanged friendly greetings with many of the Indian women, always introducing me as a "friend of the clinic," we returned to Guatemala City, where I collected my belongings and purchased additional necessary equipment before returning the next day to take up residence.

The following day, a Sunday, a chauffeur employed by INCAP drove me to the village in a jeep. He deposited my belongings in the school and left. I then walked around the village, trying to strike up conversations with people in the streets, with women drawing water at the central *pila* (public fountain), and with men lounging on the porch of the municipal office building. I asked about the mayor, expressing a desire to introduce myself to him and explain the purpose of my visit, but I was told that he was absent from the village that day. The previous day I had asked the nutritionist to introduce me to him, but he was working on his *milpa* and did not return before we left. Although the people were polite, they maintained their distance, and I felt very alone and somewhat ill at ease, though not discouraged.

The day appeared to go without serious mishap, but the chauffeur, in a very excited state, returned from Guatemala City that afternoon to inform me that I must vacate the school immediately upon the demand of the mayor. The mayor, apparently, had complained to INCAP about my proposed occupancy of the schoolhouse, because he felt my presence would deprive the local children of the bathing facilities available at the school. The chauffeur, an urbanized nonresident Indian, felt that I should return to the city as it was late and as there appeared to be no place for me to sleep that night. Two Ladino women then stepped forward to offer me a place in their homes, and an argument broke out as to which offer I should accept. At this point, one of the Indian men suggested that I sleep in the clinic, since that building belonged to INCAP with whom they presumed I worked. I quickly made a decision, moved my things into the clinic building, and stayed there for the next two months.

On weeknights I shared the building with two practical nurses who arrived at the clinic on Monday mornings and left on Friday afternoon of each week. Neither objected to the arrangement, which proved to be felicitous and practical for all of us. I assisted in buying and preparing food for the three of us during this period, and in return the girls provided valuable introductions to the townspeople, translations from "Indian" Spanish to my "textbook" Spanish, and friendship and moral support during the first trying days of my first field-work experience. On those nights when the nurses were in the city, I had the privacy to catch up on data recording or simply to relax and plan my next day's activities.

Active Research

Since my primary purpose in undertaking the project in Santa Maria was to gain field-work experience and to improve my Spanish, I contented myself with outlining only the most obvious aspects of community structure, utilizing key informants as well as those data accumulated by previous investigators that were made available to me through INCAP, Richard Adams, and the Instituto Indigenista of Guatemala. I then concentrated on the problem of acculturation in relation to dietary and medical practices and beliefs, with particular attention to the impact of the clinic and the nutrition-research projects that had been conducted in the village during the previous three years.

This topic seemed appropriate, because of my background in nutrition and because of my sex. Nutrition was a topic on which I could rely almost exclusively upon female informants, and during that particular part of the year (July and August) the men were absent from the village most of every day except Sundays. Given the short period of time I had for field work, it was simpler for me as a woman to gain rapport with other women than it might have been for a male investigator on the same topic, so it seemed wise to make an asset of this factor. Also, the topic of diet was relatively neutral, and people were accustomed to being questioned about it.

Data-Getting Techniques

At first I found it difficult to find people to talk with, because, when I approached them in the streets for information, they were usually on their way somewhere or occupied with domestic tasks. I began to spend a great deal of time in the *tiendas,* where I made friends with the owners and later inventoried their stock. When Indian women came in to make purchases, I tried to converse with them, but because they did not waste time lounging around the store, these contacts were limited in usefulness.

I then began to frequent the central *pila* where the women came to do the family washing. Depending upon the amount of their soiled clothing, they spent from thirty minutes to an hour at a time here, and it was possible for them to continue their work while I engaged them in conversation. I soon found, however, that my textbook Spanish—not highly developed conversationally anyway—was inadequate for any but the most fundamental type of communication. Although most of the women spoke Spanish, their pronunciation and grammar were difficult for me to follow, and they frequently misunderstood my halting and stilted phrases. It was clear that if I were to obtain useful data I would have to rely upon Ladino interpreters until I had mastered the Indian's way of speaking Spanish.

The clinic dispensed milk to pregnant and lactating women and preschool children twice a day. Although not all eligible women participated in this program, enough did to make it worth my while to be present at the clinic during those hours when the milk was prepared (from powdered skim milk) and served. The women frequently tarried for a while, enjoying the social aspect of meeting with their friends, and they were relatively at ease in the clinic; also I was able to call upon the practical nurses for aid in translations. The women soon became accustomed to my presence, and some proffered shy invitations to visit them in their homes. I took advantage of these opportunities, at first making "rounds" with the practical nurses who visited households to encourage the women to take part in the milk program, and to advise and assist them in case of illness.

Within a week or ten days, I was able to move freely about the village on my own, and I had established sufficient rapport with several families that I might visit their homes frequently. Children followed me about the streets and delighted in visiting me at the clinic. Sometimes they would take me to their homes, and in several cases I was invited to go along with women and their children when they carried lunches to the men working in the fields. Gradually I began to understand that I had been expelled from the schoolhouse for reasons related to village and national politics, Indian-Ladino relationships, and to the discourtesy of my not having gone through proper channels upon my arrival in the village.

In regard to politics, the village was split by factions, one of which was known as "communist," even though I doubt that anyone then knew what that term implied on an international level. INCAP had first entered the village during the time of Jacobo Arbenz, whose leftist regime was overthrown in 1954. Because of this, INCAP was associated in the minds of the people with that administration. In 1955 it was suddenly brought home to the people that the "communists" had been overthrown, and they were unclear as to what the future of the clinic would be. Some feared to be associated with it; others declined to be friendly because they dissented from the current government's policies.

The schoolhouse had been built by the national government as a normal school, but had recently been converted into a grammar school for the use of the *pueblo*. It was much larger and more elaborate than the school ordinarily found in a village of this size, and the people were, quite properly, proud of it. They resented the idea of a foreigner being billeted there, especially without their knowledge and consent.

Initially I also had some difficulty because the people considered me a medical specialist of some sort and frequently asked me to recommend treatment. I had more knowledge of Western medical practices than they did, and I occasionally made suggestions or referred them to the clinic, but I did so only when I was asked. I explained myself and my purpose in the village as a North American schoolteacher who wished to learn something of their way of life in order to promote international understanding upon my return to my own country. This explanation seemed acceptable to the villagers, and in general I was treated as a somewhat overgrown (I towered above everyone in the village—male and female alike), but well-meaning child who had a lot to learn. I traded recipes and old-wives' tales from the United States for those from the Indians' culture and amused them all with my efforts to grind corn and make tortillas. I spent hours helping the villagers shell corn as we chatted in the afternoons. This was my one domestic accomplishment, for which I paid with blisters and later calluses.

I had contact with the men of the village during the late afternoons and on weekends, but these encounters were formal, circumspect, and few. I eventually did gain the respect and even friendship of several men (including the mayor), but during this first period of field work I associated almost exclusively with women. To the barriers of language, race, ethnic group, and nationality was added that of sex.

The relationships between men and women in this society are accompanied by extreme reserve. This reserve seems related to a general concern with personal privacy that is reflected in many ways, including the high walls surrounding the homes and in a general reluctance to disrobe in the presence of others, including one's spouse. Although crowded conditions in many of the houses make it difficult to maintain complete privacy in the physical sense, modesty and shyness are characteristics highly valued in both men and women. A rigid etiquette circumscribes behavior toward all people in personal matters, but especially toward the opposite sex. Women often refuse to talk with male investigators unless their husbands are present, and sometimes this reluctance extends to women investigators as well. This never happened to me in Santa Maria, but it did once or twice when working in other Indian villages several years later.

My own upbringing, derived from a long line of puritanical New England ancestors, taught me that it was impolite to ask personal questions. "Personal" meant anything relating to home life, sex, finances, religion, disease—in short, many or most of the topics I wished to investigate. In my own society I find it difficult to ask anyone "How much did you pay for it?" or even "How old are you?," and this reluctance carried over into my field work. Coupled with my linguistic inadequacies, this reluctance made it extremely difficult for me to delve into anything but the most superficial matters. I was so reserved that I frequently worried that I might never become a really adequate field worker. I later realized that my initial reserve was interpreted as appropriate behavior and "good manners" in this society, and I now believe it contributed substantially to my final acceptance. I was told, even during this original stay, of a male Guatemalan sociologist who had asked a great many questions concerning relationships between the sexes, and who was deeply resented by the villagers as a result. I myself spoke too freely with one informant about what appeared to be an imminent birth. When I asked her when she expected her baby, she denied being pregnant. The child was born two weeks later. As a single woman without children, this was deemed an inappropriate question for me to ask, and my own grandmother would have agreed, although for different reasons. It was not until my return to the village some seven years later, and by then the mother of two, that I was able to elicit data from a few women concerning sexual activities and childbirth. Even now I would not discuss such subjects with males in this society. In 1955 politics was also a sensitive topic, so soon after the 1954 revolution, and I learned not to discuss the subject except with a very few men whose wives had become my friends.

During this original field stint, I concentrated on visual observation, supplemented by indirect questions on "safe" topics. As the people became more accustomed to my presence, they frequently initiated topics of conversation in which they knew I was interested—specifically diet and child-care. Genealogies were relatively easy to collect through direct questioning, and these enabled me to understand a little of the social structure by observing which people associated with my informants and on what occasions. I was most successful in collecting data concerning the daily round of activities, which I carefully observed, and on the physical structure of the village and its environs. I counted, measured, timed, and photographed incessantly—frequently for no good reason. I collected much useless information and some data that became meaningful only later as I grew to know the culture better.

Research in 1962

My two months in Santa Maria in 1955 went by all too quickly. By the time I left I had been asked to become a sponsor (*madrina*) for a child, and I felt that I had been relatively successful in establishing rapport and securing information on my selected topics. This impression was confirmed when I revisited the village in 1962. I found that my old informants remembered me well—even many whose names I had forgotten. Some youngsters had grown up, married, and now welcomed me into their new households. By this time I had two children of my own, which gave me a new and higher adult status and which aided my investigation of childbearing and childrearing, which were the topics I concentrated on in 1962.

My rather unorthodox field techniques in 1962, necessitated by obligations to my household and family in Guatemala City, yielded results that would have been most difficult or impossible to obtain without an initial residence period. During 1962, when I was actually employed as a research anthropologist by INCAP, I drove to the village three or four days a week, usually arriving shortly after 8 o'clock in the morning and leaving at any time between noon and 5 P.M. I often made arrangements in advance to meet with certain people on succeeding days, which gave my informants an opportunity to prepare themselves for my visits. However, I remained flexible enough to cope with the unexpected. Sometimes informants were not home on the appointed day— either because they had something else they had to do, or because they forgot my appointment. A constant danger in field work under these circumstances is that the investigator may unconsciously impose on informants who are involved in their own domestic tasks. My earlier residence in the village gave me an idea of the daily rhythm of activities, and the people knew that I did not expect them to drop whatever they were doing to devote themselves entirely to me. Ordinarily courtesy dictates that one receive a visitor graciously, providing him with a chair, perhaps a tortilla or a piece of fruit, and one's undivided attention. In Indian villages other than Santa Maria where I also did field work without an earlier period of residence, I found this attitude particularly difficult to overcome, and my home visits were necessarily curtailed by my reluctance to keep the family members from their work.

In addition to scheduled interviews or visits, I made a point of walking around the village, chatting with people on the streets, in the stores, or at the fountain, and catching up on events since my last visit. Usually I would find a friend or acquaintance who would invite me to accompany her home, or I might be hailed from a courtyard as I passed by. Sometimes I might encounter an informant on her way to the bush to cut firewood and I would accompany her, taking the opportunity to talk as we went along.

In Santa Maria there are no restaurants or other commercial resources for securing lunch. Although it would have been possible to arrange with a Ladino woman to eat at her home, I found it more convenient to bring food with me, even though most days I was offered enough by my informants to sustain me. Sometimes I would share what I had with a family, in return for their offers of coffee, a plate of beans, or a few tortillas. In other cases I ate my lunch with the practical nurses at the clinic if they were in town, and sometimes I escaped to the outskirts of the village and picnicked by myself, taking the opportunity to jot down notes on the morning's activities. Children from the village would frequently join me at such times, and I learned much from them also, not only by watching their behavior with one another, but by checking with them data of which I was unsure —identities, residences, names of plants, etc. Since most of these children had attended school, they were more fluent in Spanish than their parents, and I had less difficulty communicating with them. When the men and older boys are working in the fields, it is the custom for wives and daughters to carry their midday meal to them, and the entire family eats in the fields together. Many times the village might be practically deserted at noon, and I would therefore confine my interviewing to older persons, the sick, or Ladinos.

By taking advantage of contacts made seven years earlier, and with my improved Spanish and a series of particular problems to investigate, I was able to collect a large amount of data on my daily visits. However, because I was unable to maintain hour-by-hour or day-by-day continuity, it was difficult, although not impossible, to assess the normality of various occurrences.

This nonresident method of securing data is not unknown in anthropology, but it is probably used less frequently than methods involving the investigator's living in the community. It is also probably considered to be less efficacious than the latter. It need not be so, if the situation is carefully appraised and utilized for all it is worth.

PART II: THE CARIBS

Problem, Theory, and Research Design

After my research among the Cakchiqueles in the summer of 1955 I returned to the United States for further course work and again sought a grant from the Doherty Foundation to return to Guatemala for a full year in 1956–1957. During my first stay in Guatemala, I had learned about the Black Carib culture of the Caribbean coast of Central America and had visited Livingston, the only Carib village in Guatemala. I was impressed by the fact that this culture had never been studied in Guatemala by anthropologists, and I was intrigued by the existence of such an apparently distinct community in this land of Indians and Ladinos. The Guatemalan Caribs seemed to be relatively isolated from other social groups in the country, yet they had strong ties with Caribs in Honduras and British Honduras. I determined to do a community study of Livingston to explore the culture in general and to learn more about how it had maintained its distinctiveness in a foreign environment. At the same time I was interested in studying the relationship of this community to Guatemala as a whole and to other Carib communities in the neighboring countries.

Aside from the general aims stated above, I had no specific problem to investigate and no specific hypothesis to test. The anthropological literature on the Black Caribs was limited, the work of Douglas M. Taylor in British Honduras being the only monograph in existence (1951). My initial objective was simply to describe the community as a whole, but after residing there for several months I became more problem-oriented. It seemed to me, as I studied, that the specific relationship between household structure and the economic patterns was an important key to understanding the position of the community in the broader social context of the nation and the region. This then became my focus, but only after I had been immersed in the culture for some time.

Passive or Adaptational Research

The Black Caribs of Guatemala live primarily in the village of Livingston at the mouth of the Rio Dulce, at one time the primary port and gateway to the interior. Their residence there and in other villages strung out along the Caribbean coast of Central America dates from the turn of the nineteenth century, when they were forcibly deported from the island of St. Vincent in the Lesser Antilles by the British. Although those living in Guatemala, Honduras, and Nicaragua have Spanish surnames, speak Spanish as their second tongue, and belong to the Roman Catholic Church, their culture is composed of a blend of traits inherited from their Carib-Arawak Indian and African ancestors—a combination reflected in the name by which they are known. They also had considerable contact with British and French culture as represented in the general Caribbean area. Black Caribs living in British Honduras usually have Spanish surnames and adhere to Catholicism, but they do not speak Spanish. (See Solien, 1959, and Taylor, 1951.)

The Carib settlements are as close to the sea as possible; often their houses are built just a few yards back of the sandy beach. The climate is tropical—hot and moist. There is no rainy season, for it rains all year round, although July and August are slightly drier than the other ten months.

Although the Black Caribs still fish and cultivate manioc, their economy today is largely dependent on migratory wage labor. In 1955, Livingston had a total population of about 2,500, of whom 1,800 were Black Carib, according to a census I carried out at that time. The remainder were Guatemalan Ladinos, plus a small colony of East Indians, known locally as "Coolies," and a few Chinese businessmen. The town boasted two schools, several general stores and taverns, a small hotel, a pension, a movie theater, telegraph office, military barracks, an ice plant, and a small generator that provided electricity seven or eight hours a day. Many of the businesses were owned by one enterprising and very wealthy Ladino family who also owned considerable property in Guatemala City, but who preferred to live in Livingston. Some of their interests—the hotel, for instance—were not very profitable, but were maintained in part as hobbies and in part in the hope that someday Livingston might become popular as a resort town. At one time the town had been quite important to the country's interior, but this prominence had declined and almost disappeared with the rise of Puerto Barrios and the building of a railroad line from that city to the capital, Guatemala City.

Livingston stands on a slightly elevated promontory, and thus presents three "faces" to the sea. The main wharf, with its small customs house, is adjacent to the main business section, which stretches along one street from the shore and up a steep hill to a level where most of the Ladinos have their homes. There is no central plaza or square, and the *municipio* offices are somewhat separated from the business section, which is extended, although not dispersed. The military barracks is sharply set apart from the rest of the town, yet it overlooks the sea. The postal and telegraph offices are adjacent to the barracks and the Catholic church is also isolated from the business section and the government buildings. The houses of the Caribs are scattered over a large area in what, at first, appears to be an almost random fashion. Some are oriented to the sea, others are grouped in small compounds, the doors facing inward toward the yard, and others face a street or path. Most yards are unfenced or have only low structures that obstruct neither the view nor access to the yards.

For several generations Black Carib males have left their homes periodically to obtain wage labor up and down the Caribbean coast of Central America. Some have worked aboard ships that have taken them to the United States and to Europe, and many have settled permanently in New York, San Francisco, London, and elsewhere. Basic literacy among males approaches 100 percent, and a large number of women under forty years of age can also read and write. Great emphasis is placed on education in general, particularly on foreign languages. One of my principal informants spoke five languages—Island Carib, Spanish, English, French, and Kekchi (one of the many languages spoken by Indians in Guatemala).

Because the women are often temporarily left alone while the men are away on wage work, their status is extraordinarily high in the culture. They may own property, such as houses and house sites, travel freely according to their own desires, make decisions in regard to domestic matters, and when angry feel free to curse and even strike the men. Many women operate their own small businesses—selling lottery tickets, making and selling various prepared foodstuffs, smuggling, dressmaking, and selling garden produce. Some purchase fish which they salt and take to Puerto Barrios or even Guatemala City to sell at a profit. Cash obtained by women through any of these means is theirs to spend as they see fit.

Women also influence community policy, largely through their women's organizations, many of which are sponsored by the Catholic church. These groups serve as channels through which news of general interest is transmitted, and when an individual or group wishes to introduce a new idea, voice a complaint about existing circumstances, or simply plan a community excursion to another town (a common form of recreation and also a business), it is the better part of valor to broach it first to the women at their meetings. They will discuss the issue at length, hear pros and cons from outsiders (men) invited for this purpose, and either condemn it or offer their support. These women's groups cultivate plots of land and sell the produce to raise money for church festivals, needy members, and burial expenses.

Entry Problems and Initial Copings

My first visit to Livingston took place at the end of the summer of 1955 when I had lived in Santa Maria. I was returning to the United States by ship from Puerto Barrios, and I decided to go to the nearby Carib village for a three-day visit before sailing. There are no roads leading to Livingston; one can reach it only by sea. In 1955, and still, to my knowledge, there was only one public launch to Livingston each day. It left Livingston at 4 A.M. for Barrios and left Barrios again at about 10:30 A.M., arriving in Livingston at noon. On my first visit, I missed the 10:30 boat, but managed to talk some young Carib men into taking me in a smaller craft, much against the advice of all observers. Halfway to Livingston our motor failed, and my two companions and I were stranded in a fairly heavy sea. We strung up a white shirt on a fishing pole as a signal and were fortuitously rescued by a government yacht carrying a team of malaria researchers to Lake Izabal, via Livingston and the Rio Dulce. My arrival among the Caribs was therefore accompanied by some fanfare, and I never afterward lived down the story of my brave, but foolhardy expedition. The escapade favorably impressed the people among whom I would later live for thirteen months.

When I returned in June, 1956, to make arrangements to live in Livingston, I was no stranger, even to those whom I had not met the year previously. I first asked about housing at the Ladino-owned hotel where I was temporarily quartered, but when I indicated I was interested in living in one of the Carib districts, the manager was shocked and said he could do nothing to help me. I next asked a Carib man who had served as cook on the yacht that rescued me the year before, and he quickly found an ideal spot for me. I rented a small (12' × 15') house situated among several others in a compound occupied by several siblings and some of their descendants. The eldest daughter of the eldest sister in this sibling group took me under her wing, washing my clothes, seeing that I was fed, guiding me about town, and serving ultimately as one of my most trusted friends and informants. From my back door I could look out into the common patio of the compound, and from my front door I could watch the activity on one of the most important routes to the beach and to a well. A public water faucet was located just outside my door, which was not only a personal convenience, but a favorite gossiping place as people waited their turn for water.

After making these arrangements, which the Caribs did not seem to think were strange, I went to Guatemala City for four days to buy equipment and re-establish contacts made the year before. On my return to Livingston, many persons volunteered their services to carry my baggage the half-mile or so (partly uphill) to my new abode and help me get settled. They refused any monetary compensation. Contrary to the situation in Santa Maria, where I might never have met an Indian had I not made an effort, in Livingston the people came in droves to my house to see and meet the oddball *gringa*. Rapport was then easy to establish, and in a very short time I was able to probe any area of the culture in which I was interested.

Active Research

Although the Caribs are certainly less reticent with and less suspicious of strangers than are the highland Indians of Guatemala, their attitudes and behavior toward me were not typical of their treatment of most other Caucasians—either Latin Americans or North Americans—with whom they came in contact. The Caribs are not above exploiting Caucasians by charging outrageous prices for goods and services, or even by robbing them when the opportunity arises. They enjoy making tourists and local Ladinos both in Livingston and in Puerto Barrios the butt of their jokes, although in the presence of tourists their demeanor is polite unless they feel offended. I am certain that my rapid and successful establishment of rapport was greatly facilitated by the circumstances of my initial visit to the village. I had proved my "fearlessness"—both of the sea (which was based more on ignorance than bravery) and of the Carib—and I had indicated that I lacked concern for the physical comforts usually demanded by Caucasian visitors and had a sincere interest in visiting their village at any cost. My later behavior was consistent with their interpretation of our first encounter, so I came to be treated almost as an equal. I too became the butt of jokes, but at least some of them were to my face.

The Carib did not hesitate to offer me their foods, which I never refused, even though some were not really acceptable to my palate, and they were delighted to find that I appreciated the local rum as much as they did. When I visited other villages in the company of some of my informants, I slept in a hammock, on the floor, or sandwiched in between the members of the family in a common bed. I was willing to make long-distance, sometimes overnight, journeys by dugout canoe, and I was not above smuggling soap, cigarettes, and other small items back into Guatemala just as they did. In their dances, I was never able to overcome a certain amount of built-in Western inhibition, but they recognized and appreciated my efforts. (On a return visit in 1962, I was able to teach *them* the twist!)

Fortunately for my field work's success, the exuberance and extroverted behavior of my Carib hosts helped me to overcome my own hesitancy to ask the personal questions required in my research. When they felt no qualms about asking me about my personal life, it was easy to retaliate, but this is not to say that there were no codes of etiquette or areas about which they were somewhat reluctant to speak. Personal quarrels were matters of some privacy, and witchcraft was more difficult to explore than most other subjects, but researching even these became possible with selected informants. Most importantly, there were no closed doors or fences. People simply appeared in each others' doorways, and I too was permitted this freedom. The only area in which I was unable to participate was fishing, which is almost exclusively a male activity. On one occasion, when I insisted upon taking out a small dugout canoe alone, an activity in which women do not typically indulge, I amused a crowd of on-lookers by rolling it over several times before I managed to keep my balance. I heard of this escapade for months afterward, and I was good-naturedly joshed for having assumed such an unfeminine role.

During my thirteen-month stay in Livingston I collected data through a variety of techniques. I accompanied various women of the compound during their daily rounds of activities. I attended social gatherings of all sorts, including dances, wakes, mass at the local Catholic church, rituals in honor of dead ancestors, women's meetings, cooperative rice-harvesting sessions, and cassava-making. I spent time just sitting about in the compound watching the activities there and questioning my hosts about things I did not understand. In time, I queried selected informants on special subjects, often in prearranged interviews either in their homes or, more often, in my house. I usually was able to take notes in their presence, since these were all people with whom I had previously built up rapport. With the assistance of three young men whom I trained for the job, I took a census of the entire Carib population in the town to determine family and household composition, age distribution, migratory patterns, and sources of income.

In the company of my primary woman informant, and sometimes alone, I made trips to nearby Puerto Barrios where I interviewed Caribs and non-Caribs and learned something of the history and operation of the United Fruit Company in that area. I also made a six-week trip to Honduras and visited many Carib villages and towns, always seeking relatives of my friends in Livingston, who never failed to give me a warm welcome. I made a similar trip to British Honduras, where I traveled along the seacoast in a small cabin cruiser of the Public Health Department visiting Carib villages otherwise inaccessible. During this trip I stayed in Belice for a week perusing the archives of that colony and learning something of the Creole culture and the interrelationships between Caribs and their non-Carib Negro neighbors in that colony.

With borrowed equipment I recorded music of different types, both traditional and modern, and I made a collection of items of material culture and took pictures of the methods of manufacturing them. At the local municipal offices I went through the birth, death, and court registries, and I collected information from schoolteachers on school attendance, curriculum, drop-out rates, and so on. In short, I tried to immerse myself as completely as possible in the life of the people of the village. Each evening, unless some late activity deterred me, I typed notes that I had recorded during the day in small $3'' \times 5''$ notebooks. I filed paper slips ($5'' \times 7''$) containing typed data in a metal filing box. I tried to go back and review all my notes at least once a month, so that I might discover unrecognized relationships or inconsistencies to be checked further.

Obviously, one never gets all the data about everything in a community, and the problem becomes one of defining an area of research and then covering this as completely as possible, checking and cross-checking data with different informants to improve their reliability. One of the difficulties with the so-called community study is that the researcher often has no specific problem or hypothesis to investigate and simply tries to learn everything about the community as a whole, which is a self-defeating project. On the other hand, it is often impossible to construct a meaningful hypothesis before one's entry into a new field situation. In such cases, description must precede theorizing, but often the problem can be outlined after the research has been in progress for some time. After I had been in the field for five or six months I found myself increasingly intrigued by the kinship and family systems. I noted that non-Caribs, especially of the upper classes, spoke of the immorality of the Caribs and their high rates of illegitimacy and family disorganization. They also claimed that the Carib woman did all the work while the man simply sat around in his hammock or disappeared entirely from the domestic scene, presumably because he was too lazy or too irresponsible to maintain his wife and children.

The Carib communities I observed, however, did not seem to be either vice-ridden or lascivious. I also learned to admire the Carib man's efforts to find work in a difficult employment market. I became interested in trying to understand the structure by means of which these communities were able to maintain a measure of stability in what was clearly a changing world for them. There were some areas I did not research for lack of time or experience, for impracticality, and/or because I felt they were irrelevant to my central theme. For instance, I left virtually untouched the culture of the non-Carib elements of the local population, the Ladinos and the Hindu "Coolies." I got to know well one Ladino family—the most important one in town—and I knew a few Coolies slightly, but I never delved into their culture patterns. In part this was because the Caribs were clearly a group apart. They despised the Coolies and were looked down upon in return by the Ladinos, and I did not wish to endanger my position with the Caribs by spending too much time with either of these groups. For this same reason, I was unable to obtain quantitative information from the stores and small businesses concerning volume of trade, buying habits of their clients, credit arrangements, and so forth, as the stores were all owned by non-Caribs.

Another deficiency in my study was that I never found a satisfactory method of collecting household budgets systematically because of the nature of the culture itself. Although some women were literate, they were only barely so, and most could not keep records for me. Furthermore, the sources of income were so diverse and so irregular that most people could not give me any exact accounting. Male relatives would contribute sums of money when they were working, women earned varying amounts from small enterprises such as selling cassava or candy or bread, and children sometimes contributed money earned by running errands or doing odd jobs. Besides, much of the domestic economy depended on fish, which were either caught by members of the household itself, donated by relatives, bartered for other goods, or purchased, and on such home-grown products as rice, platanos, and root crops. It was clear that those households lucky enough to have attached *employed* males lived better than those with none, but I never got exact quantitative information from a large sample of households. Instead, I relied on qualitative data from case studies and personal observation to understand how the economic system operated.

Leaving the village after having lived there for thirteen months was a fairly casual matter. From the beginning everyone knew that I was to be there for approximately a year, so it was no surprise to them when I finally fixed a departure date, which soon became known throughout the town. Many persons brought presents of sea-shells, pretty seeds, hand-embroidered pillowcases, and lithographs of saints "to remember them by."

Most, however, when they saw me in the streets would simply say, *"Te vas, entonces? Bueno, que te vaya bien!"* (So you're leaving? Well, goodbye and good luck.) In a culture such as this, where people come and go with frequency, mine was just another departure. We all assumed, correctly so, that someday we would meet again. I have made two trips back to the town since, and I have been in contact with Carib migrants from Livingston in Guatemala City. Even now some of them write to me, usually for "loans" or for help in finding jobs.

Research in 1962

I returned to Livingston twice for about a week each time during 1962 while I was employed by INCAP to do research on diet and child-rearing practices in the country as a whole. On these visits, I spent a full day visiting special friends and acquaintances, and then settled down to straight interviewing with a few selected informants. Because I already knew the basic culture outlines, including patterns of child-rearing, it was possible for me in a very short time to fill in the blank or spotty areas, check one informant against another, and check all material against former data and observations. I already knew the people personally, so I was able to control my samples' characteristics by choosing persons known to be voluble and open, yet not prone to constructing tall stories simply to impress me. The latter tendency was one I constantly had to guard against, particularly since, when I checked *some* of these seeming fictions, they turned out to be true! I learned that some informants were more likely to be forthright and honest with me than others, and for the short-term investigation of selected topics such as diet and child-rearing I chose such people.

Another project, undertaken in collaboration with a Guatemalan pathologist also employed by INCAP, was collecting blood samples to determine certain factor frequencies and to assess nutritional status. After discussing the matter before the two women's clubs and obtaining the assistance of a young Carib man, I selected eighty unrelated adults with no known non-Carib ancestry as our sample population. Each was contacted personally before the technicians' arrival, informed of the nature of the study, and asked to participate. Each was promised a report indicating whether his blood was "healthy" or not. These reports were later mailed to the individuals, and if signs of anemia or venereal disease were present, they were advised to consult a physician. This ploy was so successful that when the technicians arrived in Livington, the sampling went smoothly and with no serious complaint on the Caribs' part. Contrary to what is often presumed, these people had few qualms about allowing samples of their blood to be taken. Their major fear (apart from a fear of the discomfort involved) was that the agency we represented would profit by selling the blood. Their relative sophistication in regard to Western medical practices and their knowledge that blood for medical purposes *is* often bought and sold lay behind their objections. The Caribs have a well-developed set of native beliefs and practices in regard to curing, but they also make extensive use of Western medical facilities available in Puerto Barrios and other cities.[4] Once we explained the situation, we had more subjects than we could actually handle.

In addition to these two short return visits to Livingston, I also completed a small research project concerning Caribs who had migrated to Guatemala City. In 1957, when I conducted my census of Livingston, 12 persons out of 211 "absentees" were said to be in the capital. But in the early 1960s, when I was living in Guatemala City, I was repeatedly contacted by Caribs whom I had known during my original field work in Livingston. All maintained that by this time there was a fairly large number of Black Caribs who had come to the city to "make their futures." In 1964 I worked out a one-page short-answer schedule, and with the help of two men who had previously acted as informants, I administred it to eighty-two Carib adults living in Guatemala City. Here, as in the research carried out on a regular but intermittent basis in Santa Maria, I found that as an anthropologist I had to adapt my field techniques considerably. Participant observation, in the usual sense of the word, was impossible. My observations were limited by the fact that I did not actually live in the type of neighborhood frequented by the Caribs, and the social structure of the city itself, of which I was a part, recast the entire nature of my rapport with them. Although I was working with the same people, many of whom I had known quite well in Livingston, their attitudes toward me were altered by the new environment of the city. They now perceived me as a member of the local upper-middle class—a status assignment over which I had no control. They remained friendly and readily invited me into their homes, but it was unthinkable that I remain overnight or accompany them about the city in their various domestic and recreational activities. One of the interesting findings of the research was that the Black Caribs in Guatemala City did not restrict their social contacts to the Carib group itself, but actively sought and participated

---

[4] The results of our analysis of the sickle-cell trait and the Diego factor are reported in Tejada, González, and Sanchez, 1965.

in relationships with other ethnic groups—especially with Ladinos. Many of the men were living in marital relationships with Ladino women, and in their work situations the Caribs constantly interacted with the Ladinos. They tended to live not in a cluster, but spread out through the lower-class neighborhoods of the city. The results of this study have been presented in González (1965).

Although I was welcomed into the Carib households, it was as a temporary visitor. Thus it would have been awkward and embarrassing had I tried to push my participant observation into nondomestic spheres. As part of my newly assigned role, I was requested to make small loans, help find jobs, donate old or outgrown clothes from my household to theirs, and even help them get out of jail. In many ways, this was my role in Santa Maria, a role also defined for me by the sociocultural system itself. In my opinion, this is the single most important distinction between resident and intermittent field work.

Summary and Evaluation

Anthropologists, missionaries, Peace Corps volunteers, or others who attempt to immerse themselves in a community in a foreign culture should realize that they must always occupy a special position within the social system. No matter how friendly the "natives"—no matter how great the rapport—one is never actually a native himself. Most, if not all, societies in the world today have been visited by people from beyond the immediate culture, and they have identified these visitors as *aliens*. These aliens may or may not be citizens of the same nation, may or may not be representatives of the same racial stock, may or may not share the same language. Wherever they come from, whoever they are, the important point is that the native culture itself will have certain defined statuses into which it may cast them, thus limiting their behavior patterns in certain ways.

The resident anthropologist, even though he may initially fall into one or another of the standard "foreign" categories of persons, is usually able to create for himself a special niche—alien still—but different from all the others. In short, he hopes to be placed in a class by himself, which from the point of view of the community being studied, may never again be filled by another foreigner. As such, his behavior may vary from the behavior expected of persons in the other established statuses. As long as the anthropologist continues to occupy this, *and only this*, status, he may be permitted a great deal of freedom in establishing behavior patterns considered "proper" for this new role.

On the other hand, the anthropologist involved in intermittent field work is, in a very real sense, living a double life. It is manifestly clear to the natives that when he is not with them he is somewhere else and probably living a very different sort of life. Even this knowledge may not seriously change the situation, unless the natives chance to observe him in his "other life." If the anthropologist's "off-hours" behavior fits into a category already known to the people he is studying, they may cast him in this other role while he is in their community. Depending upon the circumstances, he may then be regarded as and treated as a tourist, an administrator, a member of the local upper or middle class, a foreign imperialist, or anything else familiar to them. Any attempt on his part to act *outside* of the expected behavior patterns for this assigned role may be met with suspicion, uneasiness, or even contempt.[5] I do not wish to imply that field work under the latter circumstances is impossible, fruitless, or necessarily lacking in rigor. There is much that can still be done, but the investigator must recognize the limitations imposed by his role in the broader culture and learn to act within them.

Other limitations are necessarily imposed by the fact that one is not continually present in the community in the physical sense. There are disadvantages, as well as advantages, of working under intermittent conditions. First, the anthropologist misses much of the minutiae of the daily round of activities, as well as some of the rhythm of the yearly cycle. Even when he is there, his presence may alter otherwise normal behavior. He is thus forced to rely more heavily on interviews with selected key informants, and he has to develop a communication network through which he is informed of future special events of importance to him in his work. These include life-crisis rites, holiday or holy-day observances, special games, elections, or other communal activities such as hunts, a cooperative house-building or planting project, and so forth. Since the anthropologist is probably not viewed as a member of the community and since the people may not be aware of his special interests, he may not be informed of these events in advance unless he takes it upon himself to see that he is. He also has to learn to look

---

[5] Even when the anthropologist lives permanently among the people while doing field work, it will be recognized that his "real life" takes place elsewhere under different circumstances, of course. But in this case, his home identity will be totally foreign to their conceptual system, and as such, will not be likely to impinge upon his relationship with them. Similarly, if he leaves for brief periods for survey work or for mental and physical relaxation, this too can be interpreted *within* the context of the role he has established.

for clues that a special event is under preparation, so that he can inquire about it and make plans to attend.

Another disadvantage is that the field worker may have no home base within the community, no place to *go* when he is not physically with his informants. If he wishes to write notes in private, bathe, change clothes after a particularly messy activity, repair an item of equipment, or simply rest for a brief period, he may find it awkward to do so without actually leaving the community. Under some circumstances he may find it possible to rent or have built for him a small house or room that he may use for such purposes or for an occasional overnight stay. Some vehicles, such as panel trucks, may also be useful as combination offices and temporary quarters.

Transportation may also be a limiting factor in field work. Having one's own vehicle—preferably one equipped with sleeping bag, canned emergency food and water, a typewriter, change of clothes, and any other measuring or recording devices one may need—is not a necessity, but it will increase the ethnographer's efficiency and comfort. Lacking this, the investigator must depend on public transportation, restricting himself to studying only those communities on direct routes. Moreover, he may have to pass up good observational or interviewing situations in order to conform to departure schedules. The amount of equipment he can carry back and forth under such circumstances is also limited.

The ethnographer who uses an intermittent method of research will find some topics that are not amenable to his method. The first of these is political organization. In most societies, power and authority reside largely in the men, and since the men may frequently be absent from their homes during the day when the researcher is present, this subject is difficult to probe. If the investigator also happens to be a female, the magnitude of the difficulty is increased. The structure of specific political institutions and their functions may be determined by questioning selected informants, but this technique is less useful for imbedded or implicit functions. The gathering of case studies to illustrate how a system actually operates may be hampered by discontinuity in direct observation, and relying on key informants may prove risky, since the latter may tend to abstract from the actual situation, thus slanting the data. Moreover, for any subject highly charged with emotion, or for those that the people themselves are unaccustomed to dealing with verbally, the lack of continuous observation may be detrimental.

If research is largely carried out during the daytime, the investigator will miss entirely those activities usually conducted in the evening. Most experienced anthropologists will attest to the value of sharing recreational activities with the natives. This sharing not only increases rapport, but offers many opportunities to observe interaction among the members of the society for the purpose of sorting out statuses and patterns of visiting and analyzing values based on topics of conversation chosen by the natives themselves. Participation in social drinking, smoking, or other activities, listening in on story-telling or planning sessions, or simply sitting around chatting with the entire family, sodality, or any other formal or informal grouping of people is often one of the most rewarding of all field-work experiences.

The disadvantages of intermittent research are somewhat balanced by a few definite advantages. Indeed, the field worker forced to carry out intermittent research may turn the situation into a very favorable one. First of all, because he is in a position to return favors offered him, he can actively promote a reciprocal relationship between himself and his informants. Most resident anthropologists are usually unskilled in the activities required for maintaining the system within which they are living. They can, of course, return favors by giving the natives gifts and money, by helping them to write letters, by interpreting the actions of administrators or other foreigners, and by advising them on dealings with the outside world. The intermittent researcher, however, can endear himself to the natives by offering transportation to those wishing to travel for some purpose of their own, by making purchases, and by carrying letters or packages to absent friends or relatives. In any community accessible enough to be visited daily, chances are that the people will be involved in a number of extracommunity relationships and will welcome assistance of this kind.

Another advantage of the intermittent investigator is that he can more easily focus on one particular topic or problem. By continually working over his notes, and by referring to library resources (assuming that these exist at the "home" base) for comparison, the chances of missing large blocks of important information on a particular topic are lessened. Also, he can schedule his visits to coincide with important events (if the precautions noted above are taken) or with certain seasons of the year. Since intermittent work is likely to be extended over a period longer than one year, observations and impressions can be rechecked at the same point in the succeeding year or years.

Informants who feel socially obligated to the investigator for services rendered and who know of his special interests and limited time may be less likely to put him off a second time. Special sessions on particular subjects may be arranged with one or several informants together, and by recording the interview, information may be secured in a relatively efficient way. I found that such sessions were always more difficult while I was actually residing in the village, because my informants, knowing that I would be there at a later hour, or the next day, or the next week, tended to treat appointments casually. Attempts to tape group sessions during my year's residence in Livingston often broke down due to the natives' embarrassment, overeagerness, or desire to play. On the other hand, during my later brief visits, sessions that I arranged specifically for the purpose of gathering information on specific topics, say, traditional songs, mythology, or health and medicine were treated more seriously because the natives knew that my time was limited. These sessions were regarded as being something of an "occasion" and were well attended. I never attempted to hold group sessions among the Cakchiquel-speaking Indians, so I cannot compare them with the Caribs in this regard.

Certain topics, especially those ordinarily researched through selected key informants, lend themselves particularly well to investigation on an intermittent basis. The technological and social patterns involved in specialist occupations, such as those of midwife, curandero or shaman, potter, and weaver, are noteworthy in this respect. Repeated visits to a particular specialist to watch him work, to talk with him, and to record his work by camera or tape recorder can build up good rapport, and this type of study suffers in no way from the fact that the researcher does not actually live in town.

Personal topics such as genealogies, case studies involving witchcraft, and sexual behavior are best handled through intensive sessions with particularly well-known informants. The Youngs (1961) have shown in data from Mexico, however, that information from key informants is *not* reliable in respect to such topics as community dietary habits and public opinion on political matters. The researcher should check information given by key informants on these subjects against other sources of data when possible, and he should remember that the danger of obtaining only one person's impression is no different in intermittent field work than in resident work. Indeed, household budgets, dietary intakes, timed recordings of work patterns, and any recorded or archival materials present in the community may be even easier to obtain if an individual works on an intermittent basis—assuming that he is seen as representing some acceptable interest or agency from the larger society.

In summary, a comparison of these two techniques of field work indicates that important and reliable information may be gathered under either set of circumstances. The resident anthropologist's status and behavior will be different from the intermittent anthropologist's, however, and this may in part determine the type of problems he can most successfully pursue. Each method has distinct advantages and disadvantages of its own, and research problems should be conceptualized and attacked within the framework of the total situation.

The field-work situations described above may be contrasted in terms of the differences between the two ethnic groups involved. In using my own research for this purpose, the nature of my residence in each should be held constant. This is somewhat difficult to do, for the bulk of my work among the Black Carib was carried out on a long-term residential basis, with only a few brief visits some years later and some work among them in Guatemala City. On the other hand, I remained in residence in the highland Indian village for only two months, and I did most of my work over a two-year period of visiting. Clearly, these differences affected the way in which I was received by the two different communities and also possibly influenced my view of the situations.

In both cases I found the people as curious about me and the culture I represented as I was about them. The Caribs were more outgoing and direct in their relations with me, even from the beginning. The probability that this stemmed more from their culture than from the nature of my presence among them is reflected in numerous ways. Unlike Santa Maria, the houses and yards in Livingston are not walled or fenced in, and there is much more openness in the everyday comings and goings of the Caribs. Family arguments are frequently conducted out-of-doors, and neighbors and passersby observe and even participate in the dispute. Gossip is frequent and opinions are openly and loudly expressed. The Caribs are not reticent about sexual relationships. Not only is there public joking about sexual behavior, accompanied by appropriate gestures, but their dancing is uninhibited in the extreme in this regard.

In Santa Maria, gossip is also frequent, but it tends to take place in whispers behind closed doors. On the surface, and in the streets and other public places, one gets the impression that the community is happily homogeneous and almost completely without personal strife. Only after rapport with individuals is established does it become clear that it is ridden with factionalism, personal enmity, and maliciousness. Witchcraft is a feature in both cultures, but it takes different forms in each. Among the Caribs, personal misfortune is frequently interpreted as the result of not properly placating a wrathful dead ancestor. Although living individuals may also cause harm to their enemies through the use of *obeah*, or witchcraft, the Carib is usually well aware of his enemies and believes he can pin down the evildoer with the aid of a shaman. Witches with innate powers of doing harm are not a conceptual entity in this culture. (See González, n.d., for a further discussion and analysis of witchcraft.)

The villagers of Santa Maria believe that certain persons may be witches, but their identity is not always known. It is widely assumed that most witches operate in secret and take pains to preserve their anonymity. This again reflects the attitudes toward personal privacy and the restricted patterns of behavior in relation to one's fellows observed in this culture.

This same restraint continues to be seen in Santa Maria when one tries to obtain information concerning land ownership, other private property, or even dietary intake. Foster (1965) has discussed this lack of communication in relation to what he calls the "image of limited good," by which he means the idea that there is only so much of a given "good" to go around in a community, and if one individual accumulates a large amount of it, he does so at the expense of his fellows and is therefore to be criticized. In Santa Maria I was told by one informant that she was afraid to give information to the nutritionists conducting dietary surveys because she didn't want her fellow townsmen to know just how much food her family consumed, for fear they would "envy" her. She also feared that the government might take away food from those who had more than others and give it to the less fortunate. There is a similar reluctance to give accurate information concerning other possessions.

This attitude of restraint is unknown in Livingston. Horticultural lands are not privately owned, although house sites and gardens in town are. Most households depend on some kind of wage labor for their livelihood, and levels of income vary with the type of job held and the number of household members working. As the prevailing wage scales for different types of jobs are well known, secrecy in such matters would be pointless. Furthermore, a great deal of pride is taken in personal property—a visible mark of success. The informant is therefore more likely to overstate his material possessions and financial status.

Finally, I found that the relationship of both groups to other sectors of the larger society differed somewhat, and this also seems to have influenced the context in which I was accepted within each community. The social and cultural gulf between the Guatemalan Indian and the Ladino has been described by many investigators (especially Tumin, 1952). To this day there has been preserved in Guatemala a culturally defined complex of behavior patterns involving obsequiousness on the part of the Indian toward Ladinos and a patronizing and paternal attitude of the Ladinos toward the Indians. This is symbolized by the Indian ritual of giving small gifts of food to those Ladinos who visit or otherwise take notice of him, and seeking Ladinos as sponsors for his children in the *compadrazgo* system.[6] These actions confer upon the Indian the right to ask small favors of the Ladinos—loans, intercession with authorities on personal or community matters, help in finding a job, and so on.

The Black Carib, on the other hand, even though they occupy a low position in the social hierarchy of the Central American coastline, are notoriously nonobsequious in their relations with non-Caribs. They are aware of their social position, and they are conscious of the fact that non-Caribs (and nonblacks) control the government and the national economy, and thus Carib chances for obtaining work and increasing their standard of living. They react to this situation not with servility, but with a braggadocio for which they have achieved a reputation throughout the area. The Caribs—especially the men—exude self-confidence, both as individuals and in terms of their ethnic group, and for good reason, for they are often better educated than most Indians and many lower-class Ladinos in the area. In the colony of British Honduras, they are highly regarded because of this, and they are widely employed as elementary schoolteachers throughout that region. The Caribs are also considered to be good dock workers, sailors, and fishermen. In their dress they have a tendency toward the flamboyant, wearing bright colors and fashionable styles when they appear in non-Carib company or on special occasions in their own town. Unlike the Indian, they do not hesitate to "tell off" a Ladino when they feel they have been crossed. Many Ladinos and non-Carib blacks express a general fear and awe of Caribs, whom they believe to be particularly adept at "'black magic." This reputation undoubtedly protects them somewhat in their personal relations with others, and at the same time helps maintain their position as a distinct social group.

These differences in personality structure, themselves reflections of the total social and cultural configurations, certainly affected the manner in which I was received in the two communities. My status and role were in part determined for me by the people I was studying, and I was successful to the extent that I was able to govern my behavior within this framework so as to maintain their respect. Among the Santa Maria Indians, themselves reserved in their behavior, I too had to maintain a certain reserve and observance of traditional formalities. I overstepped this in my first encounter with them when I bypassed the local

---

[6] *Compadrazgo* refers to the network of social relationships created by the custom of naming sponsors or godparents for various life-crisis rites such as baptism or marriage; a godparent and a real parent call each other *"compadre,"* hence anthropologists name the entire system *compadrazgo.*

Indian authorities in arranging to live at the school. I also was out of line in asking questions about childbirth, questions deemed inappropriate for an unmarried woman and a foreigner. I eventually compensated for these errors by my subsequent behavior, but only because I reacted immediately to their disapproval and withdrawal.

On the other hand, the Caribs do not respect a reserved manner, and in a foreigner they interpret reserve as evidence of snobbery, prejudice, and distaste for them and their customs. As I pointed out, the fortuitous accident that preceded my first visit to Livingston helped me to establish a favorable image among the Caribs. Later, rather than shocking the Caribs with my questions, they often shocked me, and there were times when I was uncomfortable, yet forced to hide my discomfort in order to retain their respect. They thought nothing of asking me "personal" questions about my finances, sex life, religious beliefs, and politics. In a sense, the Indians of Santa Maria and the Black Caribs presented opposite extremes in terms of personality patterns, and my own personality fell somewhere in between.

Within the limitations imposed by the general cultural situation, the field worker can, indeed must, create a special niche for himself. There is always a tendency for the natives to classify the anthropologist with other foreigners they have known. The anthropologist must alter their perception of him, so that he may work outside of the narrow boundaries imposed by their expectations. The Caribs, because of their own respect for education and their broader experience with members of other cultures, were able to understand and accept as legitimate the idea of my conducting pure research. When they asked what I was doing among them, I simply told them that I wanted to find out as much as possible about their way of life. Among the Indians such an explanation did not make sense. For them, knowledge must be for *some purpose*. In Santa Maria, I identified myself as a schoolteacher, and although I am not sure they ever really understood why I might wish to teach others about their way of life, at least this was a familiar role and one they apparently accepted. I was also viewed in Santa Maria as a representative of a nutritional-research organization whose research activities and personnel were accepted because the Indians received medical attention in return. The Indians recognized that for some illnesses Western medicine was superior to their own, and in time they answered almost any question from representatives of the agency, *provided* these representatives behaved according to the Indians' expectations and customs. Eventually, I established rapport on an individual basis with my informants, and this made it possible to probe even more sensitive areas, such as how they felt about the research activities to which they were subjected. When informants began to tell me how and why they had on occasion deceived the clinic personnel on certain subjects, I felt that I had at last carved out my own special niche.

This analysis points up a well-known and accepted principle of field-work technique—know, as well as is possible ahead of time, the culture to be studied. This includes not only the culture itself, but the social context within which that culture exists and the patterns of behavior expected of persons foreign to that culture. Within this general framework, the field worker must always be sensitive to cues given by the natives, and he must learn to adapt his behavior as rapidly as possible so as not to offend them. In this, the anthropologist must recognize that his own personality is an important factor and that some personal stress is to be expected in the process of adjustment. Furthermore, the nature of the contact itself—whether long-term residence or repeated daily visits—will also alter the entire situation, and it must be taken into account if the investigator wishes to be successful in the ultimate goal of obtaining accurate and useful data for scientific purposes.

MOHAWK
HEROES
AND TRINIDADIAN
PEASANTS

Morris Freilich

PART I: MOHAWK HEROES
IN STRUCTURAL STEEL

Problem, Theory, and Research Design

New Yorkers sometimes read in their newspapers about a unique phenomenon in their midst: the Mohawk Indians who work on the steel structures of various buildings in and around their city. Articles, at times accompanied by pictures of smiling Indians, discuss these "brave" and "sure-footed" Mohawks. The question of why so many Mohawks work in structural steel is one that is often researched by students enrolled in colleges located in and around New York. In 1956, this problem was, in fact, my first professional research assignment. I used A. F. C. Wallace's paper "Some Psychological Determinants of Culture Change in an Iroquoian Community" as the foil in my proposal for research support. Wallace's paper suggested that Mohawks lack a fear of heights, and that this lack of fear explains their involvement with the steel industry. I argued that a negative trait (lack of fear) cannot have specific positive consequences (lead a tribe into steel work). I argued further that there is no functional value in a lack of fear of heights for steel work, and that in actuality the opposite is true: a normal fear of high places leads to caution that saves lives. A more plausible argument seemed to be that Mohawks frequently act *as if* they have no fear of heights. In presenting a subsidiary problem, "Why these acts of daredevilry?" I put forth my theoretical belief that sociocultural factors explain social and cultural phenomena better than do psychological factors. I had a vague notion that Mohawks in steel work represented some kind of cultural continuity. Thus, the questions I posed were (1) Why is it good, culturally, for a Mohawk male to be a structural steel worker? and (2) How does such a cultural "goodness" relate to Mohawk cultural history?

I had no research design, although questions which colleagues and friends asked about my work could have led to one. For example, they asked me about Mohawks who did not work in structural steel and about structural steel workers who were not Mohawks. I found questions such as these interesting but irrelevant to my project. Even the question "How will I know when I have successfully completed my project?" held little interest for me, probably because of my poor training in science and methodology and because of a dominant theme in the culture of many anthropology students that one's commitment is primarily to anthropology rather than to science.

I had had some interviewing experience prior to the Mohawk project, but I had received little training in this area. During my years as a graduate student at Columbia University, science and research methods were greatly underplayed. To become a "real" anthropologist, we learned, one finds a group that can be referred to as "mine." To work with several groups simultaneously, to be concerned with controls, to worry about the kinds of proofs one is presenting for an argument were not part of anthropology, as we learned it. Good anthropologists, those staunch and wily enough to survive the rigors of "primitive" living, returned with stories that demonstrated their popularity with the "natives" and their knowledge of the social structure and culture of "their" tribe. Research designs had no role in this work.

Passive or Adaptational Research

Adaptational research begins when one attempts to get a "passport" permitting free entry, unhampered travel, and communication privileges in the community, tribe, or group being researched. It ends when the researcher can say to himself, "I will probably be able to see this project through to some kind of (more or less) successful conclusion."

The environment of the group being researched. The reservation of the Mohawks I studied, Caughnawaga, is located about ten miles south of Montreal and is regarded as "home" by the Indians. To facilitate their finding work in structural steel, the Caughnawaga Mohawks have formed several small communities in eastern Canada and in the United States. The community I studied in Brooklyn, New York, began to develop about forty years ago. It is located in an area that has a variety of advantages for Mohawks. First, it is close to the headquarters of their union: Local 361 of the Iron Workers Union. Second, the Mohawks can here be less visibly "different," for here being different is the norm. At one time or another the area has attracted Germans, Norwegians, Italians, Irish, Syrians, Greeks, Negroes, Jews, and Puerto Ricans. Third, in this working-class area with easy access to buses and subways the Mohawks can live as they wish.

Entry and initial copings. The Brooklyn community with its multi-ethnic population and its lack of formal boundaries provided no entry problems for me. Nor were there any particular problems to entering the reservation at Caughnawaga. My first real problem was knowing how and where to start work. Three related questions needed immediate answers. First, *where* should I start working? At places where the Mohawks work? In their homes? In some of their recreational centers? Should I begin in Brooklyn? Should I start interviewing the women and then get to the steel workers, or should I do the reverse? Third, *how* should I begin researching? Should I have some formal questions to pose, or might it be better initially to "play" the interested observer? I decided to start work by contacting Dr. David Corey, the spiritual head of the Cuyler Presbyterian Church (on Pacific Street), who had helped me in an earlier project with Mohawks.[1] Dr. Corey was much involved with the Brooklyn

---

[1] I had previously contacted Dr. Corey for aid, when as an undergraduate at Brooklyn College, I wrote a short paper on Mohawks in Brooklyn.

Mohawks, many of whom were members of his congregation. To make his church services more attractive to the Mohawks, Dr. Corey conducted a monthly Sunday evening service in Mohawk. However, as I discovered after several visits to the church, only a small portion of the older Mohawks were interested in Dr. Corey's innovation. The younger Mohawks could hardly talk to their grandparents in Mohawk, let alone follow a church service in the language.

Dr. Corey believed that Mohawks work in high steel because they like to travel ("they have itchy feet"), and because they want to make good wages without going through a long training period, but Dr. Corey's ideas did not explain why occupations such as salesman, which also include much travel and few training requirements, do not attract Mohawks. His explanation also raised an additional question: Why does a group that supposedly is attracted to an occupation because of its monetary rewards have so little interest in money per se?

Dr. Corey gave me the names of several Mohawks on whom I could call. He also suggested that I visit his church and meet some of the Mohawks who were regular worshipers. Although I contacted a number of Dr. Corey's friends, these Mohawks either would not see me or allowed me but a brief noninformative interview.

I decided to start looking for Mohawks at their work sites. After many hours of wandering around construction sites in Manhattan and failing to locate any Mohawks, I decided to talk to some *non*-Indian steel workers about Mohawks in structural steel. Discussions with non-Indian steel workers provided almost no new information. My informants were convinced that Mohawks and other Indians were "sure-footed" and worked in steel because of the high wages. Further questioning clearly indicated that much of what the non-Indian construction workers "saw" was influenced by what they had read in newspapers and periodicals. This is not surprising, since the Mohawks themselves had completely accepted the "white man's" stereotype of the "sure-footed" and "fearless" Indian. Somewhat disheartened, I ended my search for Mohawks in construction sites and returned to the Brooklyn community.

In Brooklyn I again interviewed several of the people to whom Dr. Corey had referred me, none of whom worked in structural steel. I met elderly women, mainly mothers of young steel workers and wives of the older "pushers" (foremen). I explained my project as "a great interest in Mohawk history" and "an attempt to discover how things have changed." These women appeared interested in my work, but claimed to know little about structural steel and its magnetic fascination for Mohawk males. Finally, I met a Mohawk male while I was visiting his mother. This young steel worker showed no interest in talking to me. After several attempts at conversation, I received a half-serious invitation to meet him in the Wigwam bar the next day. However, when I arrived at the appointed time, the young man acted as if he did not know me. I was instantly depressed.

I sat at the bar of the Wigwam, drank beer, and developed a strong doubt as to my ability to complete my project. I dawdled over my drink and began to survey the bar's clientele and resources. The bartender, an Italian, suddenly showed a special interest in me and began to tell me of a recent "big fight" in the Wigwam. Several Puerto Rican males had come in one night and had overstayed their welcome. A few Indians politely asked them to leave, but the Puerto Ricans kept ordering more drinks. As a result, the Puerto Ricans were physically attacked and badly beaten in a brawl. In the words of the bartender:

> The Puerto Ricans ran outside and got into a big car. Four Mohawks went to the corners of the car, and they picked it off the ground like it was a toy. The Puerto Ricans couldn't leave. One Mohawk yelled: "Next time you come in here we'll throw you in the car, and then throw the car." The Puerto Ricans never came back!

Whether or not this story was true is irrelevant. Essentially the bartender's message was: "Stranger, this is a Mohawk hangout; if you stay here for very long you're likely to get beaten up and thrown out." I finished my beer and left. I decided, however, that if my project was to be successful, I had to make the Wigwam my headquarters. What better place to work with Mohawks than in what appeared to be (and was) their major recreational center? My problem now was how to get accepted as a member of Wigwam society.

The fact that the Italian bartender seemed quite at home in the Wigwam indicated that one need not be an Indian to be a Wigwam member. My research strategy was to frequent the Wigwam often but for very short periods of time and to create some doubts in the minds of club members as to whether I belonged or not. My morning visits to the Wigwam aroused no apparent antagonism from the Indians. A Mohawk would periodically decide that he did not feel like going to work that day, due to ill health, to bad weather, or just because he felt like loafing. Such individuals seemed to welcome the chance to talk. Few Mohawks were present during these morning hours, and no competition existed for the various resources of the bar: chairs, tables, men, and (sometimes) women to talk to. My presence was very obvious, yet there was never a suggestion that I was not welcome to sit, drink, and talk. At night when the Wigwam was full of Indians, there were always some Indians who eyed me suspiciously and (it seemed to me) threateningly. My initial night visits to the Wigwam were frequent but brief. I would buy a beer, sit at the bar, sip slowly, and look around for Indians I had met before. If I did not see anyone I knew, I left as soon as I had finished my drink. If I saw someone I knew, I tried to get into a conversation with him. Whether or not my informant seemed friendly, I left shortly thereafter, went to a nearby coffee shop, and jotted down what I had heard and seen.

I returned to the bar about an hour later, repeating the whole process several times each night. I soon discovered that a number of non-Indians appeared to have membership privileges. These Mohawkphiles drank here, dated Mohawk girls, wore moccasins, and traveled regularly to the reservation. In short, they strongly identified with, and were accepted by, the Mohawks. This indicated that I too could become a Wigwam member.

About a week after these regular, short-duration visits to the Wigwam, I became overconfident and stayed one night for a few hours without a break. Just when I thought I was really "in," a Mohawk who could have passed easily for a professional wrestler, suggested in menacing tones that I finish my beer and leave. I agreed that his idea was sound and left. The next evening I returned to my cautious strategy. As the days passed it became more and more probable that I would meet someone I knew at any particular visit to the Wigwam. As I sat and talked to Mohawks who did not seem to treat me as a stranger, I was observed by an audience whose cumulative size grew daily. Soon I began to recognize Mohawks with whom I had never spoken, but who had been around while I was conversing with others. It became relatively easy to strike up a conversation with these men. At times I heard Indians ask each other, "Who is he?" A typical answer was, "I don't know, but he seems to know a lot of people around here."

Within a few weeks, a young Indian (I will call him Joe) began to show signs of friendship. Joe was invariably broke, and after we ran out of my limited funds he began "bumming" drinks for the two of us. He invited me to his apartment, and I met (what I later found out to be) his commonlaw wife, his sister, and her commonlaw husband. To Joe, I was a nice kid, although I was white and a Jew. My admiration for Mohawks was in his eyes a sign of great maturity. The fact that I would listen attentively while he endlessly recounted his exploits in structural-steel gangs, his travels all over the country, his drinking bouts, his sexual exploits, and his beating up of men twice his size made my company desirable. However, he quickly indicated that my work at the university was of no interest to him. To Joe and to the large majority of the young steel workers whom I got to know, the university world was quite unimportant. More accurately, for them it did not exist. I learned to avoid any topic that dealt with my professional career, and I slowly developed the role of Joe's sidekick.

My acceptance in Mohawk Wigwam society was now steadily growing through a daily improvement in my friendship with Joe and a daily increase in numbers of Mohawks spoken to and in numbers who observed me speaking to Indians. Complete acceptance occurred once I had traveled to the reservation and lived in a Mohawk house as Joe's guest.

The prelude to this trip was as follows. While sitting in the Wigwam one Friday afternoon Joe asked me whether I had ever been to Caughnawaga. I said "No," and he then told me that he was going there within the next hour or so and asked me to come along. Although I knew that this trip would be important for the project, I had made some other plans for part of the weekend that I was not eager to break. I also thought that, since I had received this kind of an invitation once, I could get it again at some later date. Indeed, I had several rationalizations for not going to Caughnawaga that day. These reasons were all connected to the fact that middle-class Americans rarely leave the country at an hour's notice. My initial reaction to his offer was then not of the anthropologist expressing his glee that he had finally been successful in getting an invitation to spend a weekend with a good informant and his Indian friends, but rather that of a typical middle-class American, uneasy at the prospect of having to change his plans at the last minute and travel a great distance with minimal funds.

I told Joe that it really was a pity that he had not mentioned this trip earlier, but that I couldn't go because of lack of money and previous plans. Joe, who was accustomed to traveling all over the country with very little money and to changing major plans at a moment's notice, expressed disdain for my excuses. He said that a number of cars would be going to Canada that afternoon and evening, so that transportation would not be a problem. As to my financial situation, Joe indicated that when a group of Indians collectively had enough money to get to Caughnawaga almost anything one threw in the pot to help would be acceptable. He also mentioned that I could eat and sleep at his mother's house and that, if necessary, he would help me to borrow some money. I offered no further arguments and instead expressed my gratitude for all his help.

As the Mohawks discovered that I was off to Caughnawaga that day to stay with Joe, my position in Wigwam society began to change. Within the hour I heard someone refer to me as "Joe's friend." Although I was not aware of it at the time, an interesting process was beginning. Joe's early friendly come-ons had been the prelude to a sort of adoption process that other "whites" had gone through. His offer to "take" me to the reservation symbolized a certain stage in this process; he was broadcasting to his group that I was the type of non-Indian that one can accept. Whether or not they would accept me depended partly on Joe's status in the group and partly on how I continued to behave as my interactions with group members became more frequent and more intimate. As it turned out, my adoption by Joe was very fortunate, due to the status Joe held in Wigwam society and due to the role of Joe's mother in Caughnawaga. Although Joe was one of the smallest of the Mohawk steel workers, he was held in high esteem by the group due both to his "wild" fighting habits and to the role his mother assumed.

Ma Joe, a woman in her late forties, enjoyed having Joe's friends in her home. Her house was almost a structural parallel of the Wigwam bar in Brooklyn. At any time between 9 A.M. and midnight or after, one might find a young group of Mohawks sitting in Ma Joe's house, drinking, joking, swearing, and story-telling. Ma Joe was treated as one of the gang, and she loved it. During my first weekend at Caughnawaga I met about thirty young Mohawks and my living in Ma Joe's house itself almost assured me of membership in Wigwam society.

After my return from the reservation I was no longer a stranger; my new name, "Joe's friend," had stuck. People referred to me thus both directly and indirectly. It was clear that I now had acceptance by the group as a white man who was almost good enough to be an Indian.[2]

Once I had a legitimate right to be around Mohawks at almost any reasonable time and had achieved adequate rapport to talk to them as a nonstranger, I began to wonder how I could best work actively toward a successful completion of my project.

Active Research

The kind of active research activity that appears feasible in a given project is directly related to the kind of rapport achieved during the adaptational period of passive research. It is neces-

---

[2] It is interesting that historically Mohawk warriors used to capture men of non-Iroquoian tribes and frequently adopt them into their society. Thus, I, together with a number of other non-Indians, filled a legitimate role with a long history. Although I had told my name to dozens of Indians, as far as I can recall only four Mohawks ever used my real name or acted as if they knew it: Joe, Joe's mother, and two other young Mohawk males, the latter being rather marginal members of Mohawk society.

sary to consider *what* one has rapport to do, *with whom, when,* and under *what specific conditions.*

The rapport achieved and problems of rapport maintenance. A rule of thumb generally given to graduate students in anthropology is, "Be honest, present what you are doing in simple language, but present it as close to the truth as practically possible." I attempted to present myself as a graduate student in anthropology, very interested in Indians, particularly in Mohawks and their "glorious" history. Although I repeated my story to a considerable number of Mohawks, no information seemed to be passing from me to them. They either did not know who and what I was, or claimed not to *until* I became "Joe's friend." In their eyes, I had no social existence until I was adopted; before adoption I had no rapport. After adoption I had *adequate* rapport (for my project goals), but I never really achieved more than this, except in a few cases.

Once I had become an accepted member of Wigwam and Mohawks-in-Brooklyn society I tried to revert to the role of anthropologist. This attempt was generally fruitless. It was soon clear that any anthropological symbol was tabu to this project. I could use no pencils, notebooks, or questionnaires. I even failed in attempts to play the semianthropologist. For example, I tried saying, "Now that is really interesting; let me write that down so that I don't forget it." Suddenly my audience became hostile, and the few words I jotted down cost me much in rapport for the next few days. To continue doing research with the steel workers I had to keep a small notebook in my hip pocket and periodically go to the men's room in the bar or the outhouse at Caughnawaga and write notes to myself. As frequently as possible, I would go to a coffee shop to write down longer statements that could turn out to be important.

In short, during the active research stage I could play only the role of the "adopted Mohawk" if I wanted to maintain membership in the young Mohawk clique—the group that did structural steel work. To play this role, I had to fulfill certain obvious requirements: (1) I had to identify completely with Mohawks, including making frequent "broadcasts" of Indian superiority over all other groups and wearing some Indian clothing; (2) I had to make periodic trips to the reservation in the company of Mohawks; and (3) I had to have a high frequency interaction with Mohawks.

The data-getting strategy that paid off was simply being around Mohawks, watching, listening, and slipping away to write down any information collected. I did not adopt this strategy immediately for obvious reasons. Emotionally, I did not enjoy playing the equivalent of the undercover agent. Ethically, I had my doubts as to my right to work this way. And professionally, I had been taught that it was wise to remain "above board." Furthermore, I wanted "my tribe" to know that they had an anthropologist in their midst. Such knowledge would have legitimized the work of my first anthropological research project and would have been supportive during the *rite de passage* into the profession.

Data-collection techniques. After my fruitless attempts to write down information in the presence of Mohawks, I used another fruitless, but less harmful, approach. I began asking Mohawks direct questions concerning their fear of being up so high on narrow ledges. "Don't you ever see the newspapers? Haven't you heard about us before coming here? Indians are afraid of nothing. Steel work is in their blood. Indians are surefooted." This was the typical response to this line of questioning. In short, in terms of direct questions concerning fear of heights, the Indians presented the same statements that appear in the press about them. They were brave, surefooted daredevils, who were afraid of nothing and who had steel work in their blood. They had accepted the stereotype given them by the white man; they almost had me believing that the Mohawk was a fearless daredevil.

I next decided simply to stay around the Mohawks and talk about steel work whenever possible. Good ways of "staying around" Mohawks included (1) getting a job in structural steel work; (2) spending long periods of time daily in the Wigwam; and (3) riding up to the reservation with Mohawk steel workers. Getting a job in structural steel involved two problems. First, it is very difficult to get membership in the appropriate union, and, second, the more time one spends at a specific job site working with a relatively small number of Mohawks, the less time there is for staying around the Wigwam. I decided against trying to get a job in structural steel and concentrated my work activities in the Wigwam with periodic trips to the reservation.

As my task became more clearly defined in the Wigwam, to be a human camera and tape recorder, I began to observe some interesting phenomena I had previously overlooked. Prominently displayed around the room were drawings of Iroquois warriors and war scenes. Intermingled among these drawings, which included one of Custer's Last Stand, were helmets of structural steel workers who had fallen to their deaths. In one corner stood a large juke box filled with popular American records, and in another part of the barroom there was a small mechanical "bowling" game.

Although the Mohawks who frequented the Wigwam spent

most of their time just sitting, drinking, and talking, periodically there was some roughhousing. I observed that the younger Mohawks would frequently go out of their way to annoy a given individual and that after a few verbal bouts, the annoyer and the annoyed became antagonists in a physical battle, generally of short duration. After some fighting, with rare attention to Queensbury rules, the antagonists were separated by some of the audience, furniture was put back in place, and the group got back into the drinking-talking pattern. I was initially surprised at the lack of ill feeling that existed between the "fighters" after any given bout, particularly since there was much body-hurt involved. Joe, my adopter, described one of his fights as follows:

> After a lot of arguing, Angus hit me on the nose, then when I fell he gave me the boot in my face. I got up and knocked the —— out of him. . . . He came at me again. I hit him with a large beer bottle, right in the head. [Joe laughed heartily.]

As far as I knew, Joe and Angus remained as friendly after their bout as they had been before. Nor did the fights between other Mohawks lead to any permanent hostilities between either individual Indians or cliques. Further observations led me to conclude that these short fights almost invariably occurred between Mohawks who were roughly equal in size and weight. In fact, the only small Mohawk I ever saw attack a large Mohawk was Joe. Joe weighed about 150 pounds, stood about 5 feet 5 inches, and was quite muscular. It was not unusual to see him throw himself at a much larger man, get in a few blows, receive several blows in return, and then kid his way out of the "fight." Because of this behavioral pattern, Joe was known as "wild," or "crazy," but he was very much respected for his courage and fighting ability. The Mohawks found Joe somewhat unpredictable, and he enjoyed "being different" and the prestige it provided.

It seemed clear to me after observing a number of such fights that the younger Mohawks were playing a pecking-order game. As a young Indian began "feeling his oats," he believed he could take on someone who had beaten him previously and would engineer a bout. This kind of "fight" need not be long or drawn out. As soon as it was obvious who was superior, the group separated the combatants, so that the "game" could not disrupt the group by generating ill feelings between the antagonists. Joe, with his unorthodox involvement with men who greatly outsized and thus outranked him in the Wigwam, seemed to bypass the pecking-order game completely. Mohawks who were roughly equal to Joe in size and strength avoided "quarrels" with him, since he was known to attack the toughest Indians in the group. The big and very strong Indians seemed to respect Joe's ability to get in a few fast blows. However, no prestige was attached to fighting with a person who was so much smaller and thus lower in rank than they. Joe's unusual situation in the Wigwam gave him considerable notoriety and gave anyone closely associated with him—like myself—considerable publicity.

It should have been obvious to me that if a pecking-order game was really a part of Wigwam society, and if I was accepted as a legitimate member of this society, then I must expect to be asked to "play" by Mohawks who were roughly of my size and weight. It wasn't, and therefore, my first encounter with a gauntlet-throwing Mohawk was both distasteful and confusing. Bill, a muscular youth of about twenty, slightly taller but obviously much stronger than I, had been talking to me on and off for about fifteen minutes. He seemed to be angry about something. Finally he made the critical "play."

> BILL: How old did you say you were?
> MF: I'm twenty-eight. (I had not mentioned my age previously.)
> BILL: I can't believe you're that old. No, you're
> no more than twenty.
> MF: Why do you think I'm not twenty-eight?
> BILL: A guy of twenty-eight would not talk stupid like you do!

I was obviously being challenged to fight. I pretended to misunderstand the challenge and continued receiving insult after insult. I parried verbally with statements such as "What gives you the idea that I'm stupid?" and "In what ways do I act silly?" Bill finally decided that he had "won" without showing his physical prowess. He announced it was a waste of time talking to me and walked off.

Bill was the first of several young Mohawks who in various ways made it clear that they were eager to fight me. Only a considerable amount of pride-swallowing prevented me from being badly beaten. The young Mohawks who were goading me to fight not only had much experience in this type of encounter, but they were also in excellent physical condition.

It soon became clear to all the Mohawks who frequented the Wigwam that I was no threat to the status of any Indian, large or small. I had placed myself on the lowest rung of the group's status system. My low rank was valuable because any higher rank would have required me to fight periodically with those just below me in order to maintain my rank. My loss of status in playing the cowardly "I will not fight" role was partly compensated for by being "Joe's friend" and partly balanced by the fact that I was not really Indian; if I were, it would have been almost impossible for me to attain the low-rank position without at least one fight.

The pecking-order game seemed to serve two major functions for social life in the Wigwam. First, it set up a ranking system: when a given Mohawk was throwing his weight around the bar, those who outranked him could easily get him back in line; those lower in rank had to put up with his abuses. Second, it permitted a Mohawk to play the role of "tough guy," a role that appeared to give them great personal satisfaction. Playing the tough-guy role was not limited to the situations involving the pecking-order game. Mohawks frequently went out of their way to annoy non-Indians in situations where such abuses were *almost* appropriate: police officers who stopped them would be treated with considerable hostility; young men who were trying to get served in stores or restaurants ahead of them would be abused and so forth. Whenever Mohawks felt that abuses and annoyances could be escalated into fights that they could win, they did so. Such fights were not the "friendly" bouts of Mohawk versus Mohawk; they were fights in which the combatants could be critically injured.

For example, Jack, an Indian in his early twenties, proudly related how he and his friend had "beaten up a couple of guys" in Canada. During the fight Jack pulled a knife and stabbed his antagonist. He was completely unconcerned that the man was in the hospital on the critical list. He said: "I like to fight. . . . That's how I have fun." His real concern was expressed as follows: "I can't go back to Canada, because the cops are looking for me." He was particularly upset because a Mohawk friend was getting married shortly, and he was unwilling to attend the wedding and risk getting arrested.

In the "tough-guy" role the Mohawks communicated to their associates the degree to which "the Hero" could be physically destructive. Their stories of wrecked cars and of breaking up "joints" in various cities showed a complete disregard for personal safety. At times a Mohawk would "act out" in a manner like the following to show he was tough:

> Late one evening, Jack, an Indian in his early twenties came into the Wigwam looking angry and drunk. He asked the barman for a bottle of beer. The barman, not wishing to serve him, did not reply. Jack jumped over the counter, took a bottle, drank half of it and then started toward the bathroom. The jukebox was playing as he passed it. He pulled back his arm and threw a long right-handed punch at the glass. The glass cracked and his hand bled profusely. When the barman yelled at him in anger he tried to fight the barman. Several onlookers (including myself) tried to get Jack to a nearby hospital. Jack, who was losing blood at a fast

rate, refused to go. The barman gave him a towel to wrap around his hand, and Jack yelled "I don't want your pity." (A few Indians made him wrap it around his wrist and hand.) Two Indians then grabbed Jack and told him they were going to take him to the Catholic clinic nearby. On the way, we (the group now included four Mohawks and myself) ran into several girls Jack knew. He waved the bloody towel at them and said he would not have his hand fixed unless they came along. When the now large group arrived at the clinic, Jack swore and cursed as the nuns were fixing his hand. He received an injection, four stitches, and was bandaged up. As we were leaving, Jack kept trying to indicate his disdain for everything that happened with respect to taking care of his hand. His final act of "disdain" was to urinate on the front door of the clinic. Later I asked Jack, "Why did you break the glass?" He replied: "I did not like the record that was playing."

Wigwam society included, besides the pecking-order system, a he-man role and an *esprit de corps* based on the notion that Mohawks were the greatest people in the world. My own membership in this system was tenuous, as exemplified by the following event:

I entered the Wigwam at about 10 o'clock one morning and found the place full of Mohawks. The weather was fine for structural steel work. It was dry, clear and warm; and it seemed strange that so many Mohawks should feel like staying away from work all at the same time. I asked a Mohawk sitting next to me why so many of the men were not working today. Suddenly most of the conversation that was going on stopped, and everyone seemed to be looking at the Indian next to me to hear what he would say. The young Indian took "center stage," as if on cue, and began telling me a long historical tale. In serious tones he discussed the death of a famous chief many, many years ago. "Chief (a garbled name) was a great and fearless Mohawk warrior," I was told. "Today is the day he died!" The Indian went on to describe how solemn a day this was for all Mohawks, and how very disrespectful it would be to the memory of their great chief to work on this sacred day. He concluded by saying that it was customary for the Mohawks who happened to be in Brooklyn on this day to come to the Wigwam and quietly drink to his memory. As the Mohawk spoke I tried hard to remember every word he was saying. This appeared to be important data on cultural persistence. Fortunately, near the end of his monologue I noticed an Indian near me suppress a smile. I realized then that this was a group joke, and I was expected to make some foolish reaction. I replied in a manner that indicated my understanding of the "joke"; everyone laughed heartily, and the typical barroom conversational buzz resumed.

After this incident I became more on guard for possible future put ons, a few of which occurred. However, none of the latter were as dramatic as the event described. I did not realize at the time that my low-status position in the pecking order, actually almost an outcast role, made me highly susceptible to the role of group's goat.

Activities found valuable for data collection. My trips to the reservation were most valuable for getting data on how a group of young Mohawks behave when they remain together continuously for eight or ten hours. A typical trip to Caughnawaga began with a sort of planning stage. Everyone in the Wigwam knew that a number of cars would be leaving some time on Friday for Caughnawaga. The problem for any given Mohawk who wanted to go was to find out exactly who was planning on driving, how many people were traveling with him, and who these passengers were. Mohawks wishing to leave would thus try to get in with a group they enjoyed that was leaving at about the time they wanted to leave. Although, according to Joe, any amount of money one had could be thrown into the pot for car expenses, the Mohawks who arranged the car pools tried to get about $15 from each passenger for the round trip. As far as I know, Mohawks with less than $15 were not turned away, but Mohawks who paid the $15 and did not return in the same car did not receive refunds. There were not, then, the many bookkeeping transactions common in middle-class American society.

Drinking started before the 400-mile trip, carried on during the trip, and helped celebrate its conclusion. The possibility of being stopped by police for drinking while driving occurred to the Mohawks, but it did not deter them from drinking. This type of behavior was part of a pattern of indirect challenges to authority figures to "do something about it," coupled with the implicit announcement to other Mohawks present that "I'm afraid of nothing." During the ride to Caughnawaga, the Indians boasted of their great recklessness in driving. For example:

Joe boasted that he and his buddy Ronnie had been in eleven accidents together. Each time they managed to almost completely wreck the car they were in: "At one time we tried to turn over a Buick which was supposed never to turn over. We turned it over!" Another time Joe dared Ronnie to hit a pole at high speed. He did. In a third "accident" they attempted to break the accelerator. "We did not manage that, although we drove 120 miles an hour." Indians were supposed to be great drivers. They only smashed up cars for the fun of it. There was also usually much boasting about how fast a given Indian had made the trip from Brooklyn to Caughnawaga. One young Indian claimed to have done it in 7½ hours.

The talk also invariably touched on wild sex escapades and Indians who broke a law and went to prison and the smarter ones who did not get caught. One of the groups I rode with included three Mohawks who boasted that they had been stopped by a couple of Canadian Mounties a few years before and accused of drunken driving. "We beat up the Mounties, took their guns and their wallets, and got away."

The trip to Caughnawaga always included a stop at Hoff's Diner in the Albany area. Hoff was an Indian, and most of the Mohawks traveling to and from the reservation would stop there. In the friendly atmosphere of Hoff's Diner, it was easy for the young steel workers to play the hero. They wisecracked with the waitresses, made passes at girls, and generally acted as if the diner belonged to them.

The next major event was crossing the border. Here again the Indians would go out of their way to let me know that they did not expect to be detained or annoyed in any way. Just before we got to the Canadian border an Indian would tell me to say I was a Mohawk. "That will stop any other questioning." They were special people. Apparently, the officials at both the American and Canadian sides of the border had been frequently annoyed by the Mohawks, and the effect was a minimal delay.

Upon reaching the reservation, the Mohawks would in some manner signal their arrival. One time a Mohawk got out and fired a hunting rifle several times into the air; usually the driver would start to honk the horn of the car. A group from Brooklyn had arrived, and they wanted all to know it.

Keeping Field Data

While doing observation-participation field work, I carried a small notebook and pencil and whenever possible jotted down a few words in the notebook to serve as mnemonic devices. I would periodically go off to get a soda or coffee in a nearby café, write my notes to myself, and then go back to the bar. When I got home I would attempt to reconstruct the events of the day with the help of my notebook.

There are, of course, a number of problems with this kind of field work. For one thing, it is possible to get caught, and for another the researcher must rely heavily on his memory. Although a small notebook can easily be hidden in a back pocket, situations arise when a notebook can become visible to the informants. It is thus essential that nothing be put in the note-book pocket, since when taking out the other item the notebook may fall out, and that the notebook not be in one's pocket when one sleeps in the house of an informant. While half asleep on Joe's mother's couch in Caughnawaga, I noticed that someone was going through my clothes. It turned out that Joe's drunken step-father was looking for my wallet to get money for liquor. Because he was drunk, he paid no attention to my little notebook, but his perusal of it might have had serious repercussions on my future field work.

After a certain amount of experience with this work I found that my memory served me far better than I expected. I tried to have in my notebook (1) the names of people I spoke to, (2) the subjects discussed, (3) the time of day, (4) any unusual occurrence, (5) any statistical data that I might quickly forget, such as the wages of a given man, ages, frequency of going to the reservation, etc. After going through the notebook and re-constructing events by the name, subject matter, time sequence, and occurrences, I usually felt fairly certain that little of the information I had received on a given day was lost.

Bowing Out

I did intensive field work with Mohawks during the months of June, July, August, and September of 1956. By the end of September, I was spending perhaps ten hours a week in research, although my wife and I spent several days in September at the reservation. I told many of my informants that I was going to do more work in graduate school and that I would try to be around as often as possible. "Bowing out" was essentially a simple process with the Mohawks for several reasons. First my apartment was no more than a forty-minute subway ride from the Wigwam. Second, the Mohawks were well accustomed to having someone "disappear" for several months (such absence never entailed mail from the absentee). Mohawks would get steel jobs all over the country and in Canada. When their assignments were completed they usually came back to Brooklyn. However, the absence might be as long as six months or even much longer. From October, 1956, until March, 1957, I spent very few hours a week at the Wigwam. Indeed, many weeks passed without my going there at all. During the spring of 1957 I periodically met with a few Mohawks either in their houses or in the Wigwam. I had developed a correspondence with a Mohawk who stayed in Caughnawaga, and I continued to write to him and receive mail from him through May, 1957.

Results: The Modern Mohawk Warrior

The social life of the Mohawks, be it in the reservation, traveling to and from the reservation, or in and around the Wigwam, seemed to center around a role in which Indians reveled: *fearless hero*. The "fearless hero" indicated at every opportunity that he didn't give a hoot for safety, law, authority, and the culturally accepted propriety rules of other groups. This became clear to me from observation of and participation in Mohawk social life and from many long discussions with Mohawks who were involved in structural steel work. My information concerning Mohawks at and around work came from more limited sources. Such information did not include observing Mohawks at work, but came from discussions with Mohawks about work and from discussions with several non-Mohawk officials of Local 361 of the Iron Workers Union. Indirect information also came from discussions with teachers of Mohawk children as to the work ambitions of Mohawk youth.

Discussions with Mohawks working in structural steel were frequently very unrewarding. That the work in steel was important to them quickly became evident, but the how's and why's of the work were difficult to establish, since the Mohawks would generally only talk about it in a highly idealized fashion. The mundane aspects of steel work were never brought up. What seemed to be always at the core of talk about steel were the possibilities of daring exploits and how such possibilities were at times translated into action. Thus one Mohawk discussed the famous exploits of a work-gang leader whom I will call "Pusher Bob." According to this Mohawk steel worker:

> Bob was a real man. He was a pusher and did not call up and say 'Do so and so.' He came up and showed you. He would often swing around just hanging by his feet and when he pushed a pin in, it went. He would push them in [steel pins] with his bare hands.

Stories such as those were told to "prove" what great and fearless steel workers the Mohawks were. They were usually accompanied by statements such as "Caughnawaga Indians are the best steel workers in the world. It's in their blood." Or, "Steel work is in our blood; that is why we do it. I did not tell my son to go into construction work, but that is what he is doing."

Questions concerning Indians who were not in steel work led to information about structural steel work that was more plausible. Again, direct questions about a given man not working in a construction gang led to general answers, such as "I don't know, he just doesn't like steel work.... He likes something else.

. . . That's his business." Indirect probing led to such statements as "Jack was *no good;* he was scared to be on the bars." And, "Some Indians are not in steel work; *they couldn't make it.*" It quickly became apparent that it was not Jack's *fear of heights* that made him no good. Rather, it was Jack's letting his fears keep him from doing real man's work—work appropriate to the Mohawk male. Therefore, the Indian *who made it,* who lived up to the group's definition of what a real Mohawk male was like, worked on high narrow steel ledges and, like Pusher Bob, died with his structural steel boots on. The Indians who *couldn't make it* were those in occupations other than structural steel.

Data collected in this project indicated clearly that *Mohawks have a normal fear of heights.* I was fortunate to be in the Wigwam when a few inebriated Indians were discussing this very subject. Russell said, "I pray every morning that I'll come back alive." The others agreed that when they are up there on the outside of a building, they are afraid. Joe Ringer said, "I've yet to meet the man who's not afraid up there. . . . If you were not afraid you would not be a good steel worker as you would not be careful."

Usually, it is impossible to get Mohawks to admit fear of height for two reasons. First, the Indian has completely accepted the white man's stereotype of him as the "surefooted, fearless Indian." Second, a warrior is not afraid! A frequent statement of the Mohawks is, "Indians are afraid of nothing." Their fear of heights is the normal one of men who know that work on the girders is dangerous; however, just as the possibility of death did not deter the warrior from the warpath, it does not deter his descendant from structural steel work. In both cases, participating in dangerous activities is the sign of being a man.

In terms of Mohawk culture, a *man* is daring, fearless, and frequently destructive. He seeks rather than flees from dangerous activities. He challenges authority figures. This behavior was evident around the Wigwam, in Brooklyn, traveling to and from Caughnawaga, and in and around the reservation. It came to me that a shorthand formula to describe this behavior was, *To be a Mohawk male = to be a warrior = to be a steel worker.* This formula made much historical and current ethnographic data understandable. Historically, the Mohawks were frequently involved in small group warfare, and the male role *warrior* had become both extremely prestigious and socially rewarding. "Playing warrior" in the 1950s was simply a case of social structural persistence. The formula *warrior = steel worker* stems from (1) the essential similarities of the two ways of life and (2) the impossibility of playing "real" warrior. To analogize this to today's context, steel workers, like their warrior ancestors of old, leave for dangerous assignments with their gang of young men and an older leader (the pusher). There is a chance that some of them will not return alive, for steel work is dangerous work requiring all the ingredients of the warrior role: courage, strength, firmness of limb, and a willingness to face death. Those who do not die after the successful completion of an assignment come home and receive the praises of the camp. This analogy helps explain why Mohawks will spend sixteen to twenty hours traveling to and from the reservation to be there for perhaps but forty hours. The reservation is their real home, and when possible they want to hear the home folks sing "see the conquering hero comes."

The juxtaposition in the Wigwam of the helmets of the dead steel workers and the pictures of fighting Indians began to make more sense when I thought of structural steel workers as the *modern Mohawk warriors*. The concept *modern Mohawk warrior* also helped me to understand the meaning of a number of similar bits of false information I had been given. A number of Mohawks in the Wigwam, all middle-aged, had told me that they were "Big Chiefs" in the tribe. Upon checking this information I discovered that *none* of these men held any special chiefly tribal position. However, I found out that *all* of them were in charge of small structural-steel gangs; they were all "pushers." If one translates "big chief" not as important tribal chief but rather as "warrior chief," then the information I had received from the older men was not false. That is, the equation *war chief* = *pusher* makes Mohawk cultural sense, given that *warrior* = *steel worker*. Both the war chief (leader of the war party) and the "pusher" lead a party of young Indians to an assignment where they can play "hero" and return with booty to the community to receive its applause.

If love of the warrior role was a major explanatory principle for Mohawks in structural steel work, then one would expect Mohawk youths to shun all other types of employment. This expectation is indeed justified. My discussion with Mohawk youths and with their teachers in Brooklyn indicated that the Mohawk male can rarely be interested in continuing his schooling after completing the minimal requirements. He has fixed a goal in mind: *to be a steel worker*.

Evaluation

This study of the Mohawks in structural steel represents the classical "sink-or-swim" approach in anthropological research.

Very little training in research had been forced on me, nor did I seek it. The project was successful despite this, for a number of reasons. First, I was not isolated from my own cultural environment or from my colleagues and teachers. After a certain amount of intensive field work, I was back at Columbia University talking incessantly about Mohawks to anyone who would listen. I lectured, argued, debated, and told stories about Mohawks. I was trying to put together a variety of data, collected in a disorganized, unplanned fashion.

Second, I believe my extroverted personality fitted in nicely with the extroverted, "I-can-take-on-the-world" Mohawk warriors who frequented the Wigwam. True, I wouldn't fight, but I would do almost anything else. I was an intense, energetic, and highly motivated graduate student, determined to "make it" in anthropology. And, if "making it" meant driving at high speeds in old cars with drunken Mohawks, that is what I did.

Although I was constantly discussing my field work—a most rewarding technique—I did not do something that might have been extremely helpful: I did not make periodic summaries of what I thought I knew at a given time. Such summaries are helpful in predicting that a given set of phenomena will occur and in using such predictions to validate given data. Further, such predictions facilitate future adaptations to the culture the researcher is learning. For example, had I made summary statements concerning the pecking-order game, I would have been able to argue as follows:

> I hypothesize that a pecking-order game is here in progress and that all members of the system are involved in it. Further, I hypothesize that, most frequently, it is the younger members who must fight it out to maintain or increase their rank. I also believe that I have been accepted as a member of Wigwam society. *Therefore,* I must assume that I will be brought into this game and challenged to fight. What will I do when such a challenge occurs?

Had I summarized in writing what I thought I knew and considered its logical implications, I would not have found a particular challenge confusing and would not have had to make an on-the-spot decision as to how to answer it. Perhaps I would have decided to get involved in a few "fights," after talking to Joe about the situation ahead of time, and persuaded him to stop a fight as soon as it looked like I was likely to be hurt. A few fights of this kind with some of the lowest ranking Mohawks would have given me all the advantages of non-fighting (being thought below everyone) and in addition given me a more secure position among the Mohawk "warriors."

I believe that I also should have reverted to the role of anthropologist after I had obtained as much data as I could in the role of "adopted Mohawk." Put differently, after a point in the field work, I really had nothing (or very little) to lose by assuming the role of anthropologist. I could have devised some schedules or questionnaires and tried giving them to a cross section of the Brooklyn community. At worst I would have lost my status of adopted Mohawk. At best I might have obtained a lot of good information on exactly how the role of structural steel worker is equated with the role of warrior.

Some of the older Mohawks had indicated to me that the younger Mohawks were disinterested in the Mohawk language and in many aspects of the "old ways" and were not respectful to the older people. It might have been interesting to look into this schism between the generations and perhaps find in it an historical relation to the young Mohawk warriors who would rather be on the warpath than help in the more mundane activities of the tribe.

In short, my research time in the last few months of work with the Mohawks was not efficiently used. When there were only a few Mohawks around the Wigwam or the nearby Spar Bar, I could have spent the time talking to the older people. I could also have tried to gather more statistical information through the use of schedules. I was afraid, however, to lose the position I had attained, although at a specific time in the research project I could have well afforded to take the risk.

Due to a number of favorable accidents, namely, my personality, my "adoption," and my remaining alive, the work with the Mohawks was completed with a certain amount of success. Such "luck" can be hoped for, but it can rarely replace the carefully designed and planned project used by a well-trained researcher.

PART II: TRINIDADIAN PEASANTS AND THE NATURAL EXPERIMENT

Problem, Theory, and Research Design

Does geography determine men's lives? This problem has intrigued scholars and laymen for centuries; in modern times it has been the subject of many heated exchanges among social scientists.[3] Anthropologists, although rarely answering the question with a simple Yes, have often turned to environmental deterministic theories for an answer. Indeed, some fundamental ideas in cultural anthropology are closely connected to environmentalism: culture area, the study of man in his "natural habitat," and cultural evolution.

The anthropological belief that culture is the prime determinant in human affairs has been neatly linked to environmentalism by the concept, cultural ecology. Cultural ecology —a theoretical orientation developed by Julian Steward—isolates technology as the major cultural determinant of change and problems of survival as the critical change factor within the environment. An environment is then seen as presenting a group with subsistence problems that must be solved. Solutions to these subsistence problems depend upon the level of the group's technology. Given a set of subsistence problems *(S)* and a set of technological accomplishments *(T)*, certain cultural forms *(C)* must be developed. That is, according to cultural-ecological theory, adaptations to environments by use of specific technologies constitute "creative processes," or $S \times T \rightarrow C$.

Cultural ecology has made an important contribution to anthropological theory and methodology, because testable propositions can be derived from this framework. For this very reason I was attracted to cultural ecology. My Mohawk study, though satisfactory, did not leave me with the kind of surety—that I-knew-I-knew feeling—that I wanted from my research. With the Mohawk material I was a captive of my intuition and post facto logic. I wanted to stand on firmer ground in my second research assignment, and cultural ecology seemed to provide a more "scientific" framework for it. The argument basic to this research project is as follows: (1) Given two groups with extremely different cultural traditions, and (2) given that both these groups finally settle in the same community and make a living in the same way, (3) both these groups should develop similar cultural forms *caused by* the same problems they face in making a living, if the cultural-ecological approach is correct. Or, in cultural-ecological language, two groups that share both a subsistence problem and technology for solving it should also share many basic cultural forms.

In a recent paper (Freilich, 1968), I described the design for this study as *after-only multi-experimental*. In other words,

---

[3] For an historical summary of approaches to environmental determinism, see my paper "Ecology and Culture: Environmental Determinism and the Ecological Approach in Anthropology," *Anthropological Quarterly*, 40:26–43, 1967.

it is an example of a study where two experimental groups have been subjected to similar causal factors and where data on the two groups became available only after the causal factors entered.[4] Research that uses experimental designs under natural conditions falls under the general category of "natural experiments."

Natural experimenters work in "man-found" rather than "man-made" laboratories. Therefore, my first problem was to locate a community with the characteristics described. I did not solve this problem by taking a quick "look around the world." At the time this study was being developed, I was a member of a Caribbean Seminar jointly run by Columbia University and the Research Institute for the Study of Man (RISM), which was preparing graduate students for field work in the Caribbean with special emphasis on research problems in Trinidad. I expected to receive a research training fellowship from RISM that would get me to Trinidad for the summer of 1957. If this materialized, I planned to spend some of that summer searching for the kind of community required to test my cultural-ecological hypothesis.

My readings on Trinidad indicated that this island would probably have several communities with the required characteristics, for Trinidad has a large population of East Indians whose cultural tradition is significantly different from that of the island's majority population, Creoles, or local Negroes. A number of mixed Indian-Creole communities also exist in Trinidad. In Trinidad, many Creoles and East Indians earn a living in the same manner and have done so for several generations, and this was just the special type of situation I required.

---

[4] The classical experimental design has a before and after *experimental group* and a before and after *control group*. It is frequently symbolized as follows:

	Time	
	t_1	t_2
Experimental group	x'_1	x'_2
Control group	x_1	x_2

x and x′ are identical in all critical variables; x′ but not x is subjected to the independent variable.

In this study there is no adequate data for the "before" period (t_1). Although there are no control groups as such, each experimental group functions as a "control" for the other. The after-only multi-experimental design can be symbolized as:

	Time	
	t_1	t_2
Experimental group 1		x_2
Experimental group 2		y_2

I received a fellowship from RISM as well as research funds from the Social Science Research Council (SSRC). Thus, by the beginning of June, 1957, I was financially prepared for a prolonged stay in Trinidad and had digested much of the published ethnographic materials on the Caribbean.[5]

Adaptational Research

An anthropologist preparing to do research in a tropical climate is well advised to spend considerable time planning for climatic adaptation. Early in the planning stage, time should be allowed for whatever series of injections are required for the area. He must also plan for special clothing needs—strong, light shoes for walking, light outer clothing, and some rainproof garments. There may be special sleeping problems requiring tents, sleeping bags, and mosquito netting. Transportation problems requiring the purchase of a jeep or a functionally equivalent item must be looked into also. Most anthropologists take a considerable number of pictures so a camera expert's advice should be sought on the type of camera and film most likely to do the best job in a given climate. It is also important to have a special container for camera and equipment to protect them from the elements. Today a variety of inexpensive but highly effective tape recorders are available, but these too must be chosen with care, keeping in mind the special climatic conditions of one's research. Matters of general notekeeping that provide no problem at home are at times overlooked by the inexperienced researcher, but it is possible to arrive in an area where pencils, ball-point pens, paper, and note cards are both extremely difficult to get and then most expensive. I did not plan as adequately as I might have for my tropical trip and ran into unnecessary problems. Perhaps the best rule of thumb is to spend some time with an anthropologist who has worked in the general geographical area of one's research.

I arrived in Trinidad in June, 1957, and made my initial headquarters in a rooming house in Port-of-Spain. A few days later, while looking through a local telephone directory, I discovered a third cousin on the island and was invited to stay at his house for a week until my summer research began. This was a most welcome piece of luck. The culture shock one generally receives in the adaptational period of research in a foreign land

[5] I am much indebted to both the Research Institute for the Study of Man for this fellowship and to the director of RISM—Vera Rubin—for many helpful and much-needed assistances at various stages of this project and to the Social Science Research Council for their grant permitting me to do this natural experiment.

was greatly reduced for me by being around my newly-found family. My cousin Jacob, a man of about fifty who had worked as an engineer and now ran a rooming house and a restaurant, was most knowledgeable about the island, its geography, its politics, and its economic problems. He was an avid reader of newspapers, journals, and books and knew many Trinidadian officials personally. I quickly became friendly with him and his immediate family and with a close relative of Jacob's who was a manufacturer and an importer and exporter. In long discussions with these people I came to see the island through the eyes of some of its middle-class, long-time residents. Jacob, an aristocrat at heart, generally took the upper-class white man's point of view on most topics. He had rare intuition, however, and understood many of his prejudices in favor of businessmen and the land-owners of large estates. He thus frequently spoke of matters from both the Creoles' and the Indians' points of view. His rooming house was integrated, and he had had many opportunities to learn how the middle and lower classes feel about island affairs.

The field-training fellowship from RISM required that I spend a few months of research in a lower-class sugar-estate community—let me call it Sugarville—not far from Port-of-Spain. Before settling in Sugarville, RISM's field director planned trips for the seminar members, so that the group could see the island as a whole before we settled into our respective work sites. These trips around Trinidad, parties at the field director's house where we met the local intelligentsia, and our study seminars were all useful adaptation mechanisms to a very non-Protestant-ethic society.

With my wife, who was interested in collecting culture and personality data in Trinidad, I settled in Sugarville two weeks after arriving on the island. The Sugarville community was useful for my later research, because it was a mixed community of Indians and Creoles. In Sugarville, I also had an opportunity to make "cultural mistakes" before moving to the place where my SSRC research would be conducted. Many of the mistakes researchers make are a function of the differences between their culture of orientation and the research culture, and since my research culture in Sugarville was similar to that of my natural-experiment community, I had the opportunity to make "mistakes" in Sugarville that I would know better than to repeat later in my experimental research.

I could plan few data-gathering events that included both Creoles and Indians, since these two groups had a strong mutual dislike for each other. It was also obvious that research approaches toward Indians and Creoles would have to be very different because of the fundamental differences in the two groups' cultural traditions. Exactly what strategies would pay off well I did not discover until I had left Sugarville, but my experiences there at least alerted me to the types of problems I would be facing later during my stay in Trinidad.

In Sugarville I spent much of my spare time collecting information about the locations of ethnically mixed communities. I wanted to study in a peasant farming community, and information and advice collected from taxi drivers, schoolteachers, newspaper reporters, government agricultural experts, and lecturers in the College of Tropical Agriculture indicated one direction: to go east to a highland area known as Tamana. In this eastern highland area I discovered several villages that might meet my requirements, but the village I selected—Anamat—seemed the best choice for several reasons. First, its head teacher was extremely interested in my work and even offered to do a rough population check of the Creole and Indian peasants and to obtain some economic data on these groups. Teacher Ram—an Indian of Presbyterian faith—seemed quite popular in his village, and his interest in my work appeared to be a favorable sign for a successful project. Second, Anamat was a relatively isolated community. It had no electricity, gas, telephone, or major highways nearby, so that extraneous variables would not have to be controlled. Except for voting in major elections and participating in Carnival celebrations, the Anamatians were minimally involved with island culture. Third, a vacant building (a former school) was available to house us. It was an ideal house for my purposes, because it was located approximately in the center of the village and adjacent to the new school building and post office. Much village life could be observed through the windows of this structure. Fourth, several Anamatian peasants to whom Teacher Ram introduced me appeared cooperative and pleased about my prospective stay in Anamat.

After giving Teacher Ram about ten days for his initial survey, I visited him again and received the following information. First, the "average" Indian peasant of the village owned about the same amount of land as the "average" Creole peasant. Second, the major cash crops for all the peasants were cocoa and coffee. Third, all the Anamatians seemed to have similar ideas about how to cultivate their land. I was overjoyed with this information, because, although I realized that Ram's findings would have to be carefully checked, Anamat seemed to be *the* community for my study. Ram added one fact that he thought might prevent me from going there. He had understood that I wanted to be in "one community," but he had doubts as to whether Anamat filled this requirement. Some peasants, he told me, lived far away from the schoolhouse and the village shops,

and some were rarely seen at village functions. I replied that
this did not worry me particularly, keeping to myself the information that anthropologists, together with other social scientists, do not really know what a community is and thus can
never be sure they are in one.

I decided to move to Anamat and told Teacher Ram to
spread the word that I was writing a book about life in Trinidad
and would start my studies there. I began to make inquiries in
Port-of-Spain as to how one obtains permission to use a piece of
government property: namely, the ex-schoolhouse. I was told to
contact a certain government cabinet minister. Although interviewing government officials is far simpler in Trinidad than it
is in America, many precious field-work days were lost cutting
the red tape involved in getting the use of the ex-schoolhouse.
My persistence and unorthodox ways of approaching high-
ranking government officials finally produced a favorable decision. The dilapidated building was useless to the government,
and the minister and his staff must have been glad to get me out
of Port-of-Spain.

The move into the ex-schoolhouse was in retrospect a mixed
blessing. The government had passed an income-tax law shortly
before my arrival in Anamat. When I, claiming to be an anthropologist, arrived in the village and moved into a government-
owned house, most of the peasants quickly jumped to the conclusion that I was a government tax spy. Their suspicions grew
as I went about trying to obtain data from them from which I
could deduce their incomes. In terms of my natural experiment,
I had to determine (1) if the size of the land holdings of the
Creoles as a group roughly equaled the total land belonging to
Indians, and (2) if the model size of each group's holdings was
roughly equal. I therefore asked all the peasants how much land
they worked, how much of it they owned, and how much (if any)
they rented. I also inquired into crop yields and other related
matters. My questions, which I regarded as impersonal, were,
much to my amazement, met with great suspicion. I later realized
I was a tax spy in the eyes of the peasants, but even so I should
have realized that questions relating to income are personal and
almost invariably "tricky," since few groups like to divulge their
earnings.

The Indians generally avoided my economic questions. Instead, they talked at length about the wonders of the Hindu
religion and of their good family life. The Creoles similarly
avoided economic questions, speaking instead about fêtes and
the joys of Carnival.

I decided, temporarily, to stop all questions pertaining to
the ecological adaptations of Anamatian peasants. I also decided

to stay in Anamat and do a traditional community study, should statistics later indicate that the experimental controls, which I assumed existed, were absent. I still did not quite understand why the ecological questions received such a poor response, but I accepted the fact as a temporary failure. I began to follow the more traditional anthropological approach, which favored not pursuing anything specific in the early period, getting to know people, time patterns, and interactional settings, and in general trying to gain enough rapport for the more specific aspects of the study. I had made the mistake of rushing things because of my concern with the availability of specific controls for my natural experiment, and because I wanted to make up the time I had wasted in Port-of-Spain getting permission to use the ex-schoolhouse.

The rate at which rapport can be established with a people is in part a function of how quickly the researcher becomes involved in public events. I was fortunate to have moved to Anamat just prior to the deaths of the grandmother of one neighbor and the mother of another. My wife and I were invited to partake in the rituals associated with the two deaths, and we were quickly placed "on stage" where we were clearly visible to many community members. The presence of an anthropologist and his wife in Anamat soon became public knowledge, and introductions to many community members quickly followed. Within a week of these events, Ma Mac—one of the most respected members of the Creole community—visited us, a sign I took (though wrongly) of acceptance by the Creoles of the community. We returned Ma Mac's visit in short order, and my visits to her house were frequent throughout the study.

I began capitalizing on my wife's presence in the community. While I went around introducing myself to the farmers of the village and to anyone else I happened to see, my wife made friends with farmers' wives and daughters. Several of the neighbors' wives then visited us at our house, and their visits were quickly reciprocated. We met several other women at our neighbors' homes, and Teacher Ram's wife, an intelligent and helpful woman, became a most valuable friend. Like her husband, she was well liked in the community, and introductions coming from her helped my wife establish rapport with the peasants.

The Rams not only directly helped my research but were of considerable indirect assistance. The teacher and his wife were culturally intermediate between the peasants and my previous associates from Columbia University, so this couple's friendship provided a cultural and psychological bridge to the community. The Rams had spent most of their lives in a much larger and more urban community close to Port-of-Spain, and they were able to empathize with our feelings of isolation. Our friendship with this couple made life much happier in rural Anamat.

Shortly after settling in Anamat, I developed a friendship with one of the richest Indian peasants there, Mr. Rapas. I expected this friendship to "open up" the Indian community for research, but this did not occur. It took about a month of collecting and decoding vague bits of information received from both Creole and Indian Anamatians to reach the conclusion that Mr. Rapas was one of the most disliked people in Anamat, particularly by the Indians. My friendship with Mr. Rapas made my work with the other Indians more difficult, but as my ties with him weakened (due to conscious efforts on my part), relationships with other Indian peasants seemed to improve.

My rapport-getting was much facilitated by my ability to play an adequate game of cricket. The British had introduced cricket to Trinidad, and the sport was popular with young and old. My knowledge of the game soon brought me into contact with Mr. Ed, a rich Creole who had started one of the local cricket clubs. Mr. Ed's house was a hang-out for many of the Creole peasants, particularly for those who were directly involved in playing cricket. I was soon practicing with this group and their sons on late afternoons and weekends. After cricket practice we would all stop at Ed's house and have a scotch or two, and I would invite those present to "drop in" at my house any time they were in the vicinity. When the talk veered toward my work, as it invariably did, I took the opportunity to explain my research aims. My "explanation" usually went as follows: It was important for world peace that people get to know about each other, and I had been sent to obtain information about how Trinidadians live, so that a book could be written telling the world about them. I explained that since many people in Trinidad are engaged in farming, it was necessary for me to spend some time studying farmers, and that the friendliness of Anamat and its head teacher had made me select it as the headquarters for my research.

I slowly developed rapport to the extent that I could return to sensitive topics, but the research included a structural problem that was never completely solved: the Indians and the Creoles disliked each other so intensely that the better my relations developed with one group, the more the suspicions of the other group grew. It took the Anamatians a long time to accept the fact that I could honestly like both Creoles and Indians. I later found out that the peasants had concluded that my "strange" behavior had something to do with my work. The behavior they found strange was not only my friendship for Creoles *and*

Indians, but my regular attendance at Catholic, Presbyterian, Baptist, and Hindu prayer meetings, my perpetual readiness to assist an Anamatian—from driving him into a nearby market town to helping him repair his house—and the fact that all and sundry were given friendly hospitality whenever they visited our house.

One of my adaptational problems was simply how to manage my time. During our first week in Anamat, I was overwhelmed with the idea that I had one year in which I could do anything I wanted to. This tremendous freedom was somewhat frightening, and I spent several days worrying about how best to use my time. This in itself was rather a ridiculous waste of time, since I did not have the information to make an effective decision until much of the field work was completed. I finally decided to use my evenings for writing up field notes, to try and meet farmers on their land holdings during the mornings and early afternoon hours, and after a while to make specific appointments for interviews in the late afternoons.

At first I roamed the village with a small notebook and pencil looking for farmers and frequently not finding them. However, in my wanderings I noticed that Anamatians regularly congregated at a variety of village sites, the post office, rum shops, Benny's Shed (where the Village Council meetings and Agricultural Society meetings were held), the schoolhouse, at one of the three local stores, at Salmadie corner (where the two major roads of the village crossed), at the Catholic Church, and at one or other of the two cricket fields. At one of these village centers one could, by careful choice of time and place, meet and gossip with the locals. I used the centers as "information stations" and tried to spend some time each day at one or more of them.

As my village contacts grew, and as more and more Anamatians seemed willing to cooperate with me, I became optimistic as to the study's final outcome. In terms of the concepts I used, I had successfully completed the adaptational stage of the study. However, in other terms my adaptational research in Anamat never really ended, for I never completely adapted to living, thinking, and feeling in three cultures: Creole, East Indian, and White American.

Active Research

During the adaptational period, the anthropologist talks to people on subjects they wish to discuss and in ways they select, and he terminates such conversations in accordance with cues they provide. Data collection at this time is thus accurately described as "passive," and the actual data collected are generally only indirectly related to the problem being investigated. The anthropologist is thus eager to arrive at the active research stage as quickly as possible. Since a premature entry can, however, adversely affect the whole research program, it is well to look carefully for signs indicating the informants' readiness for active research. When the anthropologist approaches a typical group of informants and notices that his presence does not seem to change the information flow—they continue talking in essentially the same manner as before—he has a good sign that the adaptational period can be concluded. Other signs include receiving house invitations from informants of diverse social status and being invited to restricted community functions. In Anamat everyone was considered welcome at a funeral, at a wake, at the house of a sick individual, at a cricket match, and at a meeting of the Village Council. "Sunday breakfasts" (parties after church early on Sunday afternoon), birthday parties, wedding receptions, and Indian *pujas* (family prayer meetings) were all restricted community functions, participation in which was by invitation only. Invitations to the restricted functions of well-to-do Anamatians were particularly good signs of having successfully passed through the adaptational period.

About six weeks after arriving in Anamat, I returned to an active role in the research setting. That is, I questioned some informants on specific topics, interviewed in a planned manner, and continued discussing a topic long enough to get a satisfactory closure on the subject. This meant ignoring informants' cues that indicated their desire to change the topic. During this early entry stage into active research my rapport was not equally good with all the Anamatian peasants. With some informants it was excellent. For example, according to my field diary, I spent four hours walking over Mr. Dowell's estate and questioning him on highly specific matters. Our discussions included such sensitive topics as how good a farmer he considered himself to be, how he ranked himself vis-à-vis other Anamatian farmers, his average income from various crops, his regular expenditures on his estate, and many other related questions. Our discussions were cordial, and Dowell in no way indicated that I should change my line of questioning. In fact, he seemed to enjoy our talk, and he invited me to visit him one evening the following week so that he could explain how his records were kept. He kept figures on all his expenditures and on various income-producing activities, and his records, which he permitted me to examine at length, were a gold mine of excellent data. I achieved maximum rapport with Dowell, and I could count on his aid and advice throughout my stay in Trinidad.

With most of the community the rapport achieved six weeks

after "entry" was nowhere near as good as that achieved with Dowell. With some Anamatians my rapport was good only when discussing a limited number of topics. It began to decline when I brought up sensitive subjects. With some other informants I achieved only a minimal amount of rapport, and these weak relationships permitted neither controlled interviews for long durations nor interviews on sensitive topics.

The "whys" of this differential rapport are hard to pinpoint. My best informants in Anamat, at all stages of my study, were atypical in one way or another. Dowell was proud of his achievements in agriculture and of his abilities to successfully plan ahead and meet the goals he set himself. His involvement in agricultural matters, which included serious attention to government pamphlets and government agricultural officers, made him happy to "teach" agriculture to me, his (high-status) pupil. From very poor beginnings, Dowell had acquired one of the largest land holdings in the community. He reminded me frequently of the American "self-made man." My good rapport with him was partly a function of his willingness to broadcast his successes to me and partly due to the fact that his drive and energy were channeled mainly into work, which other Creole Anamatians did not think was the way a good Creole should live. Dowell thus had very few close friends in the village, and I was able to fill an important slot in his life: I admired him for that which he believed merited admiration.

Another example of an excellent informant who was somewhat apart from the group was Ma Mac, who considered herself part of Anamat's "aristocracy," and whose husband had left her enough land to live well. Her family's long history of wealth (as locally defined), her kinship connections to other well-to-do Anamatians, her daughter's marriage to a schoolteacher, and her son's passing the exams for the Trinidadian police force all gave substance to her aristocratic air. Mr. Ramli, another excellent informant, was much involved in "scientific" agriculture, was self-educated in Hindu scriptures, practiced Hindu religion in a highly orthodox manner, and held himself aloof from Creole-Indian conflicts. Mr. Bool lived alone, rarely involved himself with community affairs, gave long lectures (when given a chance) on the hypocrisy of the Catholic Church and the futility of any kind of religious worship, and generally considered himself the "philosopher" of the village. Mr. Brown was a bachelor who did not care enough for his estate or show enough interest in women to meet the community's approval. His great passion was horse racing rather than woman chasing, and as a result he was thought of as a "sissy" by community members.

It is important to distinguish between the problems of rapport achievement and maintenance with Indians and those with Creoles. Throughout my study these problems were quite different. Among the Indians my general rapport, my acceptance by the group as a short-duration member of the community, was largely a function of the total time I spent in the community. My general rapport grew over time both in size and in quality. In terms of size, I received ever more privileges as a "local" or, as one peasant put it, "one of us." In terms of quality, the general rapport I achieved with the Indians grew ever more "solid": my position with this group became ever less vulnerable as time passed. Various incorrect, inappropriate, or unappreciated acts on my part were ever less likely to result in a significant loss of previously achieved rapport. Differently put, my rapport "investment" with the Indian community as a whole became "safer" as my stay in the community lengthened.

Although my general rapport with the Creole community grew in size as the time I spent in the community increased, qualitatively the rapport did not become ever more "solid." That is, the rapport achieved at a given time remained quite vulnerable. My rapport investment was less "safe," and it was subject to decline if my interactions with the public decreased. My nonattendance at a Village Council meeting, at a cricket match, or at a fête had much more serious consequences from the Creole community than from the Indian community.

The specific rapport I attained, i.e., that achieved with specific individual members of Anamat—was also different between Indians and Creoles. Good rapport, once attained with a given Indian family, was rarely lost for the total duration of the study. With many Indian families I was treated almost as a family member and, in several, addressed by the younger people with a kinship term: "father's brother." Once I had attained these close ties, they were minimally influenced by interaction rates, specific acts on my part, or my positions on Trinidadian political matters.

Although I had many close friends among the Creole peasants, too, these relationships were more fluid than my ties with the Indians. For example, if I had not visited a typical Creole peasant for a week or two, some of my rapport seemed to have evaporated and some rapport building was necessary before getting down to serious (active) data collecting.

Associated with the solid rapport achieved with the Indians and the fluid rapport achieved with the Creoles was what I called a *differential spreadability factor*. Solid rapport was functionally related to maximum spreadability. That is, a good relationship with one Indian family greatly increased the probability of developing good relationships with another Indian family. A good relationship with a Creole family helped in developing relationships with other Creole families, but minimally so. Thus, although Ma Mac was highly thought of among the Creoles of Anamat and although my relationships with her and her family were excellent, these relationships did not appear to help me in developing ties with other Creoles. However, my equally good relationships with Ramli and his family helped me considerably to establish rapport with other Indian peasants.

Regular attendance at a variety of village public functions was a most useful technique for maintaining general rapport and for building on the specific rapport attained with Anamatians who attended the functions. Perhaps the most important village organization was the Village Council. This pseudogovernmental advisory organization was considered a waste of time by many Anamatians, and only ten to fifteen adults attended Village Council meetings with any regularity. However, all the village adults were concerned with what the Village Council was doing, and most Anamatians made infrequent appearances at the meetings.

Who the regular attenders were depended largely on who was currently running the Village Council—that is, whether the individual was a Creole or an Indian, whether he supported the People's National Movement (PNM) or the People's Democratic Party (PDP), and whether he lived at one end of the village (called "Salmadie") or at the other end (called "the Village"). Although formal authority within the Village Council lay in the hands of an elected chairman, the actual person who "ran things" might be the secretary, the vice-president, or any one of several officers who talked well and convincingly and seemed to know how to run an organization. The regular attenders were mainly those with some kind of social link to the man who "ran things"—a neighbor, friend, relation, or co-party member.

As in most organizational participations in field work, the anthropologist's strong identification with a given group has both positive and negative consequences for the research. The benefits I received from my strong involvement with the Village Council were as follows: my regular attendance at meetings was, for most Anamatians, a sign of real interest in the community's problems and its developmental plans. Those who believed this believed (wrongly) that my work with the Village Council was purely altruistic and unrelated to the basic objectives of the research. I was thus frequently complimented for the interest I showed in village affairs. At various special meetings I was asked to take the chair. This meant that I was supposed to begin proceedings by saying a few words. My speeches invariably included a plug for anthropology and its importance to world affairs, a statement of thanks for the great help I was receiving from the people of Anamat, and a reaffirmation of my willingness to help the Council in all its goals. The Village Council thus gave me the opportunity to speak publicly about my work, to publicly praise community members for past assistance, and thus to indirectly ensure that such assistances would be forthcoming in the future. Even when I did not chair meetings, my presence was still somewhat of a "commercial" for the project.

To those who considered the current political élite of the village misguided and (according to some Anamatians) working for personal rather than village goals, I was foolishly spending time doing the wrong things with the wrong people. For these Anamatians, a "broadcast" through local informational channels of my activities with the Village Council adversely affected my general rapport. However, on balance, I believe (and this is hard to demonstrate) that my work with the Village Council added to the rapport I achieved at any given time and greatly helped in rapport maintenance.

Some of my problems that were directly related to my Village Council activities were perhaps more of my own making than necessary outcomes of the involvement. One such problem related to island politics. Most of the "regulars" of the Village Council belonged to the PNM. My own political leanings favored this party also, and I made known my feelings to all who asked me a direct political question. I thus developed a special social persona for the community members: I was an anthropologist, actively involved with the Village Council clique, and an admirer of the PNM. My political stance had the advantage of getting me involved in long political discussions with many members of the community and in long political arguments with many others. These discussions and arguments provided good data on island and local politics. However, I also created some ill-feelings between myself and a few of the local peasants. Perhaps more careful thought to the impressions Anamatians were getting of me and greater skill in impression management might have led me to be more guarded about my feelings, especially in the area of politics.

In this context it is well to remember that an anthropologist in a field setting spends much of his time "on stage." People are looking at him, talking to him, and watching him talk to others seven days a week for long hours each day. In such a work setting it may not be wise to attempt more than a minimal amount of impression management. Impression management includes a certain amount of deception, which if discovered may badly hurt the research program. Our informants in the field, though frequently lacking in formal education, are not lacking in sensitivity and insight. They are capable of making and do make exceedingly accurate judgments about the researcher and his activities. Therefore, it may be wise for the field anthropologist to be himself in terms of personality, likes, and interests, as much as he can. Since I generally enjoy actively participating in groups with which I work, it would have been most difficult for me to stay away from Village Council involvements, and it would have been false to present myself as only an objective observer of island politics.

Although I lost some rapport with a few Anamatians because of my involvements with the Village Council and with island politics, I believe I came across to the village as "honest." The statements of an honest anthropologist are more likely to be accepted by the community at large. Statements such as, "These data I am collecting are all confidential, and you will never be associated with anything you tell me," must be believed by one's informants in order to get valid data. Thus a policy of honesty in presentation of self is for the researcher pragmatically the best policy.

It is fortunate for this study that most of the Creoles favored the party I supported, the PNM, that most Anamatians, Creole or Indian, were not strongly involved with island politics, that those who were strongly in favor of the PDP were Indians, and that my strong political stance did not emerge till late in the field work. That is, by the time all the Indian peasants knew my political inclinations, I had developed fairly good ties with them. Given that "solid" rather than "fluid" rapport could be and was developed with Indians, my favoring the PNM did minimal damage to relationships in Anamat. Fortunately, I had *not* supported the PDP, which would have politically antagonized many of the Creoles.

I regularly attended Catholic Church services (every other Sunday morning), Presbyterian Church services every Sunday afternoon, meetings of the local Agricultural Credit Society, and meetings of the Friendly Society. These centers were all useful for maintaining and developing rapport and for gathering much valuable ethnographic data.

Although most informants improve with time, some Anamatian peasants remained difficult to work with for the duration of my study. In a traditional anthropological study an informant who proves difficult can be substituted, for one can argue that someone else of similar age and status will probably provide equivalent information. However, in natural-experimental research the anthropologist is much concerned with the controls that exist for his experiment. A specific group of people must be worked with—in my case *all* the peasants of Anamat—and specific sets of information must be obtained. In short, having defined this study as a natural experiment I could not "give up" on any peasant in the community, no matter what problems I had getting data from him.

The natural-experimental approach had an additional requirement: I had to spend the large majority of my time in the village *with the peasants* in order to maximize the possibility of getting all the information I wanted from all the peasants of Anamat. Thus, in situations necessitating a choice of activities, the peasants always had first call on my time. For example, if I was invited to two "Sunday breakfasts" on the same day, of which one was given by a peasant farmer and the other by a nonpeasant, I invariably went to the former. My decisions in favor of the peasants rarely caused problems. The peasants represented the "upper class" of the community, and the Anamatians found my behavior understandable. It was reasonable to them that a white man should spend most of his time with people closest to his own class. A problem that was not so easily solved was what to do when a function among a group of East Indian peasants conflicted in time with a function among a group of Creole peasants. I sometimes went to both functions, staying a short time with each group and satisfying neither. More often, however, I attempted to alternate visits to Indian and Creole functions.

Our Creole housekeeper proved so valuable for my research that I promoted her to research assistant. Tina had lived in the village all her life and was surprisingly well-informed on local history and culture and even on small details of the lives of the Indians. In her short life she had been a teacher's assistant and had lived with four husbands, each of whom had left her with at least one child. Her constant good humor made her liked, even by those Anamatians who attacked her morals. Through her husbands and their families, her father and his family, her stepfather and his relatives, and her mother's family, she was related to a large number of local Creoles. Thus, her being identified with my research was of considerable value for rapport maintenance and development.

My "upranking" of Tina from housekeeper to research assistant was well accepted by the community. It was generally felt that I had given Tina the opportunity to "make good," and both she and the community were proud of her as she walked around with her notebook, setting up appointments for herself and for me, and giving interviews. Had Tina not been so generally liked it would have been necessary to hire an Indian assistant also, so as not to appear to be favoring the Creole community.

The job vacancy of "housekeeper" was of interest to Tina's friend Lee, and I was interested in hiring her. Although an Indian woman seemed to be preferable for this position, no one from the Indian community was available. I began the hiring process by asking people of the village about Lee and what they thought of my plans to hire her. Most of them said she would be a good person for Tina's old job, but several Anamatians disagreed. After much prodding, I was told by some of the latter that I would not be happy with Lee, since she was too much of a gossip. This information made me more interested than ever in hiring Lee, for out of the mouths of local gossips come many rewarding leads for anthropological investigations. Lee was hired, and her presence in the house was generally advantageous for the research. Lee, like Tina, had a family in the village, several members of whom became good informants. Her interest in talking about goings on in the community did indeed prove useful, but I discovered that a gossip in one's house is a two-edged sword: many happenings within the house become well known in the community.

Having two Creole women working for me, rather than one Creole and one Indian, was determined by the unavailability of Indian help when I needed it. This situation, however, did have some advantages for the project. First, the two Creole women got along well with each other and gave me no labor problems. An Indian assistant working alongside a Creole might have created considerable tension within the house, given the general antagonism between Creoles and Indians. Second, given the differential problems of rapport maintenance for Creoles and Indians respectively, stronger ties with the Creole community were established via my labor force.

Data-Getting Techniques

How much control over critical variables is necessary before a study merits the designation "natural experiment"? This question perhaps has no categorical answer.[6] From its designation as a natural experiment the work derived several benefits, for the label forced me to "think experiment." Thus, I was constantly comparing my own efforts with work performed in the

---

[6] For a comprehensive treatment of this and related questions, see my paper "The Natural Experiment: A Strategy for Anthropological Research," Ms. (1968).

laboratories of physical and biological scientists. I forced myself to be aware constantly of the reliability, validity, and comparability of the data I was collecting. By thinking experiment I remained concerned throughout my research with programing my research activities in a scientific way.

The problems I identified at the beginning of the active research period were as follows: (1) to find out exactly who belonged in my sample; (2) to get to know these people well enough so that they would answer very specific and often quite personal questions; (3) to know what questions to ask and how to ask them. I was helped in all these matters both by special informants and by hired help.

With the help of Teacher Ram I developed a list of fifty-seven peasants. This list, which was later augmented because of additional information, represented all the peasants Ram knew. (A peasant was defined as a farmer who worked only for himself and who derived the large majority of his income from working the land.[7]) I prepared a large work sheet with columns headed name, land owned, land rented, house location, first interview, date, subject discussed, second interview, date, subject discussed, and so on, with a final column for problems. Throughout the study this master list helped me keep track of work accomplished, work yet to be done, and major problems of the research. As I developed formal questionnaires I added them to the work sheet by title, so that I could keep track of who had received and answered a given questionnaire.

Use of special informants and hired help. Ram was very friendly with eight of the peasants and offered to accompany me to their houses on my first visit. His presence helped me to establish rapport and permitted me to initiate a dialogue between him and the peasant on the subject with which I had previously had difficulties obtaining information: the agricultural practices of Anamatians.

I asked both Ram and Tina to introduce me to peasant farmers whenever the opportunity arose, even if I had met the individual before. Although I had seen and met many peasants by this time, I still had difficulty in matching names with faces.

In several long interviews with Ram I questioned him on what he knew about each peasant on my list. This information was useful both for achieving better rapport with the peasants

---

[7] Many of the Anamatian peasants had side lines that provided extra income. Examples of such side lines include buying oxen and renting such "bulls" to those who need them to pull lumber out of the forest, working the "bull," and hunting wild animals.

and for checking on information that they later provided. Ram took his job as Head Teacher of Anamat very seriously. His deep interest in the education of the village children was in sharp contrast to the attitude of the previous Head Teacher, and Ram was greatly respected for his many educational efforts on behalf of the villagers. In his frequent contacts with Anamatians he came to know a great deal about local affairs, including how well given farmers were doing economically, and how they felt about a variety of phenomena from the running of the Village Council to attempts to set up a second cricket club. Ram found it neither embarrassing nor unethical to provide me with considerable data pertaining to the life-styles of the peasants in my sample. In exchange—so to speak—I made it clear that his information would be treated with complete confidence and that I would be happy to help him and his family in any way I could. Throughout the study I presented Ram with questions, problems, and hypotheses relating to the research, and he was always willing and able to help me.

I developed similar close working and friendly relationships with several Anamatian peasants, who as a group could be referred to as "special informants." The special informants differed in terms of the subjects they were willing and able to discuss at any length. They had in common, however, a special interest in my work and a wish to assist me in it. Among the best of my special informants were Dowell, Ma Mac, Brown, Ramli, Bool, and Paluk.

Dowell was a most valuable source of agricultural data. Through him I learned much about the types of soil in Anamat and about the scientific method of farming particular types of land. Although Dowell's notions of scientific agriculture were not completely in accord with those of various members of Trinidad's College of Tropical Agriculture, he did know the standards used by the Anamatian peasants. Further, he discussed in great detail the many things the local peasants did wrong, from not providing enough drains for their land to not removing trees that rarely bear, and from overloading their holdings with too many subsidiary crops, to not harvesting in the proper manner.

With Ramli, one of the better Indian farmers in Anamat, I developed good rapport and was always welcome in his house. If I visited on an evening when he had made no plans to go out, he would spend considerable time discussing his favorite topic: Hindu religion. He was particularly concerned with the irreligiosity of many Indians in Anamat. They did not make regular *pujas*, they were unconcerned with getting proper mates for their children, and their relationships with members of their extended families left much to be desired. According to Ramli, the young people were forgetting the traditional Hindu precepts. The "old times" were much better, and to Ramli there seemed no way to reverse the trend.

Ma Mac too eulogized the days "when the old heads were alive," when the island in general and Anamat in particular had "better living." She described the good times she had had as a girl in her father's house and often mentioned the private parties and dances that the "old heads" used to give. In the old days, "girls of reputation" were closely supervised. They were not allowed to go anywhere alone, unlike the girls of today.

Bool, whose fifth wife was Ma Mac's sister, gave me a less idealized version of the old days. He spoke at length of the troubles with the Indians when the latter were still indentured servants, with the difficulties people had in making a living, and (his favorite subject) how the church helped the poor to remain downtrodden. He was antagonistic to me and my work even before meeting me, and this had made it quite difficult for me to get to speak with him alone. After several unsuccessful efforts to use Ma Mac as a go-between[8] and several other unsuccessful ploys, I hit on an approach that worked. I went to him and, remembering that he considered himself a philosopher, told him I would prove to his satisfaction that I (then thirty) was actually older than he (then seventy). He found this topic quite fascinating. Briefly put, I argued that age should not be calculated in terms of how frequently we had taken a "ride around the sun" but rather in terms of the number and diversity of our experiences. In terms of the number and diversity of my experiences, I argued that I was older than he.

Bool was interested enough in this topic to spend a whole afternoon telling me his experiences. He did not appear overly interested in mine, and we never really settled the matter of who was older. However, I told him that our discussions that day were of great value to me as an anthropologist and that, since he seemed to have enjoyed our talk, he would probably enjoy future discussions with me. Although I could rarely get Bool to visit my house, he was always happy to see me in his. Data received from Bool were particularly valuable in the areas of local history and attitudes and activities of Creoles with respect to religion and marriage.

The data from Ramli, Ma Mac, and Bool helped me to re-

---

[8] This is a good example of the minimal spreadability of rapport among Creoles. Bool was not only a relative of Ma Mac but a good friend as well, yet my good relationship with her did little for me with respect to developing ties with Bool.

construct village social life as it had been when these informants were children. These data were also valuable as the basis for developing *history* questions dispersed among several questionnaires.

Paluk, Ramli's brother, was generally recognized as the village "healer." Paluk, a man accustomed to thinking deeply on subjects in which he had an interest, was initially quite skeptical about my explanation of what I was doing in Anamat. However, he indicated an interest in anthropology, and I spent considerable time discussing both my research interests in Anamat and anthropology's general aims. In a short time Paluk's skepticism vanished, and he became an admirer and disciple ready to do anything in his power to help in my work. He provided data on local medicine and people's attitudes and activities with respect to sickness and helped me to meet many of the peasants of Anamat. Since he "treated" Creoles and Indians alike—taking in recompense only what each individual could afford, usually in the form of produce—Paluk was greatly admired in the community, and his introductions and "certifications" of my role were extremely valuable to my study. In addition, Paluk was a talented mechanic who was able to repair my second-hand Morris Minor. His firm stand that payment for "just doing a little ting on the car" would represent a denial of our friendship forced me to reciprocate in other ways. I took him to the beaches in my car and transported him to Indian weddings and to various community functions to which we were invited. Paluk, like Teacher Ram, could discuss a variety of problems pertaining to my research, but unlike Ram, he was not happy discussing Creole activities and culture at any length, and our talks were generally restricted to matters that pertained only to the Indians of Anamat.

Brown frequently came to our house in the evenings. He lived alone and so particularly enjoyed our invitations for dinner, followed, at times, by some three-handed poker. As a special informant, Brown was most valuable in providing data on the beliefs, goals, values, and typical activities of young adult Creoles—those in approximately the 18–30 age bracket. Many of the young bachelors of Anamat considered Brown's house their hangout; thus the data he provided had a strong factual basis.

I had decided to use Tina as a sort of "Girl Friday" research assistant. She was set up with a "desk"—made by attaching two long planks to a wall—some "filing cabinets"—made from boxes obtained in the local stores—and pencils and paper and instructed to write essays on every peasant in the community. The essays were supposed to follow categories traditional in ethnographies—history, work, family and kinship, religious activities

—and to include anything else she considered interesting. In essence, I was using Tina as a paid special informant and asking her to discuss a far larger range of topics than I discussed with any particular nonpaid special informant. In order to save time I had her write the data, rather than tell it to me.

Lee, too, was most valuable as a special informant. She was particularly useful in helping me to understand the sex and mating habits of my subjects. She had a common-law husband and many "friends" and willingly discussed her sex life, what she expected from a given relationship, and her marriage and family goals. We talked at great length on these matters. Unlike Tina, who would rather write me an essay on these questions than talk about them, Lee enjoyed the verbal give and take. She "took" each of several pilot questionnaires I developed on mating and marriage, and her work contributed greatly to a final (very productive) questionnaire on mating, marriage, and the family that I gave to all the peasants.

Long discussions with special informants and hired help not only helped me to isolate significant matters for my formal questionnaires but helped me overcome a linguistic problem. Specifically, this problem—perhaps describable under a category such as "Terminological Traps for Field Workers"—is the temptation to think one knows a language, when the language he knows and the one spoken by his informants are referred to by the same word, say English. In Anamat, the locals spoke English and my native tongue is English, so I initially assumed that I had no communication problems. When I had prolonged conversations with the locals on fairly specific topics, however, I found that many of the messages that went from me to them were not being decoded in the way I had intended. Further, some of the messages I received from them did not make sense: I too had decoding problems. For example, certain statements made by the Anamatians have the same tonal sequence Americans use for questions. However, for the Anamatians most of these statements are not questions. Thus, "Jones, a fête-man, yes?" simply means that Jones likes to spend a lot of time, money, and energy having a good time. No *question* is here implied. Another difficulty was that many words had meanings quite different from the one I gave them. For example, "Smith a socialist, yes?" means that Smith likes to do a lot of socializing and has nothing to do with his politics.

By the time I developed formal questionnaires I was able to communicate quite effectively with my informants. However, in order to get reliable and valid data in Anamat, I found that I needed to have more than good rapport and an understanding of communication patterns. I needed an awareness of social reality as seen through the eyes of Creoles and Indians themselves, for I found that answers to my questions were only as good as the questions themselves. I also found that, for any given topic, the more diversified were my data-collecting procedures, the more valid were the data on that topic. Take for example my data on divorce with respect to the Creole peasants. After collecting some data on legal marriage, I assumed that the reason most Creoles seemed to favor common-law marriage was that to leave a legal wife required a divorce, whereas to rid oneself of a common-law wife, the husband simply left her. Because I had discovered, after achieving considerable rapport with most of the Anamatian peasants, that *no peasant in Anamat had been divorced,* I believed that very few had been legally married. However, I subsequently discovered that my data were *not valid,* because what I meant by divorce was not the same as what the peasant meant by this term. I had not tapped Creole social reality on this subject. I was led toward the collection of valid data on legal marriage in the following manner. During a visit with a Creole peasant I had a long discussion with his wife while my host was talking with a neighbor. My host had previously informed me that he was legally married and that his wife was still living. I therefore assumed that my hostess was my host's legally married wife. The information I received from her, however, was that (1) she was legally married, (2) her "lawful husband" lived in another village, (3) my host and she had been living happily in common-law marriage for several years, and (4) neither she nor my host had gone through any kind of divorce proceedings. I followed up this discussion by reinterviewing a number of peasants on the subject of divorce, querying them on the difficulties and expense of getting a divorce in Trinidad and the risks of abandoning a legal spouse. These discussions occurred within a variety of frameworks: informal interviews, group discussions, focused interviews, and, finally, as part of a formal questionnaire. The data I collected indicated quite unequivocally that (1) approximately one-third of the Creole peasants of Anamat had been legally married at some time, (2) most of the peasants did not currently reside with their legal wives, (3) no Anamatian peasant had ever received a legal divorce, (4) it was common practice to live with a common-law wife after leaving a legal wife, and (5) a given peasant's common-law wife is often some other man's legal wife. In brief, good rapport and poor questions initially provided reliable but invalid data on legal marriage.

For data to be comparable it obviously has to be valid. The problems of comparability, however, go beyond validity, since they entail covering similar areas of social reality for all groups being compared. I soon came to the conclusion that, to get this kind of "coverage," I would have to use (among other data-collecting procedures) formal questionnaires capable of eliciting both *statistical* and *normative* data. Statistical data would answer questions such as: How many acres of land do you own? How many children do you have? How often do you go to a fête? How óften do you go to a *puja?* These kinds of data, which varied with the opportunities, abilities, or knowledge of the respondents, had to be analyzed in terms of averages, percentages, and frequencies. Such data, therefore, had to be obtained from every member of the sample, for unless everyone reveals, say, how much land he owns, it is not possible to compare accurately the average Creole land holdings with the average Indian land holdings.

Normative data I wanted to obtain were the rules Creoles and Indians followed. These included (1) *definitional rules* (What is considered a good fête, a good *puja,* a good cricket match?), (2) *operational or procedural rules* (How does one go about getting a wife, getting membership in the Village Council?), and (3) *evaluational rules* (How do you rank given scarce resources in order to know their relative importance?). I planned to obtain the same *amount* and *kind* of normative data from each member of my sample. However, I was not worried about a few poor responses to normative questions. That is, if a rule is really a rule then one gets at it long before all the members of the sample have answered questions about it.

Developing formal research tools: focused interviews and formal questionnaires. My first questionnaire was "Use of Time." After administering it to several informants I realized that many of my questions were not well understood. I decided, therefore, to put these questions to a limited number of Anamatians in the form of a "focused interview" before continuing with the formal questionnaire. During the focused interview I asked the informant several related questions in a chit-chat conversational manner. To minimize the fears of my informants, or just their reticence to talk "for the record," I did not record their answers during the interview. As soon as the interview was over I found some private place and wrote down a shorthand version of it, which I later transcribed for my files.

The focused interviews were given in a variety of settings. The most successful ones were those that occurred while I visited farmers on their holdings. I was often able to lend a hand in the work being done, and while we worked I probed for information. In addition to questions on the "topic of the day," I also inquired about their various trees and crops and listened admiringly while they discussed the many improvements they had made. Periodically, we rested, sucked citrus fruits, and discussed village affairs.

The focused interviews were facilitated by the rapport I had previously achieved, since it was necessary to keep an informant focused on limited subject matter often involving highly personal information. This work continued, with some minor interruptions, throughout October, November, and December. Before discussing the next stage of my study, it is necessary to describe these minor interruptions, since they represented important aspects of "living in the field."

Early in October Ram spoke to me of his efforts to bring educators to the village as part of an adult-educational program he was developing. I told him I would be delighted to participate in his program, and we quickly made up several posters to hang in the post office, at the two rum shops, and at the two general stores. The posters informed the public that all were invited to a free lecture on anthropology to be given at the school house, at 7:30 on October 22, as part of a series of lectures sponsored by the Anamat Adult Education Program. My first lecture was essentially the first lecture most anthropologists give in an introductory course. The turn-out by the community was far beyond my expectations; all the seats in the hall were filled, and many people were standing. As I later discovered, there was considerable drinking going on in the back rows, and many who came thought something was going to be given away. The second lecture, given on November 5, had a much smaller audience and was concerned with the different ways of life found in human societies. The third lecture, on "Race," on November 19, was better attended than the second, but not as well as the first. I later discovered that the size of my audience was, in part, a function of lunar time: the well-attended lectures were given on bright moonlit nights when the villagers like to be out. In addition to presenting some of the basic concepts and theories of anthropology, I tried to impress the Anamatians with (1) why it is important to be a good informant, and (2) how to be a good informant. In other words, I preached the value of anthropology: its contributions to world understanding, to racial peace, to mental health, and to understanding crime and criminals. The Anamatians were left with the distinct impression that about the only thing that anthropology could not do was to get a rascal into heaven. I'm sure they also believed that mine was almost a priestly calling and that those who gave me assistance were involved with God's work.

The Christmas season provides another minor interruption. By the middle of November many Anamatians were talking and planning for Christmas and forming *parang* groups: small groups of musicians who serenade their friends and neighbors with Christmas carols. Any house is fair game for a parang group, which can visit at any time from early evening till four or five o'clock in the morning. The hosts are supposed to provide the musicians with food and liquor, and the entertainers stay as long as things are lively. For data-collection and rapport maintenance reasons (and because I enjoy singing) I joined a *parang* group that included a guitarist, a drummer, and a cuatro (a four-stringed instrument) player.

The celebrations of the Christmas season were by no means all related to work, but as a resident anthropologist one is forever on stage and a central subject for community gossip. One never ceases to remember the hugeness of one's project in relationship to the time and energy available for its completion, and one is always on guard against behavior that might adversely affect the project. The state of being constantly on guard is physically, mentally, and emotionally exhausting, and by the end of December my wife and I decided we had to get away from the village for a short vacation.

Our plans for a vacation were favorably viewed by the locals, who gave us much useful information as to enjoyable places to visit on Tobago. Some of our informants had kin in Tobago and we said we might drop in if we had the time. We planned not to have the time, since visits to relatives of informants are but an extension of regular field work. We left the village on January 8 and returned on January 15.

The Tobago vacation was valuable in at least three ways. First, it provided a most needed rest. Second, although we were away for but a week it was possible to recapture on our return some of the feelings of strangeness we had when we first arrived in Anamat. After a prolonged stay in a community, many things are taken for granted, and many important sociocultural phenomena once considered "strange" and thus noted carefully begin to appear "normal." Seeing the village as strange again is thus a valuable help for observational-participational research. Third, and perhaps of greatest importance, many Anamatians believed we had left for good. Our return to the community was thus a rapport-getting device in itself. It was now much more convincing when we said "We really like it here in Anamat." And now we could add "Yes, Tobago is really very pretty, but here we have friends and can do our work well."

Formal questionnaires and changing work times. After returning from Tobago I carefully reviewed the data obtained in the focused interviews, revised the questionnaire I had earlier developed, and constructed additional questionnaires that were then administered topic by topic in the following sequence: (1) Use of Time, (2) History and Agriculture, (3) Food and Budgets, (4) Mating, Marriage, and Family, (5) Religion and Magic, (6) Work, (7) Fêtes, and (8) Income. Most peasants were not willing to sit through more than one questionnaire per visit, so most peasants had to be visited at least eight separate times. The formal questionnaires represented but a minimal set of stimuli to which all the peasants responded, and our discussions on the "topic of the day" frequently went on to many other topics as well. The questionnaires are reproduced in the appendix.

To several of the more verbally skilled peasants I gave a "class" questionnaire and used the data obtained therefrom as a base for several "seminars" on the subject of class. I would invite three or four peasants to my house, ostensibly to "have a little drink and exchange a few ideas." After the rum had loosened their tongues, I would raise questions about the class situation in Anamat. I asked such questions as, "Who would you say is of a higher class, Teacher Ram or Mr. Eddy?" After they had reached some consensus, I raised questions about the *criteria* that they used for the ranking. "Why do you put Ram higher than Eddy when Eddy is obviously much richer than Ram?" "Because Ram is *known all over;* he is known by the government," I was told. Also, "When Ram is sick he still gets paid. He has a regular income and does not have to work for it under the cocoa." Although the peasants were initially reticent to discuss community members, they invariably warmed up to the "game" and came to enjoy the discovery process involved in a cultural analysis.

To the wives and daughters of the Anamatian peasants, my wife gave (1) a life-history questionnaire, (2) a child-rearing questionnaire, (3) a questionnaire on woman's roles, (4) Thematic Apperception Tests, and (5) Rorschach tests. In some of this work she was assisted by Tina. Tina also administered all my questionnaires to a representative group of Indians and Creoles who were *not* peasants. In addition to these data-collecting activities Tina was responsible for checking all of my kinship data on the Creole community, which I was convinced was overly simplistic and in some areas completely in error due to my use of reliable but nonvalid data. I spent long hours with Tina, Lee, and several special informants on subjects such as (1) the relative advantages of common-law as against legal marriages, (2) sexual behavior of the Creole males and females, and (3) the differential attachments of Creoles to their nuclear families and their matrifocal families, respectively.

Tina's checking of my kinship data indicated precisely what

I had suspected. The Creole peasants almost invariably understated the number of wives they had lived with and rarely mentioned "outside women" with whom they had been intimate during given marriages. In most cases Tina was able to provide the names of specific women with whom Anamatian Creole peasants had lived, the length of these unions, and the (general known) reasons for their dissolution. She also knew of most of the "love affairs" (involvement with outside women) of the local peasants. However, she provided the latter information with considerable hesitancy, and only after I had myself discovered the sexual musical-chair game that was going on in the village.

I gave considerable thought to the question of trusting Tina to check my kinship and mating material. A "blabber-mouth" assistant with access to my writings could easily ruin the project. However, in terms of Tina's reputation in the village, and in terms of the experiences my wife and I had with her while she worked for us as cook and housekeeper, we decided she was a "safe risk." We never trusted Lee with any ethnographic data, because her reputation as a gossip was justified. Although I received much ethnographic data from her, I had to be most careful as to what was said or done when she was nearby.

Tina had an agile mind, she strongly identified with the project, and she showed an amazing ability to grasp the fundamentals of the anthropological approach to research. To my knowledge she never passed on any information she obtained.

I discovered the sexual musical-chair game referred to above through a change of routine in field-work procedure. Except for days when a special community affair had been planned, or when I had a specific invitation to the house of an Anamatian, I used my after-dinner hours to relax, receive visitors in my house, and write up the day's field-work data. I found this routine quite valuable: it provided some cultural continuity with my life in America, coming home from work and relaxing with the family; it kept me up to date with my data write-ups; and it made it possible for me to tell Anamatians, "You're welcome to drop in to my house anytime; but the best time to find me in is after dinner." And, indeed, several of my better informants did drop in to the benefit of this research.

Early in April of 1958, Peasant Jones had been taken to the hospital, and I decided to visit his wife to ask how he was. I arrived at her house at about 8 P.M. and found Mrs. Jones sparsely clad, in intimate conversation with an Anamatian male. I stayed for only a few minutes, since I had the distinct impression that my presence was an embarrassment to both my hostess and her guest. I discussed this incident with Tina the next day, and her initial attempts to make nothing of this incident led me to question her at length with reference to Mrs. Jones and her "lover" and to similar affairs in the village. Tina's information—essentially that many men had "lovers" in the village and that most of the wives knew what was going on—led me to begin roaming around the village in the evenings. My own observations and discussions with Tina and several Creole informants led to the isolation of the following subsystem: A certain man leaves his house on an evening to visit a girl friend or to have a fête with the boys. His wife, now alone, can be visited by one of her admirers. The second male, by leaving his wife alone in his own house, provides a place for a third man, and so forth.

These data—which shed great light on Creole mating and marriage and which were "a secret" only to me—were collected due to a change in my work patterns. The lesson is clear: fieldwork routines must be changed during the research period, so that the anthropologist gets a maximal understanding of community time rhythms.

Summary and Conclusions

Two major types of data—ecological and cultural—were collected from both the East Indians and the Negroes. The ecological data were collected to verify that the adaptations of East Indian and Negro peasants were indeed similar. The cultural data were collected in order to observe to what extent similarities in ecological adaptations had led to similar cultural practices in areas of social life not directly connected with subsistence activities. The data collected showed that the East Indians and the Negroes had the same general environmental conditions and made specific ecological adaptations that were similar enough to be considered the same for the purpose of this natural experiment. In brief, both groups:

1. shared the same climatic conditions
2. worked land of similar acreage
3. worked with similar biotic and edaphic (soils, relief, and drainage) features
4. spent similar amounts of time working the land
5. used the same folk-science technology
6. used the same kind and number of personnel (head of the house) to do most of the farming
7. worked to produce the same cashcrops: cocoa and coffee
8. worked to produce the same crops for home consumption (root crops)
9. shared the same market and transportation facilities
10. obtained similar incomes from their subsistence activities

Cultural data were obtained from both groups on economic practices, marriage, the family, extended kinship ties, authority patterns, leisure activities, expressive symbols, religious practices, involvement in social and political community affairs, and the various roles in their respective systems. The cultural data collected showed that East Indians and Creoles respectively were members of very different cultural systems.

Money was spent differently by East Indians and Creoles. Although the average Creole household contained only one child and the average East Indian household had three or four, both groups spent similar amounts for food and clothing. Thus, per family member, the East Indians spent far less on food and clothing than the Creoles. The East Indians, however, spend more money on housing and on education than the Creole. At the time of this study, two sons of East Indian peasants were studying in universities in England, and one other East Indian youth was planning to go to England. None of the Creole peasants had sons studying in a university, nor did any of the Creole youths plan on going to a university.

The Creoles spent more money than the East Indians on "fêtes": events where at least two of the following elements, people, talk, rum, music, dance, and sexual play, were available. If all or most of these elements were present at a given party, the Creole would consider himself to be at a "big fête" or "fête-for-so" (Freilich, 1961). The East Indian spent more money than the Creoles on religious matters. These usually took the form of the *puja*, a family prayer meeting held in the house or the yard of the person "making" the *puja*.

In short, Indians spent more money on capital items that would affect their future (housing, education, religion), while Creoles spent more money on noncapital items that were fairly quickly consumed. Going along with a different use of money by East Indians and Negroes was a different use of time: the East Indians were future oriented, whereas the Creoles were much more concerned with the present. The East Indians lived in a joint family setting: a household of three generations, with patrilineal inheritance, patriarchial authority, and patrilocal residence rules. Although the joint family household frequently split into nuclear households, the latter were usually placed within close proximity of each other, and close contacts were maintained between the members of a joint family. Although a given Indian might be living in his own house and be relatively independent economically, the directives of a father or an elder brother were still orders and not suggestions.

The Negroes lived in nuclear households but had strong affectionate ties to a matrifocal family: a three-generation consanguineal unit with a minimal membership of a mother, her brother, her sons and daughters, and her daughters' children. Authority patterns were here equalitarian. Directives were given by elder members of the family in the form of advice rather than orders.

The marriages of the East Indians were arranged by their elders, and the father of a young Indian girl would attempt to find a husband for his daughter who was of "good family" (i.e., of a caste which was at least of equal status with his own) and who lived in another village. The marriage was supposed to last for life. The Negroes selected their own mates and understood that a given marriage was supposed to last only as long as man and wife "cooperated"; when one or both parties thought that the proper "cooperation" no longer existed, it was time for them to separate. As the Anamatian Negro put it, a marriage was a "now-for-now" affair.

In terms of associational patterns the East Indians maintained a sharp separation of the sexes in all social activities. Be it at a family *puja* with fifty or more people congregating in and around one house, or during a friendly visit of a man and his wife, Indian women rarely interact with any of the males present. The Indian women understand and accept the fact that their place is with the other women who are present. The Indian men would similarly consider it improper to have social intercourse with the women on these occasions. Social intercourse across sex lines was greatly limited in Indian culture and occurred mostly between a man and his wife when they were alone. For Creoles a get-together without members of the opposite sex represents a very dull party. The associational activities of the Creole peasants in Anamat thus usually included interactions between members of both sexes.

The sociocultural systems of these two groups can be summarized as follows: East Indians are future oriented in time, use village space for most of their interactions, but extend such space to include the villages of the members of their extended family, are members of a joint family, possess a hierarchical authority structure, exchange goods and services by using money as a medium of exchange, exchange women (indirectly) with joint families of other villages, exchange information by the use of the English language, have supernatural, polytheistic sanctions, and have "family improvements" as a major goal.

The Creoles are present oriented in time, use the village space for most of their interactions, but extend this space, mainly by traveling to fêtes in other communities where they interact with friends, are members of a matrifocal-consanguineal family, possess a loose, equalitarian authority system, exchange goods and services by using money and the sexual services of women as media of exchange, exchange women (indirectly) with other matrifocal families on a temporary basis, exchange information by the use of the English language, have social tabus and fatalism as major forms of sanctions, and regard "being in a big fête" a major goal in life.

Elements that are similar in the two systems, such as use of the village for most interactions, use of money as a medium of exchange, and use of English as a means of exchanging information, cannot be related to the shared mode of cultural ecological adaptation. The use of the village for the majority of interactions is very similar to village life in most cultures: it cannot therefore be related to the common adaptations of the East Indian and Negro peasants. The use of money as a medium of exchange and the use of the English language are also unrelated to cocoa and coffee farming. The money (British West Indian dollar) and language used in Anamat are used all over Trinidad and are directly related to the fact that till recently Trinidad was a British colony.

The hypothesis that two groups of peasants—East Indian and Creole, respectively—who share a common mode of cultural ecological adaptation will also show a significant number of cultural similarities outside of economic-adaptive life, had to be rejected.

Bowing Out

By May of 1958 the Anamatians began to ask me when I was planning to leave the island. I answered that I would probably be leaving the village about the middle of June, when I had finished my work. At these times I spoke of my interest in spending a few days in each of several other Caribbean islands in order to get some ideas on Caribbean society and culture, greatly praised the inhabitants of Anamat, stressing my sincere gratitude for their help, discussed my intentions to keep in touch with my friends in the community by mail, and indicated that I hoped to return to Anamat as soon as I had the opportunity to do so.

Several Anamatians became quite involved in various details concerning our departure. I was given advice on to how to sell my car and receive a fair price for it. (The Anamatians had long realized that I did not fit their stereotype of the white man as an individual with lots of money.) They helped me to obtain two large trunks for the goods that I was taking back to America —including an Indian drum, two cutlasses, and some deer skins, all made by Anamatians. I was also provided with a truck and many willing hands to load and get these goods to the docks in Port-of-Spain.

Several days before our departure the Village Council gave a large going-away party in our honor, and teacher Ram's wife had a small dinner party for a few close friends. The long intensive interactions that my wife and I had with many Anamatians made leaving the community a deeply emotional experience, and we still remember well the last greetings between us and a representative group who came to see us off at the airport.

Evaluation

Many of the shortcomings of this study can be attributed to the following set of factors: attempting a too-ambitious project (the comparative study of two *complete* systems); not allowing enough time to do it; not having more funds for the work; and not being more concerned with experimental methodology, particularly experimental design. These factors are obviously related. If, for example, I had limited my study to comparing family and kinship relationships among peasants in Anamat who made a common ecological adaptation, I would have had plenty of time. If I had been more concerned with experimental methodology, I would have realized the great difficulties inherent in scientific comparisons of total systems and might well have limited my study. Given these problems, it is understandable that I rushed things in the adaptational period. The large amount of work facing me and the relatively short period of time I had to do it were facts I was conscious of throughout the study. I was pushing hard all the time, and this produced a state of mind not conducive to excellence in data gathering, particularly in the early periods of field work.

I could have obtained superior data had I been able to spend more money for paid assistants. Several of my special informants would have made first-rate research assistants, and I believe I could have got some of them to do this work for me during their non-busy farming periods. With extra funds I could have hired students and/or faculty from the College of Tropical Agriculture in Trinidad to do part-time research on the agricultural aspects of my study. Ideally, I should have spent the September through Christmas period doing *adaptational research*. Starting in January, 1958, I then could have had a complete year for active research. This additional time would have permitted more relaxed thinking time that could have been used to work out a superior comparative framework. A longer adaptational period would have probably changed my approach to village politics. Although I have argued for honesty in presenting one's self to one's subjects, my honesty in local politics should have been more subtle and less verbal. There were many political discussions in which I could have played a far more passive role than I actually did. Further, I could have presented my position less strongly and in a more comparative framework. That is, I could have said something like, "In my country I generally vote for the party that is more liberal and more socialistic in its approach to social problems. If I were a Trinidadian I would perhaps do the same. Given my limited knowledge of Trinidadian politics I guess I would support the P.N.M. However, I may be wrong about the benefits for Trinidad of P.N.M. politics."

The many problems I encountered in this study—how to design anthropological experiments, how to collect data for such, how to develop "rulers" (models) for comparing total systems, —had an unforeseen positive consequence, for they have provided me with work goals for the past ten years. Indeed, these problems are still foremost in my mind and may well keep me busy for another decade.

PART III: COMPARISONS BETWEEN MOHAWK AND TRINIDADIAN RESEARCH

The research done with the Mohawks and that done with the Trinidadian peasants was quite clearly very different in style, scope, and purpose. The sink-or-swim, get-your-own-tribe, participate-and-observe approach with the Mohawks was a common one for the graduate-student researcher in anthropology. Its manifest function was clearly to get research experience and raw data. Its latent function was (and perhaps still is) to weed out the anthropology-for-kicks student from the serious would-be professional. As an unsure graduate student relying more on energy and perspiration than education and inspiration, I did what appeared necessary in the Mohawk research: I went native. For various reasons, the Mohawk accepted me and allowed me to pick up crumbs of information pertaining to my research problem. During the actual field work I had difficulties playing my assumed role, "adopted" Mohawk, and I must have cut a strange figure to the Mohawk "warriors": the "chicken warrior."

Fortunately, and good fortune did indeed play an important part in the project, I did not have to tackle many of the problems of traditional anthropological research. I did not have to set up residence in a strange country and in a strange community, temporarily stop interacting with previous associates, learn a new language, or work in a sociopolitical environment foreign to my experience. For these reasons I did not have to bear the burden of culture shock—that strange feeling of anxiety that frequently attacks researchers working in very unfamiliar environments.

The Trinidadian research had as its dominant purpose getting material for a doctoral dissertation. In style, it therefore had much in common with the work of other doctors without dissertations. The attempts to do an experiment, to find a "natural laboratory," to test the Stewardian framework, and to diversify data-collecting methods are all aspects of the anthropologist who occupies a status somewhere in between student and professional. My secondary purposes were then, to do the "great study," to help make anthropology scientific, and to please my high-status friends (the members of my doctoral committee). That I should select a goal—to do a natural experiment—that was somewhat beyond my educational and experiential abilities is understandable in terms of my marginal status in anthropology. A possible adaptive mode for marginal role players in a system is to go beyond accepted standards to prove their worth to the system.

The Mohawk and Trinidadian research are examples of "secretive" versus "above-board" research, respectively. My work with Mohawks became fruitful when I dropped the role of anthropologist and assumed the role of Joe's sidekick. This kind of unorthodox field work had all the disadvantages generally attributed to it: no formal interviewing was possible, none of the Mohawks could be used as a field-work assistant, I had to be constantly wary of my notebook being discovered, and I could only minimally plan my work. That is, I had to adapt my data-getting procedures to the exigencies of Mohawk interaction and activities. The Trinidad work was distinctly different, and partly because of its "openness" it was much more enjoyable. The presentation of myself as a research anthropologist permitted me not only to use formal research techniques but also to develop a quasi-research organization in the field. What with my wife, Tina, Lee, and several very helpful special informants I had a "staff" that regularly provided valuable data. My role as research anthropologist could (and was) easily extended to include teaching anthropologist, and teaching the members of one's sample how to be good informants is a most rewarding field-work activity. (When the anthropologist assumes the role of "teacher in the field" he will probably also have to assume the role of pupil. After teaching them how to provide good data, the brighter informants in Anamat gave me instructions on how to be a more effective researcher.)

The Trinidad study was far from the perfect experiment. Indeed, ten years later I am still working on ways to achieve maximum control in anthropological experiments. However, this research, unlike the work with Mohawks, did go beyond the pilot-study stage. That is, a problem was presented in a solvable way, and data were collected that (ideally) could answer the questions posed. That my answer is far from definitive (see, Freilich 1960, 1963) does not imply that mine was merely a pilot study. Unlike a pilot study, which becomes more definitive with additional data-collecting activities, my study does not suffer from a lack of data. Its shortcomings stem rather from a lack of theoretical sophistication on my part as to what data to collect and how to use what I collected. When I analyzed my data, I did not know how to compare total systems. I thus was not able to state categorically that Creole and Indian peasant cultures in Anamat represent systems so significantly different that no causal effects can possibly be attributed to their shared mode of exploiting a basically similar environment. Nor could I say that systems similar to those of Anamatian Creoles and Indians in adapting to an environment similar to Anamat's by methods described in my study *would not* experience culture change due to their cultural-ecological adaptations. I am still hopeful that "lawlike" generalizations are possible in anthropology, and I still believe that anthropologists will have to do experimental work to arrive at laws of sociocultural change.

APPENDIX: QUESTIONNAIRES ADMINISTERED

Use of Time

1. What time does each person in the family rise in the morning?

2. Who prepares the meals? Gets water? Cooks? Washes up?

3. What time does each one leave the house for work? How long does it take to reach work?

4. What are the household tasks of each person living there?

5. What time is each meal? Who eats with whom at each meal?

6. What is usually eaten for tea, lunch, supper?

7. Does the family like wild meat better than shop meat?

8. How often is meat eaten?

9. Does anyone go fishing? How often? How often is fresh fish eaten? Are eggs liked at home?

10. How many eggs are used each week?

11. What time do grown-ups go to bed at night?

12. What things are done on Monday, Tuesday, Wednesday, Thursday, Friday, Saturday, Sunday? By each family person?

13. What sports do members of the house do? How often do they do it?

14. What is the busiest day of the week? Why?

15. What is the slowest day of the week? Why?

16. What day do you enjoy most? Why?

17. What day do you enjoy least? Why?

18. What time of day is enjoyed most? Why?

19. What time least? Why?

20. What month of the year do you like most? Why?

21. What month of the year do you like least? Why?

22. List the months in the order of your preference for them.

23. To what family gathering would some people from the house always go? Sometimes go?

24. Who would go in each case? Give preference: Who always? Who sometimes?

25. To what district gatherings would some people always go? Sometimes go? Who would go?

26. Who in the house has attended an Indian dinner (prayer meeting)? At whose house?

27. Who is the closest relative you have? Second closest? Third? Fourth? Fifth? (List as many as possible.)

28. How often do you see these people? Where? When?

29. Who visits you frequently? When?

30. Who do you visit? When?

31. Who do you like to be with best? Second best? Third best?

History and Agriculture

1. How much land do you work?

2. How much do you own?

3. How much do you rent?

4. How did you come by the land you own? How much was inherited? How much was purchased? Date of Purchase? From whom? Price? How much was paid in cash? How and when was balance paid?

5. How much land is owned jointly with other family members? With whom?

6. How would you describe the soil on your land?

7. What work do you regularly do on your land?

8. What work do you do that is seasonal?

9. Does your land have good drainage?

10. If not, why not? (Why don't you dig good drains and maintain good drains?)

11. What trees, plants, and shrubs do you have on your land? How many of the following?

Cocoa _____	Pewa _____	Coconut _____
Robusta coffee _____	Bread fruit _____	Cush-Cush _____
Arabica coffee _____	Pommecy-there _____	Dasheen _____
Banana _____	Avocado _____	Mango _____
Citrus fruits _____	Cashew _____	Mangosteen _____
Tonka beans _____	Cassava _____	Mahogany _____
	Cedar _____	Shatain _____
		Tania _____
		Yam _____

12. Any others?

13. From where did you get your agricultural knowledge?

14. Do you hire people to help you with some of your agricultural work? If Yes, why? If No, why not?

15. Who would you say are the best farmers in Anamat? What makes these people so good in agriculture?

16. Who are really poor farmers? What makes them so bad in agriculture? [My dichotomy of good versus poor farmers had to be changed. The Anamatians distinguished between poor, good, and very good farmers.]

17. How do you like agricultural work? [Here I probed on why this work was satisfying. This question usually led to a long discussion on such matters as the relative advantages of agriculture over other kinds of labor, the attitude of the "young generation" toward agriculture, and what the government should do to help farmers.]

Food and Budgets

1. How often is food bought? How much is bought?

2. How much is spent for clothes in a year, for yourself? How much for your wife? How much for the children?

3. How much is spent in a year for traveling and for fêting?

4. How often do you pay the shop?

5. How often do you make a big Sunday breakfast for friends or family? (For Indians, how often do you make a *puja*?)

6. How much does it usually cost you?

7. What is the biggest amount of credit you ever took?

8. Who controls money in the house? Who keeps it until it is needed? Who decides what to spend it on? Who is mainly responsible for saving?

9. Who goes to sell in the provision market? How often? How much money do you think you make a year from the market?

10. Do you buy more clothes for your family than your father did? Why?

11. Who entertained people in the house more, you or your father? Why?

12. In times of trouble, who would help you?

13. What things have you bought for the house in the past three years? Cash or credit?

14. Is there anything you are planning to buy for the house in the next few years? How will you pay for it?

15. Is there anything you are planning to get outside the house (like land or a new house)? How will you pay for it?

16. Who do you think will mind you when you are too old to work?

17. How much salary each two weeks would a person have to give you to get you to work in town?

18. What is the most money you ever had in your name in a bank book?

19. Do you expect your children will be richer than you? Why?

Mating, Marriage and Family

1. (a) "Better a good living than a bad marriage." Explain. (b) At what age should a man first live with a woman?

2. At what age should a woman first live with a man?

3. Which is better: trial or marriage right off? Why?

4. What benefit is there of the other?

5. What are the bad things about trial marriage?

6. How many trials should one make?

7. (a) Why don't some men get legally married? (b) "Marriage is a society." Explain. (c) Forgetting about the religious side, what is marriage?

8. Why won't some women get legally married?

9. Do you want your sons to make trial first? Why not daughters?

10. Why do men wish to marry? Why do women wish to marry?

11. Some couples lived together but never fought until they got legally married. Is this true? If so, why?

12. What should a man have before asking a woman to marry him legally? Why? Should any changes be made in an old place?

13. Who is supposed to bend more to make things work out? Why?

14. Is there any preference for marrying a virgin?

15. Is it better to marry a woman (or man) who has had many husbands (wives) before?

16. Why did you leave former wives (husbands)?

17. In whose house were the children brought up?

18. Whom did you ever advise to marry? Why?

19. Who ever tried to influence you to get legally married? Why?

20. If you had brought home any outside children, what would your mother say and do? Your father?

21. Does legal marriage make a man more respected?

22. What about a woman?

23. The difference between a natural child and a bastard is _____.

24. How old were you when you got your first keeper?

25. What are the duties of a keeper? Of a common-law husband? Of a mistress? Of a legal husband?

26. If you have no house of your own, where is it best to live?

27. Why are parents more vex (angry) if a daughter brings home a child than if a son does so?

28. Is American dating system better or here where girls meet boys in secret when they are living at their mother's house? Why or why not? What are advantages of each way? Bad things about each?

Religion and Magic

1. How many of the following functions have you attended in the past twenty-four months?

    a. Wakes. Whose, and who else from your family did go?

    b. Weddings. Where and who else from your family did go?

    c. Christenings. Whose and who else from your family did go?

    d. Prayer meetings (*pujas*). Whose and who else from your family did go?

    e. Any other big function. Whose and who else from your family did go?

2. The Christmas festivities usually cost you how much? (Give big items: liquor, food, clothes, furniture.)

3. How do you usually spend Good Friday? Easter Sunday? Easter Monday? Queen's Birthday? Carnival? St. Joseph's Day? Discovery Day? All Saints Day?

4. How do you keep a. *Magh Nahaan?* b. *Phagwa?* c. *Pitra Paksh* (lent)? d. *Devalli* (or *Lakhmi Puja*)? e. *Kartig Nahaan?* f. Are there any other Hindu Festivals, that you keep? Which ones? How?

5. Has prayer ever helped you or your family in times of trouble? Give examples. How often do you pray? For what reason?

6. Have dreams ever given you warnings? Foretold the future? Given you any other information?

7. How do you guard against *maljo* (the evil eye)? What can cure *maljo?* Why do some people usually get *maljo?* Did you or your family get it? From whom?

8. I know people who have been cured of different ailments by bush medicine. What bush has helped your family or you? Who got it and prepared it for you? How did they learn about this?

9. People have showed me *sukreyant* marks and have told me they saw *Papa Bois* and other spirits. Have you ever had any experience with these? Do you believe these people are telling the truth or lying? Explain.

10. Would you sleep in a cemetery for a whole night for a bet? Why, or why not?

11. Did you ever hear of the "Bucks of B.G.?" Was anyone you know ever helped by them?

12. Some people try to trick you out of money. How can one tell that an *Obeah* man really knows his science?

13. Why do you think God permits evil to stay in the world?

14. How can you prevent people working *Obeah* on you? What cures *Obeah?* Why are some people attacked this way?

15. How many pilgrimages have you been to in the last twenty-four months? Where to?

16. How many pilgrimages were you invited to and did not go? Why not?

Work

1. At what age did you leave school?

2. At what age did you work for a salary? Who got the money?

3. At what age did you keep your own salary? Why at this time?

4. At what age did you leave the house where you were brought up?

5. Do you work more hours each day than your father did? Why?

6. Do you work more days a week than your father did? Why?

7. How many times do you work on a Saturday afternoon? Why?

8. How many Sundays do you work during crop time? At other times?

9. Some men are very rich yet they still work hard. Are they foolish? Why?

10. How often does your wife help bring some money into the house? How often do your children?

11. A man should never work more than —— hours per day. Why?

12. If you won $50,000 on a sweepstake, how would that change your life (how would you live differently)?

13. What kind of work would you like your son to do, daughter?

14. "We should shoot work; kill him dead." Comment.

15. "To work hard is to be a slave." Comment.

16. When did you work hardest in your life?

17. Does hard work weaken a man's body?

18. In about 100 years from now machines will do all our work for us. (a) Will that be a good time to live in and why? (b) If things were like that today how would you pass the time away?

19. Why don't you want your sons to do agricultural work?

20. Do you like job work or day work better? Why?

Fêtes

1. How old were you when you started going around to (a) dances, (b) wakes, (c) prayers?

2. How often did you go to these before you got a wife (husband)?

3. How often are you in a fête these days?

4. Were you in many more in your younger days?

5. Some people get bad tempered when they drink and some get more cheerful and entertaining. How does rum affect you?

6. Did your father (mother) do more fêting in his time than you? Why?

7. How about your grandfather? (grandmother?)

8. Some say that when they fête they like to have a good fête man (woman) with them. What is a good fête man (woman)?

9. If you saved all that you spend, fêting, how much more money would you have today?

10. People say "Trinidad is a paradise." Do you agree? Why?

11. If a man earns $200 a month and it cost him $100 a month to eat and maintain his family, how much can he afford to spend on fête? Why?

12. Some people have money but don't enjoy it. Why make money if you can't enjoy it?

13. How often do you go to the pictures?

14. How often do you go to Sangre Grande? To Port-of-Spain? To the beach? To St. Benedict?

15. How often do you see family who live a good way off?

16. At whose house in Anamat did you ever take Sunday breakfast?

17. Work has to do with serious business; *fête* has to do with ————? (Informant was asked to complete this sentence)

18. How many godchildren do you have?

Income

1. Discuss yields from various crops.

2. Discuss income for the past six years. [Questions on income representing "sensitive" topics, were differently put to each informant, depending on my relationship with him and his mood at the time of the interview. Some informants with whom I had excellent rapport *were asked* for their records. Some others, after a long and tiring interview, made a statement such as "I'm too tired to go on with this; if you come back next week I'll have it all down on paper for you."]

OPEN NETWORKS AND NATIVE FORMALISM: THE MANDAYA AND PITJANDJARA CASES

Aram A. Yengoyan

The Mandaya of the Philippines and the Pitjandjara of western Australia have radically different cultural elements and social institutions and radically different ways of conceptualizing environmental and social phenomena. Among the Pitjandjara of the western desert of Australia, for instance, linguistic designations for marriage groupings and arrangements, tribal "segments," moieties, and semimoieties are widespread and clearly definable. Ideological conceptions of the Pitjandjara's social world are mental constructs that are verbally expressible.

The Mandaya of southeastern Mindanao, Philippines, however, present a different case, for they have no linguistic categories for territorial and social groupings. Yet, individuals and families combine for social action, form groups that are of a temporary nature, and get jobs done in a context in which permanent formal groupings for joint action are absent. Groups form to achieve certain ends and disband upon completion of the goals. In this situation, the ethnographer must analyze territorial groups and social activity in laymen's terms, not in Mandaya or social anthropological terms.

My research design, techniques, methods, and analysis differed in both cases, yet I did attempt to maintain a certain amount of standardization in them. There are types of data that are basic to social anthropology, and ideally the categorization and analysis of this information may lead to general propositions. I hope that in this comparison of two societies whose adaptational, ideological, and sociological modes of existence are markedly different I can make clear both the differences and the similarities in design, approaches, and analysis that characterize them.

PART I: THE MANDAYA

Problem, Theory, and Research Design

The Mandaya are a non-Islamic, non-Christian population inhabiting the eastern cordillera and coastal areas of the provinces of Davao, Agusan, and Surigao del Sur in Mindanao in the Philippines. Earlier accounts of the Mandaya indicate that they once numbered between 25,000 and 35,000 and represented one of the most powerful warring groups in eastern Mindanao. The only definitive account of the Mandaya is by Fay-Cooper Cole (1913), who spent seven months in the Davao Gulf area in 1910. Other early sources are Garvan (1931), the *cartas* of the early Jesuit missionaries, and various travel accounts.

My own work among the Mandaya took place from 1960 to 1962 and again in the summer of 1965.[1] By the early 1960s I knew something of the general features of Mandaya sociocultural organization, so my research did not start from scratch. My original problem was to enumerate and evaluate those spatial environmental variables such as rainfall, topography, soils, leaching processes, erosion, and vegetation that, as the popula-

[1] Financial support for the first field work (1960–1962) came from the Ford Foundation Foreign Area Training Fellowship Program. The Agricultural Development Council, New York, supported the 1965 field work.

tion adapts to them, effect observed variations in social organization. In other words, mine was an ecological study of shifting cultivation, and my problem was to qualify and quantify the major environmental and demographic factors that structure Mandaya social organization.

The Mandaya are shifting (i.e., swidden) cultivators of upland rice, root crops, vegetables, and fruits, and I hoped that my study would provide information applicable to Southeast Asian shifting cultivation, as well as a means of testing some general propositions on shifting cultivation set forth by Conklin (1957), Leach (1950), and Pelzer (1945). I also planned to make a detailed analysis of environmental factors as they relate to demographic composition, subsistence activities, and social units of exploitation.

I chose this particular problem and area for a number of reasons. First, traditional ecological approaches in anthropology have assumed that the presence of cultivation turns environment from a "limiting" into a "creative" factor in cultural development. It has been said that environmental influences on hunting-gathering societies mold a population's subsistence and social activity, but that with cultivation, even of a neolithic type, environment helps to develop new and varied cultural responses to different situations. Although this may be true in the over-all evolutionary perspectives of cultural growth, there are a number of shifting cultivation populations whose structures and responses are still regulated, directly or indirectly, by environmental factors. Furthermore, the socioeconomic unit of exploitation among shifting cultivators may be smaller and more flexible than the role of the band or horde in hunting and gathering societies. In comparing them, one finds a number of parallels between food-collecting peoples and simple food-producing economies that can be traced to environmental variables.

I chose eastern Mindanao and the Mandaya partly because of the lack of contemporary anthropological work in the area, and partly because Cole's and Garvan's earlier accounts suggested that the tribal peoples of eastern Mindanao are somewhat different from the tribal populations of western Mindanao (e.g., Subanun) in having an active warfare pattern and a political system based on organized warfare. Although warfare ended in the 1920s, I collected sufficient information from older informants to present in my doctoral dissertation (1964) a general description of warfare patterns and their relationship to man-land ratios.

One of the first tasks I undertook upon arriving in Mindanao was to survey the upland Mandaya areas on the Pacific coast cordillera from Mati, Davao, to Bislig, Surigao. I also surveyed

Mandaya areas near the upper Agusan River communities of Compostela and Monkayo. I collected survey information by hiking for six to eight weeks through the upland and coastal foothill areas of the eastern Davao municipalities of Mati, Manay, Caraga, Baganga, and Cateel, as well as Lingig and Bislig in Surigao, recording data as I went on cropping patterns, areas of cultivation, settlement size, routes of trade and exchange, and various traditional practices.

It soon became apparent to me that the Mandaya were no longer an economically homogeneous population. Along the eastern Mindanao coast and foothills, they were involved in the cultivation of abaca (Manila hemp) as a cash crop. The commercial commitment to abaca production varied with specific areas and within the same regional population. In most cases, they still cultivated rice and/or corn, though in a limited way, and they planted garden crops for subsistence.

My next problem was to decide which of the two modes of environmental and economic adaptation—the subsistence-based rice-cultivating upland area or the cash-oriented abaca-cultivating foothill area—to choose as my research site. My surveys indicated that I should study both areas if I wished to demarcate, analyze, and explain the organizational responses to varying ecological factors and external pressures. I chose, in 1960–1962, to analyze traditional Mandaya cultivation in the upland rice areas, and I returned in 1965 to study the foothill abaca areas.

Although on my first field trip I dealt primarily with the upland areas, I also collected comparative data on the foothill populations. I devoted the summer of 1965 to studying marketing networks and other economic processes among the abaca cultivators.

The eastern Mindanao coast is a high-rainfall zone where the basic contrast between wet and dry seasons is not marked. As one moves from the coast to the upland interiors, any wet-dry contrast becomes even less obvious. The upland groups around Pagpawan and Toacanga (upper Manay and Caraga) practice shifting cultivation, but, because of the extensive rainfall, they are unable to burn or "fire" the cut growth effectively.

The mean annual rainfall in the uplands for the period from January, 1961, to January, 1962, was 168 inches in 224 days of rain. The longest period without rain was five days, but this "dry spell" occurred only once in that twelve-month period. In the absence of "firing," there is, of course, a limited amount of ash return, and what ash there is has to be highly leached to extract the alkaline elements that are essential for rice cultivation. Thus, I realized that I must alter my original research design to account for these variations in terms of man-hour/

yield ratios, man-hours per swidden cycle, labor outputs, and total yields per swidden.

With my surveys completed and my original problem and research design reanalyzed, I had to choose a specific locality for study. The typical situation was represented by the eastern cordillera population, who had not had intensive contact with the lowland Bisayans. Most of the Mandaya in the upper Agusan River drainage were involved in a lowland social network. With the exception of Mati municipality, none of the other four east-coast municipalities are connected to one another by roads. The only means of transportation between east-coast settlements are outrigger powerized *bancas* or launches carrying copra, hemp, food supplies, and commercial items among the settlements.

Environment of the Group

I selected the upland areas of Manay and Caraga municipalities for study. The uplands (generally called Pagpawan) could be reached from the coast in a two- or three-day hike. Furthermore, the upland rice-cultivation systems were operative, and the Mandaya were not yet fully involved in the lowland Philippine social system that characterizes many of the coastal towns and villages. Also access to Mati and the other east-coast municipalities was still possible.

In eastern Mindanao cocoanuts are farmed on the coastal lowlands and in the mangrove swamps; grasslands and secondary forest rise to an elevation of 1,500 feet in the foothill areas; and the interior uplands are of mixed primary and secondary forest growth. With the exception of the Baganga and Cateel areas, the flat coastal lowlands are not very extensive, since the foothills at times approach the Pacific Ocean. A number of rivers and streams originating in the uplands dissect the foothills, and communication in the foothills is generally difficult for this reason. In the foothills are small-scale dispersed abaca cultivators who also grow rice, corn, root crops, and vegetables. Upland areas are mountainous, thickly forested, and marked by swift flowing streams and rivers that empty into the Pacific Ocean. The high rainfall in the uplands creates exceedingly muddy and damp conditions.

The settlement pattern of the upland Mandaya rice cultivators makes it difficult for the ethnographer to move from one family to another, since nuclear families occupy a single dwelling that is adjacent to their swidden (rice field). Swiddens are occupied for only one cultivation cycle, thus each family changes its residence every year. I found that the combination one-family one-household one-field one-year occurred 96.4 percent of the time during the 1960–1962 period. Because the population is scattered, highly distributed, and mobile, I spent a vast amount of time hiking from one household to another. (Households are anywhere from a half-kilometer to two kilometers apart.) Compact population clusters with fields radiating from them are emerging in some of the foothill populations, where sedentarization is increasing due to the intensive cultivation of abaca, but in the uplands I often felt frustrated when I tallied up the time I spent in just getting from household to household.

When town officials asked me what the reasons were for my prolonged stay in the area, I explained to them, as well as to the uplanders, that I was interested in investigating the problems and methods of shifting cultivation (*kaingin*) in terms of crop productivity, labor, exchanges, and related matters. They assumed from this that I was concerned with such practical ends as how to increase rice production and control *mosaic* (a virus that seriously debilitates abaca plants). I was never squarely confronted with specific questions on these practical matters, and in most cases I attempted to avoid such discussions. Since national and provincial officials have shown no interest in the east-coast Davao populations, my presence and investigations were assumed to be of some benefit. Furthermore, most lowland people in the Philippines were friendly toward Americans in 1960–1962, when the CIA scare had not permeated to these rural areas. In 1965 one of the village teachers asked me if I had any connection with the CIA. Friendliness toward Americans has markedly decreased in the past few years.

Active Research

After I stated my general and vague field aims, the town officials agreed to provide assistance, and through them and Catholic missionaries in the towns of Manay and Caraga I had an entrée to householders in the uplands. Although uplanders have little permanent contact with coastal populations, most of them acquire certain material goods such as kerosene and clothing from foothill and coastal merchants.

I settled in Capasnan, because, first, it was on the main trail to Toacanga and Lemento-og and had access to foothill abaca-cultivating communities. Also, Capasnan provided environmental and economic variation in terms of differential forest cover, varying field sizes, and cropping patterns.

An abandoned dwelling in Capasnan was loaned to me by one of the older and better known household heads. Although the owner continuously rejected any form of payment or service for the dwelling, I gave him a number of small gifts such as kerosene lamps, liquor, Chinese medicinal wine, and canned goods.

My house, like all houses in Mandaya, was perched atop a dozen or so posts about six feet above the ground. The walls and roofs were constructed of native grasses and palms woven and matted together. The walls and roofs usually last about a year, since they decay quite rapidly in that humid climate. When the householder moves to a new swidden site, he takes with him the pilings and the roof beams.

One of my major problems was obtaining food. Since the uplanders are on a subsistence economy, staples cannot be purchased for long-term use. Rice accounts for less than half of the yearly family diet, with root crops providing the bulk of family subsistence needs. I bought rice, canned goods, and catsup in Manay town and transported them to Capasnan by horseback or human carriers. (Catsup was an important part of my diet, if for nothing more than to make the food palatable.) For nearly six months I obtained most of my subsistence needs from Manay, except for root crops, fruits, and vegetables. As time went on, this method of obtaining food became so time consuming that I abandoned it, except for two necessities, catsup and liquor.

Conversing in Mandaya took longer than I expected, and initially I used an interpreter. When my proficiency increased, the interpreter's function became less important, but I was never able to dispense with him entirely. Mandaya is fairly close grammatically to Cebuano, the *lingua franca* of eastern Mindanao, and learning Cebuano in the field facilitated communication and allowed me to "plug in" Mandaya vocabulary when needed.

I usually had two assistants in the field. One was an Illongo speaker from Cotabato, who had accompanied me on my early surveys and whose reliability I had already assessed, and the other was a Mandaya in his mid-twenties, who was well known to both the uplanders and the foothill populations. I first met Gerardo, my Illongo field assistant, in Compostela, a logging town in Northern Davao Province, when I was visiting personal friends there. Since my salaries for field assistants were better than labor wages, the young man agreed to assist me during my field work, provided I would use my contacts in Davao City to guarantee him a job after the work was fully completed. Malang, my Mandaya assistant, was recommended to me by the elders in Pagpawan as one who was reliable and perceptive, though somewhat restless. I paid equal salaries to both assistants. As time went on, Gerardo and Malang were anxious for me to discuss my observations and ideas with them, which I readily did. I found this type of discourse most fruitful in checking my "ethno-bias."

I had almost no trouble with either assistant, for they had different roles to play in terms of the Pagpawan uplanders and so there was no conflict or competition between them. The assistance provided by each differed depending on what types of problems were being investigated. Malang, who lived with his parents and spent most nights in my house or out courting young girls, provided information on gossip, gambling coalitions during the post-harvest period, and marital problems and feuds among the uplanders. I rechecked most of his observations to assess their reliability. Gerardo helped me to obtain quantified data on yields, acreage, and labor exchange.

Establishing Rapport

Problems of rapport are difficult to enumerate and discuss. For one thing, rapport is always being "gained" and "lost," so one never feels that rapport problems have been surmounted. In the initial stages of the work, people knew that I was interested in methods and problems of cultivation and other sociocultural factors affecting the modes of subsistence. At the time, rats were plaguing the uplands of Manay and Caraga and significantly reducing rice yields, and many felt that my interest in cultivation might alleviate the condition. Because many welcomed me on this account, rapport was easily established. The quality of the uplanders' responses was "restricted," by which I mean that their replies, comments, and statements were only in terms of precisely what I asked—nothing more or less. The general attitude of the Mandaya, as I perceived it, was that the sooner I obtained the information I required, the sooner I would have a "solution" to their problem.

At first, I established rapport primarily through the male elders in Pagpawan, who introduced me to different household members and explained why I was there. These introductions became unnecessary after a while, for my presence and purpose were soon widely known. When interviewing a respondent for the first time, I always inquired about crops, cropping activities, and techniques utilized, for I found these topics provided the best means to start my work. In all conversations throughout the entire project I inquired first about particular events or acts and gradually moved into abstract realms. The Mandaya are very detail conscious and always asked me if I had recorded all details correctly. On the level of generalizations where rules are not always rigidly applied, the Mandaya often throw out statements for debate. In group interviewing, the discussions and disputes that resulted from such general statements were most fruitful in revealing how various individuals perceived the social alignments of which they were a part. I participated in these general discussions by reviewing past cases and observing how interpretations of what had happened changed, depending on the flow of the conversation.

One of the best examples of this process is litigation. There are few hard and fast rules or legal norms that cover many cases, but the particulars of how cases are settled are important, and the various contestants in litigation will bring up those cases that are relevant to the point they are making, using them to support their position. I had recorded a number of cases and could use these to argue against the Mandaya to understand how they would respond. The details in each particular case are spelled out very clearly, and the focus is on those cases from which a general settlement emerges. In future cases pertaining to similar problems, the principle of settlement is not utilized, but the particular cases are cited again.

After three or four months, most uplanders felt that I was saturated with information and would depart. But problems and questions led to new inquiries. Furthermore, during this period, I had participated in a series of the drinking bouts that accompany most rituals. My participation in these sessions markedly increased my rapport with the Mandaya, and my fame spread far beyond the confines of the area of investigation.

By expressing an interest in and striking up a conversation about such "neutral" subjects as cultivation techniques, flora, fauna, and cropping patterns, I eventually led the Mandaya into more subjective and personal aspects of their social life. The only major concern of my informants was that I would turn over my data on field sizes and yields to the tax officials. This doubt did not fade during the entire 1960–1962 period. On my second trip to Manay in 1965, however, the doubt had been assuaged, since no increase in taxation had occurred during my three years' absence.

Once my general purpose was known to the Mandaya males, I was able to proceed with my investigation of shifting cultivation and its social concomitants. With the assistance of my field associates, I collected information on interaction networks, exchanges, and "neighborhoods." Most Mandaya could not conceptualize why I wanted to know who talks with whom about what, or whom one asks for services and loans. In general, the more abstract my inquiries became, the slower were the responses. To maintain what rapport I had achieved and to expand my inquiries to new topics, I unconsciously and consciously changed the directions of my probings, switching from abstract topics to more concrete ones, such as the number of rice varieties planted, what a "good" harvest means, types of wild foods collected, medicinal plants and their uses, and forecasts on rain. Inquiries of this type evoked wide enthusiasm; young boys even began to collect wild foods and medicinal herbs for me. Once their interest was partially restored, I moved again into more abstract realms. My respondents would discuss and argue over most of my questions, and a few with whom I became very close gave me deep insight into these matters.

With Mandaya women, rapport was very poor. Female *ballyan* (part-time medical practitioners and mediums) either limited their conversations with me or totally avoided me. Even in questioning them about "neutral" subjects such as the time spent in planting, husking rice, and so forth, their replies were short and uninformative. Furthermore, females systematically kept me from observing the rituals surrounding the planting and harvesting of rice. In most cases, these rituals were held in areas inaccessible to me, or I was told about them after they were over. This secretiveness among the females was most effective in excluding me from these areas of Mandaya culture.

During no time in the field did I so much as consider obtaining a female field assistant. Since I was unmarried at the time, hiring a female assistant would have implied that I wanted her services for purposes beyond my basic field interests. To avoid gossip on such matters, I seldom dealt directly with females and interviewed them only in the presence of their husbands, male siblings, or fathers. My behavior was interpreted as a sign that I was a homosexual, since in the eyes of the locals all men at my age (twenty-five) should have access to an occasional female companion. I had none, and this bothered some people.

The rapport I gradually gained with the females of Mandaya was severely damaged in July, 1961, when a *hadji* (Muslim religious teacher) came to the eastern Davao coast.[2] Although the Mandaya are in general a non-Islamic population, in Davao some Mandaya communities around Mayo Bay were converted to Islam during the late nineteenth century, but this conversion did not entail that the converts completely deny their original tradition. Islamic and Mandaya supernatural categories are basically the same, but the former's are more embracing and more powerful. The female *ballyan* asked me to tell the *hadji* to go away because his activities would disrupt the existing cultural life, but I refused to do so, for I believed that his presence

---

[2] The Mandaya use the term *hadji* to mean a proselytizer for Islam. Among Muslim populations, *hadji* refers to the pilgrimage to Mecca.

would have little impact on the Mandaya culture. Nevertheless, I was tagged by the females as not being concerned about Mandaya modes of life. For six or eight months after this event, I was continuously kept from observing rituals and other major religious activities, except for the ceremonial sacrifices that accompany the planting and harvesting of each swidden. The males recognized what was occurring, joked about it to me, and told me not to worry for all would soon be healed. The breach was, however, never completely healed.

I refused the *ballyan*, because I felt that it was not my concern to force the situation. In the past, other *hadji* had come to Pagpawan, and their impact had always been short-lived and superficial. My involvement would have disrupted a previous pattern and might have generated the *hadji's* antagonisms toward the Pagpawan population and me with the possible long-range effects of more rigorous proselytization. Although I was thereafter ostracized from religious activities, I still think that my course of action was the only choice I had.

On my second trip in 1965, the females were somewhat more open, but they were still uncertain about my intentions. Needless to say, my information on women's activities, except in regard to rice cultivation and economic activities, is poor or nil.

Data-Gathering Techniques

I used various techniques to obtain and record data. I employed a standard questionnaire for collecting information on each rice field (swidden) occupied or recently occupied. This questionnaire contained mainly inquiries that could be quantified or answered with a simple Yes or No. Information on rice yields, crops grown, and varieties per crop was gleaned from the questionnaire. Besides providing a useful as well as simple means for collecting and combining vast amounts of quantified data, the questionnaire allowed me to go through my data periodically to recheck certain features and to determine how these features were related to other phenomena. Although the questionnaires were most useful in gathering data amenable to quantification, they took a good deal of time to administer. In most cases, they could not be fully completed in a single encounter with an informant. Usually informants became restless after an hour of interviewing, and most questionnaires took three or four meetings with an individual before they were fully worked out. The ideal is a fully completed and perfected questionnaire, but only seldom did I obtain a significant number of completed schedules.

I also took a genealogical census covering every family in

the district. This census permitted me to infer changes in mobility and interaction among kinsmen and nonkinsmen. The aim of a genealogical census is to obtain data on a particular individual and to note his relationships with kin and nonkin, but the real strength of this approach depends on the extensiveness of the information collected. Primarily, one collects information on a respondent and all his kinsmen, fictive and nonfictive, in terms of birthplace, age, sex, occupation, marriage (wife's name, family, when married, where married and circumstances of marriage, number of offspring per wife, and living offspring), source and amount of income and what the respondent thinks is the source and amount of income of his kin, expectations of services, inheritance, support, and friendship from others and vice versa, the property held by others, and the kind, amount, location, disposition, and possible inheritance of the property by the respondent.

Within this approach, the respondent not only lists his relationships to others, but relates how he views each of these individuals in terms of the categories listed above. I attempted in this broad collection of data to get away from the relatively static approach that usually plagues the collection and interpretation of genealogies. As the respondent places himself within the larger context of kin, fictive kin, and nonkin, he defines his own social position and enumerates his expectations of and demands on others and of others on him. Since the Mandaya population is highly mobile, this genealogical data allowed me to evaluate the importance of kin relations vis-à-vis spatial distribution in determining how each respondent manipulates the surrounding human resources.

I conducted most open-ended interviewing during the evenings, since the natives worked in their fields during the day. My house in Capasnan became a nightly meeting place for most males. Nearly every night anywhere from two to ten men would come over and spend a few hours talking, smoking, and drinking. My kerosene lamp, flickering in the darkness until 10 or 11 P.M., as well as a good supply of tobacco and liquor, induced them to stop by to talk about their activities and my work. I also did most of my intensive interviewing in this setting. With the pressures of daily activity at a minimum, the men could relax and talk.

In most cases, two or three men would listen in as I administered the questionnaire or conducted interviews on points of mutual interest. Most questions were not discussed by the bystanders, but some inspired great interest in all concerned. Long discussions resulted from questions on bride price, bride service, amounts paid in various cases, and, most important, divorce and its social consequences. Divorce is rare among the upland Mandaya, and the men usually had little or no precedent in arguing from and for different positions.

Other occasions also permitted interviewing and group discussion. During rice rituals many distant families gathered for collective activity, accompanied by the drinking of rum, Chinese medicinal wine, and *tuba* (fermented cocoanut sap). In fact, these settings were most important for obtaining primary information and for observing the responses of others to my questioning and the arguments that certain points sometimes provoked. These discussions and arguments never resulted in a consensus, which is indicative of how the Mandaya view the decision-making process. As the Mandaya conceptualize it, a consensus does not occur naturally; thus they see no reason for striving for it. Each person states and holds a position to the bitter end.

Other forms of activity permitted observation. After the final rice harvest and prior to the selection of a new swidden site, Mandayas from various neighborhoods meet in a central location within the *bagani* domain for feasting, dancing, courting, and gambling. Gambling is a favorite pastime, but it is only during the postharvest period that the intensity of betting reaches its peak. Betting on cock fights is widespread in the uplands, as is betting on painted bones or match sticks and their various possible combinations. Nearly all male household heads within a domain participate to varying degrees in these gambling bouts, which may last for five or six days.

Gambling often determines coalition formations and differential support of individuals. Nearly all men who have harvested rice or who own extra pigs or chickens utilize these food items for gambling. Initially, the process of sorting out the early losers is swift. As the players gradually lose segments of their harvest, they shift their bets and resources to another player who is known to be an astute gambler. This pooling of resources occurs after the first day. After the first three days, only six or eight players out of perhaps as many as eighty survive. It is at this point that the real drama starts, since the surviving participants become more cautious and continuously re-evaluate their resources and strategy. The Mandaya claim that the ideal gambling bout ends when one man, or at most two, controls the full range of goods that were bet from the initial play. If this end is realized, all those who backed the winner at various stages claim what they contributed and what their capital acquired in the winning process. In actuality, most of the earnings of the winners are redistributed so that each player regains his original investment. Gambling may thus be interpreted as a means not of financial gain, but of demonstrating male skill and prowess.

I did not directly participate in gambling for a number of reasons. First, the rules of play were unknown to me, and I did not wish to hold up the activity while someone explained them to me. But more important, I think that my active participation would have made the other players self-conscious about what they did and who they backed in varying circumstances. Through observation I was able to capture the picture and process of gambling and its socioeconomic structure. One of my assistants participated in the gambling with two sacks of *humay* (unhusked rice), which I contributed. He was eliminated within the early rounds, but was told by the elders that if I would contribute more rice he would be readmitted. I was regarded as an unending source of food items, which was not the case.

Observing the gambling permitted me to evaluate the differential importance of kinship relations, space, and skill in the process of temporary coalition formations. Everyone knows who the most skilled gamblers are, but the shifting of resources to various parties does not take place until at least half of the original contestants are eliminated. The first coalitions among individuals are based on spatial factors, with individuals residing within the same neighborhoods pooling resources as each individual thinks his end is in sight. As players are gradually eliminated, the bonds of kin and space give way, and the onlookers support men who are the most skilled and whose resources are not in jeopardy of dwindling.

Techniques for recording and storing data. I did not record questionnaire data in duplicate, and this was a mistake, for had I lost the data I would not have been able to reconstruct it from memory. All field notes should always be recorded in duplicate or even triplicate. Extra copies should be mailed to someone who can store your notes until your return from the field. The duplicating of questionnaire information is a tedious job, but it should be done.

I recorded interviews by hand, then wrote them up in a legal-size ledger. I cross-listed all cases so I would have a check on how information collected in one interview fitted with other interview information. I made carbon copies of all recorded interviews. I did not use a tape recorder in the field, but recorded observation in a small notebook for transcription at a more convenient time.

I recorded most data on punch cards (Unisort Analysis Card, Burroughs, Form Y-9). These 5″ × 8″ punch cards are easily stored in metal or cardboard file boxes. Each card contains information for a particular culture category. The information is typed directly on the card and the attached carbon. After the data are typed in, each card is punched with a hand-punch. Form Y-9 has ninety-one single categories; thus an almost infinite variety of possible combinations can be punched. The establishing of categories and their numerical designations requires one to maintain category uniformity throughout the study. I originally started out with forty to fifty categories, but as my work progressed, I abandoned some of the original categories as unnecessary and subdivided other categories into finer units. For example, I found the category "native flora" much too broad; more precise designations were needed. After four or five months of field work, I had established categories that I maintained throughout the study. In most cases, a particular card was punched for three or four categories, but in other cases the full range of a social event might require up to ten particular categories.

The great advantage of hand-punch cards is that the data are not particularized or atomized into smaller meaningless units. Each event, observation, or fact is typed directly onto the cards as it occurs, and thus the unity of the event is maintained. Yet the categorization allows the researcher to determine how certain phenomena, such as household economic output, are related to, say, interaction with various kinsmen. If these data are recorded in a regular notebook, then a number of cross-listings with other items is necessary. The punch-card method avoids excessive cross-numbering in numerous notebooks, yet allows one to analyze the notes easily when needed. With a hand sorter, one can go through his notes quickly in attempting to get at what information he has on a particular phenomenon and how it relates to other events. The cost of cards, punch, and hand sorter amounted to $30 in 1960.

All typed cards should be punched immediately and filed in the appropriate category. One thus has access to his notes at all times, whereas the recording of information in more sophisticated ways requires expensive, nonportable, and highly technical machinery.

I recorded genealogies on wrapping paper, listing precise information on each individual on separate sheets under a numerical designation. Most of my genealogies are woefully incomplete. With the high rate of population mobility, most families moved out of neighborhoods before I could recheck particulars. Also, by mistake, I took several genealogies twice.

I found it profitable to take one or two breaks during my field stay. This permitted me to reassess my original problem and to reread my notes in order to discern common features and patterns. By staying too close to the data at all times, the field worker may miss the larger setting until it is too late to recheck important events and facts. During the 1960–1962 trip, I took a number of short breaks down to Manay town or to Davao City. These short trips are also beneficial for maintenance of sanity. They permitted me to get in touch with the outside by reading newspapers, writing letters, drinking cold beer, and talking to the inhabitants of Manay about recent national and international political events. I found myself reading novels of various types in the field and would suggest that each field worker take a number of cheap paperback volumes with him. The reading of nonanthropological materials may provide a balance to one's becoming emotionally and intellectually overextended.

If possible, copies of notes should be sent to someone who knows about your work and topic, and who will read them and return comments and constructive criticism. The perceptions of another worker are unique and useful in posing new problems for investigation.

Departing from the field in 1962 was not traumatic. When I made preparations to leave, a number of men hinted that they would like any items that I was abandoning. I announced that I would dispose of my possessions but only when a number of people were present. I distributed these items a few days before my departure, taking no payment for them, since their value was practically nil. Yet, my turning over of the commodities to the males was in a way a token payment for their assistance in my field work. I had paid none of my informants in cash or goods, though I had distributed tobacco and occasionally liquor generously. A few women sought my kerosene lamps, which I gave to them.

I knew that the men with whom I was on very friendly terms were discussing the matter of my return among themselves. During my last week, they asked me if I would return. I told them that I would like to come back in three or four years, but that I would spend most of my time investigating abaca cultivation in the foothill areas. Most of them could not accept my plans for returning and laughed at my answer.

On the day of my departure a number of men and boys accompanied me to Manay town. They stayed in Manay for a few days until my plans were finalized. I gave my United States address to a few town merchants and a Catholic priest in Manay in case someone wanted to contact me. In April, 1962, I left Manay for Davao City.

During the interim period from 1962 to 1965, I occasionally received letters from coastal people relating recent events among the upland Mandaya. I also received requests for shoes, with tracings of feet enclosed, during my three-year absence. A number of these requests were filled.

In 1965 I returned to upper Manay, much to the surprise of the Mandaya. Acquaintances were renewed with little difficulty. The uplanders gave me running accounts of the past years' happenings. Field work during the second trip was much easier, since I knew how to avoid preliminary problems and mistakes. Since my departure in 1965 I have received letters on recent events and still maintain contact with a few coastal families.

Summary

As noted earlier, my original intention was to make an ecological study of upland rice cultivation with emphasis on how environmental variables influence social organization and spatial mobility. After surveying the eastern Davao coast, I selected the Mandaya of Upper Caraga and Manay for study. I found, however, that upland Mandaya shifting cultivation is not typical of this part of Mindanao due to the wet climate, which precludes the normal burning process in the agricultural cycle. My interest focused, therefore, on a descriptive analysis of the cultivation system and its relationships to labor, production, and environmental factors. I found that variations in cultivation patterns and microenvironmental factors were related to socioeconomic units and neighborhood networks. Great population mobility and the absence of permanent social units and cognized spatial groupings reflect the demands of the cultivation system. Upland rice-cultivating may thus be regarded as an adaptation to environmental factors that combine to produce an intricate and infinite number of microenvironmental niches.

The upland rice systems are a segment of a larger complex. Shifting cultivation exists in the densely forested uplands, but the foothill Mandaya have adapted to the grasslands and secondary forest growth by cultivating abaca. Abaca production requires a new and different set of capital inputs along with increasing involvement in a semipeasant market economy. Participation in a cash economy in turn generates new demands on the household economy. In 1965, I began my work among the abaca cultivators to determine the full range of change in Mandaya social structure resulting from the economic readaptation to a new productive base. I also investigated abaca-marketing networks and other economic processes, such as the ability of household units to withhold goods and activity or interaction from the market and how price or market knowledge was obtained by household units who are not in direct daily contact with the markets in Manay, Santiago, or Caraga. Partial results of this work on rice and abaca cultivation have been published (Yengoyan, 1964, 1965, 1966a, 1966b, 1966c, and in press).

One of the major problems in working with cognatic societies like the Mandaya is determining group structure. The only Mandaya verbal category pertaining to social groups is the term for *family*. Beyond the family, there are no formal cognized social units that are capable of being linguistically blocked and verbally expressed. Domains are demarcated by natural features. The term for kindred *(kalumonan)* is verbally expressed, but it is the widest recognized kin category and is not a group. In situations like this, one must *induce* group structure by investigating interaction patterns—finding out who interacts with whom, when, why, and how often. Social networks and interaction rates must be abstracted from the detailed collecting and analyzing of sociograms.

How are these data, which cannot be attached to a formally cognized social structure, expressed? What kinds of units or groupings are utilized? In the Mandaya case, I have had to use terminology from layman's English rather than from the language of anthropology to express these relationships. I have used the terms *neighborhood* and *community* by defining them with reference to my analysis of the data. Formal anthropological categories are primarily social categories pertaining to groups based on kinship, descent, and marriage principles. For the most part, the vocabulary of social anthropology has few terms for groups based only on spatial principles.

If I were to redo my field work among the Mandaya, I think I would investigate a number of different problems and approach others in a different way. I would put more emphasis on learning the language, and on determining how individuals cognize their social and natural environments and how their cognition influences their realm of choice. In tackling this problem, I would investigate economic activities and environmental factors, articulation with neighboring social units, and the perception of rituals and their importance in noneconomic activities. In most cases, the Mandaya formally express ideal relationships with little allowance for variation. In actuality, the organizational level of activity is flexible enough to permit a wide range of choice as a means of achieving certain ends. How the Mandaya view this discrepancy and reconcile it—verbally and socially—is a major problem that needs investigation. A detailed knowledge of the language and of how linguistic categories influence verbal permutations, perceptions, and behavior is crucial and of the utmost interest.

PART II: THE PITJANDJARA

Problem, Theory, and Research Design

The Pitjandjara are an aboriginal people living in the western desert of central Australia. At present the Pitjandjara are scattered throughout the southern half of the western desert from Jigalong to Warburton Mission (West Australia), to the northwest areas of the state of South Australia, and north to Areyonga native settlement in the Northern Territory. My own work among the Pitjandjara was in South Australia from the Tomkinson Ranges east to Ernabella Mission and north to the Petermann Ranges. The native groups in this area are not unknown in anthropological literature. The early works of Basedow (1914, 1925) were followed with more definitive studies into various aspects of social anthropology. Elkin (1931, 1938–1940) has worked on kinship and social structure, Tindale (1935, 1936, 1959, 1963, 1965) on material culture, mythology, and initiation, and Mountford (1950, 1965) on legends and art.

I worked among the Pitjandjara from May, 1966, to June, 1967.[3] The Pitjandjara are fairly well known among the Australian aborigines, so I undertook a detailed study of certain social phenomena. My project goals were as follows:

1. To reconstruct and ascertain the nature of precontact local organization and more inclusive sociogeographic units. Since local organization represents a key relationship between social structure and environmental exploitation, this segment of the project would provide data on how local units adapted to varying environmental factors, both spatially and seasonally.

2. To investigate the demographic structure of various groups and how these factors are related to variations in certain aspects of social organization, such as marital arrangements and section systems. Factors such as sex ratios, age structure, marriage rates, marriage ages, fertility and mortality rates, number of eligible females per male at any one time, etc., are crucial in assessing such questions as the number of required females for optimal operation of certain marital arrangements, the nature and functioning of connubiums, the spatial distribution of eligible mates

---

[3] The Australian Institute of Aboriginal Studies supported the field work during this period. Transportation to and from Australia was provided by the Australian-American Educational Foundation (Fulbright).

and variations in prescriptive marriage patterns, and changes in social organization due to population fluctuation.

I wanted to investigate the first problem described above because local organization is the articulating unit between social organization and environmental factors. The typical and ideal description of aboriginal Australian local organization was originally set forth by Radcliffe-Brown (1913, 1918, 1930) and emphasized in a general context by Steward (1936, 1955) and Service (1962). Radcliffe-Brown's description of the patrilineal, exogamous, territorially based horde has recently been reviewed by Meggitt (1962) and Hiatt (1965), who claim that aboriginal local organization was not as structured as Radcliffe-Brown claimed and in fact that its composition and structure varied over time and space.

Although local organization in the western desert is no longer operative, this change has occurred only within the past twenty years. It is still possible to reconstruct ethnographically local group areas with the assistance of tribal elders who have recently come in from the bush. Important water sources and totemic sites can be mapped with a degree of assurance, but the evaluation of group composition and changes have to be recorded with great care. This problem will be discussed later. The focus on local organization was primarily designed to contribute additional data on this topic and the ongoing discourse on aboriginal local groupings (Stanner, 1965; Hiatt, 1966).

I chose my second problem because I have had a long-term interest in demographic analysis. Although most demographic measures and indexes cannot be utilized in small societies due to limited samples and poor data, the determination of basic population characteristics is critical to an understanding of social phenomena. This approach is not new; many scholars have discussed the relevance of demographic interconnections, but detailed descriptions are generally not available. Furthermore, Rose (1960) has provided an excellent ethnographic description of Wanindiljaugwa marriage categories, age classification, and sex distribution. His account is probably one of the first sources that demonstrate how demographic factors influence the operation of marriage rules. My own goal was to investigate similar factors in a population living in geographic and climatic surroundings different from the semitropical, densely populated Wanindiljaugwa, who live on Groote Eylandt in the Gulf of Carpentaria. In 1968, I published a preliminary investigation of the interrelationships between population size and the statistical confirmation of marriage rules, but this work was not based on my 1966–1967 field data.

In the field I followed my original research design with only minor modifications, although collecting population data was difficult for a number of reasons, the major one being that the Pitjandjara were not interested and/or did not know what I was getting at. In most cases, direct questioning on this subject was nearly impossible. A fuller discussion of the methods I used in my demographic analysis will be given later.

Analyzing local organization also proved difficult. I could transmit to the aborigines some notion of spatial entities and geographic units, and in general the tribal elders showed interest in mapping out various areas. The composition of residential groups was difficult to determine, but I tested my reconstructions to my satisfaction in a case involving the mining of chrysoprase (Australian jade) in the Mt. Davis area.

The Mandaya had had a general interest in my work since it overlapped with their own interests, but my field interest in demographic analysis and the determination of social categories was not shared by the Pitjandjara. The tribal elders were concerned, almost imbued, with the past in terms of mythology, legends, rituals, the dreamtime, and a complex symbolism.

The Environment of the Group

In the Musgrave-Tomkinson-Petermann Ranges, the average rainfall is six to ten inches per year, and thus the area is classified as a desert, though it is very different from the deserts of North Africa. In only a few localities (e.g., the Simpson desert) does one find sand-swept dunes with a complete absence of vegetation. Average rainfall figures mean little in terms of the floral and faunal composition, but drought is the rule and rain the exception. When I started field work in 1966, the center's desert flowers, grasses, scrub, and trees were responding to rainfall after a severe drought of six or eight years. Even in a wet cycle, however, vegetation is sparse. Low-lying scrub and grasses are most typical of the Musgrave area. Vast stretches of spinifix grass *(Triodia aristata)* and mulga trees *(Acacia aneura)* are common, and desert oaks *(Casuarina decaisneana)* and gum trees *(Eucalyptus rostrata, Eucalyptus papuanus)* are interspersed in sand hills and creek beds, respectively.

Faunal composition and density vary with the vegetation cover. Fauna native to the area—kangaroos, emus, euros, dingoes, rabbits, wild camels, and lizards—is in short supply, but the aborigines are able to detect species of nearly all genera by tracking dung droppings. The exploitation of fauna for subsistence is regarded as man's work, although the importance of game in the daily precontact diet was not as significant as vegetable foods, which were and still are gathered by women. However, fauna is of utmost importance in myth, ritual, and daily conversation.

The Musgrave Ranges, like most of the ranges in the western desert, are not very high, but in a land where salt pans, flat terrain, and gently rolling hills provide a routine uniformity, almost any unsual peak is named and stressed for purposes of direction. Most of the ranges contain water in the form of creeks, rock pools, and natural dams. Creeks are normally dry, but, in general, surface waters are obtainable by digging a six-to-eight-foot well. An excellent description of the environment of the Musgrave-Mann-Petermann Ranges is provided by Finlayson (1936).

Most of the states in Australia maintain reserves for their aboriginal populations; aborigines are, however, free to leave any reserve at any time. To work on a reserve, one must first obtain a permit from the organization that handles aboriginal affairs. Prior to arriving in Australia, I had obtained the necessary permits for my wife, my daughter, and myself from the Department of Aboriginal Affairs in Adelaide. These permits were checked on our arrival in Adelaide before we were allowed to proceed to the native settlement at Amáta (Musgrave Park), the major settlement on the 27,000-square-mile Northwest Aboriginal Reserve. Later, we obtained permits from the Welfare Department in Alice Springs to gain entrance to Northern Territory reserves such as Aneyonga and the future settlement site at Docker Creek in the Petermanns.

Active Research

My choice of the Amáta-Ernabella area was based on a number of factors. First, I had reports that the Pitjandjara population in this vicinity was large enough to supply good data on marriage rates and demographic composition. Second, the tribal orientation of the population still exists, though the economic structure of traditional aboriginal life has changed. Third, Amáta is about 350 miles southwest of Alice Springs, which could be my base of operation. Furthermore, permission to work at Amáta and assistance from the Ernabella Mission made some problems of introduction much easier.

In Adelaide, I obtained a Land Rover and a 6' × 13' house trailer or caravan that was to be the residence for my wife, our two-year-old daughter, and myself. This equipment was acquired from the Bureau of Supply, Commonwealth of Australia, and financed by the Australian Institute of Aboriginal Studies. In May, 1966, we left Adelaide for Alice Springs on the "Ghan," a narrow-gauge train that makes this run twice a week. The Land Rover and caravan were also loaded on the train. After a week in Alice Springs, where we bought food supplies and camping gear, we drove south to Kulgera Station and then due west to Victory Downs homestead, Mulga Park homestead, and Amáta. The initial trip took two days with the caravan, but normally the trip can be made in a long day's travel.

Amáta (Musgrave Park) is the government settlement for the Northwest Reserve. The settlement staff consists of a superintendent, nurse, building overseer, stockman, mechanic, welfare officer, and a patrol officer. The settlement was established in 1961, and in 1966 the population was not more than 350. A number of native men and women work for wages in construction and fence building. A settlement store sells basic staples to the locals, and fresh beef is sold three times a week. A herd of 300 to 400 cows is kept in neighboring paddocks.

We parked our caravan alongside a bough shelter for the duration of the field work. The hospital provided bathing facilities, and we had access to a tap of bore water. My family stayed with me until the height of the summer when I took them to Alice Springs. We bought most of our canned food from the local store; fresh vegetables and fruits were flown in on the Saturday mail plane from Alice Springs.

Establishing Rapport

Establishing rapport at the initial stages of the work was not very difficult. Most Pitjandjara are accustomed to inquiries of all kinds, and I think they have probably gone through the full range of investigation. Their interests revolve around the past as manifested in myth, ritual, totemism, and the dreamtime. Totemism, mythological beings, and creation legends are discussed almost daily by the male elders. The young men have their dreamtime, but they are not as concerned with it as the elders.

Although I did not specifically collect stories of legends and myths, any field worker must show marked interest in them if he hopes to move on to an investigation of other aspects of social organization. Once the elders recognized my patience in listening to their discussions and jotting down copious notes, they permitted me to ask them questions on other subjects, provided these were also related to the past. The natives were very cooperative in helping me to work out a formal description of group structure and marriage systems, since they view "skin groups" (sections) as possessing a mythological basis for their existence. I had great difficulty, however, in eking out suitable responses to my demographic questions on age and number of offspring, because the Pitjandjara cannot answer these types of inquiries in a formal manner. They disagree over the order of births in their families and even over the number of spouses they have had. The range of disagreement would commonly result in one or at most two points of view, so I could recheck the discrepancies in my own quantitative data.

Inquiries on local organization and territorial units were of more interest to the Pitjandjara but for different reasons. Since I had a vehicle, I could take a number of men with me to map totemic sites, water sources, and important environmental features. Nearly all Pitjandjara thoroughly enjoy going on trips, and thus my interest in local groupings and territory was matched by their interests. Their willingness and cooperation resulted in my acquiring much information on many aspects of local organization, but I had to recheck most of this data thoroughly for its factual basis.

The see-saw pattern of rapport gaining and rapport maintaining depended on how formal my questions were and how far removed they were from mythology and dreamtime. Replies to formal inquiries seldom resulted in an argument or debate, and most participating individuals simply would nod in agreement. When my probings moved into more nebulous areas, however, the group discussion increased markedly. For example, exactly how and why certain social categories are linked with other categories in terms of descent and marriage are conceptualized in a very formal manner following established and undebatable rules. However, variations of the rule are also recognized and accepted, up to a point. Certain "optional" marriages are allowed within limits, and how, when, and why these kinds of marriages occur are up for debate. I sought this kind of information to determine how far the Pitjandjara could conceptualize from the ideal cognized system.

Data-Gathering Techniques

In general, I used the same techniques for the Pitjandjara as for the Mandaya, but with more emphasis on genealogical materials, since most Pitjandjara social relationships are established within genealogical contexts. I recorded Pitjandjara genealogies with more concern for details, and so the completion of one genealogy took two to three times longer than those I recorded among the Mandaya. This time differential is due to the greater emphasis on lineality among the Pitjandjara, where actual descent may be traced back for three or four generations. Among the Mandaya, lineal emphasis is almost absent, and only those descended from a former *bagani* chief can trace their descent as far as to the grandparental generations. Determining relationships within a genealogical framework was a difficult task accomplished through a number of means, but determining all possible connections between individuals was even more difficult, since the Pitjandjara consciously obscure kinship terminology and relationships that have occurred as a result of prohibited or optional unions.

I used questionnaires only to record demographic data. Since most demographic data were also recorded in a genealogical framework, there were overlapping data depending on the strategy employed.

I conducted interviews with adults of both sexes and occasionally with children, but these were always highly unsatisfactory. In most cases, a group of elders would cluster around my trailer, and the interview would consist of a joint discussion of my inquiries. This procedure worked well on "neutral" subjects, but when I desired specific personal information I generally sought to interview the particular individual alone. I interviewed young men during the evenings after they finished their work. My wife and the nurses at Amáta and Ernabella Mission provided me with certain demographic data on the females. Male field workers are viewed with suspicion by Pitjandjara females, especially when they inquire about personal matters.

Most of the data on birth rates, deaths, infant mortality, and demographic matters pertaining to females was collected by my wife, who is a professional dietician. Her assistance in the field was very important not only in information processing, but in maintaining rapport with the females. When an ethnographer has his wife and children with him in the field, females and young children are likely to cluster around his quarters, as they did around our trailer, for conversation, tea, tobacco, and flour. I obtained much vital information in these informal gatherings. Our daughter was at first shy toward the native children but soon she was part of a play group. On other occasions my wife and she accompanied the females when they went out hunting for rabbits.

Another major source of demographic data was the birth and death records at Ernabella Mission and at Amáta. At Ernabella these records go back to 1941, while at Amáta they start in 1961. Information from these records provided me with a fairly good means of determining ages of individuals under twenty, the ages at death, recent births per female at the Mission or on the government reserve, and emigration and immigration rates from the settlement and its environs.

I did most of my interviewing in the aboriginal camp, which is about half a mile from the settlement. Males who are not working usually are in the camp until noon. In the early afternoon they walk to the settlement and would often gather at my trailer, which they viewed as a fairly good source of tea, sugar, and tobacco. In the late afternoon, Tommie Dodd's house became a focal point for discussions.[4] Nearly once a day, every male would make his way to Tommie's house to obtain information on the European staff. I often interviewed at Tommie's house and checked previously collected information there.

If I desired to interview selectively, either on an individual basis or with two or three men, I would drive them out into the "bush" for a few hours. They greatly appreciated these short trips as a means of getting away from the camp routine and hunting with their .22-caliber rifles. After a few hours of hunting, I would boil a billy can (a half-gallon tin bucket) of water and make tea before starting my questioning. Most of my "personalized" interviewing was done in this manner. In general this method was excellent, since it took us away from the camp surroundings, which permit no privacy whatsoever. Sometimes at nights a few men would visit my trailer for tobacco, and further questioning would then take place.

Techniques for recording and storing data. My techniques for recording and storing data were similar to those I used among the Mandaya. I recorded much of my ethnographic data on punch cards. I made carbon copies of all notes and sent them to a colleague in the United States. The preservation of notes and film was much easier in Australia than in the Philippines, where the humid climate quickly deteriorates them. My wife and child left in April of 1967 and I left in June. My wife's departure from the field was not easy, since she had made a number of close friends, both among the aborigines and the European staff. On my final move from Amáta to Alice Springs via Ernabella, I gave almost all my possessions to a number of men who had been of assistance during the field work. Earlier, my wife had given clothing to the women who had worked with her. Although most aborigines are illiterate, I am in communication with them through correspondence with various staff members at the Mission and at Amáta settlement. Bowing out of the field was not a problem, since most of my close informants realized that I was planning to return for further work in the near future. Also it is

---

[4] Tommie Dodd is a half-caste in his late eighties who has lived in the Musgrave area for at least thirty years. Tom's house has always been a center of activity for the old men who know that Tom is the only one who is in touch with the European staff and who knows their ways. He is thus an intermediary of information. Initially Tom was one of my interpreters, but he became much more than that. His invaluable knowledge of the environment and historic events was of immense importance to the project.

my impression that the people know that I am concerned about their activities. Recently one of the females who worked closely with my wife named her latest daughter after our daughter. This information was communicated to us through the missionary at Ernabella.

Summary

The analysis of local organization, its ideology and its composition, as stated in my original research design was difficult to achieve. Local organization is no longer operative, and its ethnographic reconstruction is difficult and not fully reliable. I mapped out territorial domains or spheres, and in general I could demarcate the Pitjandjara's notion of "country." As the Pitjandjara move away from their ancestral areas, their knowledge of minute geographic and subsistence details declines. In his ancestral area, for example, a Pitjandjara knows with a high degree of refinement where certain foods occur, in what abundance, and at what times. He also knows all sources of water and can estimate very precisely how long a given population can stay in a particular locality without exhausting the water supply, but this fineness of qualitative and quantitative information decreases as he moves into adjacent and extra-adjacent areas. The degree of the precision of their knowledge helped me in mapping out territorial units and determining their coexistence with totemic and sacred sites.

It is very difficult to establish the composition of pre-contact local groups. Residence group composition must have been flexible, since nearly all males have a wider geographic knowledge than one would assume if a strict patrilocality rule was actually adhered to. It appears that young men moved among different residence groups after they completed the basic rites of passage, such as tooth evulsion, circumcision, and subincision. Subincision usually took place when they were in their late teens or early twenties, and residential changes took place after subincision and prior to marriage, which for males is in their late twenties or early thirties. Since multiple relationships existed among all local units, it was easy to shift residence. With marriage and the birth of his first child, the male would commonly return to his ancestral residence units.

Establishing actual group composition is virtually impossible, because the pre-European economic structure is no longer operative. Yet the Pitjandjara still maintain the ideology of their area, as was made clear in 1966–1967 over the mining of chrysoprase (Australian jade) at Mt. Davis. The Mt. Davis male elders are ambivalent about the mining, one reason being that the Mt.

Davis country belongs only to those individuals who were born in the area, have *malupiti* (kangaroo) dreamtime, or have kinship relations with one who is from the area.

The third factor and its interpretation is most interesting. Many of those who claim kinship ties base their case on matrilineal or affinal linkages. Some of these claims are valid; others are slim to say the least. Distant consanguines or affines from the area are "discovered," and a case for kinship is made. The Mt. Davis elders view matrilineal and affinal ties as quasi-acceptable, but they regard some of the more distant "creations" as dubious at best. The flexibility with which kin ties are arranged with the Mt. Davis group is not a new phenomenon. In general, there is a set of varied means by which one gains access to the area. Even kinship relations in the dreamtime may serve as an entrée to the mines. In one case, a man from the Deering Hills area south of Mt. Davis with a *tjurki* (owl) dreamtime gained access to the chrysoprase mines on the grounds that the *tjurki* is related to the *malupiti*. Many people, however, were not clear on what the relationship was, if one did indeed exist.

I do not think that I could have accomplished much more than I did in my analysis of local organization. With the gradual shift into a money economy, the aborigines will not return to their pre-European economic activities, except in a sporadic and random manner. With the gradual shift from a subsistence to a "hand-out" and/or wage economy, the economic role of females, which was most important in the hunting and gathering economy, is now virtually nil. Rose (1965) discusses the present economic role of aboriginal women and its sociological consequences.

My demographic analysis was more successful. Although the population is no longer in strict equilibrium, I could ascertain the rate of population increase, despite the fact that I could not use most demographic approaches, methods, and techniques due to the small samples, lack of census materials, and incomplete data. Estimating ages is most difficult and has always been a problem in working with aborigines. Genealogical recording of surviving children among females past menopause reveals gaps that may have been caused by infanticide, death in infancy, or death in childhood. If females have a full bearing period of twenty to twenty-five years, one is then able to determine with some degree of assurance the missing offspring and thus the birth rate. By determining the rank order of births among surviving offspring, one is able to place individuals at five-year intervals and then note the gaps between siblings. In estimating ages, my errors continuously reoccurred, but the error was standardized in the same direction and roughly in the same range of years.

For males in their thirties, estimates were always lower, and for males in their forties and fifties my estimates were commonly greater. Data on death rates are even more difficult to obtain, since deceased kinsmen are quickly forgotten and their names are not mentioned. At present I am analyzing my data, but the gaps in the materials are ever-increasing, and more detailed information is unavailable.

If I were starting the project now, I would make a more detailed study of ideology and its interconnection with population dispersal and mobility. Pitjandjara mythology reflects population movements, since the spatial element of myth is stressed more than the legendary details in a given locality. The Aranda and Walbiri have a richness in the quality and quantity of their mythology in given localities, but the western desert population appears to lack this feature. Instead, myth is traced over vast tracts of land, emerges with no regularity, and the myth or dreamtime story is concerned with events as the particular fauna moved from place to place. My data on this interrelationship were collected during the latter half of my stay among the Pitjandjara and are not complete, but I think the motifs have been worked out, and a contrast with other central Australian groups may be noted.

I am not sure that more formal training in demographic analysis would have helped. The data are really not amenable to more sophisticated demographic indexes, so I think one should not force a formal analysis on them.

The Pitjandjara, like most aboriginal populations in Australia, possess a highly formalized conception of society and ideology. This extreme formalism is not only a mental exercise, but it is also verbally expressed in a number of contexts. In explaining sections systems ("skins," as they are called), a Pitjandjara sketches the ideal system on the ground in a formal graphic design and then discusses the ramifications of the system in terms of the rules of operation. At times, graphic representations and ensuing discussions approximate the formalism of Radcliffe-Brown or Lévi-Strauss in their approaches to Australian social structure. Furthermore, the Pitjandjara are able to conceptualize and to account for variations in the manifestation of rules. When optional or wrong marriages occur, kinship relationships and terminology are consciously altered to make things "straight again." Sections also reflect these changes. The only way a field worker can trace these "tamperings" is to take complete genealogies to the most ascending generation and then work back to the present. In other cases, the field worker can create fictitious situations of wrong unions, variations in group composition, sitting arrangements at rituals, etc., and observe how the people account for these differences in terms of the cognized system.

In a population like the Pitjandjara, where social units are formally cognized, linguistically blocked, and verbally expressed, an analysis of ideal social structure is not difficult. Since the arrangement of social groups and marriage relationships is expressed by specific terminologies, the field worker can describe the structure by utilizing formal Pitjandjara categories that practically cover the full range of possible groupings. Anthropological accounts of aboriginal Australian social systems are not due exclusively to our formalistic approaches, because the natives themselves are equally formalistic in their conception of how the system ideally works.

Native structural categories provide the initial basis for the investigation of group activities and relationships. *De facto* group composition, rates of interaction, the statistical confirmation of stated rules; and so forth must be analyzed quantitatively. The charter of a social system must be viewed in terms of what occurs "on the ground," and marked discrepancies between the two levels of analysis must be noted and explained in terms of ecological and demographic factors. Among the Pitjandjara, the major problem is not to *induce* group structure, which is obtained through the verbal expression of formal native categories, but to *deduce* it as it exists and operates in reality and determine to what extent reality mirrors the idealized cognized system.

PART III: COMPARISONS BETWEEN THE MANDAYA AND THE PITJANDJARA

In both cases, I used with varying degrees of emphasis such anthropological techniques as the recording of genealogies, questionnaires, and participant observation. In societies where descent is important and permanent groups are based on lineality, using genealogies to ascertain genealogical depth and alliances between social units is important. When descent is not a factor, as among the Mandaya, genealogy does not affect the formation of groups. In order to analyze the factors behind social activity and cohesion, the ethnographer must investigate the spatial arrangements of households and the cooperation among families seeking certain ends.

The particular problem of one's field work always dictates the methods and techniques employed and the varying emphasis on different ways of obtaining data. There is no single kit of anthropological tools that is utilizable in all field work, nor is there a finite number of approaches that will render "answers" in all cases. Once a set of problems for investigation has been established, the investigator must demarcate the variables that are crucial to an analysis of the problem or problems. Each variable must be analyzed in terms of the kind of data required, the units of measurement for such data, and the interrelationships of particular events. Ideally, the next step is to determine how each of the variables varies with the others. The interconnections among variables can be viewed both in a quantitative and qualitative manner. In a quantitative sense, a change in the value of one variable will influence other variables and their operation. Thus, among the Pitjandjara, verbalized marriage rules can be statistically confirmed only by observing the 600–800 individuals interacting in the system. If population size was very much smaller, these rules could not be operationalized.

Which of the various anthropological techniques and methods the researcher uses depends on the problem, the critical variables that constitute the problem, and the required data. The field worker should be familiar with different techniques, both anthropological and nonanthropological, and use those techniques that are the most meaningful in terms of his research strategy.

Although I used most anthropological techniques with varying emphasis in both field experiences, the two projects were so radically different that I had to explore fully, before making any headway, the differences in the two problems, the data I needed, and my interpretations of the data, as well as the differences in the two cultures themselves. In my initial field trip to the Mandaya, I had many problems of adjustment, and in the first six months I made many mistakes, asked untimely questions, became impatient with my respondents, and so forth. Most of these problems were ironed out by the latter half of the work. This period of adjustment was totally absent when I returned to the Mandaya in 1965. I knew most of the people and did not repeat my earlier errors. In a four-month period I accomplished what it would have taken me six months to do during the first trip.

My initial adjustments in working with the Pitjandjara were of a different order. I had learned a lesson from my past experiences and thus avoided many common errors. One of my major problems in both research areas was accepting and evaluating individuals' statements at face value. Field workers know that statements, especially general ones, cannot be accepted at face value and should be checked with other sources of information. Among the Mandaya, I had to check and recheck most initial statements. This process of sorting and resorting interview material not only reveals the basic patterns of certain activities, but also permits the researcher to determine the range of variation of socially acceptable and unacceptable behavior.

I called general statements made by the Pi'jandjara "structural" statements—accounts of how a particular activity, be it social, ceremonial, or mythological, operate. On most occasions I checked these statements with other sources and found a very high degree of consensus. They expressed the "structure" of a particular activity to me in a clear, lucid manner. Furthermore, these verbalized structural statements are abstracted by the natives from the range of events and the various means by which selected ends may be achieved. For example, the sitting arrangement for a *corroboree* (a ritual gathering) is established by kinship linkages, which are summarized through section and kin terminology. There are rules for this arrangement, but there are also acceptable variations that may be employed in case the rule cannot be manifested. The *corroboree* must be performed regardless of the absence of certain individuals. When some are absent, modifications exist to maintain the performance.

As stated earlier, the researcher's methods and data differ from case to case, depending on the problem. Among the Mandaya, my interest in interaction networks and spatial influences required my collecting information on who interacts with whom, why, when, and so forth. I obtained interaction data not only by observation but also by interviewing individuals on who and why certain individuals are selected as task-group members to achieve certain ends. Organizational data of this type cannot be systematically compared to an ideal set of rules that dictates how activities should be manifest. Variations are expected in acquiring certain ends. My interpretation of interaction data was based on how groups are formed for certain jobs, on what principles, how groups persist, and how groups change composition to meet new demands. Verbalized structural models are absent among the Mandaya; thus the observer must induce structural patterns from the data. Consequently, the abstracted structure might have no basis on how the Mandaya conceptualize their modes of activity.

To ascertain population characteristics among the Pitjandjara, I collected detailed information on sex and age distributions, fertility rates, death rates by age and sex, and so forth. Due to the paucity of the demographic data, my interpretation of it was not based on stochastic demographic models. Population features were related to the optimal operation of connubiums, prescriptive marriage patterns, and other sociological features. I interpreted organizational features—the working arrangements of a society that processes activity in terms of social ends through the manifestation of choice to meet new adjustments (Firth, 1964:45)—in terms of demographic requirements that influence the frequency with which stated rules actually occur. Thus I viewed the organization of social activity in two ways. One based on demographic and ecological features, which are prerequisites to the statistical confirmation of ideally stated rules. The other was to ascertain the gap between the structural system, which is a formal verbalized model of how cultural events should be manifested, and the ways in which social requirements are actually fulfilled.

The ethnographer is fully expected to vary his methods as his problems and interpretations vary, but in comparing the two field experiences, I believe that the differences in the cultures themselves were most important in establishing the framework of my analysis. Social structure as traditionally utilized in anthropology is concerned with analyzing formal social properties (groups and rules) based on permanency and continuity. Some cultures possess verbal categories to denote permanent social context. The Pitjandjara categorize almost all conceivable groupings for social, ceremonial, and economic purposes, but the importance of these groups is markedly different. For example, it was only during the last few weeks of my field work in Australia that I obtained the moiety designations. Moieties are functionally not important for the organization of activity; thus the terms are seldom employed. Groups are cognized, linguistically demarcated, and verbalized, and the rules for social discourse are openly stated, so the major problem for the field worker is to investigate what actually takes place and how. In such cases, one's analysis moves from the general statements and ideal system, which are expressed and moderately easy to obtain, to the particulars of how the system works, given population fluctuations or the absence of certain group members.

As stated earlier, the analysis of Mandaya social organization was quite different from the Pitjandjara, both in terms of the data collected and the analysis. Among the Mandaya, organizational activity emerges to meet specific goals, and on-going associations are absent, except in the case of warrior groups. An analysis of individual and group interaction among the Mandaya must be viewed in terms of fulfilling certain jobs and not as permanent structural entities that persist regardless of the presence or absence of tasks and goals. The absence of enduring groups—both on the ground and as cognized mental constructs—attests to the utilization of a framework based on group emergence and dispersal based on specific aims.

My personal reactions while doing field work among the Mandaya and Pitjandjara also varied. The Mandaya appeared

to be more withdrawn and less demonstrative than the Pitjandjara, not only toward me but toward each other. Most of them
were neutral toward me, responding only in terms of my inquiries, yet I had a number of Mandaya friends who accepted
me and were very open with me. It was most gratifying to be
able to communicate with at least a few individuals on personal
matters.

My initial desire to be accepted by the Mandaya evaporated
soon after the debacle with the females and the Muslim proselytizer. It was at this point that I realized that the ideal of being
completely accepted by a particular group is a romantic myth.
In most cases one ends up with a handful of warm friends with
whom communication is easy. Like most populations, the Mandaya had a segment of people who did not like me and who made
no attempt to hide their contempt. They felt that I was acquiring information about them for future use by the government.

Although the Mandaya recognize themselves as being different from the lowland Filipinos, they are aware of and make
little attempt to resist the changes that are slowly drawing them
into the orbit of a market economy and an agricultural-based
peasant population. The Pitjandjara are also aware of the impact of European ways on their society, but they possess a great
deal of pride in their mythological and ceremonial existence, and
this gives real meaning to their lifeways. This religious structure is something that the "black fella" has and the whites do
not have. They are proud of this and, when an outsider shows
interest in learning their myths and rituals, the Pitjandjara
male knows that he must take the initiative and show the novice
the true way. Thus I felt that the Pitjandjara viewed me as an
equal from another social system, not as a member of a superior
and dominant society. I was eager to learn their patterns of life,
and they were patient in showing me the Pitjandjara way.

The ethnographer who feels he is a special personality who
must be accepted and "liked" by all the members of the group
he is working with is fairly naïve. No one is liked and accepted
by everyone, even in his own culture, so there is no reason why
he should be completely accepted in an alien society. In both
Mandaya and Australia, many people did not accept me, and I
could not have cared less. Nor did this type of mutual negativism
depress me, since I suspect that there are certain personality
types with whom I could not interact, regardless of their culture and background. I see no reason to modify my behavior,
channel my thoughts, or be continuously "up tight" in the hope
of acquiring universal acceptance.

This raises the question of going "native." I felt at home
in both fields, but never more at home than in my own culture.

The Mandaya and Pitjandjara recognized that I was racially and culturally different, and their expectations of my behavior were well established. They know that whites wear trousers and shirts, are not subincised, do not have totems, and do not believe in *asuwang* spirits. It is practically impossible to immerse yourself fully in another culture, especially when the host culture has a stereotype of what you think and do. The Pitjandjara are very ethnocentric about their way of life and maintain stereotypes both of other aboriginal populations and of Europeans. I was placed in a role, and certain behavioral responses were expected of me. However, it should not be assumed that one must not deviate from his recognized cultural patterns. A cultural "straight jacket" is not the answer. One should be himself, while taking into account the norms of behavior he is studying and operating within.

Homesickness was seldom a major problem, although we became a little concerned when news from the outside was slow in arriving. Both my wife and I occasionally missed things that we were accustomed to in the States, but these were not critical. I always desired information on college football results, and eventually one of my colleagues at the university sent me clippings of game results. Most of the time I was too busy with my work to feel lonely, and my wife was too busy taking care of our daughter. If loneliness did set in, we went to Alice Springs to see friends and relax.

Living conditions in the two field areas were markedly different. My wife did not accompany me to Mandayaland, because of the limited facilities available to me. The tropical environment of Mindanao, with its great frequency of sickness, malaria, and generally hot and humid conditions, proved worse than the hot deserts of Australia, but both of us had adjustments to make in the desert. Our trailer proved much too small for the three of us, but we had no alternative. The major adjustment was keeping warm during the winter. Winter nights in the desert are very cold, and our caravan had no heating unit. Thus the winter nights proved utterly miserable, whereas heat in the summer was so intense as to virtually rule out a good night's sleep.

In Australia and the Philippines, the local and national political situation did not hinder my activities, nor did any revolutions or drastic political changes that might have altered my plans take place. Australian government agencies dealing with aboriginal affairs asked me for short interim reports that contained abstracts of my field-work progress. In the Philippines, the upland populations are not subject to formal governmental agencies, though a national integration committee exists with limited effective power.

The upland rice-cultivating Mandaya, who are not taxed by municipal officials, were initially hesitant in revealing information on crop yields, acreage planted, and other aspects of economic activity that might be used against them. The foothill, cash-crop abaca cultivators were more aware of their activities and the possibilities of being taxed. In every case, the Mandaya males underestimate their holdings and yields when questioned on this subject. Eventually, the differences between their statements and my measurements of yields and land became standardized. My data on economic activities were never seen by local officials, nor was I asked about them. On my second trip to Mandayaland, I obtained more precise information, because the people had lost their fear of my using the data against them for taxation purposes.

Before leaving for the Philippines, I had been warned that studying shifting cultivation populations is difficult because of the scattered settlement pattern and the high population mobility. This is quite true. With each Mandaya family/household separated from the others by a half to two kilometers, the amount of time spent in walking up and down hillsides and across creeks is significant. When one arrives at a household clearing, only the one family residing in the household can be interviewed. After completing the necessary inquiries, I would move to another household clearing. My hiking time between households varied from twenty minutes to an hour, depending on the distance and terrain. The people cluster only during post-harvest rituals and gambling, labor exchanges during agricultural phases, and *rites de passage*.

The Pitjandjara are now settled in clusters varying from 30 to 50 people around homesteads and between 300 to 400 live at Ernabella Mission and at the Amáta government settlement. Large semistable populations are conducive to the collecting of long-run statistical data as well as to maximum interviewing and checking and rechecking. In general, these population conditions yield more return for the time spent in the field. Also in Australia I had access to a vehicle that allowed me to "go bush" with the elders when I was working on local group areas of exploitation. In Manay municipality and the uplands of the Philippines, my legs provided the only means of transportation, since roads, trails, and vehicles were not available.

In summary, although there are marked environmental, demographic, economic, and social contrasts between these two populations, I used similar methods in both cases, but with varying emphases. A commonly recognized block of inquiries is the substance of social anthropology, and these questions are pursued in all field work. To explain the how's and why's of a particular social organization requires an investigation of cultural and noncultural phenomena that may relate to social institutions. If the investigation of these relationships is of prime concern, then one must equip himself with the necessary techniques and methods to understand the interconnections both on an empirical and a theoretical level. Ultimately, there should be no limit on the techniques and methods used by the social anthropologist. The particular set of problems for investigation will determine where he will acquire his "tools," and he should not limit himself in using methods from other disciplines when they are necessary. Nor should he be fearful about transgressing traditional anthropological domains or spheres of activity that might prove more of a burden than an asset.

FIELD WORK:
PROBLEMS AND GOALS

The anthropologist in the field needs the cooperation of the people being studied. The marginal native must have *rapport* with the "real" natives. Good research requires a planned strategy for getting and keeping rapport. To be able to do such planning, we obviously need to understand the meaning of rapport. But such understandings are not easily attained; for many myths surround this "rapport," a very "strange" thing.

To develop and maintain rapport we must keep several things in mind (see below). Basic to all our efforts in this direction, however, is *language*. The essense of rapport, we will discover, is communication; but not any manner of communication. To both communicate effectively and at the same time to increase rapport we must speak in the language of the informant.

A smart tourist knows that to get the most out of touring one needs to speak the language of the "locals." The benefits of speaking the local tongue are even greater for the anthropologist. The meaning of language for fieldwork must therefore be well understood, and this we discuss below.

To know "the language" is a great help in achieving rapport. To know the language is also of great assistance in getting to know the *culture*. Anthropology, whatever else it is, is a study of human culture. Every bit of research attempts to increase our knowledge of a particular culture, of a particular tradition. The anthropologist ever in search of new bits of culture is in a rather strange position—of not being quite certain what it is that is being sought. In reply to a specific question (like "what is culture in its essence?") we usually say "Culture is a way of life." Receiving such an answer we are put into a state which the great anthropologist Alfred Kroeber used to call "pleasant puzzlement." The researcher needs help with the concept culture.

Finally, looking toward the goals of our research we must enquire:(1) What is the purpose of our labors?, and (2) How well are our goals being met? Our purpose, we may say, is to develop laws of human behavior, social life and culture change. Our record for meeting our goals is, however, to date rather dismal. The problem possibly lies in a lack of commitment to the method which has led to much progress in the natural and biological sciences—the method of *experimentation*. Just to say that "experimentation will solve our basic scientific problems" is no solution. Yet, as I have discovered from many years of struggling with experimentation, it is at least partly a solution nevertheless. I therefore conclude part II with an account of how anthropologists can utilize experimental ideas.

As we better get to understand the meaning and value of *rapport, language, culture* and *experimentation*, we will get ever closer to developing a scientific anthropology. In a world filled with problems—of race relations, ethnic conflicts, class struggles, revolution, poverty, crime and mental illness—the usefulness of anthropology should need little discussion. But we must move into these areas with something more than good intentions, sophisticated intuitions and cross-cultural experience. We need a *scientific methodology*. Hopefully the discussions in these pages will aid in reaching these goals.

1. Rapport

Without rapport, peaceful social interaction is impossible. Without rapport, fieldwork would be a nightmare. Without rapport the data collected are almost valueless.

Rapport is to research what milk is to a baby. We need rapport to survive and to do science while in the field. Yet anthropological reports describing successful fieldwork—situations where the researcher must have gained excellent rapport—provide but vague clues as to what really is this elusive phenomenon. From many writings we get the impression that some researchers are *naturally* good with people. They have some inborn quality which makes them handle social relationships with charm and tact. Whether the natives want to or not, they are almost forced to find the researcher, so well endowed, as likable, agreeable, fun to be with, charming. In the hands of the charming marginal native the real natives become, almost, putty to be used whenever and however the needs of anthropological research dictate. Anthropologists without these talents, it would appear, should switch to some other line of work—computer programming, perhaps, or bricklaying.

This model of rapport—a model I call *humanism*—focuses on the common humanism which links researcher to informant. The humanism model suggests that because we all want to be liked, admired, and "charmed" the anthropologist must continually act like a dog trying to become his master's best friend. The humanism model underrates the intelligence of the natives and overrates the acting abilities of the anthropologist. Moreover, if the only people anthropology could use as researchers were those with inborn charm we would quickly run out of researchers. The humanism model must be rejected for a more realistic model, one I call *engineering*. The researcher, it is well known, "engineers" people and situations to get the type of data required by the study. Rather than being basically agreeable, charming and likable, the researcher is really a creature with an insatiable appetite for information. He constantly wants more information, and to get ever more requires careful well-planned action rather than natural impromptu charm. Research, as even our youngest and most naive informants soon discover, is work; not just getting to know and to like people. Being liked helps, but it is not the most important ingredient of "research." In the field what we actually "say" to our informants is not "like me," but rather "work with me." If they "reply" (directly or indirectly) "Yes, I will work with you," it is because they believe that the *risks* involved in *communicating* with a stranger are more than balanced by the *rewards* from such communication.

In short, when informants work with us we call it having rapport with them. Such rapport involves three basic variables —*communication, risk and reward*. Communication, risk and reward form the bases of my engineering model of rapport. This engineering model has several basic assumptions which need to be well understood: (1) that rapport can exist between two people without either liking or admiring the other; (2) that rapport always includes a willingness to communicate; (3) that communication always involves *risk-taking*; (4) that different types of communication are associated with more or less risk-taking; and (5) that we must always *reward* those who take risks with us. Rapport can therefore be defined as a *conditional agreement to communicate at a given level of risk*. The "conditions" on which this agreement to communicate are based include the receipt of various kinds of rewards, as discussed below. Rapport is *greater* when the parties doing the communicating take greater risks; rapport is smaller when the parties communicating take smaller risks.

To assist researchers in developing and maintaining rapport I will distinguish five (5) levels of rapport, labelled respectively (1) image rapport, (2) social rapport, (3) confidential rapport (4) secret rapport, and (5) intimacy. When we realize that rapport actually has five distinctly different "faces" we can better appreciate why this concept has appeared so difficult to fathom in the past. We thought it had but one face! If you are told "Smith has rapport with X," you must ask *How much* rapport does Smith have?" To answer this question we need the help which the following paragraphs will provide. Essentially, however, what we will learn is that to understand richness we *count valuables*, but to understand rapport we *weigh risks*.

1.1 The informant as risk-taker

To give another person information is to give someone power, power to help or harm us. When a child does not want to speak to a stranger we say (often) "the child is shy." We should say (more accurately) "the child is smart." Information, once given, cannot be taken back—it becomes the property of the receiver, to do with whatever he or she desires. Until we know, well, the intentions of information-receivers it is not smart to provide them with information. The more we know about a person the safer we feel in giving information and the safer we actually are. In these areas of information-sending, gut feelings provide an excellent guide to the actual reality.

The anthropologist moves into a strange community with a strange mission. Other people build houses, drain swamps, fix wells or do a host of different, obviously practical things. The anthropologist just walks around and asks questions. This is a stranger one must view with considerable suspicion. Indeed, as I have elsewhere documented, the anthropologist generally begins a project defined as a *spy*.[1]

To reach the lowest level of rapport, the anthropologist must be able to move around the community and be seen as an "honorable person." He or she must have *the image* of a good person; someone with whom one can chat without getting the feeling of being a traitor to the community. To achieve this image of goodness and "safeness to talk to," the anthropologist must spread the word (somehow) that the work being done is honorable and noble. With the help of local leaders, of letters from people respected by the community and (if possible) of newspaper articles on the work to be done, the researcher should quickly be able to escape the almost inevitable label of spy. By these methods and by carefully restricting the subjects of inquiry, the anthropologist can quickly achieve *image rapport.*

With image rapport, and nothing more, little actual research can be done. This is the beginning without which no climbing to greater rapport heights is possible. With image rapport, the anthropologist can move around the community and meet the people. He or she can exchange social niceties such as "How are you, my name is X, what is your name?" When researchers have achieved image rapport, the natives will not run the other way when approached with a friendly "Nice to see you today."

Once image rapport has been achieved, it is relatively easy to raise the level of interaction to *social rapport.* A person with what I call social rapport can request and easily obtain public information—information to which anyone *of that society* has direct access. A member of a given social system can "hang-around" and listen-in on all manner of social discourse which everyone around defines as "public." We often refer to this information as "common knowledge," and so it is. What I here want to emphasize is that one must (usually) be an accepted member of society S to be up to date on what S- people refer to as common knowledge. Once able to hang around community centers of interaction—the post office, local places of worship, junctions of highways, etc.—the anthropologist discovers what people are talking about and can then join in. The anthropologist too can then engage in "gossip" and "small talk" about

---

1. For further material on the anthropological spy problem see *Marginal Natives: Anthropologists at Work*, pp 500-504.

recent births and deaths, about the harvest to come or the one just finished. In receiving and moving such public information the anthropologist cements himself or herself into the local communication system—becoming an additional link in a long communication chain. When I achieved social rapport in Trinidad, I was told (over and over again) "You one of us, Yes! You really know what's happenin' around here." My handling of public information in the proper manner—getting to know when to talk about what and with whom—was beginning to make me acceptable as a member of the community. My social acceptability did not mean I could go delving into all manner of subjects. But it did mean that having achieved social rapport I could begin to aim for something higher.

The anthropologist who has social rapport will notice that, for some reason or other, some community members are more often available for "chats" than others. In modern parlance we say that some people have "time to kill." We should say "some people have more free time than others: time not already elsewhere committed." People with "more free time" value each bit of time spent with a stranger less than those more pressured for time. It is with this type of person that one can best begin to push toward *confidential rapport. Requesting* confidential material is usually easier after the researcher *offers* some confidential material concerning either personal history or events in the recent past. The anthropologist here "says" in effect: I am prepared to take risks with you and offer you data "in confidence." The hidden message then becomes "let's exchange confidences."

The anthropologist with confidential rapport shares confidences with a number of natives and gains access to information that is moving around the community's hidden channels of communication. The risks taken by informants are still not high; because most members of the community know this information anyway. But there is some risk nevertheless because confidential information concerns data which runs counter to established norms for community living. In Trinidad, as previously discussed, much went on which was not "proper." Information such as who was sleeping with whom and why could not be discussed in public. Knowing such information made the anthropologist more of a community member; but the data had to be "moved" carefully so that community members did not lose face.

The successful keeper of confidential information broadcasts an important message to the community: "I can handle community secrets—when you take the risk of talking to me about confidential matters you will come to no harm and never be embarrassed." As this message moves around, as the researcher becomes ever more the subject of gossip and small talk, ever more people will be ready to exchange confidences with the anthropologist. Let us note that in exchanging public and confidential information people are not, usually, telling things they don't know. Rather, such information gets moved around because people enjoy telling and retelling stories. We have an important message here for the researcher; part of the reward provided natives for their risk-taking is to be a *good listener*. As any psychotherapist will attest to, it is far from simple to develop good listening habits. Differently put, from one point of view the natives and the researcher have something important in common: they enjoy telling some stories and the researcher needs to hear them.

The researcher with confidential rapport soon feels able to ask questions which relate only to a given subgroup. The researcher is now probing for "secret" information, data which according to Junker is what is known to members of an in-group who avoid letting it be known to an outsider, since its exclusive possession is important to an in-group's solidarity and continued existence.[2]

The more people of the community know and believe that the researcher has proven his or her ability to keep community secrets, the more of them will be ready to provide secrets pertaining to their subgroup. It is clear that one's behavior on a level of rapport below the one aimed for needs to be perfected before trying to "climb higher." And *secret rapport* is (usually) as high as the average anthropologist needs to climb. The researcher who is able to tap information sources concerning family life, business activities, political organization, religious activities and life in the areas of class or caste returns from the field, usually, with everything required for a successful project. The next level, *intimacy*, is only necessary where psychological material is needed by the project.

Whether we need to or not, we usually attain intimacy with some of our informants. Differently put, along with doing research while "in the field," we make deep and lasting friendships and share intimate and personal thoughts and feelings. How strange that we can do this with people from another world; from another culture!

1.2 Rapping, risk-taking and reward

Much has been said about rapping or communicating and risk-taking; we must now look to the problem of rewards. What does the anthropologist have to offer in exchange for the risk-

---

2. See, B. H. Junker 1960 *Fieldwork: An Introduction to the Social Sciences*. Chicago: University of Chicago Press, pp. 34-35.

taking and time-spending done by the natives? He or she has "capital" to offer and some items of such exchange capital are obvious.

1.21 "Obvious" Capital

a. money
b. specialized knowledge—proficiency in writing, first aid ability, techniques in dealing with governmental red tape, information for educational opportunities for the native, etc.
c. use of personal property—car, camera, gun, fishing equipment, tent, etc. .
d. use of the anthropologist as "laborer"—assisting in hunting, harvesting, house-building, etc.

1.22 Non-Obvious Capital

e. hope capital

Aram Yengoyan had Mandayan informants who believed that his research in agriculture could help them rid their community of the rats which plagued them and reduced their yield of rice. My own agricultural discussions with Trinidadian peasants often included remarks pertaining to my belief that scientific agriculture would in time rid them of all kinds of problems. This kind of hopeful outlook toward the future is very basic to anthropology. To give someone hope for a better future is, surely, a real contribution to their welfare. Both by temperament and training anthropologists are well equipped to provide such hope.

f. confirmation capital

Confirmation can be defined as *a person's desire to be appreciated*.[3] And the highest form of appreciation, clearly, is emulation. The anthropologist in the field attempts to live and think like the natives. To understand their culture, an attempt is made to put its rules into daily practice. As this generally well-educated stranger takes on ever more local roles and values, the real natives become ever more impressed with their own culture. The argument is logical and obvious: "If

---

3. My statements on confirmation capital are indebted to the work of Craig C. Lundberg, particularly his paper "A transactional conception of fieldwork" *Human Organization* volume 27 no. 1, pp 45-49

this educated stranger finds our ways valuable, then they must truly be valuable!" Each time the anthropologist interacts with a native the latter receives this same flattering message.

g. therapy capital

A stranger who is able and willing to keep secrets can be (and often is) used as "therapist." Problems which natives find difficult to discuss with other real natives are more easily presented to marginal natives. The researcher must be careful here to give only what can be given. Differently put, the native usually does not want advice and the researcher is generally not trained to give it. The native wants a sympathetic listener; a sounding board which legitimizes feelings and a mirror which makes big problems appear small. With smiles, nods and a little reading in Rogerian nondirective techniques, the researcher can alleviate some suffering.[4]

1.3 Summary and Conclusions

Many successful researchers will find the engineering model of rapport far less flattering than the humanistic one. Although these people may be as gifted as snake charmers, it is not their lovable personality characteristics that, I believe, led to success. Following the engineering model, I am forced to identify successful marginal natives as rational opportunists who manipulate other people, situations and themselves. Research is serious and difficult work. It deserves to be treated realistically rather than romantically. In fieldwork, "nice guys" do not finish at all. We are not *just* nice people touring strange places and having fun with informants. We are not part of the good-natured minority wanting to share in the lives of exotic peoples. We are not restless Westerners looking for new kicks. Nor are we nature freaks trying to return to a simpler and more "natural" lifestyle. We are Machiavellian manipulators working for a prince called "truth." The prince is a tireless taskmaster and we need much training, hope and courage to but stay "in service." Nice guys finish last!

We manipulate people without embarrassment. Our "excuse" is simple: we need valid cross-cultural data to develop a science of humanity. And we need to achieve a science of humanity quickly; before there are no more humans either to do research or to be researched. That peculiar primate called *Homo sapiens*

---

4. See, Rogers, C. R. (1951) *Client-Centered Therapy*. Boston: Houghton Mifflin.

has a new toy—atomic power—which can kill its owners. Understandings from anthropological work, linked to those from other disciplines, may provide ways to discipline this strange beast. We and our informants, in brief, have the common goal of survival.

Our informants are not simple-minded "primitives" flattered by attention received from scholars. They are not children to be charmed and played with so that they can be asked to give up their possessions—possessions called "data." The real natives, like us, are risk-takers. Under given conditions they will take all manner of risks with us. As we manipulate them, so they try to manipulate us—into providing ever more exchange capital as the risks of rapping increase. Within the dirt and grime of the informational market place anthropologists and natives sometimes reach deep and affectionate understandings. Much of the time, however, our daily business is just that—business. And our business as marginal natives is exchanging valued items for information.

2. Language

To truly understand a group of human beings we must live with them. This anthropological message cannot be repeated too often. Many social scientists look for short cuts. Their work with questionnaires and surveys, as the only data-getting instrument, keep many people busy and hardly make an impact on the major social problems of the day. We must fully participate in the worlds of the peoples studied (i.e., the natives). By sharing their environments we discover what is considered joyful and what is sad. We get to know what it means to be a man, a woman, a child, a leader, a follower and a human in general. To be allowed to share in an environment which "belongs" to another group, the researcher needs rapport and a good command of the language of the locals. The problems surrounding rapport achievement and maintenance have been discussed. I now turn to *language*.

All animals communicate, but the human animal specializes in communication. We communicate by facial expressions, by hand and arm movements, by making eye contact and by avoiding eye contact. We communicate by wearing certain kinds of clothes or by disrobing. We communicate by attaching adornments to the ears, the nose, the lips, the hair, the penis. And we communicate with pictures, music, art, architecture and dance. In these and related ways we send each other messages while doing "other things." That is, these messages are generally transmitted without "senders" being fully aware that they are indeed sending messages. Moreover these messages have a vagueness about them: there is no one-to-one relationship between the symbol (say a bit of clothing) and some meaning. Such is not the case with language.

Language is a system specialized for communication. With language there is a conscious awareness of message sending and receiving. With language there is the possibility of making our meanings quite clear to another person—if he or she understands the code. For language requires us to *encode* messages —to put them in the correct form for sending—and to *decode* messages—to translate sounds into meanings. Technically speaking, language is *a communication system with a channel (sound) and a code*—a set of rules which define the usable sounds and the permissible ways of putting them together.

By knowing a language our ability to achieve a high level of rapport is greatly facilitated. When we have secret rapport and possess a good command of the local language we can successfully collect whatever data our particular project requires. Language is the most effective communication system currently known; but it is more than that. Language, like a flag, is also an identification symbol—a statement of who one is, what group she or he belongs to. A good command of the local language therefore tells the natives: I care about you and feel some identification with you. Language also orders the universe of a group —categorizing given phenomena in a way peculiar to that group. We, for example, have many words to distinguish slight "differences" in color. In some languages it is only possible to distinguish three colors: black, white and red. *Our* interest in color has led to many words in this area, while our relative disinterest in, for example, snow provides but one word: "snow." The Eskimo, for whom knowing the differences between different types of snowfall is very important, has many words for "snow."

To know a language well is to know much about the culture of a group. Earl Rubington, in "The Language of Drunks" and Paul Dredge in "Social Rules of Speech in Korean," well illustrate the importance of language for knowing "the culture." The "alcoholic language" once learned provides the researcher (pp 291-301) with a key to the complex world of the alcoholic. It directs us to the typical and recurrent situations that "drunks" experience; who helps them or provides the "ace in the hole," and who reports them, playing the role of "citizen." The types of drinks and the kinds of drinkers are all uncovered by the language as are the dire aspects of their strange existence. Every culture will have its own terms for drinking and drunks as well as a host of terms providing their particular approach to different types of drinking situations. Similarly, every culture will have its special vocabulary for each subarea of social life:

kinship, religion, economics, politics, community interaction and so forth.

But the words we use give us yet more information, as Dredge shows us. At times we must be polite and show deference to someone who is "more important," or simply "older." At other times I (Ego) am given deference by the person who is speaking to me (Alter). Knowing the language permits us to follow the social niceties which differentiate the well-mannered from the bore or idiot. Knowing the language also helps us pick up anger, frustration and upsetness that people feel when something has not gone the expected way. To learn a foreign language well enough to understand the many subtleties that constitute human interaction is a great challenge. But that challenge must be met by all those who would do anthropological field work.

3. Culture

The world, said Shakespeare, is a stage. His idea, while helpful for crowding theatres has been of doubtful value for anthropology. But many think otherwise. Many have accepted the wisdom of the Bard and have used it to build models of human life. Humans (for them) are simply "actors" playing parts called "social roles." The total play then becomes *culture*. Those who think in this manner believe that "a genius is a genius is a genius." They believe that the writer of great drama must surely understand humans! The discrepancies between this view of culture and our everyday experiences make it necessary to refer to these ideas as "Shakesperian myth."

Humans, we all know, are not just puppets mouthing lines that our "culture" has written for us. We are not just mechanical machines programmed for a play called "our culture." While we share "a culture" in common with those around us, there is yet something individual about each one of us. Just as each of us is different from everyone else in the world genetically, we are each different socially and psychologically. Our behavior, although *influenced* by culture, is yet *ours*. We decide to act in a given manner, taking cultural rules into account, certainly—but also taking into account personal needs, desires, goals and other environmental factors. If it is hot, we may take off certain items of clothing; although "the culture" may define certain behavior as "immodest." If we interact with a small group we may drop certain culturally defined ways of addressing other members. If we are ravenously hungry we may grab some foods with our hands when "culture" would have us use utensils. To well understand the humans with whom we do research we must appreciate human freedom.

The human animal must be seen as a decision-maker, not as a slave wrapped in cultural chains. We must start again and naively ask "What is culture?" and "How did we get this concept?"

Professional anthropology found "culture" with many meanings attached to it. In attempting to mold the concept for their own purposes, anthropologists kept adding meanings. So that today hundreds of definitions exist for the important idea of "culture." How did our science get into this kind of a mess? Let's put the initial "blame" on the Romans. The word comes from the Latin *cultura* and *cultus*; *culture* originally designated *cultivation*, as in *agri cultura*, the cultivation of the soil. But culture soon soaked up additional meanings such as "training," "adornment," "worship" and "cult." From its root meaning of *doing something* (an activity), culture was slowly transformed to mean *having something* (a condition). Culture became the state of being cultivated; the superior condition of those who appreciated music, the arts, philosophy and similar noble pastimes. Throughout the Roman empire culture became synonymous with *humanitas*—the human as against the animal condition; with *urbanitas*—the urbanite as against the inferior peasant; and with *civilitas*—the good manners of the sophisticated in social life.

The Germans picked up the ideas of superiority in framing their own notion of *kultur*; but they defined "being superior" in ways quite different from the Romans. Working out of a philosophical tradition the Germans linked their concept *kultur* to the word *bildung*: the development of a deep inner life with spiritual qualities. For them the good manners of the "civilized" were but a superficial layer of sophistication. Really superior humans, they said, were profound with a deep spiritual existence.[5]

Where exactly the Humanists, such as Matthew Arnold, went to get their insights into culture need not concern us here.[6] Suffice it to say that in this literary tradition "culture" stood for what is most perfect in human achievement. Culture was here a condition of absolute superiority; a state that is known and that could be used as a measuring rod to separate the cultured from the inferior. The Roman, Germanic and Humanistic traditions left their marks on early anthropological definitions.

---

5. For Additional Historical Material See, J. W. Stocking, Jr. *Race Culture and Evolution*. New York: The Free Press (1968). And, Erick Kahler "Culture and Evolution" (In Culture, Man's Adaptive *Dimension*. Edited by M. F. Ashley Montague, London: University Press, 1960.

6. More on Humanistic "culture" can be obtained from reading Raymond Williams, *Culture and Society 1780-1950*, Garden City New York, 1960.

Understandably so; because old conceptualizations never die —they slowly fade away. And in the fading process they creep into the works of many scholars too seeped in their own intellectual milieux to notice. It therefore took anthropology some time to climb out of the ethnocentric approach of "superior" and "inferior" cultures to an approach which claimed that: *All groups are culturally equal until and unless proven otherwise.*

Sir Edward Tylor—recognized by most anthropologists as their intellectual father—was stuck with many ethnocentric views of culture. Indeed, he saw his professional mission as helping to eradicate "the last survivals of savagery and barbarism from civilized European society." Like many evolutionary thinkers of his time Tylor really believed that three types of cultures existed: savage, barbaric and civilized. "Savages"—those who practiced savage culture—had evolved only minimally from an animal life style. "Barbarians"—those who practiced barbaric culture—had rude manners and thought in childish ways. Not that these people were incapable of civilized living; rather they had not yet reached that high pinacle of human existence. If Savages and Barbarians lived such "lowly lives" can it be said that they actually had culture. In much of his writings Tylor seems to say "Yes"; but his definition of culture leaves some room for doubt.

> Culture, or civilization, taken in its wide ethnographic sense is that complex whole which includes knowledge, belief, art, morals, law, custom, and any other capabilities and habits acquired by man as a member of society.

Does "Culture, or civilization" mean that Tylor equated culture with civilization? If it does then it would contradict Tylor's other writings which claim that culture is a human universal. If culture does not equal civilization, then why does Tylor say "Culture, or civilization" rather than "Culture taken in its wide . . . ?" The best answer, surely, was that Tylor did not quite know what to do with culture. His ignorance is certainly more forgivable than ours—one hundred years later!

To describe the many "wrong turns" taken by anthropologists since the days of Tylor would require a complete book on culture. We linked culture to basic needs, to ecology, economy, technology and history—all without touching on its basic essence. As anthropologists spread into academia they took their favorite concept, culture, with them. Culture therefore became a concept for all scholars; a solution for all problems. Definitions of culture began to sprout like weeds in an unkept garden. Understandably, as definitions increased in number, "culture" decreased in value. Sending an anthropologist into the field to study "culture" was almost like sending a child to the zoo to find unicorns. The reader who has been told culture "is a way of life" or something equally vague should no longer be surprised at the vagueness. The history of cultural discussions has put a foggy cloak on this concept. And two modern scholars would even have us accept this fuzziness. Culture, they write, "is a class of phenomena conceptualized by anthropologists in order to deal with questions they are trying to answer."[7] Culture, following these gentlemen, is a slimey thing which wriggles into different forms in response to different questions!

But the essentials of culture *had been identified* as long ago as 1917. Culture, wrote the anthropologist Alfred Kroeber[8]

> rests in the past . . . [and] exists only in the mind. Gunpowder, textile arts . . . [etc.] are not themselves transmitted from man to man or from generation to generation, at least not permanently. It is the perception, knowledge, and understanding of them, their *ideas* in the Platonic sense, that are passed along.

Here sat culture unmasked, as: (1) tradition—something old; (2) ideas—something in our heads which *guides* action; and as (3) related to but not actually behavior.

Messages have their time and style. Kroeber's message on culture was ahead of its time and in the wrong style. His words seemed to make culture something mystical and mysterious. His 1917 paper, although widely discussed, was not accepted as aiding in the definition of culture. But more recent writings show that Kroeber was on the right track. Identifying almost the same set of variables, Clyde Kluckhohn and W. H. Kelly described culture as

> historically created designs for living, explicit and implicit, rational and irrational, and non-rational, which exist at any given time as potential guides for the behavior of men.[9]

To get the message across let us use modern style. In current language something which "guides behavior" is *a guidance system*. Moreover, something which is "historically created" is something which comes to us "out of history," or "out of our past." Simply put, such a thing is "old." Culture then is *an old guidance system*. What does this old guidance system

---

7. David Kaplan and Robert Manners, *Culture Theory*: Englewood Cliffs, N. J.: Prentice Hall 1972; p. 2.
8. Alfred Kroeber "The Superorganic," *American Anthropologist* 1917 volume 19, pp. 163-214.
9. Kluckhohn, Clyde and W. H. Kelly 1945 "The concept of culture" In, *The Science of Man in the World of Crisis*. Edited by R. Linton. New York: Columbia University Press.

"teach us"? Well it does not necessarily teach us to do that which is *rational*. The logical, reasonable, effective, or efficient way, may not be cultural way. We learn this as children, when on a hot and sticky day we are forced to "dress up" to visit relatives. It is much more reasonable to *undress* for the weather; that is the *smart* thing to do. But we are forced to *dress* for the family; because that is the *proper* thing to do. Culture, an *old guidance system,* teaches us what people around us consider "proper." Culture, can therefore be defined as: *an old guidance system for proper behavior.*

It is relatively easy to demonstrate that old guides identify the proper *because they are old.* In other words, it takes a long time to "make something" proper. If you and your group keep doing something over and over again (for whatever reason), that becomes "the thing to do." All of you become accustomed to do "the thing". And becoming *accustomed* is just another way of saying that the group has taken on a *custom.* Custom, culture, and "that which is proper" all mean the same thing. They mean doing something "for its own sake"; doing it because everyone thinks it's correct. Since that which is old and which continues to "survive" becomes "proper," we can now define culture more simply. Culture becomes a guidance system for the proper, or *proper guides.*

When we act according to proper guides (when we follow cultural guides, that is) we feel apart from nature. Other animals must adapt to nature by acting smartly to survive. Their social life must be rational and pragmatic. We adapt primarily to each other—to the members of our society. Together we create a set of rules called "culture"—rules which help to make our lives more predictable, more rhythmic, more artistic and more meaningful. When thinking of ourselves as cultural people we temporarily lose sight of the beast that lurks beneath our veneer of culture. Culture helps us to hide the animal. We eat at mealtimes, not when we are hungry like other animals. We sleep at bedtime, not (necessarily) when we are tired. The rest of our lives is similarly given an artificial (non-animal, non-natural) flavor as culture helps us to conceal the fact that like the animals we have physical needs —and that like the animals, we die.

But humans cannot and do not live by culture alone. The beast clothed and elevated by manners, customs, conventions and other human niceties still obeys the first law of animal existence—the law of survival. Proper guides give the beast "meaning," "morality" and "beauty" transforming animal passions into human feelings. But the proper way is often ineffective when survival is at stake. Humans, therefore, develop a second guidance system; a system oriented specifically to solve *immediate* problems pragmatically. This second system of *social* guides is shared by a community, just like culture. But there the similarity ends. For the logic of social guides is the logic of *smartness*. Like the rest of the animal kingdom the human too must at times adapt smartly—do the practical thing, that which works. Smart guides *reveal* animal needs; especially the need to stay alive. Smart guides are *young* ideas; notions which can be tested empirically to see if they are really useful.

We have reached a critical point in this discussion. For generations, social scientists have assumed that humans follow the beat of but one drummer called *culture.* In the language of sociology, it was assumed that humans have but one set of *norms* called culture. Further, that when we do not "follow culture" we are deviants. It now appears that we were wrong. Humans certainly follow culture—this guidance system is often an influence in human action. But there is a second major influence; what I call *social guides*—guides for smart behavior. Human life is monitored by *two sets of guides*. And we are never quite sure whether to be proper (by following cultural guides) or to be smart (by following social guides).

We return to Shakespeare who is *almost right* so often. In *Hamlet* he was inches away from a brilliant sociological discovery and he "muffed it." The Bard told us that for humans the problem is "To be or not to be." In actuality the human dilemma is but a minor modification of that famous phrase. Each human, in every society, almost daily asks himself a more difficult question, namely *"To be smart* (and survive and prosper) or *to be proper* (and feel good and noble.)"

The anthropological researcher working in strange and often difficult environments needs a clear conceptual scheme to facilitate fieldwork. This analysis of culture may be helpful in providing such aids. First, the human animal must be seen as a decision-maker, forever chosing between alternatives. Choice means freedom, a great and wondrous thing. But choice is also anguish, worry and indecision. To be forever forced to choose is to act as a real human—with dignity and purpose. But the anxieties surrounding decision-making leave their marks on us. Psychiatry to the contrary, to be a human (anywhere) is to be neurotic!

Second, human alternatives always include two sets of guides: *guides for proper behavior* (i.e. "culture") and *guides for smart behavior* (i.e. social guides). At times the proper guide and the smart guide are the same. As, for example, the current American (U.S.A.) rule to drive at 55 miles per hour or less on highways: it is "correct driving" and also "safer" or smarter driving. More often than not the proper way and the smart way are quite different. And researchers must be sensitive to the conflicts that these two guidance systems engender in a society. As more and more people are guided by the "smart" and avoid the "proper," *the smart is transformed into the proper.* Our current proper guides were once smart guides. At some previous time the proper guides came into the system because they worked; now they are there because we have become *accustomed* to them. Unfortunately, a guide which was based on practical reasons, previously (i.e. a smart guide of a past era) is now (most probably) no longer practical. The environment has changed; what was "smart" before is "smart" no more!

Third, human *behavior* is neither culturally determined (i.e. *determined* by rules for the proper) nor socially determined (i.e. *determined* by rules for the smart). Human behavior is always an action by an individual which tells us as much about the individual as it does about a given society and culture. Certainly the individual is *influenced* by the society ("smart guides") and by the culture ("proper guides"). Indeed, the individual is subject to multiple influences; many guidance systems *attempt* to "push" people around. The *climate* is a guidance system, as is "personality" and size of the interactional group. But at base the individual *selects* a bit of behavior and thereby broadcasts to the world, and to himself, "This is me." Human will, dignity, courage, despair, hope and futility must all be brought back to anthropology. Only then will we catch real people, living real lives in a tension-filled arena called a "socio-cultural system." Within this model of culture we will escape two false myths currently plaguing social science. The first says: Since man (*Homo sapiens*) is an animal, then humans must be thought of as just another group of animals. The second says: Since humans and computers both do (at times) similar kinds of work, then man (*Homo sapiens*) is just a machine.

Humans are neither *just animals* nor *just machines*, although they have some characteristics of both. Humans are rather self-transforming systems plagued and blessed by big brains, which make any problem (sooner or later) solvable. The anthropological researcher must be able to bring this realistic hope to the people with whom fieldwork is done. As a prophet of hope armed with the tools of science, the anthropologists can become truly relevant in a world fast approaching 1984.

4. Experimentation: the Natural Experiment as a Modern Research Tool

Anthropology is flooded with facts but can boast of few laws and theories. Our sorry state, as I have suggested, is due to the minimal use of experimentation, the very approach which ushered in modern science. To do experimentation without manipulating people we must utilize the "natural experiment" (Festinger and Katz 1953). The value of this approach as well as some of its problems are discussed in this section. More specifically I will describe four of my own natural experiments. The first two are but briefly summarized since they are more fully discussed elsewhere (chapter 4). The last two, both dealing with Hasidic culture, will be presented in greater detail.[10]

4.1 Natural Experiments 1 and 2: Mohawks and Trinidadian Peasants

The natural experiment is a research strategy in which the researcher *selects* a situation for study where *change of a clear and dramatic nature has occurred*. Such change is then considered as the *independent variable* ("the cause") of additional changes. Working within the general framework of cultural ecology (Steward 1955), I hypothesized that modern Mohawk culture was quite different from ancient Mohawk culture because modern Mohawks "made a living" in ways quite different from their ancestors. In the language of cultural ecology, my hypothesis was that *a changed mode of cultural ecological adaptation has led to culture change functionally related to adaptational changes.*

The data on modern Mohawks indicated that although culture change had occurred, the change was of a limited nature. Moreover, many of the new patterns were quite unconnected to cultural ecological changes; there was considerable persistence of old cultural patterns. My research with Mohawks led to the rejection of my hypothesis. To better understand the data I developed the concept "social adaptation" to handle change due to differences in the social environment. Armed now with two adaptational concepts—cultural ecology and social adaptation—I went to Trinidad to test a second hypothesis.

In the Trinidad study, I selected a community where Creoles and East Indians shared a similar cultural ecology (both did cocoa and coffee farming) and a similar social environment. I formulated an hypothesis: *The common adaptational problems of Creoles and East Indians will lead both groups to develop a similar culture.* As shown in figure 1, the cultural systems of Creoles and East Indians are quite dramatically different. This hypothesis therefore, also had to be rejected.

10. I am indebted to the New York State Museum and Science Service; Columbia University; the Social Science Research Council and the National Institute of Mental Health for the various grants which made these studies possible. The studies outside of Israel are more fully described in the following works: Freilich 1958, 1960a, 1960b, 1961, 1962 and 1963.

FIGURE 1

A Comparative Model for East Indian and Creole Cultural Systems

Points of Reference	Cultural Systems	
	EAST INDIAN	CREOLE
Time	The future	The "Now"
Space	Village; Extended by Permanent Villages of Kin	Village; Extended by Temporary Fête Centers
People *Kinship Unit*	Corporate, Consanguineal, Patrilineal	Noncorporate, Consanguineal, Matrilineal
Associational Patterns	With Family	With Friends Freely Chosen
Authority	Patripotestal, Rigid Hierarchal	Loose, Equalitarian
Exchange *Goods and Services*	Money Medium of Exchange	Money and Sexual Services Media of Exchange
Women	Indirect, Permanent, Between Joint Families	Indirect, Temporal Between Matrifocal Families
Symbols	English	English
Sanctions	Supernatural, Polytheistic	Social (Natural) Plus Fatalism
Goals	Family Improvement	Fête

To explain the data collected in Trinidad I suggested that two kinds of adaptational situations existed—*deterministic* and *permissive*. Trinidadian farmers lived in a permissive environment. Under these conditions each group could continue to practice its own ancient ways and remain culturally different from its neighbor, irrespective of environmental similarities. It appeared clear to me that cultures could be thought of as either *specialized* (functionally related to but one type of environment) or *generalized* (functionally "linkable" to many types of environments). My first two natural experiments were successful insofar as I was "pushed" to explain the facts and (almost) *forced* to develop new concepts. Future research could identify cultures and environments more fully and (I believe) more accurately (see figure 2). As of now I think that

(1) Environments could be *deterministic* ecologically (d)— the way a group made a living could *force* them into certain cultural patterns;

(2) Environments could be *deterministic* socially (d_1)— the way a group had to interact with other groups, tribes and nations could necessitate given cultural patterns;

(3) Environments could be *permissive* ecologically (p) permitting great leeway for any group living therein to practice whatever culture they desire;

(4) Environments could be *permissive* socially (p_1).

Logically, if a group entered into a dd_1 situation the deterministic "economic" and social forces would soon lead to culture change. However pp_1 situations would tend to allow for cultural persistence. Moreover, under all conditions of change a generalized culture could more easily adapt than a specialized culture. In terms of this model, the hypothesis tested in Trinidad may have been rejected because of a pp_1 environment, because the adapting cultures were both generalized or because of both these factors combined.

FIGURE 2

A Modified Cultural Ecological Model

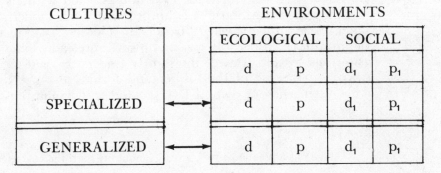

CULTURES	ENVIRONMENTS			
	ECOLOGICAL		SOCIAL	
	d	p	d_1	p_1
SPECIALIZED	d	p	d_1	p_1
GENERALIZED	d	p	d_1	p_1

Key:
d =deterministic cultural ecology
p =permissive cultural ecology
d_1=deterministic social environment
p_1=permissive social environment

4.2 Hasidim in Suburbia: Natural Experiment 3

In Rabbiville, New York, Hasidic Jews inhabit an environment sharply different from that of their ancestors in Eastern Europe.[11] Here was change of a clear and dramatic nature and its effects could be studied as a natural experiment. Modern Hasidim[12] are the cultural descendants of Israel Ben Eliezer, better known as the *Baal Shem Tov* or *Besht*, who was born in 1698 in a small town in the Carpathian Mountains.[13] As a young man he travelled widely throughout Galicia; and he spent several years in the Carpathian mountains quarrying lime. There he developed a great love for nature and learned how to use plants for healing purposes. It was in the role of healer that the *Besht* began to expound his religious ideas.

The central theme of the Besht's teachings was *love of God in a direct, person-to-God, relationship*. God he taught, was everywhere and accessible to everyone: the poor, the lowly, the deformed, the sinner and the saint. God, the loving and caring father, wanted people to come to him in joy and gladness; with dance and music mixed with the language of the market place. The *Besht* died in 1760 and left his environment with a two-fold legacy: a way of living and praying called Hasidism and a group of disciples dedicated to spreading the teachings of the Master.

4.21 Rabbiville: Place, People and Culture

Rabbiville, New York, is a very different community from the Hasidic *shtetl* (little town) of Eastern Europe. Here 74 nuclear families live in rows of Cape Cod houses, each with its own little garden. Each house is equipped with such modern conveniences as are considered "basic" in middle-class American communities. Noticeably absent, however, are radios and television sets. Rabbi David, the saintly leader for these people, frowns on the use of the former and forbids the use of the latter. Hence no one owns a T.V. set, and only 25 families have radios.

---

11. Rabbiville is a pseudonym for a real community with the characteristics herein described.
12. Basic texts on Hasidism can be found in the bibliography. Of special value are the works of the modern mystic, Martin Buber.
13. Much concerning the life and teachings of the Bal Shem Tov comes to us by word of mouth; and has been subject to the mythological processes which "attach themselves" to the life histories of all great minds. His name *Bal Shem Tov* (literally good master of the name of God) refers to *a man* believed to possess exceptional spiritual powers, *who was able to work miracles and to heal through the use of the ineffable name of God.*

Rabbiville, although superficially an American community, does not fit our image of American middle class life. The men have long beards, *payos* (long ear curls) and wear large, black, felt-rimmed hats. The women generally wear dark and drab-looking clothes, *sheitels* (wigs) and head scarfs. Following the religious injunction that a woman should not appear attractive to "other" men (other than the husband), Rabbivillian women make themselves look much older than they really are. Their actual ages range from early twenties to middle thirties. Community life is oriented toward religion; a strict following of Old Testament laws and additional injunctions of Rabbi David. Men, women and children have their own special tasks to perform and Rabbiville itself is seen as something unique in the strange environment called suburbia. The outside world is seen in various degrees of impurity.*

The men work in a great variety of occupations: they are proprietors, professionals, artisans, "learners" (those who sit and study all day) managers and laborers (see Table 1). Average incomes are between 400 and 500 dollars per month.† The women have one major role-goal to reach—becoming a *bal buster* (a mistress of her house). This role keeps women busy from morning till night cooking, cleaning, sewing, making clothes, and caring for children (four to five on the average).

The roles played in Rabbiville are essentially those found in its Eastern European counterpart. In addition there are the new positions of mayor, deputy mayor, councilman, village secretary, village postman and busdriver. In terms of social status, Rabbiville still has its *shayne* (1st class), *balabatishe* (second class) and *prosteh* (third class) *Yiden* (Jews). And each group has its special section in the synagogue. The criteria for class is still the same: *Yiches* (or family), learning and wealth.

American culture slowly but slyly slips into Rabbiville, thus far making but a few dramatic inroads. There is the "committee" complex with people wanting to form subgroups to solve specific problems instead of just asking Rabbi David's advice. Ideas of democratic government are seeping in with the notion that one should give to Caesar (Rabbi David) only his due (submission in religious matters). There is the growing realization that an education in "English" subjects (mathematics,

---

*Going from the least to the most "impure" there are: (1) Hasidim who do not live in Rabbiville; (2) religious Jews who are not Hasidim; who do not attach themselves to a Holy man or *Zaddik*; (3) non-orthodox Jews and (4) non-Jews. Marriage is permitted only with Hasidim; preferably those from Rabbiville.
†1961-62 figures.

TABLE I
Occupations of Household Heads of Rabbiville

Type of Occupation	No.	(%)	Explanation
Rabbi and Learners	6	(8.1)	Rabbi David, his son and son's friend, the Rov and two others
Proprietors	23	(31.1)	Selling; books, eggs; manufacturing; caps, dinette-sets, thread and iron specialties; jewelry making and repairing; silver engraving; operating a travel agency; running a "bargain store"; doing textile printing and electrical repairs, and selling used cars
Professionals	12	(16.2)	Mainly, teachers in Rabbiville or in nearby Jewish schools, and assistant rabbis in nearby communities
Artisans and Skilled Laborers	21	(28.4)	All work in the diamond industry
Semi-professionals Managerials	4	(5.4)	A typesetter in a leading American newspaper; a shoe salesman; a factory manager; the community's bus driver
Laborers (Including those on partial relief)	8	(10.8)	Includes post office workers, factory workers (in needle trades, knitting and textiles) and odd job men
Totals	74	(100%)	

history, English language and literature) can lead to a more prosperous future.

The Rabbivillians associate on the basis of several principles: (1) a separation of the sexes (2) praying done primarily by men (3) one should stay with people of one's class (4) one should never insult another person (5) people of one's nationality are "better." Although people have their different associational

FIGURE 3

Hasidic Culture: Eastern Europe and Rabbiville, U.S.A.

	Eastern European	Rabbiville	Change Index*
1. *Time Orientation*	Past	Past + Future	3
2. *Space:* Of Functioning	*Shtetl* (small community) some "movements" for trading, visiting, etc.	Community+ Regular trips to Urban centers	4
Transformation	Minimal	Much	5
3. *People:* Segments	Rabbi; Hasidim 1st, 2nd and 3rd class	Rabbi; Hasidim 1st, 2nd and 3rd class	1
Basic Kinship Unit	Nuclear Family	Nuclear Family	1
Major Roles	Rabbi, Ritual Assistants Business people, laborers	Rabbi, Ritual Assistants, Business People Mayor, Deputy, Trustee	3
Associational Groupings	Along sex lines, along class lines	Along sex and class lines, also by place of birth	3

FIGURE 3 (cont.)

	Eastern European	Rabbiville	Change Index*
4. Authority	God→Rabbi→Hasidim Women→children	God→Rabbi→Hasidim Women→children Also per political office	3
5. Exchanges: Symbols (i.e. linguistic)	Yiddish, primarily	Yiddish + English	2
Economic	Money the medium, few material possessions	Money, many material possessions	4
Marriage	Arranged marriages between Hasidic families	Arranged, between Hasidim	1
6. Sanctions	Primarily religious	Religious and Social	3
7. Goals	Survival, health, "life upliftment" via ritual	Health, "life upliftment" Economic improvement	3

Totals 36

*1=no change; 2=slight modification; 3=small change; 4=great change; 5=very great change; 36÷by 13= approximately 3 cliques, everyone is allowed (indeed encouraged) to pray together 3 times each day: at the morning, afternoon and night services. Because of these prayers and due to the little chats that follow a prayer meeting, information in Rabbiville flows swiftly throughout the community. Whatever one Rabbivillian knows will soon be known by the whole community.

The Hasidic world is orderly and dualistic. Each week has two parts; work days and holidays. And each week has at least one holiday; the Sabbath. Each month has regular Sabbaths and one special Sabbath; the one just before the new moon. The year can also be subdivided into times of regular holidays (Sabbath and minor festivals) and special holiday times (Passover, *Shevout, Succot,* New Year and *Yom Kippur*).

Hasidic life in Rabbiville shows both change and continuity with the past; as shown in Figure 3. The indices presented refer to the following scale:

Degree of Change

None	Slight	Small	Great	Very Great
1	2	3	4	5

Each index is understood within the following guidelines:

Time—index 3. A growing concern with the future while not letting the past "go." Planning for educational and physical plant changes is slowly getting general support.

Space
  Of Functioning—index 4. Much more travelling done both for work and for recreation.
  Degree of Transformation—index 5. Rabbivillians in charge of a 140 acre community (Rabbiville is an incorporated village) have both the ability and desire to change their physical environment.

People
  Social Segments—index 1. No change.
  Basic Kinship Unit—index 1. No change.
  Basic Roles—index 3. There are new roles in the system.
  Associational Groupings—index 3. Change here due to the fact that Rabbivillians come from a number of different European backgrounds and the concept of *landsman* (person of my nation) affects interaction.

Authority System—index 3. Rabbi's rule is being weakened by "committee" complex and by democratic ideas of American culture.

Exchanges

Symbols—index 2. People are but infrequently using English. Many of them have difficulty speaking English.

Goods and Services—index 4. A much greater interest in comfortable and aesthetic surroundings. Also a great use of "modern" home conveniences at least in comparison with Eastern European Hasidic women.

Women (in Marriage)— index 1. No change.

Sanctions—index 3. "Friendly" social sanctions coming from friends and neighbors of the Rabbivillians are pushing the community away from the isolationism of the Eastern European Hasidic Shtetl.

Goals—index 3. The old idea of "No bread, no Torah" or eat only enought to keep body and soul together to do God's bidding, is changing. The value of physical comfort is appreciated ever more as well as the importance of making money. The system can be described as having changed "a little"; index 3 is the arithmetic mean. Since Rabbiville is a fairly new social system, the 3 index location is quite meaningful. It is reasonably assumed that many years in the American environment of upstate New York will push this community into yet greater change.

4.22 Results of the Hasidim-in-Rabbiville Study

Rabbiville is an excellent example of a specialized culture in a pp_1 environment. The "specialization" of the Rabbivillians is religion (Hasidic Judaism) and submission to a religious leader. The cultural ecology is permissive since many ways of making a living are possible for the Hasidim. And the social environment is permissive in that (1) the larger society is a democracy and (2) the Hasidim "own" their own community —their houses are bought and the land is now part of an incorporated village, under their own direction. Situations of pp_1 permit cultural persistence; and specialized cultures tend to persist or "die" (just as do specialized animals). An index of 3 was calculated; which represents "small change." It is well to list the forces making for change and non-change respectively.

Forces for change:

1. New problems which relate to running an incorporated village
2. New problems of budgeting (which pertain to living in a high cost-of-living area)

3. Problems of running a showplace: a self-governing Hasidic village
4. Problems pertaining to integration of multi-national Hasidim: Hasidim from Hungary, Poland, Russia, etc.
5. Influence of American culture: materialism, separation of religion and politics, "committee" complex

Forces for Non-Change:
1. Strong religious emphasis of the group
2. Continued power of Rabbi David, the Zaddik (Holy Leader);
3. Information pooling abilities of the system; keeping people "in line"
4. Marriage endogamy—within Hasidic communities
5. Control of the educational system by the community
6. Maintaining own language, Yiddish
7. Keeping many American influences out by banning T.V.

The above model for change and non-change related to two culture-types (specialized and generalized) and to several possible combinations of either deterministic or permissive ecologies and social situations (pp_1, pd_1, dp_1, dd_1). With all the complexities of the model, it was still too *simple* to pick up the possible paths a socio-cultural system could take when its environment changed. I modified some of my ideas relating to culture change but before this I did another experiment with a Hasidic community. This one was situated in Israel, its name was *Moshav Hadash* (a pseudonym).

4.3 Experiment 4: Moshav Hadash, Israel

A *Moshav* is a cooperative agricultural settlement. Agriculture is a new mode of adaptation for Hasidim. Agricultural work, then, could be considered as the "independent variable" leading to other changes in Hasidic life.

4.31 Historical Background and actual Work Patterns

The Hasidim of Moshav Hadash left Europe after World War II. Under direction from their Rabbi the Zaddik, Rabbi Zev, they were directed to go to Israel to create their own community. I had questions concerning the early days of communal living in Israel and concerning the problems of setting up an agricultural community, and these were generally avoided, with brief, indirect replies. Not making much headway with questions concerning their life as farmers I began to study farming behavior directly. Walking around the community, I was surprised to discover that few of the Hasidim were actually working as farmers. Almost invariably, my question "Can I talk to Mr. X?" received the same answer: "Mr X had to go to town today." I came to a tentative conclusion after weeks of not finding the farmers at home or in the fields: *Very few of the Hasidim were actually practicing agriculture.* For some reason or other they wanted to be known as "farmers" but their income came from other sources.

I confronted the Hasidim with this data and they said "you are partly right; actually about a third of our people lived completely from their agricultural labors; one third were part time agriculturalists and a third did nothing in agriculture." Very few would admit to what my data actually showed: that of the original 74 moshav members only 13 were engaged in full time agriculture (17.5%). Further that the community had grown from the original 74 families to 170 families and that of the now 170 families only approximately 7.7% (13 out of 170) were full time agriculturalists. The way community members actually earned their livelihoods is shown in Table II.

My problem had now changed from the one proposed while I was still in America—*what effects will agricultural life have on Hasidic culture*—to the one provided by the field data. Now I had to investigate *what factors led this group to give up agriculture even though their Rabbi had directed them to form an agricultural village.* I had a number of hypotheses: first, that Hasidic cultural practices were contradictory to an agricultural life. Second, that this group coming from various parts of Europe had only the common bond to their Rabbi to bind them to each other and this was not enough to lead to the kinds of cooperative efforts required to successfully run a Moshav. Third, that urban dwellers cannot adapt to Moshav living. Fourth, that orthodox Judaism presents great problems to the would-be farmer. Fifth, that farming was looked down on by Shtetl Jews as being *prosteh arbait* (low class, common type work). A few of my hypotheses were quickly put aside after several interviews with agricultural experts working for the *Sachnut*—the Jewish Agency. I was told that although urban people have difficulties living in a Moshav, many highly successful Moshavim existed in Israel which were run by people who were previously urban. Indeed most of the new immigrants (post-Israeli war of liberation) were from nonagricultural backgrounds and most of them were settled in Moshavim.

I returned to my first set of questions concerning agriculture in the early days of Moshav Hadash. Armed with data on actual work practices I now asked, more forcefully, (1) Have you experienced difficulties in working in a cooperative agricultural setting? (2) Do you find agricultural life inconsistent with Hasidic beliefs? and (3) What precisely took you out of agriculture? My new data indicated that working *cooperatively* was never a problem for the Hasidim and that agriculture was considered proper work since Rabbi Zev had ordered them to do it.

Table 2
THE MAIN SOURCE OF INCOME OF
HOUSEHOLD HEADS OF MOSHAV HADASH

Occupation Providing Main Source of Income	No.	Percent
Professionals (mainly teachers)	65	38.3
Sales People (mainly working in shops in urban centers	21	11.9
Community Employees	20	11.8
Unskilled Laborers	18	10.7
Farmers	13	7.7
Skilled Laborers and Artisans	10	5.9
Managerial Work	9	5.3
Pensioners	8	4.8
Proprietors	4	2.4
Learners	2	1.2
Totals	170	100%

The Hasidim had picked a site for their Moshav which had easy access to a large city. With the help of Rabbi Zev they came to the conclusion that if their Moshav was near a city they could pick up some work in offices and businesses. This was extra security for people without any training in farming. The argument in short was that "if farming does not suit us we can get jobs in the city." With all good intentions about creating a farming cooperative, the Hasidim found the work difficult and unrewarding. Whether due to poor instruction, lack of adequate water facilities or absence of talent for farming (all reasons given me) little profit was made from agricultural work.

After nearly a year of unsuccessful experiences with agriculture it seemed evident to the Hasidim that they would not be able to support themselves and their families by farming. The Hasidim thus started searching for other kinds of ways to make a living. That they were successful in their search was partly a function of their previous planning in the selection of the site, partly a function of the duality of their goals, and partly a function of Hasidic culture. Having discussed the "previous planning" factor, let me turn to the latter factors.

Duality of goals and Hasidic culture

My question "How is it you have gone against your Rabbi's wishes and are not working in agriculture?" received two answers from everyone who was asked. First, I was told that they had all received permission from the Rabbi to leave agricultural work after they had told him that they could not support themselves this way. Second, I was informed that creating an agricultural village was only one of the goals of their Rabbi and that perhaps his more important goal was to spread Hasidism.

In spreading the Hasidic way of life, the Hasidim used two strategies: first, they gave lectures and sang Hasidic melodies in various nonreligious communities; second, they set up schools which were staffed by their people so that the young children of Israel could be trained in Hasidic thought and culture. The goal of spreading Hasidism took away time and energy which might otherwise have been used for agricultural training, work and planning. It also provided urban type jobs for the Hasidim—teaching—and gave many Hasidim the opportunity to leave agriculture.

That many Hasidim were fit to be teachers is a factor of Hasidic culture which needs some elucidation. An individual in this system—a Hasid—is expected to perform the various *mitzvot*—religious prescriptions—*more than completely*. A Hasid is supposed to go beyond the minimal requirements of action and belief. He is supposed to dig deeply into the meanings of ritual and religious observances so that religious acts can be performed with gladness and joy. The role of teacher of religion comes easily to the average Hasid; it is simply teaching others what one had to learn for oneself.

I asked people "Why did a small minority of Hasidim stay in agricultural work?" Answers received can be summarized as: (1) *Intrinsically*, agricultural work was *prost* (lower class). (It became somewhat less *prost* when Rabbi Zev directed people to that occupation.) (2) People were attracted to other more *balbatishe* (middle class work). But all members of the community could not make it in *babatishe work*. (3) Some people with talent in agriculture, having the blessings of the Rabbi to stay as farmers, found the work congenial and profitable.

I then began investigating the problems of social adaptation. Specifically, I needed to know (1) Was the Israeli government fooled into believing that this was a real Moshav? Discovering from government officers that they knew what was going on right from the start I enquired (2) How it was that an agricultural community in which over one million Israeli pounds was invested was being allowed to run as a non-Moshav? Answers to this question were difficult to come by. But I persisted and discovered the following.

The Hasidim are contributing to the Israeli scene in an important way. They brought a strong religious fervor which many found inspiring. They provided an idealism which the country needed: an antidote to the growing materialism which urbanization was bringing. Moreover, many powerful political figures had strong attachments to Hasidic life. As was often mentioned to me by Israeli officials: *To get an audience with high-ranking members of government is not difficult in Israel: but the Hasidim get what they want soon after the interview*!

The failure of Moshav Hadash (as a Moshav) might lead to the conclusion that Hasidic culture (a specialized culture) cannot persist in an agricultural setting (a deterministic ecology) even though the social environment was permissive. In shortened form: *In a situation of dp_1 a specialized culture tries to "move" to a situation of pp_1*. The conclusion, in my opinion, is *almost* correct. Many orthodox and several Hasidic communities exist in Israel as *Moshavim* (plural). In Moshav Hadash itself *some* Hasidim manage to both practice their traditional culture and to be farmers. The conclusion needs to be modified to: *A specialized culture can persist in dp_1 situations. However, difficulties in adaptation will lead the system to try to "move."* The fact that many in Moshav Hadash could "move" out of agriculture and toward urban occupations appears to be a function of several factors:

1. Rational planning by leaders to situate near an urban center
2. Initial agricultural failure, leading people to look to the city
3. The goal of spreading Hasidism taking time from agriculture
4. The ability of the group to manipulate its social environment

To summarize the data, the Moshav Hadash, a specialized culture transplanted in a new nation, tried to find an ecological niche which would do two things: (1) permit Hasidim to follow their Rabbi's directives and form an agricultural community; (2) maximize opportunities for change should agriculture create economic and social hardships. Due to having political power and because of their special contribution to Israeli life, the group was successful both in getting what they wanted and then in "leaving" agricultural work. The system's missionary goals and the inexperience of its members with agricultural work made agricultural failure highly probable. Moreover, cultural definitions of agricultural labor as *prost* made failure in farming easy to take. Availability of city work made it unnecessary for the Hasidim to persevere too long in farming.

4.4 Lessons from Experimentation

The natural experiment attempts to set up the contrived experiment as its model; there is the assumption that science progresses only if experimental work is done. The anthropologist working in the tradition of natural science *and* being part of a moral order finds enormous difficulties in manipulating people to follow an experimental design. The natural experiment provides a way out. Some control is lost by allowing "nature" and normal social events to give us independant variables. But this work still forces us to solve problems which all the sciences face. How do you describe a situation accurately enough so that you know when and if it changes? My model for description (Figure 3) surely needs to be modified; but it captures much of importance in socio-cultural life. Time, people, space, authority, exchange and goals are basic elements in every human society. Each of these elements must be dealt with, providing a second problem which the natural experimenter will have to solve and this is: How shall we *consider these elements*? Can we simply ask "What is the basic time orientation of the group? Toward the past, present or future?" Or, is it not better to enquire "What is the time orientation for each area of social life: for economics, politics, kinship, religion and recreation?" How does one measure "degree of transformation of space"? What guidelines can we develop accurately to assign change-index numbers? My questions all deal with the issue of measurement; an issue forced upon us when we attempt to experiment.

Experimentation forces us to describe formally and to develop measuring devices; it does more. Our initial feeble approaches in natural experimentation will probably lead to some wrong hypotheses. The events predicted will not occur; we will be forced to develop other concepts to better explain socio-cultural processes. Differently put, a failed experiment has much value for an infant science. It forces the researchers to improve methodology and concepts. Our new understandings of *culture* as rules for proper behavior need to be fed into new experiments; so does the notion of *social guides*, rules for smart behavior. Humans are decision-makers influenced rather than determined by social and cultural rules. New problems will lead human actors to invent novel solutions. Any novel solution is potentially a trigger for much related social and cultural change. In future natural experiments it would be well to consider change as something "natural" and normal in socio-cultural events. Irrespective of whether environments are codeable as dd_1 or pp_1 (or whatever); and whether cultures are specialized or generalized we must assume change. Assuming change, we ask "How much change will occur?" "What areas will change most and what least?" and "What rate of change can be expected?" Assuming change requires us to develop more sophisticated change models. The challenge for the natural experimenter is great.[14]

14. The ideas developed in this paper received their inspiration from (among other works) "Experimental Design in the Study of Culture Change" by George Spindler and Walter Goldschmidt, *Southwestern Journal of Anthropology*, volume 8, Spring 1952.

SOCIAL RULES OF SPEECH IN KOREAN: THE VIEWS OF A COMIC STRIP CHARACTER*

C. Paul Dredge

All languages are spoken with reference to social rules. This paper attempts to clarify socially determined conventions that govern speech in the Korean language. The analysis is based on sample speech patterns taken from a popular Korean newspaper comic strip entitled "Ko (a common surname) Pa-u Yong gam."[1] Its hero, Ko Pa-u, is an astute commentator on Korean society, culture, geography, government, and social problems as they are reflected in current events.

In comparison to speakers of other languages, speakers of Korean are forced to choose from an unusually wide range of alter-

---

* This is an edited and much shortened version of the paper which first appeared in *Korea Journal* in January 1976
1. A comparable American comic strip is "Blondie."

natives in order to fit the form of speech to the social situation. The most important decision a Korean speaker must make, comparable to the French choice between pronouns, is whether to use the plain form of the verb or the polite form.[2] The choice is influenced by age, authority, social status, intimacy and kinship. As shown in Table 1 the same form of speech is not used every time one speaks to a given person. There is, however, a typical way of speaking to someone, and when this proper-way is not used some additional information is being sent. It is typical for a husband to speak to his wife using *plain* forms and for a wife to speak to her husband using *polite* forms. When a wife uses a plain form to her husband it is generally a sign of anger.

Table 1
Plain and Polite Forms in Korean
as taken from 150 comic strips of Ko Pa-u

Sender of Message	Receiver of Message	1950's Plain	1950's Polite	1960's Plain	1960's Polite
Husband	Wife	13	3	25	6
Wife	Husband	2	19	2	28
Adult	Child	32	2	9	0
Child	Adult	9	17	1	5
Child	Child	20	2	2	0
Employer	Employee	15	0	22	5
Employee	Employer	0	9	0	20
Human	Self	30	1	35	0
Human	Animal	0	0	1	0
Friend	Friend	34	8	43	16
Tradesman	Customer	1	15	0	33
Customer	Tradesman	4	8	12	12
Professional	Client	1	7	1	9
Client	Professional	2	6	1	2
Charity-solicitor	Giver	1	5	0	1
Giver	Charity-solicitor	7	1	3	0
Stranger	Stranger	10	6	0	7
Younger relative	Older relative	0	0	0	3
Older relative	Younger relative	0	0	3	0
Woman	Man	0	0	0	4
Man	Woman	0	0	0	3

2. Plain vs. polite is a simplification of the true situation, but one which Koreans themselves readily resort to in summarizing the speech level system.

Traditionally, a marriage in Korea was a contract between two families. The husband and mother-in-law had considerable power over the wife; and the speech patterns reflected the power relationships. Many things have changed since World War II; but family relationships have remained much the same. A child still uses polite forms to his parents. At times the plain form will be used to the mother (a lesser authority figure) either because the child has not yet learned the correct form or focusing on the intimate loving relationship between mother and child. The indulgence in this kind of speech gradually disappears as a child attends school and becomes familiar with proper speech behavior. The two instances (Table 1) of an adult using a polite form to a child represent, respectively, sarcasm (by a chauffeur to his boss's son) and a request for a favor (by Ko Pau to a newspaper boy).

The employer-employee dyad illustrates a true power-dominated relationship. The employer will use polite forms when he wants a special favor or when speaking to a group of employees. The general rule is that when addressing a group the polite form is used unless every member of the group is an obvious subordinate, as in the case of a gym teacher talking to his students.

Humans talking to themselves and to animals use plain speech styles. Close friends use plain forms with each other, whereas acquaintances tend to use polite forms until their relationship becomes more intimate. Tradespeople and customers use polite forms to each other. In keeping with the Confucian tradition of scholarship and government service, any person who holds a doctorate—medical or "of philosophy"—or who is a high government official ranks in the highest class of society. Even if such a person has no authority over his "client" and though he may be of the same age he should be addressed with polite forms and he may respond with plain forms. A professional will speak in polite style to an elder.

When high status is linked to poverty, continued use of polite forms lends a touch of satire to the communication. This is illustrated when Ko visits his neighbor, a Ph.D. in dire economic straights, and asks him in the polite form: "What are you doing with your books lately?" He is answered in the proper plain form: "I am seeing if my ox can survive by eating books."

"Charity solicitor" is usually a euphemism for a beggar, who must use polite forms and is answered with plain forms. Strangers generally use polite forms to each other; although a much older stranger may use plain forms with a much younger person. The large number of plain forms shown in Table 1 between strangers are examples of intense emotional situations; such as when someone is drowning and asks for help with the plain form. In times of anger, fear and jesting some reversals of the rules are possible.

The man-to-woman dyad indicates two things. First, little speech interaction occurs between men and women who are non-kin. Second, the authority of the male sex rarely extends outside the home. A man talking to a woman acquaintance uses the polite form, just as she does to him.

The diagram shown in figure 1 summarizes the cases in the sample data (150 comic strips) and also is in accordance with opinions of Korean informants. It is to be understood as follows: A person older than me is addressed with polite forms; a child in plain forms. If the person's age is equal or less than mine; it is a question of authority—superior authority requires polite forms. Equal or inferior authority makes it a question of general status—superior status requires polite forms, inferior status requires plain forms. If the statuses of the speakers are equal, it becomes a question of intimacy. Intimates use plain forms, others use polite forms.

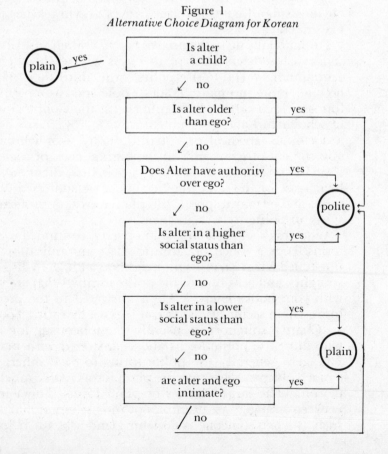

Figure 1
Alternative Choice Diagram for Korean

THE LANGUAGE OF
DRUNKS*

Earl Rubington

Language, in part, is composed of categories. These categories
may be official and conventional, or unofficial and unconventional. Official categories are used in formal situations when
people of divergent social statuses mix, e.g., writing, lectures,
speeches. Conventional or informal categories are used in everyday life, most often when people meet as equals. Official terms
can sometimes be used, but more often a set of terms emerges
which make for common understanding among equals.

Unconventional categories exist for both equals and unequals
who live outside the controls of either formal or everyday social

---
*Reprinted from *Quarterly Journal of Studies on Alcohol* vol 32 No. 3 Sept.
1971. The original source gives a list of over 500 alcohol-related terms.
Examples include **bar drinker** One who drinks only in bars. **bar fly** A per-

life. Some of the users of unconventional speech are members of the underworld, jazz musicians, teen-agers, juvenile delinquents, narcotics users, hoboes, tramps, bums, Skid Row people, Blacks and members of other ethnic subcultures. But whether official, conventional or unconventional, categories organize social life.

At present, such a thing as an "alcohol language" exists. Formed in part by laymen and in part by professionals, it takes either an oral or a written form. For instance, there is a language of Alcoholics Anonymous which one can hear at A.A. meetings or read in the A.A. literature. Similarly, there is a whole set of terms which might be called "drinking slang," and this too is both oral and written, though probably more often oral than written. Finally, there is also a "drunk language" which is almost wholly oral. This is the language of people variously designated as Skid Row alcoholics, homeless men, chronic drunkenness offenders, "drunks," and the like.

Such social types participate, to greater or lesser degree, in deviant groups. To participate at all they need to learn some of the terms. Since the culture of "drunks" is relatively simple as compared with, say, the narcotics user, the number of terms and the array of people, places, things and events covered by

---

son who frequents bars. **barreled up** Intoxicated. **bat** Extended drinking bout. **bathtub gin** Gin produced illegally in bathtubs (or other large vessels) during Prohibition. **bats** Delirium tremens; e.g., " . . . is in the bats." **belt** A drink, usually from a bottle [either as verb or noun]. **bend the elbor** Imbibe freely. **bender** Extended drinking bout. **B-girl** A paid companion in certain bars who induces men to buy drinks and who may or may not engage in prostitution or other illegal activities. **big head** Hangover. Also BIG SKULL. **bindle stiff** A hobo who works, drinks socially if at all, and carries his belongings in a bedroll. **bing-bang** Gasoline and milk cocktail, alleged to be popular on Philadelphia's Skid Row; also *gasso*. **binge** Drinking bout. **bit of the hair** Short for the *hair of the dog that bit you*. **blackout** Alcoholic palimpsest, amnesia [either as verb or noun]. **blase** Intoxicated. **blind** A respectable façade which conceals some illicit enterprise; e.g., a dry-cleaning store which is in reality a gambling office. **blind pig** Illegal liquor outlet. **block and fall** Inexpensive fortified wine. "So named because you walk a block after a drink of this wine and then fall." See also *Sneaky Pete*. **blood** Port wine. **blotto** Intoxicated. **boilermaker** Same as a *ball and a half*. **bombed** Intoxicated. **booster** First drink in the morning, the *eye-opener*, the *starter*. **booze** Any alcoholic beverage, especially distilled spirits. **booze fighter** An alcoholic. Also BOOZEHOUND, BOOZER. **boozing** Drinking alcoholic beverages. **booze talk, the booze talking** Grandiose statements made only when the speaker is intoxicated. **bottle drinker** Member of a *bottle gang*; one who does not drink in bars. **bottle gang** Men who have pooled their resources in order to obtain alcohol for the group. **bottle off** Same as *taper off*. **bottom** Lowest limit of alcoholic degradation. See also *high-bottom, low-bottom*. **bouncing** To be on a drinking bout; e.g., "I hear . . . is still bouncing." **Bowery bum** Man who lives on the Bowery in New York City; by extension, any inhabitant of a Skid Row. **break a seal with** Drink sociably; so called because it is necessary to break the seal on the bottle before drinking. Also *split a few seals with*.

them are not very diversified. Nonetheless the language, such as it is, exists and serves its purposes. Firstly, it is a vehicle for communication, particularly about drinking and its consequences. Secondly, it is a badge, revealing membership, including and excluding at one and the same time. And thirdly, it has its expressive uses.

Similarly, the language of "drunks" can have its purposes for those who are not members of groups which understand and use its terms: to students of language it can be of interest in its own right; for sociologists and anthropologists, it can be studied to learn exactly how "drunks" organize their lives and deal with the typically recurrent situations which make up those lives. It may also have possible uses in communication when nonmembers of "drunk groups" seek to persuade and influence members to defect from their peculiar style of life.

The Vocabulary of Drink

At least two compilers of dictionaries of slang have noted that the act of drinking and its consequences have probably spawned more slang terms than any other social act (1, 2). A good deal of these terms are organized around drinking as an action system which has five phases: procurement, consumption, repair, punishment and reintegration (3). Many of the terms "drunks" use for discussing these phases, their cycles and their peculiar problems are not unknown to lay people.

This may well be the case because of the nature of slang and its social action. Slang deals with the immediate, the present, the colorful, the different, the novel. More often it is expressive rather than abstract or denotative like scientific language. For example, persons observing others who are intoxicated have had occasion to remark the effects of alcohol on behavior and to invent or borrow colorful terms for describing that behavior which departs from etiquette. Slang is particularly useful, when drinking is involved, as a language of disparagement. Persons who parade their worst selves before others open themselves to attack, criticism and ridicule. The terms of slang are especially helpful in handling these expressive problems and conveying the contempt and disgust the onlooker feels.

Slang itself represents a departure from cultural rules on how to use conventional language. As such, it says something about the person who uses it. Like obscenity and profanity, slang is a form of deviant behavior in its own right, from the point of view of those people who make and seek to enforce the rules on language. At the same time, slang creeps into common usage in time because it meets needs which conventional language often cannot supply. The officially appropriate language tends toward the abstract and the distant. Slang expressions make it possible to talk about matters of immediate importance about which there is strong feeling but some doubt about appropriate phrasing. These are the same conditions which seem to have produced obscenity and profanity.

The argot of the underworld, narcotics users, jazz musicians, and Skid Row alcoholics arose in response to a similar set of needs. This language is a basic part of the culture of deviant groups. Occupational subcultures, similarly, have their own special languages. For instance, one historical argument is that lawyers spoke in Latin so that their clients would not know what they were saying. The same reasoning applies to the development of underworld argot. As a matter of defense, so the argument runs, it became necessary to talk with colleagues without arousing the suspicions of legitimate people.

The vocabulary of "drunks" is made up of strands of all of these languages—lower-class idiom, underworld argot, and the vocabulary of drinking slang. However, because drinking is at the forefront, "drunks" think, feel and act mainly in terms of its categories. They have created a linguistic environment which largely influences the way they deal with alcohol and alcohol situations. This is an old, shared, linguistic tradition and not likely to die easily.

Some small elements of deceiving listeners or impressing them with a romantic way of life may be involved. But this will certainly be less often the case since "drunks," compared with participants in other deviant groups, are rather well aware of their low status. Turning their own language against their peers is perhaps the only way of deflecting attention from themselves.

More important, however, are the functions of this language within their own wide circle of drinking acquaintances. For this language not only deals with all the aspects of drinking episodes (including activities, objects, states of mind and body, and people involved in them) but likewise contains a moral evaluation of the objects so designated.

Some part of the language may arise out of the personality characteristics of alcoholics or the prolonged effects of drinking on speech functions and perhaps even on thinking—this hypothesis awaits clinical research. However, language is a group product and does not depend upon the properties of individuals. It has much more to do with the situation and the common problems that groups confront. It is one of the more important means of solving problems that were originally formulated in its own terms.

No small part of the success of A.A. depends on the fact that it has coined a special language by which alcoholics desirous of abstinence are able to communicate with one another with a simple set of terms which reveals a common understanding of the dilemmas of recovering alcoholics. New members are able to take on this way of thinking because it ,makes sense of their past and their immediate experience. Many nonalcoholics who have had intimate contact with alcoholics are able to understand and communicate with alcoholics very well. They do so because they put themselves in the place of the alcoholic by trying to see his world from his point of view. In the process, they cannot avoid using his language. This is how they put him at his ease, establish rapport, show quickly and immediately in the simplest way that they are aware of his situation: they speak his "lingo."

The mechanics of adopting "drunk talk" are probably no different from those underlying the acquisition of a new language in a new situation. Students do it all the time. Putting themselves in the place of their instructors, they now try to look upon the course materials through his eyes, which means employing his concepts, his language. As Bloomfield (4) pointed out, this is how elegant language is probably learned and transmitted in the first place. One admires and imitates, often unwittingly, another person and in so doing takes on his attitudes, his actions, his speech.[1]

---

1. Very early in the course of a study I became fascinated by "drunk language." Convinced that it was more than a curiosity, more likely a very important center around which the "drunks" understood and organized their lives, I set to work to collect information on and about this language as systematically as I could, given the field-work situation. Accordingly, whenever I heard anyone use a term I did not understand, I repeated it over to myself silently, tried to get its meaning from the context in which it was used, ultimately asked for a definition, and then listed each word together with its definition on an index card. Later I added to this another piece of information. I would list the name of the man who first used the term and the date of use. At the end of each period of field work I listed new terms and added the names of men who used old terms. This information is useful on two accounts: (*a*) it tells which persons are more immersed in "drunk culture" and (*b*) which are the key terms of that culture. References cited: 1. BERREY, L. V. and VAN DEN BARK, M. The American thesaurus of slang. New York; Crowell; 1942. 2. WENTWORTH, H. and FLEXNER, S. B. Dictionary of American slang. New York: Crowell; 1960. 3. RUBINGTON, E. The bottle gang. Quart. J. Stud. Alc. 29: 943-955, 1968. 4. BLOOMFIELD, L. Language. New York; Holt; 1933.

A GUIDE TO PLANNING
FIELD WORK

Morris Freilich

I. Introduction

Knowledge concerning the pragmatics of cross-cultural field work varies greatly. Therefore those who are well versed in such matters as how to (1) select a good graduate program, (2) become a competent researcher, (3) get grants, (4) make travel arrangements, and (5) plan for good health in the field are advised to skip this guide.

II. Selecting a Department for Graduate Studies

The importance of selecting an appropriate department for graduate studies is facilitated by certain pragmatics.

    1. Follow news of departments of anthropology in the *Fellow*

Newsletter. Available from the American Anthropological Association, 1703 New Hampshire Avenue, N.W. Washington, D.C. 20009

2. Get the *Guide to Graduate Programs of Anthropology* an annual bulletin of the American Anthropological Association.
3. Attend as many anthropological meetings as funds permit. Information on these annual meetings is also available in the *Fellow Newsletter*. Some of the major annual meetings by months include:
   a. Southern Anthropological Society, February/March
   b. Northeastern Anthropological Association, April
   c. Southwestern Anthropological Association, April
   d. American Association of Physical Anthropologists, April
   e. Society for Applied Anthropology, April
   f. Central States Anthropological Society, May
   g. Society for American Archaeology, May
   h. Canadian Sociology and Anthropology Association, June
   i. International Congress of Anthropological and Ethnological Sciences, September
   j. International Congress of Linguists, August/September
   k. American Anthropological Association, November
4. Once at an anthropological meeting, it may help to become a participant-observer and do focused interviewing. Interview anthropologists on what their departments are like, what studies are considered "in," what parts of the world are best covered in their course offerings, how stable their faculty is (given the "musical chair game" in academia, high faculty turnover is "normal" in many departments), which theoretical approaches are considered "scholarly," and any other related information you can get.
5. Visit the university that you think may best serve your interests before applying. Do participant-observation work with the graduate students; as low-status subordinates in an organization they are likely to give you much useful data.

III. Research Scholars Are Made Not Born

Programming onself for a successful career in field work necessitates planning and self-discipline. The following guides should be useful.

1. Keep a thought notebook. While reading, keep a notebook on problems that appear to exist within the material being digested. This approach serves various purposes: deeper insights are achieved, and problems are thereby "collected" for many purposes. Such a "problem collection" becomes invaluable for a professional career, especially in summarizing understandings achieved via one's problem collection. C. Wright Mills' *The*

Sociological Imagination is an excellent guide for the creative use of problem development.

2. Expertise in methodology. A modern anthropologist must beware of being fooled by labels. Field work today often involves the use of quantitative and qualitative statistical analysis, computer programming, and related approaches. It is therefore wise to make oneself expert in all areas of social-science research.

3. Experience in field research. A good way of learning research is by doing research. It is important, therefore, to try to become part of some on-going project. It is also valuable for gaining research experience to find a group with an unusual historical and cultural background and to do participant-observation research.

4. Developing different and new relationships. People whose age, religion, socioeconomic background, culture, experience, interest, and goals are very different from the researcher's provide both an intellectual challenge and useful rapport training.

5. Role-playing. It is valuable to get involved with some kind of theatrical group which puts the researcher on stage in front of an audience. This kind of role-playing is not very different from role-playing in a native community, where the anthropologist is on stage for extensive periods of time.

6. Planning for mental health. The cross-cultural researcher needs mental health. One starts with getting as much psychotherapy as is financially possible. Most universities have free counseling available. In large cities, a variety of facilities are available through numerous mental-health associations.

IV. Guide to Grantsmanship

Most research is funded. It is, therefore, necessary to learn the sources of these funds and the correct procedure for obtaining them. Grant-proposal forms generally follow a predictable pattern modeled after textbook interpretations of scientific method. However, each agency generally has its own peculiar instructions as to how their application for funds is to be filled. Read such instructions carefully. Most grant proposals include the following basic information:

1. Biographical information, including names, dates, addresses, institutions of higher education attended, degrees, and honors received.

2. Formal title of the project
3. Research plan
    (a) Introduction—general background of the research proposed
    (b) Justification—relevance of the problem to on-going research, theory development, etc.
    (c) Methodology—clear statement of the problem to be studied, sampling and data-gathering procedure and techniques, plans for data analysis
    (d) Objectives of the research
4. Total amount requested for the grant and detailed budget
    (a) Salaries—project leader, assistants, clerical aide
    (b) Travel expenses
    (c) Maintenance
    (d) Supplies and services
    (e) Equipment
    (f) Other costs
5. Work schedule and publication plans
6. Other research that the applicant has participated in, his publications, papers, etc.

It is important to pick a fund agency that is suitable for the project. Listed below are eleven different sources for information on the funding of research projects. Additional sources can be obtained from the library. High-status friends are often goldmines of information; an experienced researcher can be of invaluable aid prior to and during the application procedure. The Office of External Research is able to supply a *Directory of Governmental Resources,* which includes information on all agencies, bureaus, and offices of the federal government with available research funds.

1. Office of External Research
   Bureau of Intelligence and Research
   U.S. Department of State
   Washington, D.C.

   Publishes the *Directory of Governmental Resources*

2. American Anthropological Association
   1703 New Hampshire Avenue, N.W.
   Washington, D.C. 20009

   Publishes *Fellow Newsletter* with information on grants and fellowships.

3. Committee on International Exchange of Persons
   Conference Board of Associated Research Councils
   2102 Constitution Avenue
   Washington, D.C. 20418

4. The Agricultural Development Council
   630 Fifth Avenue
   New York, N.Y. 10020

   Publishes *ADC Newsletter* and *ADC Researcher*
   containing information on grants and fellowships.

5. Ford Foundation
   320 East 43 Street
   New York, N.Y. 10017

6. American Council of Learned Societies
   345 East 46 Street
   New York, N.Y. 10017

   Publishes *ACLS Newsletter* containing relevant information.

7. American Academy of Arts and Sciences
   280 Newton Street
   Brookline, Massachusetts

8. American Philosophical Society
   104 South Fifth Street
   Philadelphia, Pa.

9. Human Ecology Fund
   201 E. 57 Street
   New York, N.Y.

10. Social Science Research Council
    230 Park Avenue
    New York, N.Y. 10017

11. National Science Foundation
    1520 H Street, N.W.
    Washington, D.C.

V. Natives Beware: Anthropologists Are Coming

After receiving the good news of a successful application for
funding, the often agonizing process of completing all the necessary documentation begins. The anthropologist will generally
require a passport, visas, health certification, etc.

1. Passport. A United States Passport is a travel document showing the bearer's country of origin and identity, and is issued by
the Secretary of State, or under his authority, to persons owing
allegiance to the United States, One cannot leave or enter the
United States without it (except to Canada, Mexico, or the

Bahamas). It is advisable to apply early: it often takes about three weeks to a month's time to process the application.

United States passports are now valid for five years from the date of issue. Renewal can be transacted by mail. While it is possible for members of the same family to travel under one passport (for one fee), be advised against this. In case of emergency, travel separately may be required.

Application for a passport may be made in person to the United States Passport Agency located at:

J.F.K. Building, Boston, Mass.
219 S. Dearborn Street, Chicago, Ill.
51 S.W. First Avenue, Miami, Fla.
Customs House, 423 Canal Street, New Orleans, La.
630 Fifth Avenue, New York, N.Y.
300 N. Los Angeles Street, Los Angeles, Calif.
1410 Fifth Avenue, Seattle, Washington
450 Golden Gate Avenue, San Francisco, Calif.
22nd and E. Street, Washington, D.C.

In other cities, application for a passport may be made before a clerk of a federal or state court that has naturalization jurisdiction.

2. Visas. In most countries where an extended length of stay is planned, a visa will be necessary. A visa is an endorsement on one's passport by a particular country granting entrance into that country. Requirements for a particular country can be obtained from consular representatives located in major cities (especially New York, Washington, D.C., Chicago, San Francisco, Boston). Embassies of most countries are located in Washington, D.C., and addresses of such, or of consuls, may be obtained in the *Congressional Directory*.

It is the responsibility of a traveler to obtain visas, when required, from the appropriate Embassy or consular office. The Department of State, c/o Passport Office, publishes a pamphlet (M-264, 1/68) entitled *Fees Charged by Foreign Countries for the Visa of United States Passports*. It contains information on passports and visas for 170 countries.

3. Health requirements (including vaccinations). Immunization sequences requires much time: start early! To discover the necessary "shots" for the place where research is planned, speak to your physician and write for the following booklets available (for a very nominal fee) from the Superintendent of Documents, Government Printing Office, Washington, D.C. 20402.

Immunization Information for International Travel No. FS2.2:
Im 6/2/967–68   40¢

Health Information for Travel In

Africa, Including Malagasy Republic and Neighboring Islands, No. PHS 748 D

Europe, No. PHS 748

Asia, Including Japan, Indonesia, Philippines, Australia,
and New Zealand, No. PHS 748 C

Mexico, Central and South America, and the Caribbean, No.
PHS 748 B

So You're Going Abroad, No. PHS 748 A

For re-entry into the United States, only an International
Certification of Vaccination is necessary. Most foreign countries
require such a certificate of entering travelers too.

Although each part of the world is affected by different
regulations and suggestions for immunizations, it is generally
true that for Africa and South America, yellow-fever shots are
essential; for Bolivia, Peru, Ethiopia, and Ecuador, typhus is
necessary; East of Suez, cholera immunizations are legally required; and for some areas, an innoculation for plague is recommended. Adequate tetanus and polio boosters are highly
recommended, as is gamma globulin (for hepatitis). Typhoid
vaccinations are often advisable, especially for tropical areas.

4. Hints for Travel Abroad

(a). *International Student Identification Card.* Information
concerning this card may be obtained from:

USNSTA—United States National Student Travel Association
70 Fifth Avenue
New York, N.Y. 10011
or
USNSTA
11753 Wilshire Blvd.
Suite 1
Los Angeles, California 90025

(b). *Youth hostels.* If youth hostels can be of aid, write
American Youth Hostels, National Headquarters, 20
West 17 Street, New York, N.Y. 10011

(c). *Character references.* A certificate attesting to one's
character is available from the local police in the researcher's home town and is a helpful document.

(d). *Statement of financial responsibility.* A certificate stating one's financial responsibility is an assurance that the anthropologist will not run out of money and become dependent on the host country. Such a statement may simply be a letter from those sources financing the research.

(e). *Photographs.* A number of photographs are necessary in the documentation process. It is suggested that extras be made.

(f). *International driver's license.* An International Driving Permit, recognized in most countries, is available through the American Automobile Association (AAA), or affiliated motor clubs.

(g). *Work permits.* Many countries prohibit archaeological excavations without an official permit. Some countries require permission to do field work or ethnographic studies. It is advisable to check with the embassy or consulate. An application for permission should be made well enough in advance of the planned departure date to avoid last-minute delays and disappointments.

(h). *American Embassy.* Find out where the American Embassy or American Consulate nearest to the researcher's field project is located. It may become very important during the time spent in the field. The American Embassy or Consulate is prepared to assist Americans who may find themselves in any difficulty in any country. It is often advisable that one notify the Embassy upon arrival, indicating place of residence and intended length of stay.

(i). *Luggage and weight allowances.* If one flies overseas on a first-class ticket, he is allowed 66 pounds of luggage; in economy class, 44 pounds. Other luggage may be hand carried on board. Within the United States a traveler is permitted two pieces of luggage for air flights. Excess luggage can be shipped Air Freight, often in the same plane, and at reduced rate.

(j). *Clothing.* It is important that one find out what kind of clothing will be needed for the area in which research will take place.

(k). *Embarkation taxes.* While there is no fee for leaving the U.S.A., there may be fees (head tax, passenger-service tax, embarkation tax, airport-service tax, etc.) upon arrival and departure in many countries. This is easily enough checked with the consul or embassy.

(l). *Customs.* Most countries will allow the traveler to take all personal belongings, duty free, into their territories provided they all leave when the researcher departs. However, before attempting to export anything from an archaeological or ethnographic study, authorization from the proper authorities is generally needed. *Customs Hints for Returning U.S. Residents* is a helpful booklet, available from the Bureau of Customs, Treasury Department, Washington, D.C. 20226.

VI. Survival Skills in the Field

1. Foods and liquids. It is important that the researcher learn the edible and poisonous plants, fish, and animals of the area. It is suggested that one not eat any meat that has not been well cooked. Meat that is freshly killed and completely cooked is generally perfectly safe; as is any fruit that must be peeled and any hot, cooked vegetables.

It is generally wise to avoid prepared milk and milk products. If bottled water is available, one should stick with it completely. If not, the boiling of water or water purification methods are suggested.

The United States Navy prepared a book in 1943 on survival techniques on sea, on land, in tropics, desert, or the Arctic. It is called *Survival On Land and Sea* and was prepared for the United States Navy by the Ethnographic Board and the Staff of the Smithsonian Institute, Office of Naval Intelligence, U.S. Navy, 1943. While the book is not for sale, and is not readily available, it may be worthwhile to try and locate a copy. Some researchers have managed to get this book through interlibrary loan.

2. First-aid skills and supplies. It is important to have first-aid equipment handy and to know how and what and when to use such. The American Red Cross publishes several useful guides.

The following list has been suggested by several anthropologists as *necessary supplies* for anyone going into the field:

a good first-aid kit
snake-bite kit (including antivenom)
hypodermic (disposable) needles and syringes
antidysentery medicines
malarial preventatives
antihistamines (anticold pills)

aspirin
pain medicine
tablets to purify water (halazone tablets)
tissues, toilet paper

It is important to label all medicine by name and use.

3. Drug prescriptions and glasses. If one should wear glasses or contact lenses, try to have an extra pair along, or at least a prescription. If special drugs are needed, or if a medical condition exists, please let others in the area know and have the prescriptions written in generic not commercial terms. Also, if possible, try to locate a physician with western training in the research area.

It is helpful that one keep a small card—such as the following—in one's pocket along with the International Certificate of Vaccination at all times.

Side One

Side Two

Medical Identification

DOCTOR

_____
NAME

_____
NATIONALITY

_____

_____

ADDRESS

_____
_____
_____
_____

MEDICAL PROBLEMS

_____
ADDRESS

_____
_____

_____
CONTACT IN CASE OF EMERGENCY

_____
BLOOD GROUP—Rh FACTOR

4. Travel skills. It is important that one gain skills in the transportational modes used in the part of the world where research is to be carried out. The ability to walk for long distances is a must for field work. Skills in different modes of travel and in sports popular in the culture being researched often help in rapport development.

5. Tools and equipment. Each project requires a different set of tools. The novice is advised to carefully check this out with experienced researchers, particularly those who have worked in the area of the projected study.

6. Field notes. It is important that one have a planned strategy for data collecting and recording and the storing of field notes. It has been suggested that one transcribe and, if possible, type his field notes every day. It is desirable to make a copy of all notes and mail one set home.

To summarize—plan early! All you need is a good education, research experience, funds, mental health, good luck, and a great sense of humor.

REFERENCES

FIELD WORK: AN INTRODUCTION

Berreman, Gerald D.
   1962. *Behind Many Masks*. Ithaca, N.Y.: Society for Applied Anthropology, Monograph No. 4.

Boas, Franz
   1938. *General Anthropology*. Boston: D.C. Heath.

Chagnon, Napoleon A.
   1968. "Yanomamö: The Fierce People." New York: Holt, Rinehart and Winston.

Codrington, R. H.
1891. *The Melanesians: Studies in Their Anthropology and Folk-lore.* Oxford: Clarendon Press.

Evans-Pritchard, E. E.
1964. *Social Anthropology and Other Essays.* New York: Free Press.

Freilich, Morris
1963. "The Natural Experiment, Ecology, and Culture." *Southwestern Journal of Anthropology,* 19:21–39.

1964. "The Natural Triad in Kinship and Complex Systems." *American Sociological Review,* 29:183–200.

1967. "Ecology and Culture: Environmental Determinism and the Ecological Approach in Anthropology." *Anthropological Quarterly,* 40:1:

Freilich, Morris and Peter Hirsch
1967. "Mental Health Culture in Rural Missouri." St. Louis, Mo.: The Social Science Institute, Parts 1, 1A, 2, and 3–8.

Gans, Herbert
1968. "The Participant-Observer as a Human Being." *Institutions and the Person,* eds. H. Becker, B. Geer, D. Riesman, and R. Weiss. Chicago: Aldine, pp. 300–317.

Harris, Marvin
1968. *The Rise of Anthropological Theory: A History of Theories of Culture.* New York: Thomas Y. Crowell.

Junod, H. A.
1913. *The Life of a South African Tribe.* Neuchâtel: Attinger.

Lowie, Robert H.
1937. *The History of Ethnological Theory.* New York: Holt, Rinehart and Winston.

Lubbock, Sir John
1872. *Prehistoric Times as Illustrated by Ancient Remains and the Manners and Customs of Modern Savages.* London: Williams, Norgate.

McGrath, Joseph
1964. "Toward a Theory of Method." *New Perspectives in Organization Research,* ed. W. W. Cooper, *et al.* New York: John Wiley.

Malinowski, Bronislaw
1953. *Argonauts of the Western Pacific*. New York: E. P. Dutton.

1967. *A Diary in the Strict Sense of the Term*. New York: Harcourt, Brace & World.

Mead, Margaret
1949. *Male and Female: A Study of the Sexes in a Changing World*. New York: William Morrow.

Merton, Robert K.
1957. *Social Theory and Social Structure*. New York: Free Press.

Morgan, Lewis H.
1851. *League of the Ho-de-no-saunee, or Iroquois*. New York: Dodd, Mead, 1901.

1871. *Systems of Consanguinity and Affinity of the Human Family*. Washington: Smithsonian Contributions of Knowledge, vol. 17.

Powdermaker, Hortense
1967. *Stranger and Friend*. New York: Norton.

Radcliffe-Brown, A. R.
1922. *The Andamen Islanders*. New York: Free Press.

Rivers, W. H. R.
1906. *The Toda*. London and New York: Macmillan.

1910. "The Genealogical Method of Anthropological Inquiry." *The Sociological Review*, 3:1–12.

Schwartz, Morris S., and Charlotte Green Schwartz
1955. "Problems in Participant Observation." *American Journal of Sociology*, 60:343–354.

Smith, M.
1959. "Boas' 'Natural History' Approach to Field Method." *The Anthropology of Franz Boas*, Memoir 89, ed. W. Goldschmidt. Wisconsin, American Anthropological Association, pp. 46–60.

Spencer, Sir Baldwin, and Gillen, F. J.
1899. *The Native Tribes of Central Australia*. London: Macmillan.

Spencer, Herbert
1873–1880. *Descriptive Sociology*. Vols. I–XV. New York: Appleton.

Tax, Sol
1955. "From Lafitau to Radcliffe-Browne: A Short History of the Study of Social Organization." *Social Anthropology of North American Tribes,* ed. F. Eggan. Chicago: University of Chicago Press, pp. 445–481.

Tylor, E. B.
1872. *Primitive Culture.* 2nd ed. New York: Holt, Rinehart and Winston, 1877.

Waitz, Franz Theodor
1863. *Introduction to Anthropology.* London: Longmans, Green, & Roberts.

Watkins, John G.
1965. "Psychotherapeutic Methods." *Handbook of Clinical Psychology,* ed. B. B. Wolman. New York: McGraw-Hill, pp. 1143–1167.

Westermarck, E. A.
1925. The History of Human Marriage, 3 vols., London: S. Ambaras.

Wolpe, Joseph
1962. "The Experimental Foundations of Some New Psychotherapeutic Methods." *Experimental Foundations of Clinical Psychology,* ed. A. J. Bachrach. New York: Basic Books.

1. COMPARATIVE FIELD TECHNIQUES IN URBAN RESEARCH IN AFRICA

Kluckhohn, Florence R.
1940. "The Participant Observer Technique in Small Communities." *American Journal of Sociology,* vol. 46.

Levy, H.
1947. *The Universe of Science.* Watts.

McEwen, William J.
1963. "Forms and Problems of Validations in Social Anthropology." *Current Anthropology,* 4:2.

Paul, Benjamin D.
1953. "Interview Techniques and Field Relations." *Anthropology Today: An Encyclopedic Inventory,* ed. A. L. Kroeber, et al. Chicago University of Chicago Press.

Schwab, William B.

1954. "An Experiment in Methodology in a West African Community." *Human Organization,* 13:1.

1955. "Kinship and Lineage Among the Yoruba." *Africa,* 25.

1961. "Social Stratification in Gwelo." *Social Change in Modern Africa,* ed. Aidan Southall. New York and London: Oxford University Press.

1965. "Oshogbo, An Urban Community." *Urbanization and Migration in West Africa,* ed. Hilda Kuper. Berkeley: University of California Press.

1968. "Differential Urbanization in Gwelo." *Rhodesia,* Ms.

1967. Comments on "Urbanization and Social Change in Africa" by A. L. Epstein. *Current Anthropology,* 290–291.

Stebbing, L. Susan

1948. *Thinking to Some Purpose.* New York: Penguin Books.

Vidich, Arthur J.

1955. "Participant Observation and the Collection and Interpretation of Data." *American Journal of Sociology,* 60:4.

2. VILLAGE AND CITY FIELD WORK IN LEBANON

Ammar, Hamed

1966. *Growing Up in an Egyptian Village.* New York: Octagon.

Antoun, Richard T.

1965. "Conservatism and Change in the Village Community: A Jordanian Case Study." *Human Organization,* 24:1:4–10.

Ayoub, Victor

1965. "Conflict Resolution and Social Reorganization in a Lebanese Village." *Human Organization,* 24:1:11–17.

Fernea, Elizabeth W.

1965. *Guests of the Sheik.* New York: Doubleday.

Fuller, Anne H.
1961. *Buarij: Portrait of a Lebanese Muslim Village*. Cambridge, Mass.: Harvard University Press.

Gulick, John.
1949. "The Maronites: A Study of the Indigenous Christians of the Lebanon." Cambridge, Mass.: Harvard College. Unpublished B.A. honors thesis.

1953. "The Lebanese Village: An Introduction." *American Anthropologist*, 55:3:367–372.

1954. "Conservatism and Change in a Lebanese Village." *The Middle East Journal*, 8:3:295–307.

1955. *Social Structure and Culture Change in a Lebanese Village*. (Viking Fund Publications in Anthropology, No. 21.) New York: Viking Press.

1960. *Cherokees at the Crossroads*. Chapel Hill: Institute for Research in Social Science Monographs.

1962. "Social Correlates of Urban Growth and Development." *Urban Growth Dynamics*, ed. F. S. Chapin, Jr., and S. F. Weiss. New York: John Wiley, pp. 309–315.

1963a. "Images of an Arab City." *Journal of the American Institute of Planners*, 29:3:179–198.

1963b. "Urban Anthropology: Its Present and Future." *Transactions of the New York Academy of Sciences* (Series II), 25:3:445–458.

1965a. "Old Values and New Institutions in a Lebanese Arab City." *Human Organization*, 24:1:49–52.

1965b. "The Religious Structure of Lebanese Culture." *Jahrbuch fur Religionssoziologie*, ed. Joachim Matthes. Koln & Opladen: Westdeutscher Verlag, 1:151–187.

1967. *Tripoli: A Modern Arab City*. Cambridge, Mass.: Harvard University Press.

Gulick, John, Charles E. Bowerman, and Kurt W. Back
1962. "Newcomer Enculturation in the City: Attitudes and Participation." *Urban Growth Dynamics*, ed. F. S. Chapin, Jr., and S. F. Weiss. New York: John Wiley, pp. 315–358.

Lutfiyya, Abdulla H.
1966. *Baytin: A Jordanian Village*. New York: Humanities Press.

Nader, Laura
1965. "Communication Between Village and City in the Middle East." *Human Organization,* 24:1:18–24.

Peters, Emrys L.
1963. "Aspects of Rank and Status Among Muslims in a Lebanese Village." *Mediterranean Countrymen,* ed. Julian Pitt-Rivers. New York: Humanities Press, pp. 159–202.

Sweet, Louise E.
1960. *Tell Toqaan: A Syrian Village.* Ann Arbor: University of Michigan Press.

Tannous, Afif I.
1942. "Group Behaviour in the Village Community of Lebanon." *American Journal of Sociology,* 48:2:231–239.

Touma, Toufic
1958. *Un Village de Montagne au Liban* (Hadeth al-Jobbé). The Hague.

Williams, Herbert H., and Judith R. Williams
1965. "The Extended Family as a Vehicle of Culture Change." *Human Organization,* 24:1:59–64.

3. CAKCHIQUELES AND CARIBS: THE SOCIAL CONTEXT OF FIELD WORK

Adams, Richard N.
1957. *Cultural Surveys of Panama-Nicaragua-Guatemala-El Salvador-Honduras.* Washington, D.C.: Pan American Sanitary Bureau, Publication No. 33.

Foster, George M.
1965. "Peasant Society and the Image of Limited Good." *American Anthropologist,* 67:293–315.

González, Nancie L.
1965. "Black Carib Adaptation to a Latin Urban Milieu." *Social and Economic Studies,* 14:3:272:278.

In press. "Obeah and Other Witchcraft Among the Black Carib." *North American Sorcery,* ed. Deward Walker.

Reina, Ruben
1966. *The Law of the Saints.* Indianapolis: Bobbs-Merrill.

Solien, Nancie L.
1959. "West Indian Characteristics of the Black Carib." *Southwestern Journal of Anthropology*, 15:3:300–307.

Tax, Sol
1937. "The Municipios of the Midwest Highlands of Guatemala." *American Anthropologist*, 39:423–444.

1952. *Heritage of Conquest*. Glencoe, Ill.: Free Press.

Taylor, Douglas M.
1951. *The Black Carib of British Honduras*. New York: Viking Fund Publications in Anthropology, No. 17.

Tejada, Carlos, Nancie L. González, and Margarita Sánchez
1965. "El Factor Diego y el Gene de Células Falciformes entre los Caribes de Raza Negra de Livingston, Guatemala." *Revista del Colegio Médico de Guatemala*, 16:2:83–86.

Tumin, Melvin
1952. *Caste in a Peasant Society*. Princeton, N. J.: Princeton University Press.

Wagley, Charles
1949. *The Social and Religious Life of a Guatemalan Village*. American Anthropological Association, Memoir XI.

Young, Frank W., and Ruth C. Young
1961. "Key Informant Reliability in Rural Mexican Villages." *Human Organization*, 20:141–148.

4. MOHAWK HEROES AND TRINIDADIAN PEASANTS

Freilich, Morris
1958. "Culture Persistence Among the Modern Iroquois." *Anthropos* (Fribourg, Switzerland), 53:473–483.

1960. "Cultural Diversity Among Trinidadian Peasants." Doctoral dissertation. New York: Columbia University.

1961. "Serial Polygyny, Negro Peasants, and Model Analysis." *American Anthropologist*, 63:955–975.

1963. "The Natural Experiment, Ecology, and Culture." *Southwestern Journal of Anthropology*, 19:21–39.

1967. "Ecology and Culture: Environmental Determinism and the Ecological Approach in Anthropology." *Anthropological Quarterly*, 40:26–43.

1968. "The Natural Experiment: A Strategy for Anthropological Research." Ms. 90 pp.

Wallace, A. F. C.
1951. "Some Psychological Determinants of Culture Change in an Iroquoian Community." *Symposium on Local Diversity in Iroquois Culture*, W. N. Fenton. Washington, D.C.: Bureau of Ethnology, Bulletin No. 149.

5. OPEN NETWORKS AND NATIVE FORMALISM: THE MANDAYA AND PITJANDJARA CASES

Basedow, Herbert
1914. *Journal of the Government North-West Expedition.* Adelaide: Royal Geographical Society of Australia, South Australian Branch.

1925. *The Australian Aboriginal.* Adelaide: Preece.

Cole, Fay-Cooper
1913. *The Wild Tribes of Davao District, Mindanao.* Chicago: Field Museum of Natural History, 12:2.

Conklin, Harold C.
1957. *Hanunoo Agriculture.* Rome: United Nations Forestry Development Paper, No. 12.

Elkin, A. P.
1931. "Social Organization of South Australian Tribes." *Oceania,* 2:44–73.

1938–1940. "Kinship in South Australia." *Oceania,* 8:419–452; 9:41–78; 10:196–234; 10:295–349; 10:369–388.

Finlayson, H. H.
1936. *The Red Centre.* Sydney: Angus and Robertson.

Firth, Raymond
1964. *Essays on Social Organization.* London: Athlone Press.

Garvan, John M.
1931. *The Manobos of Mindanao.* (Memoirs of the National Academy of Sciences, Volume 23.) Washington, D.C.: U.S. Government Printing Office.

Hiatt, L. R.
1962. "Local Organization Among the Australian Aborigines." *Oceania*, 32:267–286.

1965. *Kinship and Conflict.* Canberra: The Australian National University.

1966. "The Lost Horde." *Oceania*, 37:81–92.

Leach, E. R.
1950. *Social Science Research in Sarawak.* (Colonial Research Studies No. 1.) London: His Majesty's Stationery Office.

Meggitt, M. J.
1962. *Desert People.* Sydney: Angus and Robertson.

Mountford, Charles P.
1950. *Brown Men and Red Sand.* Sydney: Angus and Robertson.

1965. *Ayers Rock: Its Peoples, Their Beliefs and Their Art.* Sydney: Angus and Robertson.

Pelzer, Karl J.
1945. *Pioneer Settlement in the Asiatic Tropics.* New York: American Geographical Society, Special Publication No. 29.

Radcliffe-Brown, A. R.
1913. "Three Tribes of Western Australia." *Journal of the Royal Anthropological Institute*, 43:143–194.

1918. "Notes on the Social Organization of Australian Tribes." *Journal of the Royal Anthropological Institute*, 48:222–253.

1930. *Social Organization of Australian Tribes.* Oceania Monograph No. 1.

Rose, Frederick G. G.
1960. *Classification of Kin, Age Structure and Marriage Amongst the Groote Eylandt Aborigines.* Berlin: Deutsche Akademie der Wissenschaften.

1965. *The Wind of Change in Central Australia.* Berlin: Deutsche Akademie der Wissenschaften.

Service, Elman R.
1962. *Primitive Social Organization.* New York: Random House.

Stanner, W. E. H.
1965. "Aboriginal Territorial Organization: Estate, Range, Domain and Regime." *Oceania*, 36:1–26.

Steward, Julian H.
1936. "The Economic and Social Basis of Primitive Bands." *Essays in Honor of A. L. Kroeber*. Berkeley: University of California Press.

1955. *Theory of Culture Change*. Urbana: University of Illinois Press.

Tindale, Norman B.
1935. "Initiation among the Pitjandjara Natives of the Mann and Tohkinson Ranges in South Australia." *Oceania*, 6:199–224.

1936. "General Report on the Anthropological Expedition to the Warburton Range, Western Australia, July–September 1935." *Oceania*, 6:481–485.

1959. "Totemic Beliefs in the Western Desert of Australia: Part I, Women Who Became the Pleiades." *Records of the South Australian Museum*, 13:305–332.

1963. "Totemic Beliefs in the Western Desert of Australia: Part II, Musical Rocks and Associated Objects of the Pitjandjara People." *Records of the South Australian Museum*, 14:499–514.

1965. "Stone Implement Making Among the Nakako, Ngadadjara and Pitjandjara of the Great Western Desert." *Records of the South Australian Museum*, 15:131–164.

Yengoyan, Aram A.
1964. *Environment, Shifting Cultivation, and Social Organization Among the Mandaya of Eastern Mindanao, Philippines*. Unpublished Doctoral Dissertation, University of Chicago: Department of Anthropology.

1965. "Aspects of Ecological Succession Among Mandaya Populations in Eastern Davao Province, Philippines." *Papers of the Michigan Academy of Science, Arts, and Letters*, 50:437–443.

1966a. "Baptism and 'Bisayanization' Among the Mandaya of Eastern Mindanao, Philippines." *Asian Studies*, 4:324–327.

1966b. "Marketing Networks and Economic Processes Among the Abaca Cultivating Mandaya of Eastern Mindanao, Philippines." *Selected Readings to Accompany Getting Agriculture Moving,* ed. Raymond E. Burton. New York: Agricultural Development Council, Vol. II, pp. 689–701.

1966c. "Field Report No. 1 on Pitjandjara Fieldwork," to the Australian Institute of Aboriginal Studies. (Doc. 66/491.) December.

1967. "Field Report No. 2 on Pitjandjara Fieldwork" to the Australian Institute of Aboriginal Studies. (Doc. 67/566.) March.

1968. "Demographic and Ecological Influences on Aboriginal Australian Marriage Sections." *Man the Hunter,* ed. Richard B. Lee and Irven DeVore. Chicago: Aldine Press.

In press. "Mandaya Land Tenure." *Land Tenure Systems in the South Pacific,* ed. R. Crocombe.

FIELD WORK: PROBLEMS AND GOALS (GENERAL)

Beveridge, W. E. B.
1957 *The Art of Scientific Investigation.* New York, Random House (Modern Library).

Feigl, Herbert
1949 "Some Remarks on the Meaning of Scientific Explanation." In: *Readings in Philosophical Analysis* (ed. by Herbert Feigl and Wilfred Sellers) New York.

Festinger, Leon and Daniel Katz (eds)
1953 *Research Methods in the Behavioral Sciences.* New York, The Dryden Press.

Freilich, Morris
1958 Cultural Persistence among the Modern Iroquois. *Anthropos* 53:473-483.
1960a Cultural Diversity among Trinidadian Peasants. Unpublished doctoral dissertation. New York, Columbia University.
1960b Cultural Models and Land Holdings. *Anthropological Quarterly* 33:188-197.
1961 Serial Polygyny. Negro Peasants and Model Analysis. *American Anthropologist* 63:955-975.
1962 The Modern *Shtetl*: a Study of Cultural Persistence *Anthropos* 57:45-54.

1963 The Natural Experiment: Ecology and Culture. *Southwestern Journal of Anthropology* 19:21-39.

Steward, Julian
1955 *Theory of Culture Change.* Urbana, University of Illinois Press.

FIELD WORK: PROBLEMS AND GOALS (HASIDISM)

Buber, Martin
1931 *Jewish Mysticism and the Legend of Baal-Shem,* trans. by L. Cohen, London, J. M. Dent & Sons Ltd.
1948 *Hasidism.* New York, The Philosophical Library.
1953 *For the Sake of Heaven,* trans. by Ludwig Lewishon. New York, Harper & Brothers, Publishers.
1958 *Hasidism and Modern Man,* Maurice Friedman, ed., New York, The Horizon Press.

Dresner, Samuel H.
1960 *The Zaddik*: The Doctrine of the Zaddik According to the Writings of Rabbi Yaakov Yosef of Polnoy. London, Abelard-Schuman.

Dubnow, Simon M.
1902 "Hasidism" in *The Jewish Encyclopedia.* New York, Funk and Wagnall.
1916 *History of the Jews in Russia and Poland,* trans. by Israel Friedlaender. Philadelphia, The Jewish Publication Society of America.
1930-32 *Toldot Hachassidim,* Vol. I, Tel Aviv, Devar.

Ginsburg, Louis
1902 "Baal Shem Tov, Israel B. Eliezer" *The Jewish Encyclopedia.* Funk and Wagnall Company, New York.

Scholem, Gershon G.
1946 "Jewish Mysticism and Kabbalah" in *The Jewish People Past and Present,* S. W. Baron et al eds. New York, Jewish Encyclopedic Handbooks, Central Yiddish Culture Organization. (Vol. 1 308-27).
1950 "Devekuth; The Communion with God in Early Hassidic Literature" *Review of Religion* 14:115-39.
1961 *Major Trends in Jewish Mysticism.* Schocken Books, New York.
1961a "Martin Buber's Hasidism" Commentary 32:305-16; Discussion 33:161-3.